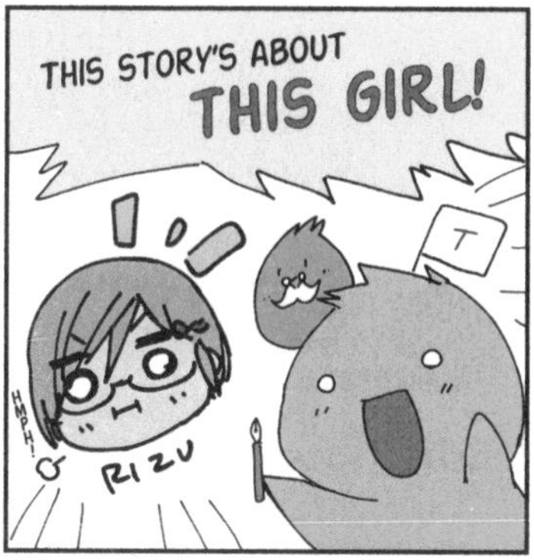
THIS STORY'S ABOUT THIS GIRL!
HMPH!
RIZU

This is Tsutsui. Thankfully, this is volume 18!

Starting with this volume, we're going to explore the question, "What if, on that night, [*X*] was...?"

The first of the parallel stories is about to unfold.

Which is the real ending? It's up to you, the reader!

I hope you enjoy!

• Taishi Tsutsui •

We Never Learn

We Never Learn

Volume 18 • SHONEN JUMP Manga Edition

STORY AND ART **Taishi Tsutsui**

TRANSLATION Camellia Nieh
SHONEN JUMP SERIES LETTERING Snir Aharon
GRAPHIC NOVEL TOUCH-UP ART & LETTERING Erika Terriquez
DESIGN Shawn Carrico
EDITOR John Bae

BOKUTACHI WA BENKYOU GA DEKINAI © 2017 by Taishi Tsutsui
All rights reserved.
First published in Japan in 2017 by SHUEISHA Inc., Tokyo.
English translation rights arranged by SHUEISHA Inc.

The stories, characters and incidents mentioned in this publication are entirely fictional.

Printed in Canada

Published by VIZ Media, LLC
P.O. Box 77010
San Francisco, CA 94107

10 9 8 7 6 5 4 3 2 1
First printing, October 2021

PARENTAL ADVISORY
WE NEVER LEARN is rated T+ for Older
Teen and is recommended for ages 16
and up. This volume contains mild
language and sexual themes.

viz.com

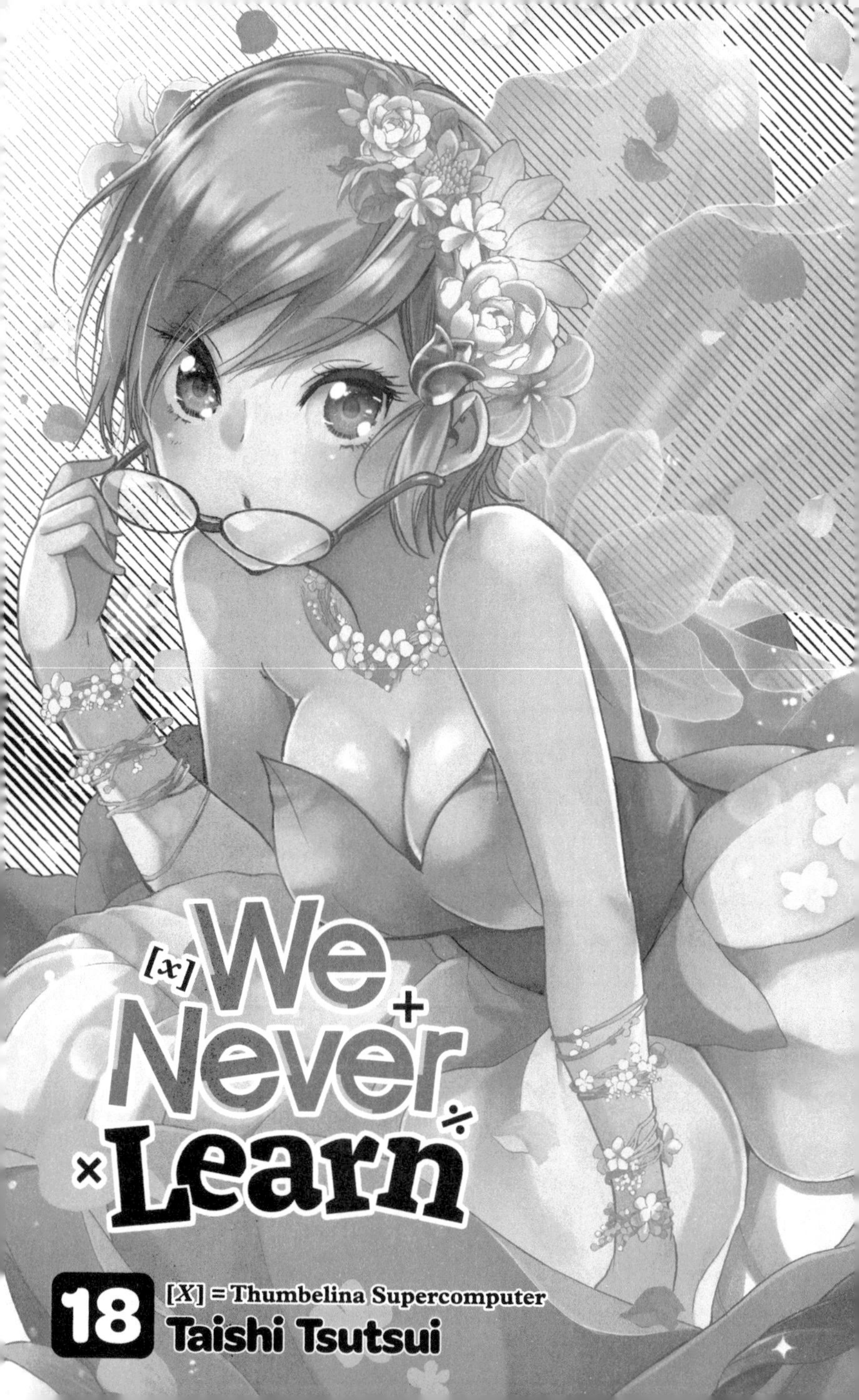
[x] We + Never ÷ × Learn
18
[X] = Thumbelina Supercomputer
Taishi Tsutsui

We Never Learn

Nariyuki Yuiga and his family have led a humble life since his father passed away, with Yuiga doing everything he can to support his siblings. So when the principal of his school agrees to grant Nariyuki the school's special VIP recommendation for a full scholarship to college, he leaps at the opportunity. However, the principal's offer comes with one condition: Yuiga must serve as the tutor of Rizu Ogata, Fumino Furuhashi and Uruka Takemoto, the three girl geniuses who are the pride of Ichinose Academy! Unfortunately, the girls, while extremely talented in certain ways, all have subjects where their grades are absolutely rock-bottom.

After successfully passing their exams, Nariyuki and Uruka end up together! But what if there are other realities where Nariyuki ends up with someone else? According to a school legend, the moment the first firework explodes on the night of the school festival, any boy and girl who are touching are destined to end up together. These alternate realities follow the parallel pathways that diverge from that moment!

NARIYUKI YUIGA

A bright student from an ordinary family. Nariyuki lacks genius in any one subject but manages to maintain stellar grades through hard work. After taking on the role of tutor to Rizu, Fumino and Uruka, he decides to pursue a teaching degree.

☺ Liberal Arts
☺ STEM
☹ Athletics

RIZU OGATA

☺ Liberal Arts 😄 STEM
☹ Athletics

Known as the Thumbelina Supercomputer, Rizu is a math and science genius, but she's a dunce at literature, especially when human emotions come into play. She chooses a literary path to learn about human psychology—partially because she wants to become better at board games.

TOKUMORI

Sawako Sekijo

Rizu's self-professed "best friend." Loves science, and looks up to Rizu, who is a science whiz.

Ogata (Father)

Runs an udon shop. Dotes on his daughter.

Fumino Furuhashi

Known as the Sleeping Beauty of the Literary Forest, Fumino is a literary wiz. She chooses a STEM path because she wants to study the stars.

Uruka Takemoto

Known as the Shimmering Ebony Mermaid Princess, Uruka is a swimming prodigy and is currently studying abroad.

Mafuyu Kirisu

A teacher at Ichinose Academy, and Rizu and Fumino's previous tutor.

Asumi Kominami

A graduate of Ichinose Academy. She is aiming to get into medical school to take over her father's clinic one day.

TITLE

We Never Learn

CONTENTS

VOLUME 18 [X] = Thumbelina Supercomputer

NAME Taishi Tsutsui

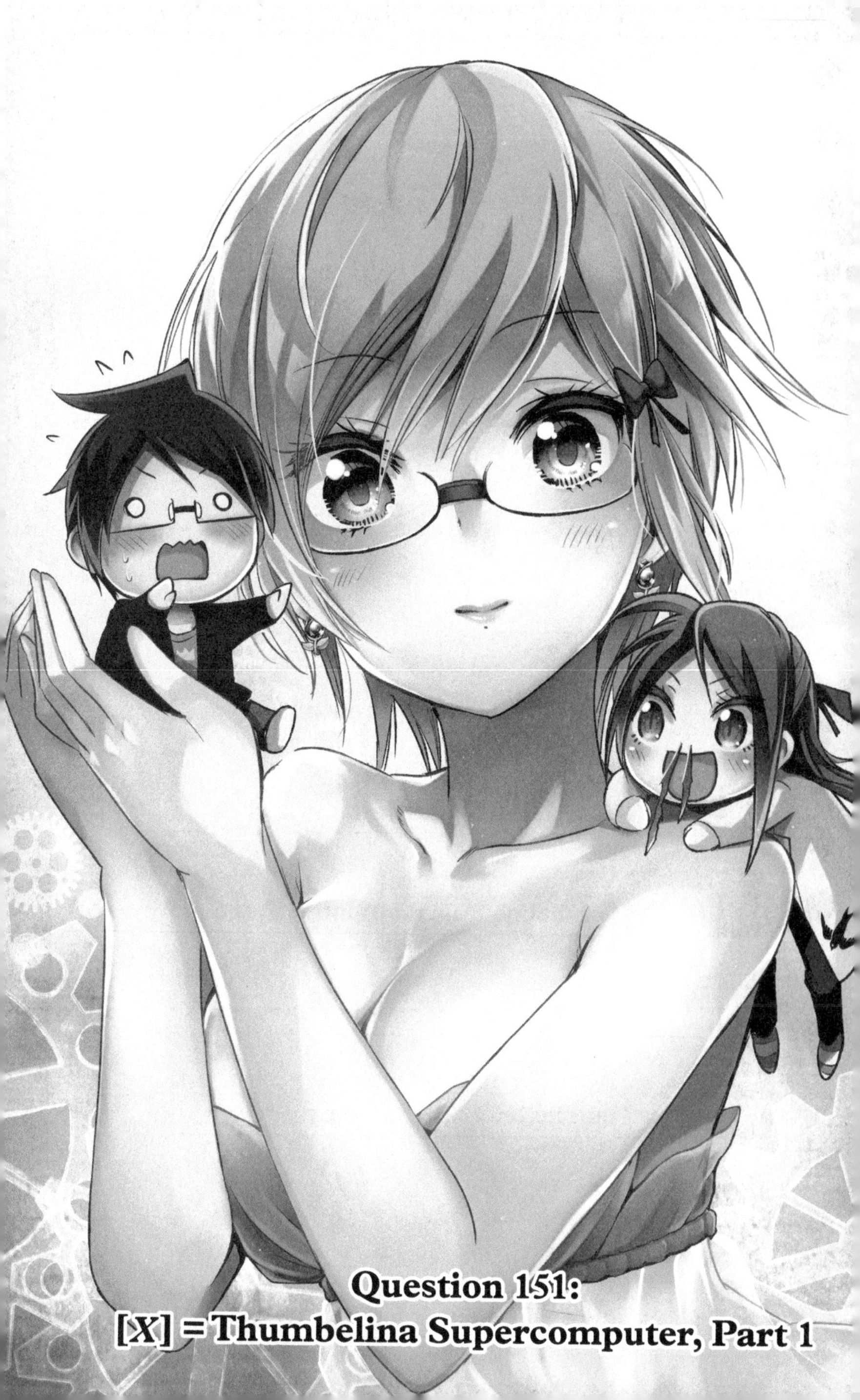

Question 151:
[X] = Thumbelina Supercomputer, Part 1

[x] We
Never
Learn

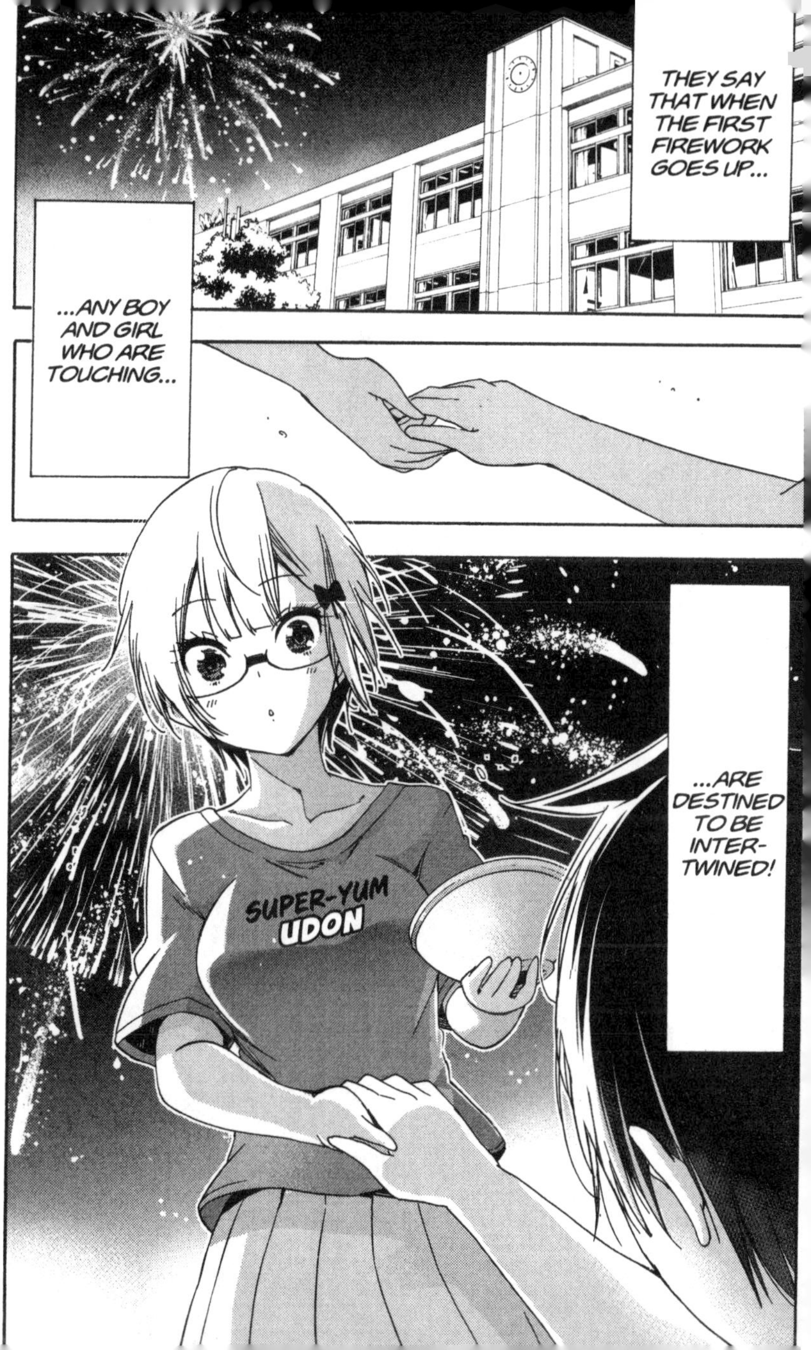
THEY SAY THAT WHEN THE FIRST FIREWORK GOES UP...
...ANY BOY AND GIRL WHO ARE TOUCHING...
...ARE DESTINED TO BE INTER-TWINED!
SUPER-YUM UDON

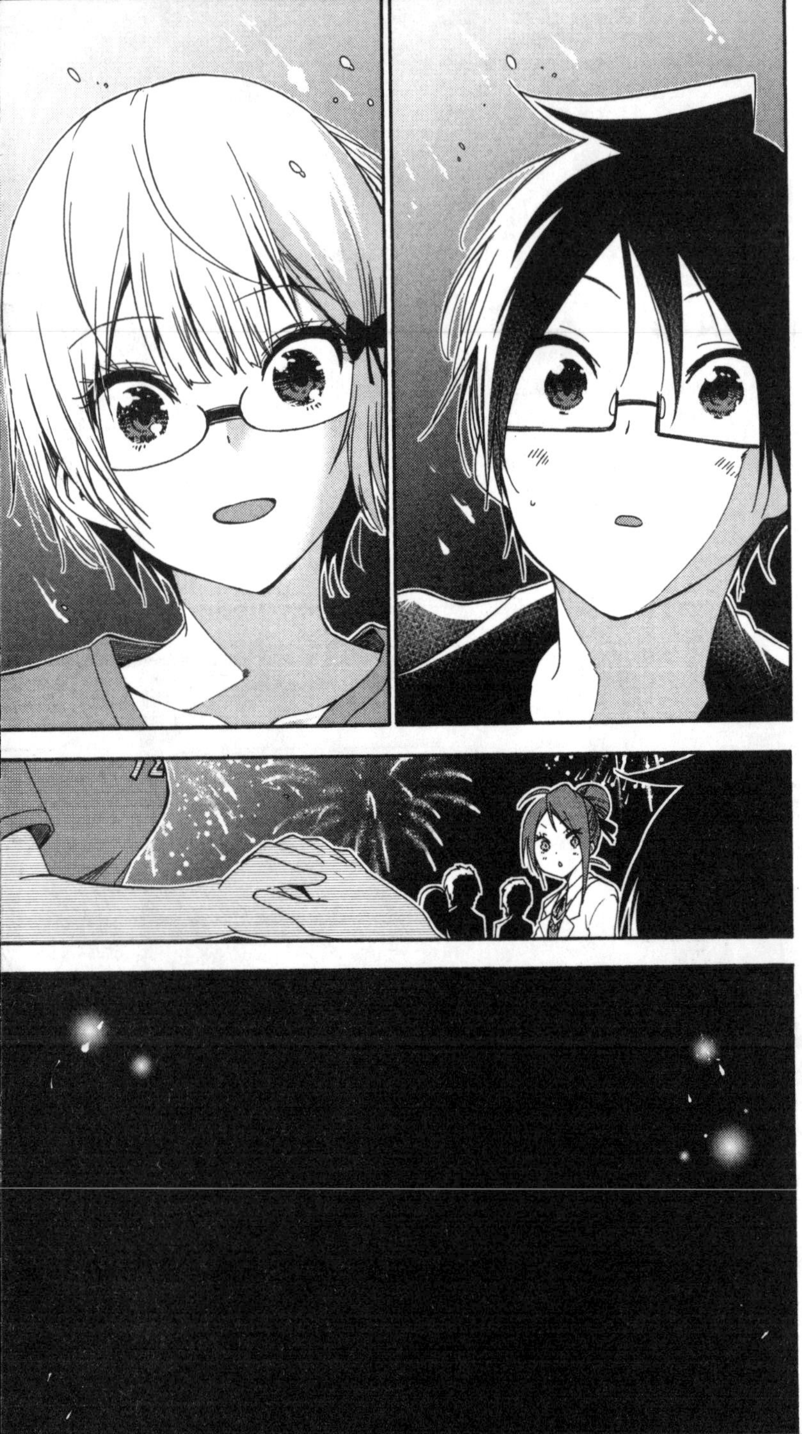

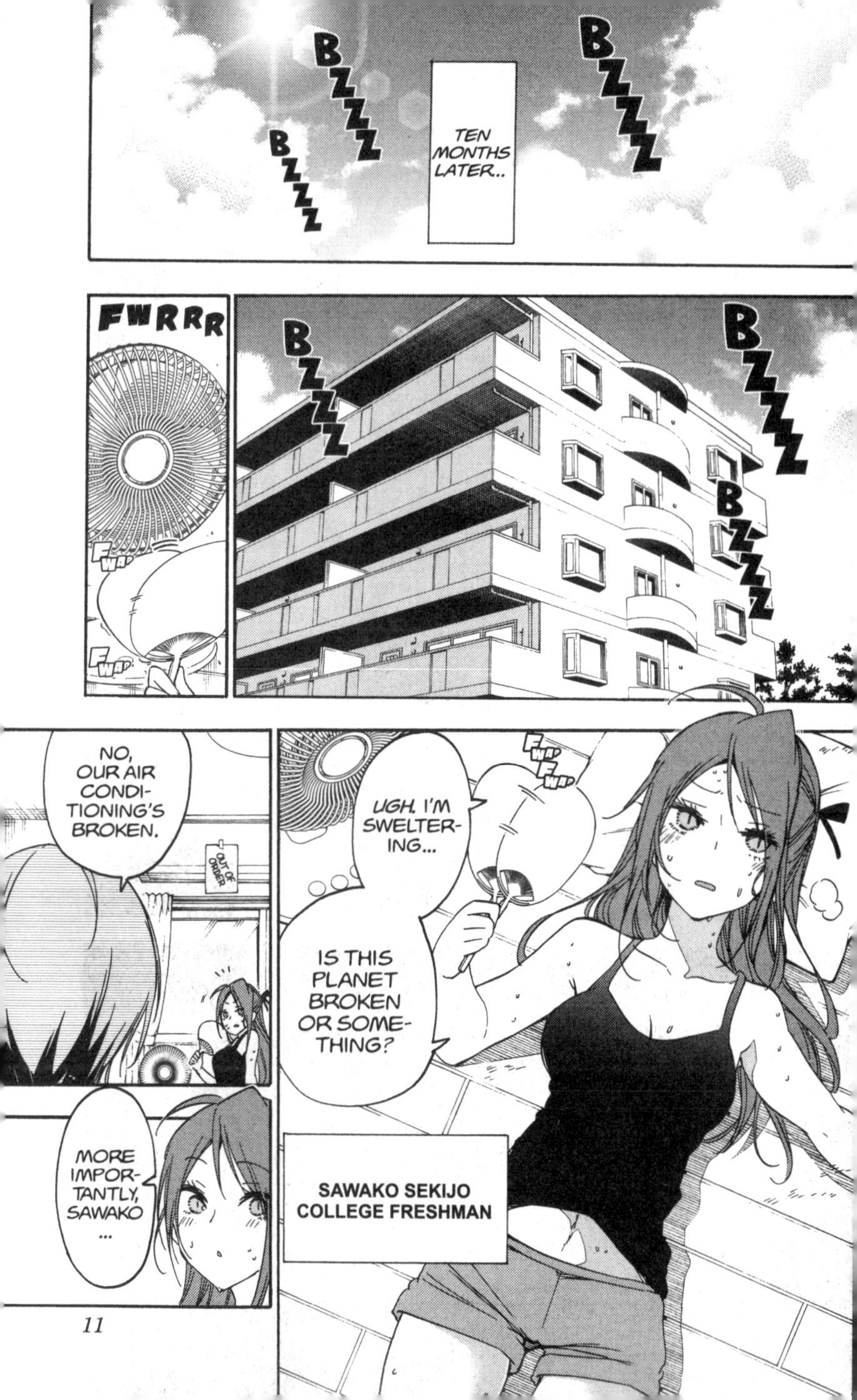
BZZZZ
TEN MONTHS LATER...
BZZZZ
BZZZZ
BZZZZ
BZZZZ
BZZZ
FWRRR
FWAP
FWAP
FWAP
FWAP
UGH. I'M SWELTERING...
IS THIS PLANET BROKEN OR SOMETHING?
SAWAKO SEKIJO
COLLEGE FRESHMAN
NO, OUR AIR CONDITIONING'S BROKEN.
OUT OF ORDER
MORE IMPORTANTLY, SAWAKO...

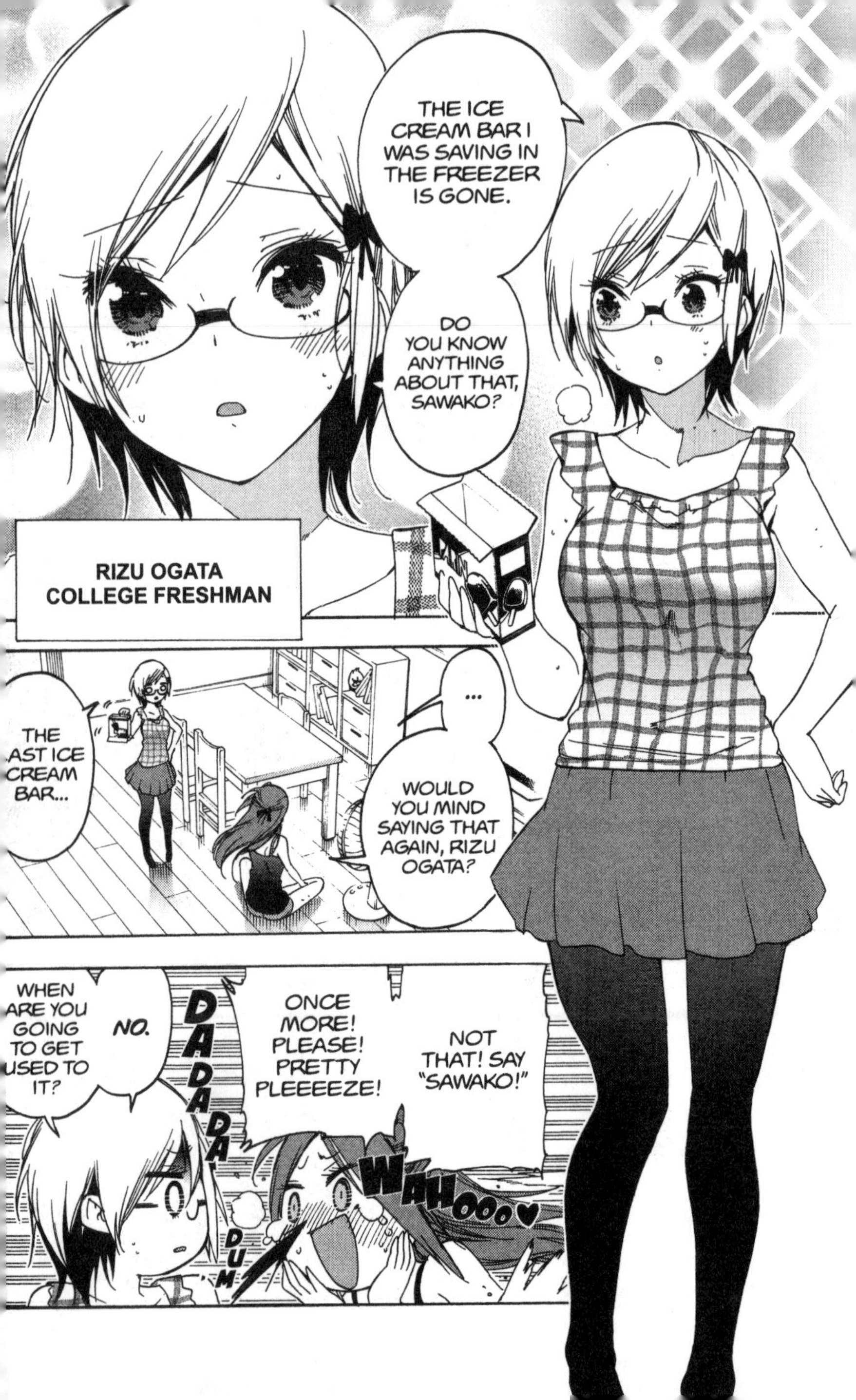
THE ICE CREAM BAR I WAS SAVING IN THE FREEZER IS GONE.
DO YOU KNOW ANYTHING ABOUT THAT, SAWAKO?
RIZU OGATA
COLLEGE FRESHMAN
...
WOULD YOU MIND SAYING THAT AGAIN, RIZU OGATA?
THE AST ICE CREAM BAR...
NOT THAT! SAY "SAWAKO!"
WAHOOOO♥
ONCE MORE! PLEASE! PRETTY PLEEEEZE!
DADADADA
DUM
NO.
WHEN ARE YOU GOING TO GET USED TO IT?

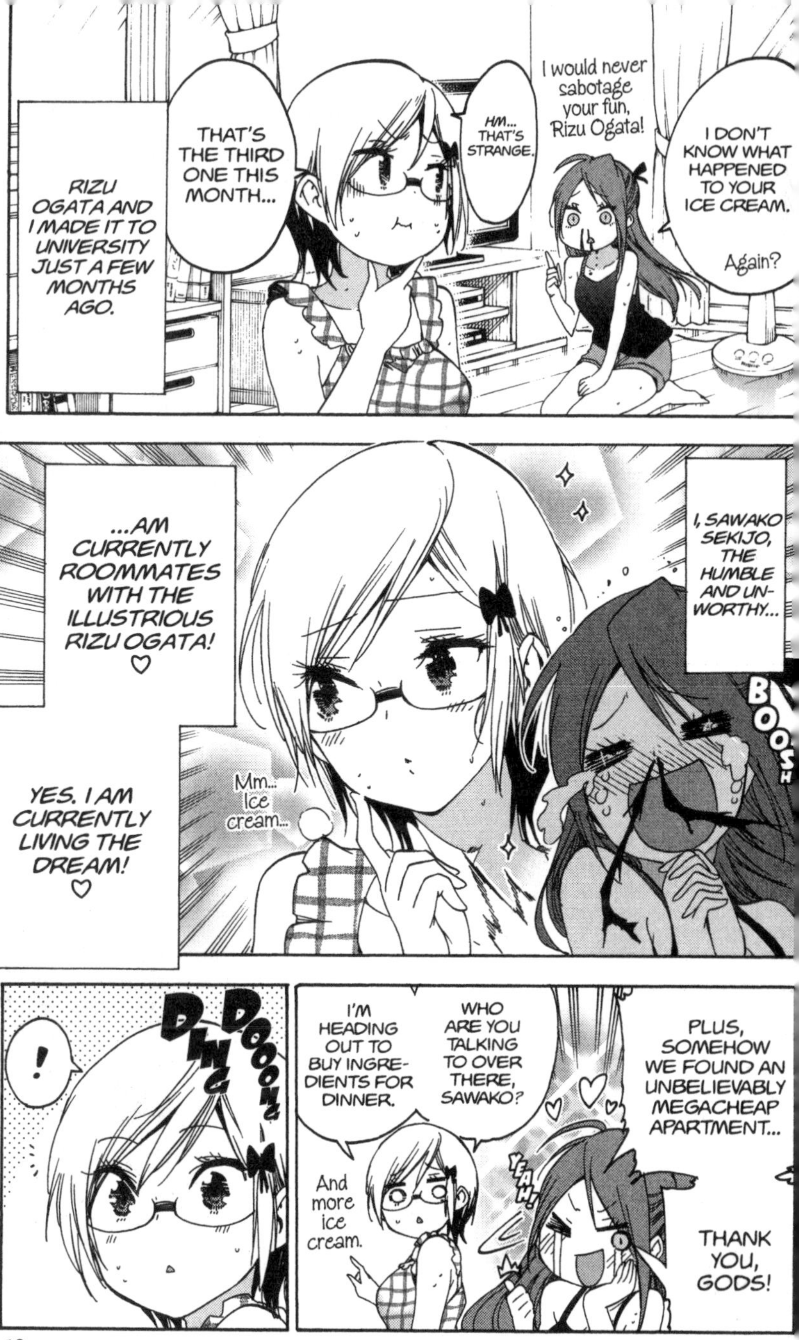
I DON'T KNOW WHAT HAPPENED TO YOUR ICE CREAM.
Again?
I would never sabotage your fun, Rizu Ogata!
HM... THAT'S STRANGE.
THAT'S THE THIRD ONE THIS MONTH...
RIZU OGATA AND I MADE IT TO UNIVERSITY JUST A FEW MONTHS AGO.
I, SAWAKO SEKIJO, THE HUMBLE AND UNWORTHY...
BOOSH
...AM CURRENTLY ROOMMATES WITH THE ILLUSTRIOUS RIZU OGATA! ♡
Mm... Ice cream...
YES. I AM CURRENTLY LIVING THE DREAM! ♡
PLUS, SOMEHOW WE FOUND AN UNBELIEVABLY MEGACHEAP APARTMENT...
WHO ARE YOU TALKING TO OVER THERE, SAWAKO?
I'M HEADING OUT TO BUY INGREDIENTS FOR DINNER.
YEAH!
THANK YOU, GODS!
And more ice cream.
DOOOONG
DING
!

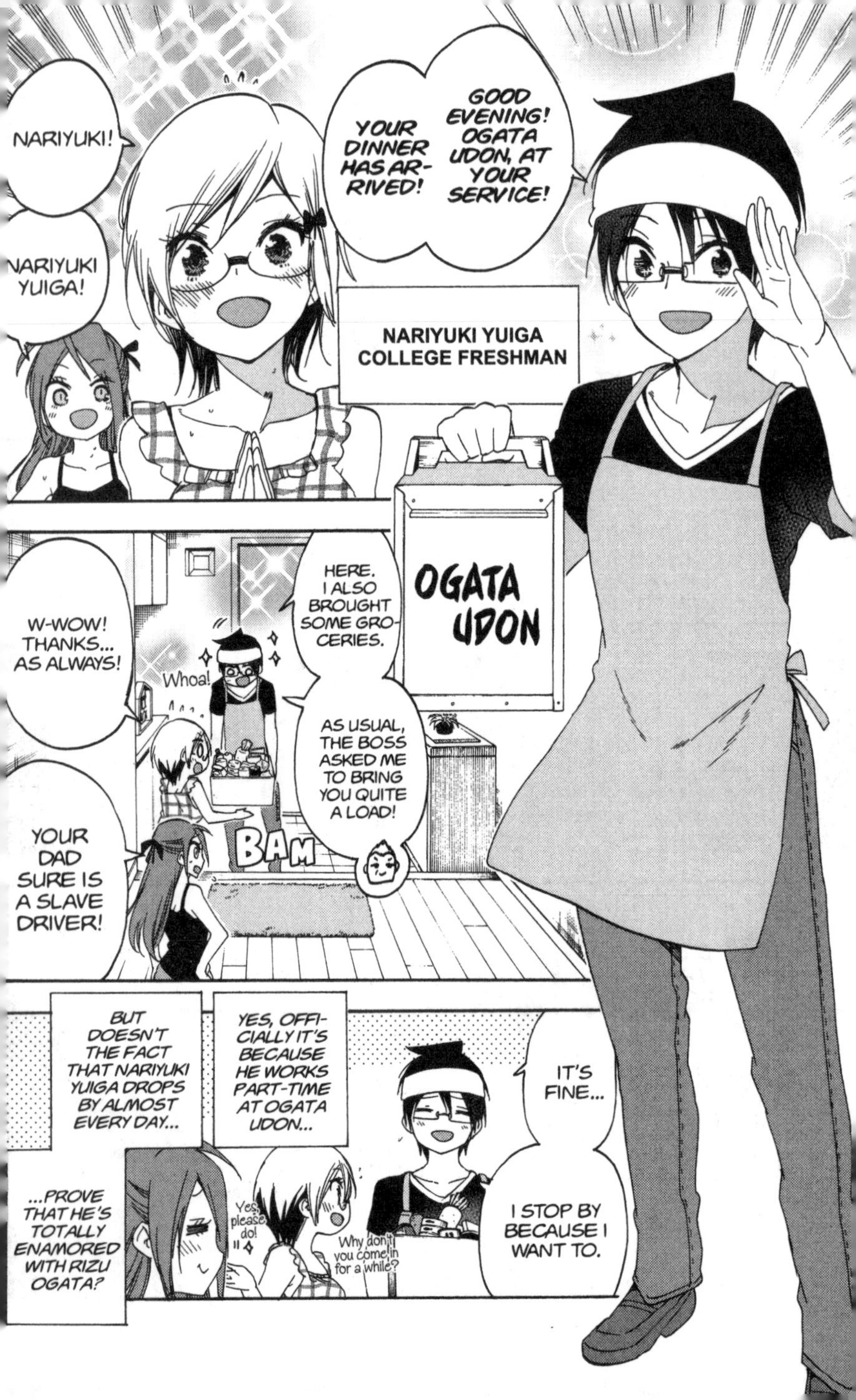
GOOD EVENING! OGATA UDON, AT YOUR SERVICE!
YOUR DINNER HAS ARRIVED!
NARIYUKI YUIGA COLLEGE FRESHMAN
OGATA UDON
NARIYUKI!
NARIYUKI YUIGA!
HERE. I ALSO BROUGHT SOME GROCERIES.
Whoa!
W-WOW! THANKS... AS ALWAYS!
AS USUAL, THE BOSS ASKED ME TO BRING YOU QUITE A LOAD!
BAM
YOUR DAD SURE IS A SLAVE DRIVER!
IT'S FINE...
I STOP BY BECAUSE I WANT TO.
YES, OFFICIALLY IT'S BECAUSE HE WORKS PART-TIME AT OGATA UDON...
BUT DOESN'T THE FACT THAT NARIYUKI YUIGA DROPS BY ALMOST EVERY DAY...
Why don't you come in for a while?
Yes, please do!
...PROVE THAT HE'S TOTALLY ENAMORED WITH RIZU OGATA?

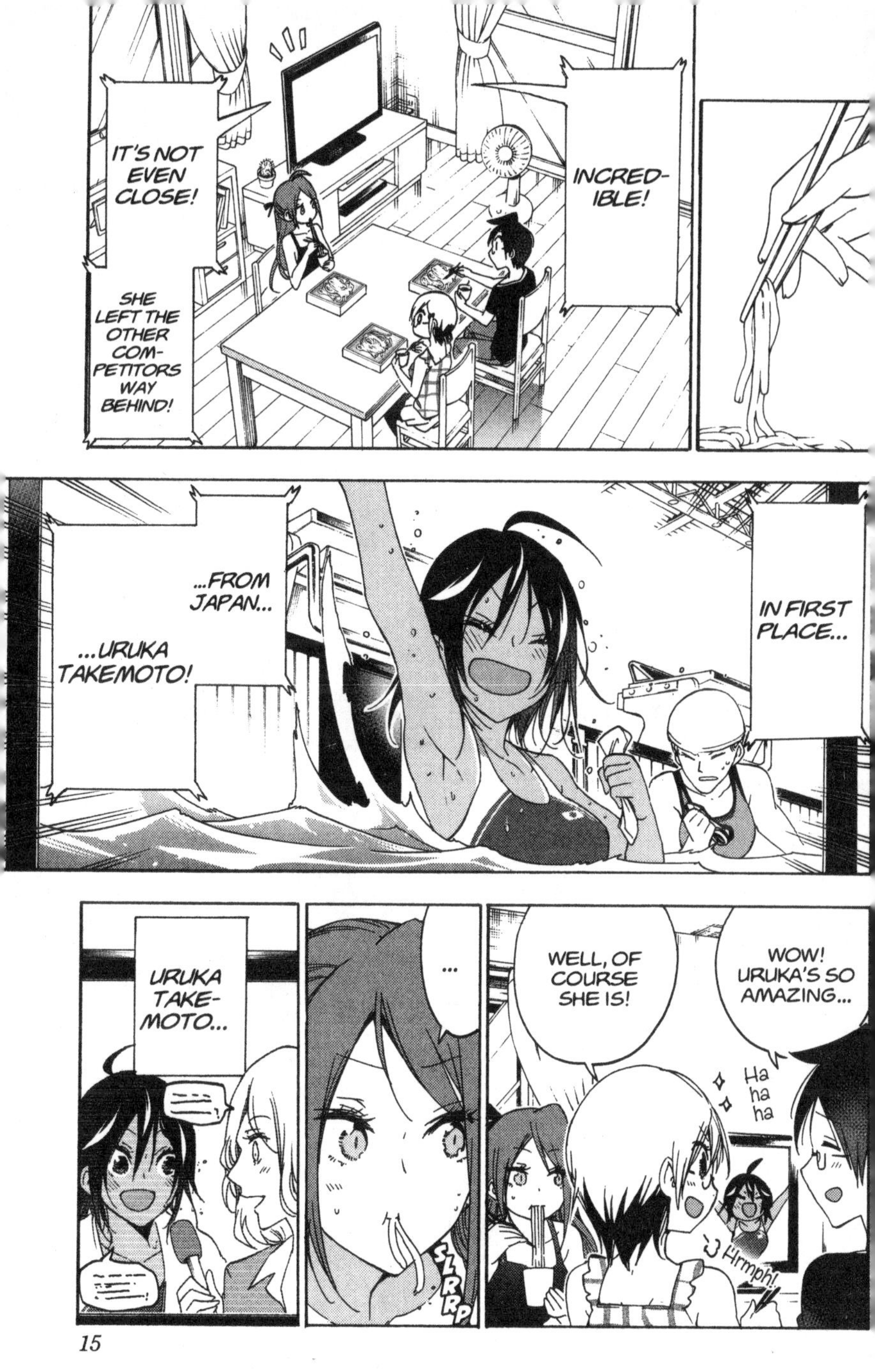
INCRED-IBLE!
IT'S NOT EVEN CLOSE!
SHE LEFT THE OTHER COM-PETITORS WAY BEHIND!
IN FIRST PLACE...
...FROM JAPAN...
...URUKA TAKEMOTO!
WOW! URUKA'S SO AMAZING...
Ha ha ha
WELL, OF COURSE SHE IS!
Hrmph!
...
SLRRP
URUKA TAKE-MOTO...

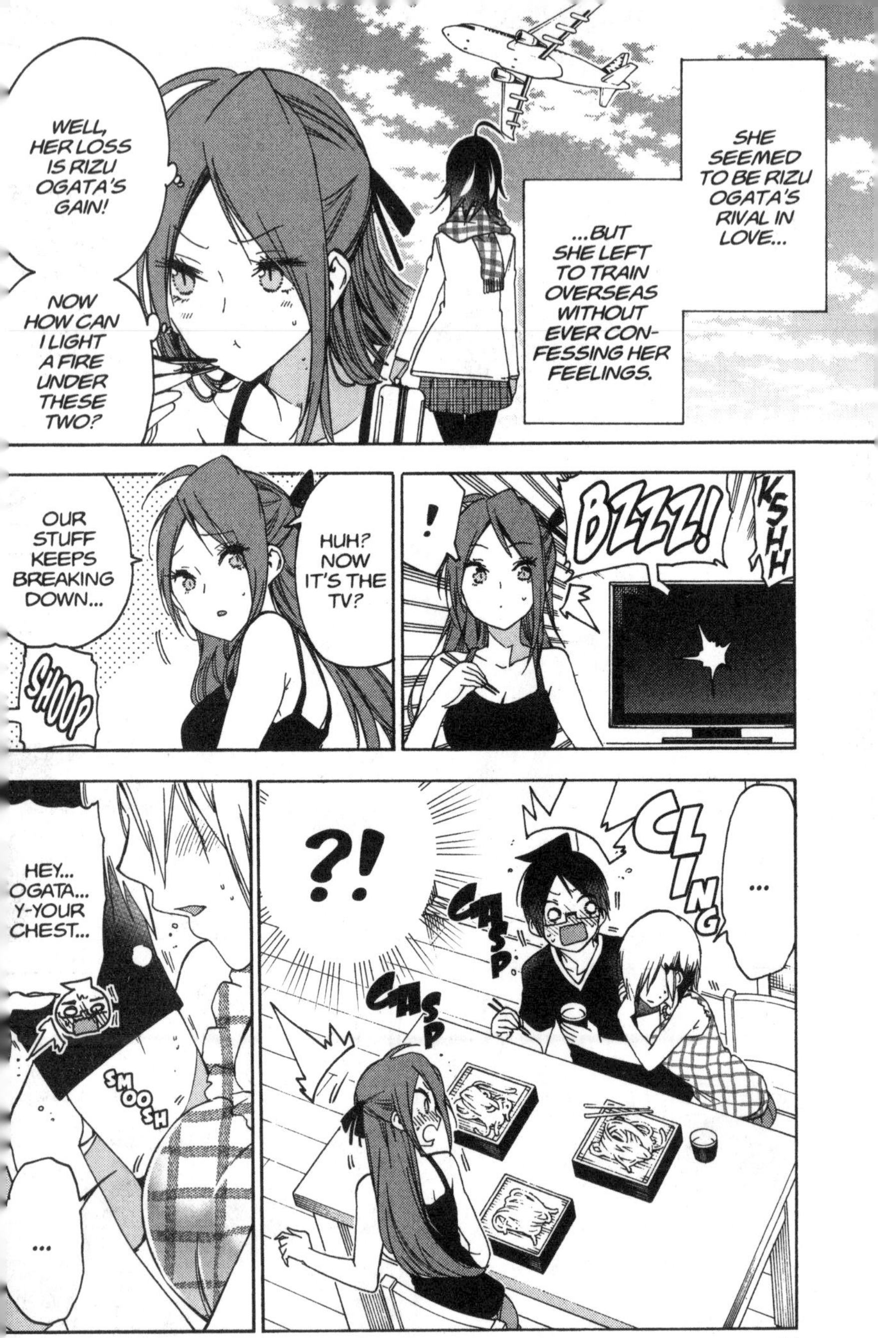
SHE SEEMED TO BE RIZU OGATA'S RIVAL IN LOVE...
...BUT SHE LEFT TO TRAIN OVERSEAS WITHOUT EVER CONFESSING HER FEELINGS.
WELL, HER LOSS IS RIZU OGATA'S GAIN!
NOW HOW CAN I LIGHT A FIRE UNDER THESE TWO?
VSHH
BZZZ!
!
HUH? NOW IT'S THE TV?
OUR STUFF KEEPS BREAKING DOWN...
SHOOP
...
CLING
?!
GASP
GASP
HEY... OGATA... Y-YOUR CHEST...
SMOOSH
...

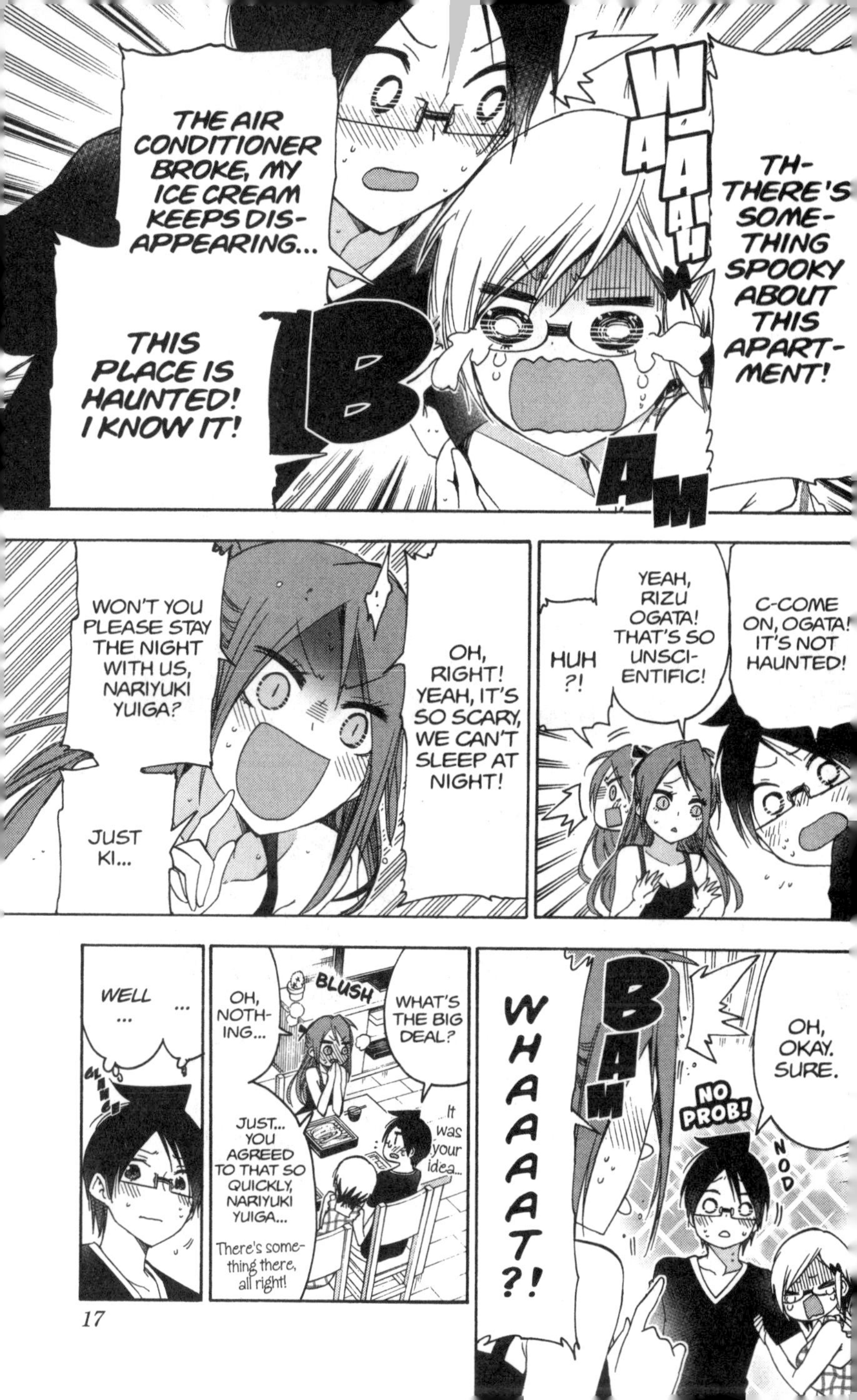
WAAAH!
TH-THERE'S SOMETHING SPOOKY ABOUT THIS APARTMENT!
THE AIR CONDITIONER BROKE, MY ICE CREAM KEEPS DISAPPEARING...
BAM
THIS PLACE IS HAUNTED! I KNOW IT!
C-COME ON, OGATA! IT'S NOT HAUNTED!
YEAH, RIZU OGATA! THAT'S SO UNSCIENTIFIC!
HUH?!
OH, RIGHT! YEAH, IT'S SO SCARY, WE CAN'T SLEEP AT NIGHT!
WON'T YOU PLEASE STAY THE NIGHT WITH US, NARIYUKI YUIGA?
JUST KI...
OH, OKAY. SURE.
NO PROB!
NOD
BAM
WHAAAAAT?!
WHAT'S THE BIG DEAL?
BLUSH
OH, NOTHING...
...It was your idea...
JUST... YOU AGREED TO THAT SO QUICKLY, NARIYUKI YUIGA...
There's something there, all right!
WELL... ...

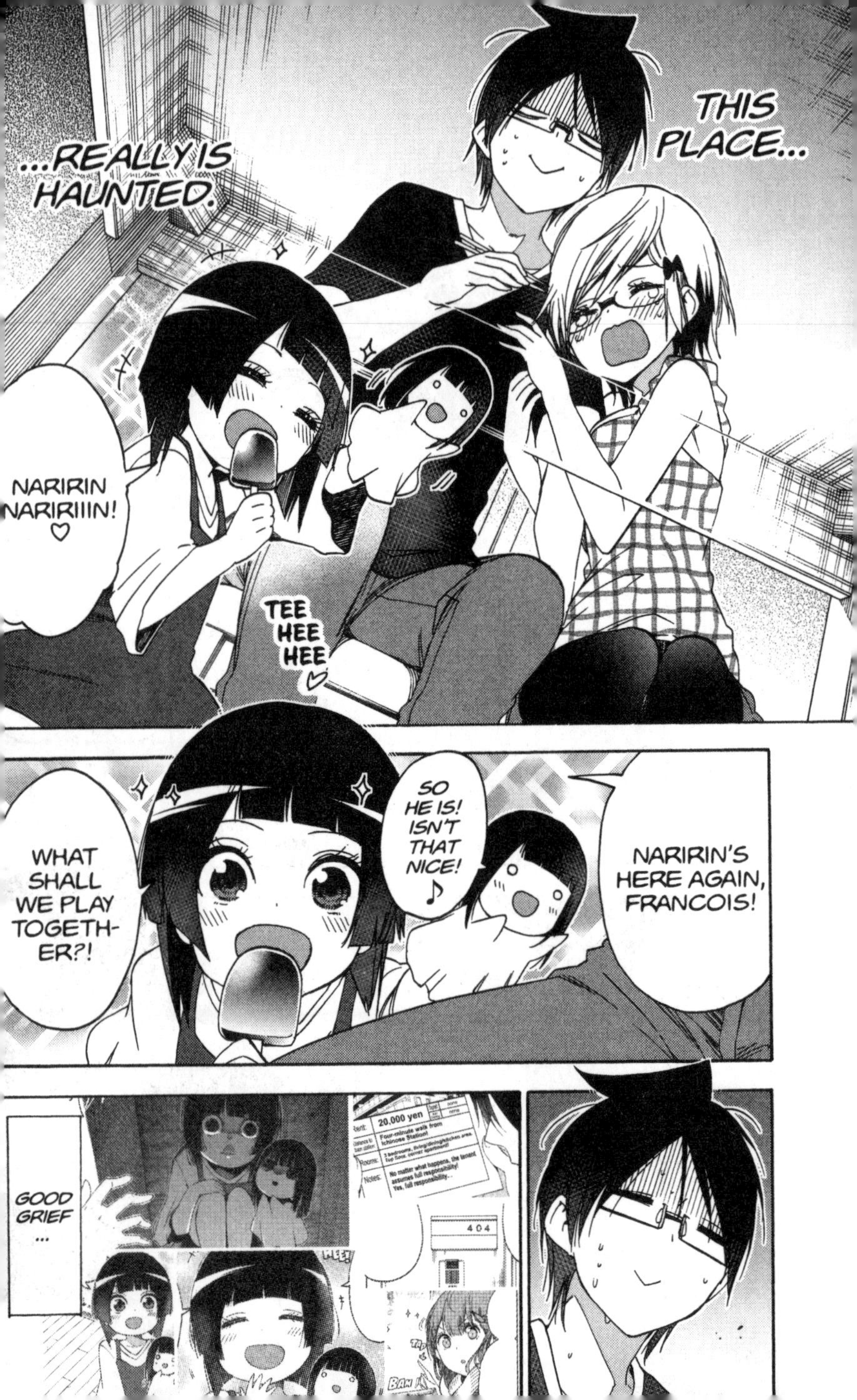
THIS PLACE...
...REALLY IS HAUNTED.
TEE HEE HEE ♡
NARIRIN NARIRIIIN! ♡
NARIRIN'S HERE AGAIN, FRANCOIS!
SO HE IS! ISN'T THAT NICE! ♪
WHAT SHALL WE PLAY TOGETH-ER?!
Rent: 20,000 yen
Four-minute walk from Ichinose Station!
No matter what happens, the tenant assumes full responsibility! Yes, full responsibility...
404
GOOD GRIEF ...

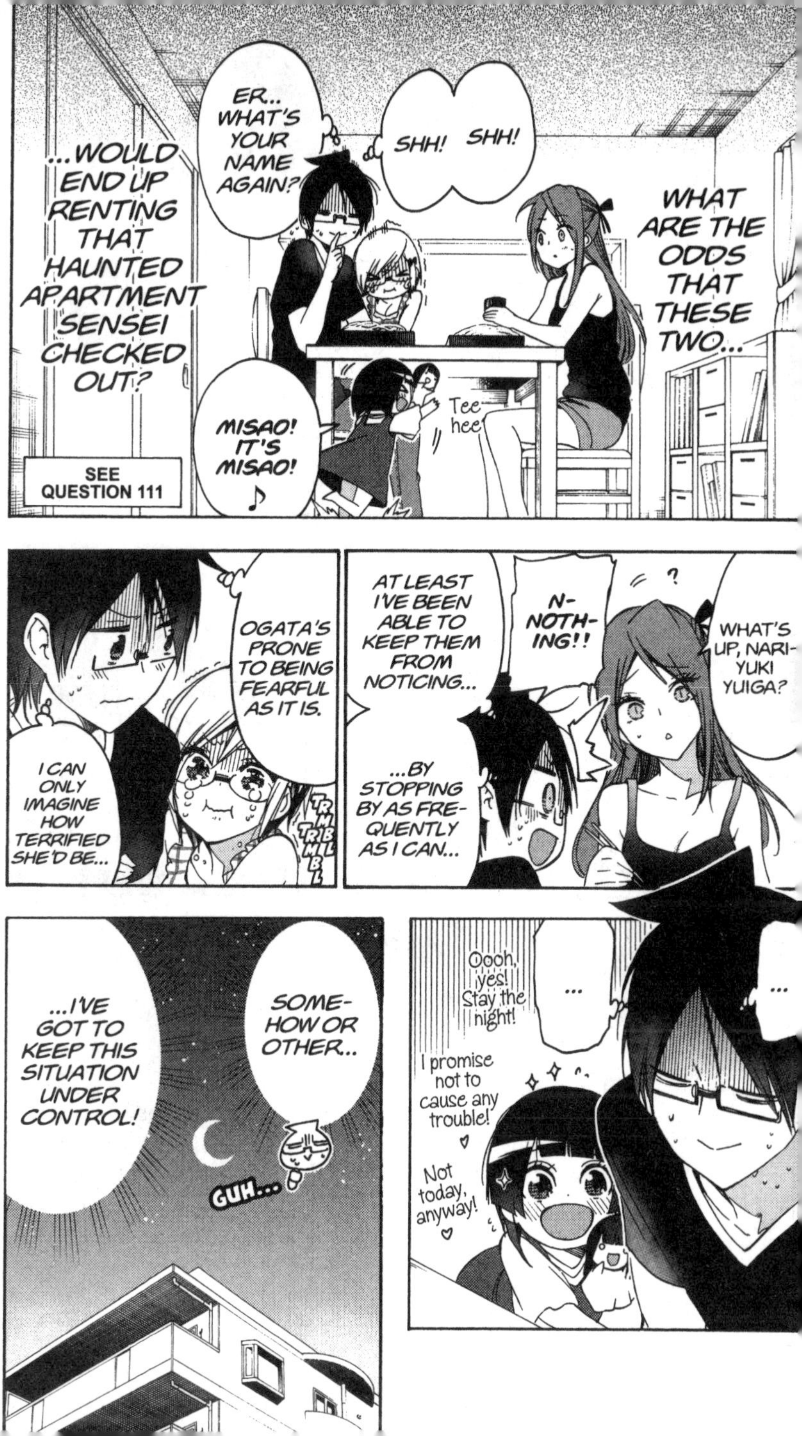
WHAT ARE THE ODDS THAT THESE TWO...
SHH! SHH!
ER... WHAT'S YOUR NAME AGAIN?
...WOULD END UP RENTING THAT HAUNTED APARTMENT SENSEI CHECKED OUT?
MISAO! IT'S MISAO! ♪
Tee hee
SEE QUESTION 111
WHAT'S UP, NARIYUKI YUIGA?
N-NOTHING!!
AT LEAST I'VE BEEN ABLE TO KEEP THEM FROM NOTICING...
...BY STOPPING BY AS FREQUENTLY AS I CAN...
OGATA'S PRONE TO BEING FEARFUL AS IT IS.
I CAN ONLY IMAGINE HOW TERRIFIED SHE'D BE...
TRMBL TRMBL
...
...
Oooh, yes! Stay the night!
I promise not to cause any trouble! ♡
Not today, anyway! ♡
SOME-HOW OR OTHER...
...I'VE GOT TO KEEP THIS SITUATION UNDER CONTROL!
GUH...

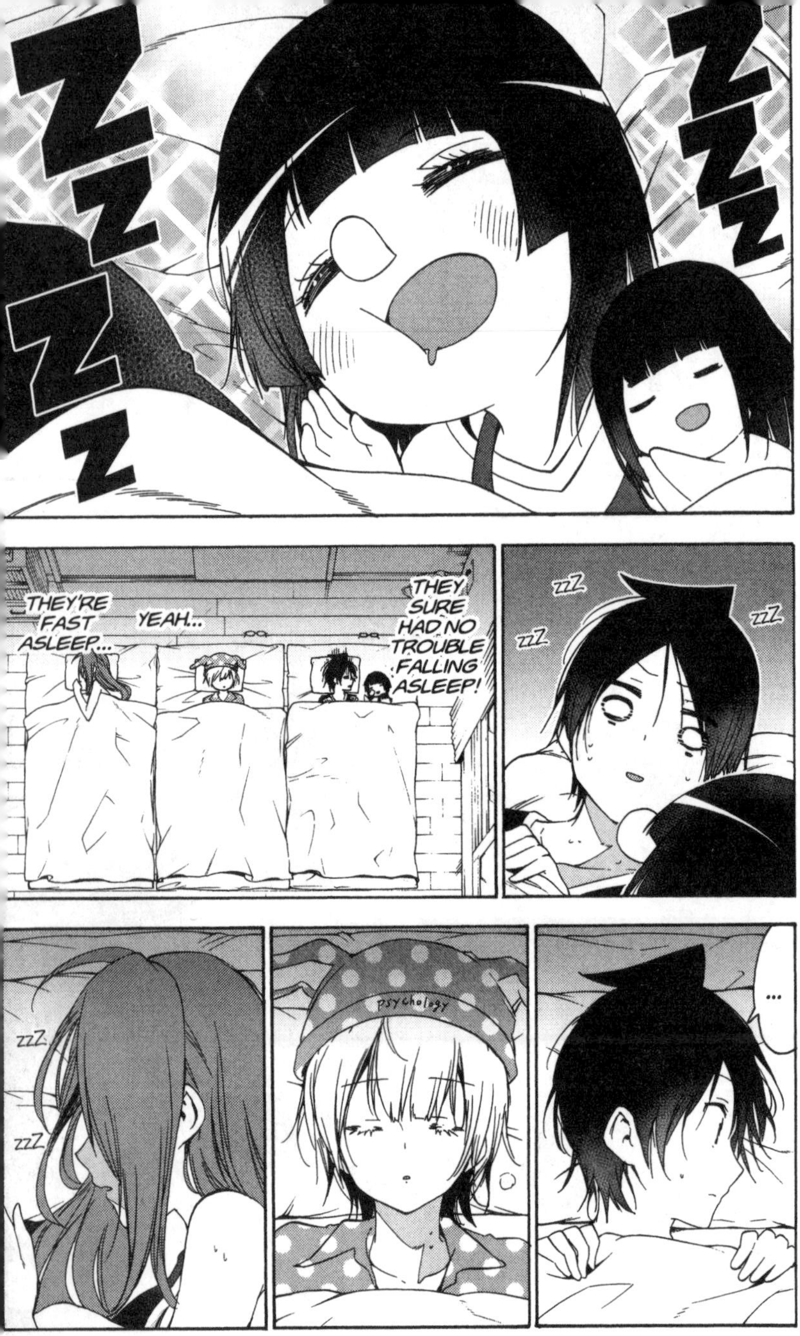
ZZZZ
ZZZZZ
zzZ
zzZ
zzZ
THEY SURE HAD NO TROUBLE FALLING ASLEEP!
YEAH...
THEY'RE FAST ASLEEP...
...
psychology
zzZ
zzZ

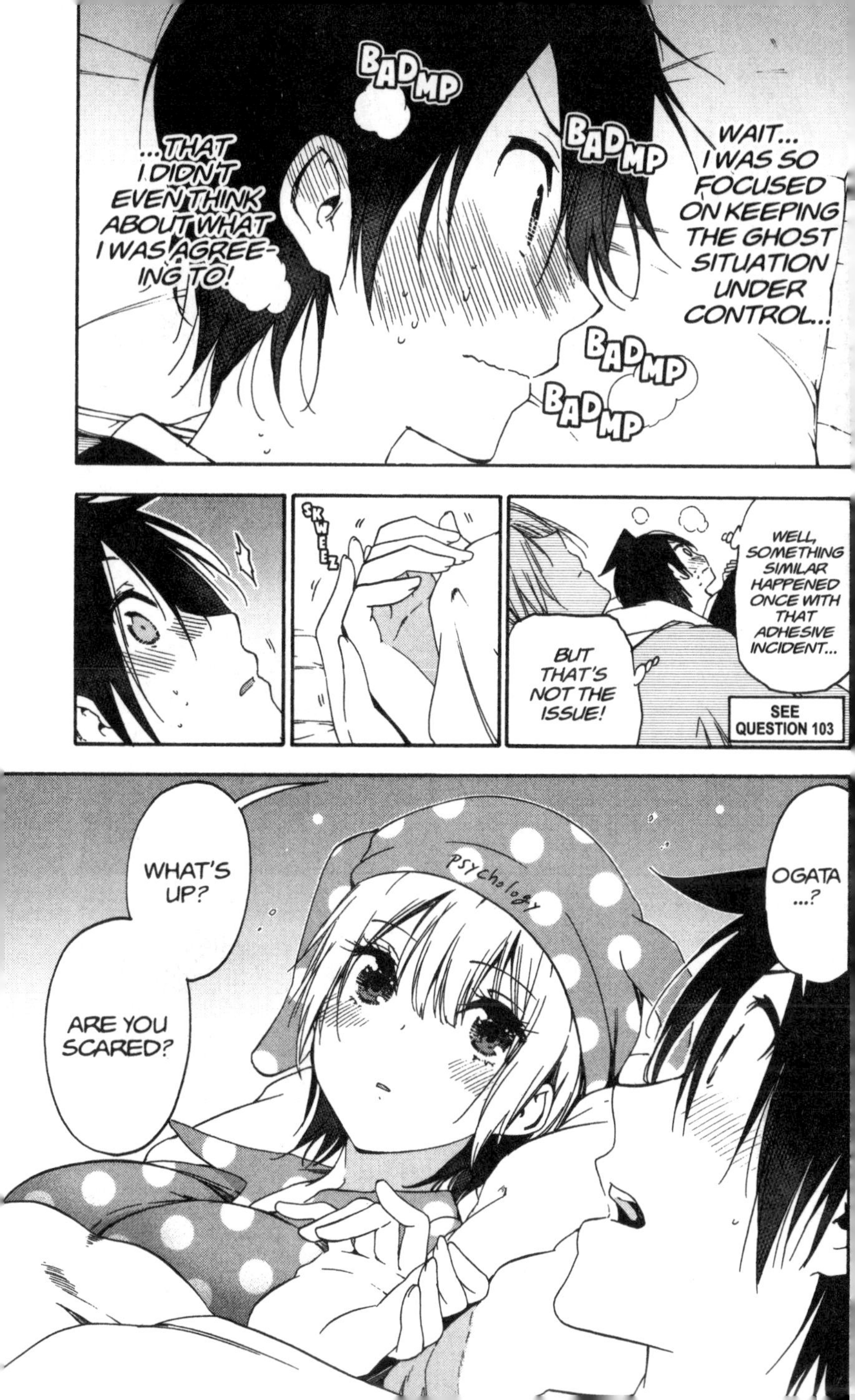
WAIT... I WAS SO FOCUSED ON KEEPING THE GHOST SITUATION UNDER CONTROL...
BADMP
BADMP
...THAT I DIDN'T EVEN THINK ABOUT WHAT I WAS AGREE-ING TO!
BADMP
BADMP
WELL, SOMETHING SIMILAR HAPPENED ONCE WITH THAT ADHESIVE INCIDENT...
BUT THAT'S NOT THE ISSUE!
SEE QUESTION 103
SKWEEZ
OGATA ...?
Psychology
WHAT'S UP?
ARE YOU SCARED?

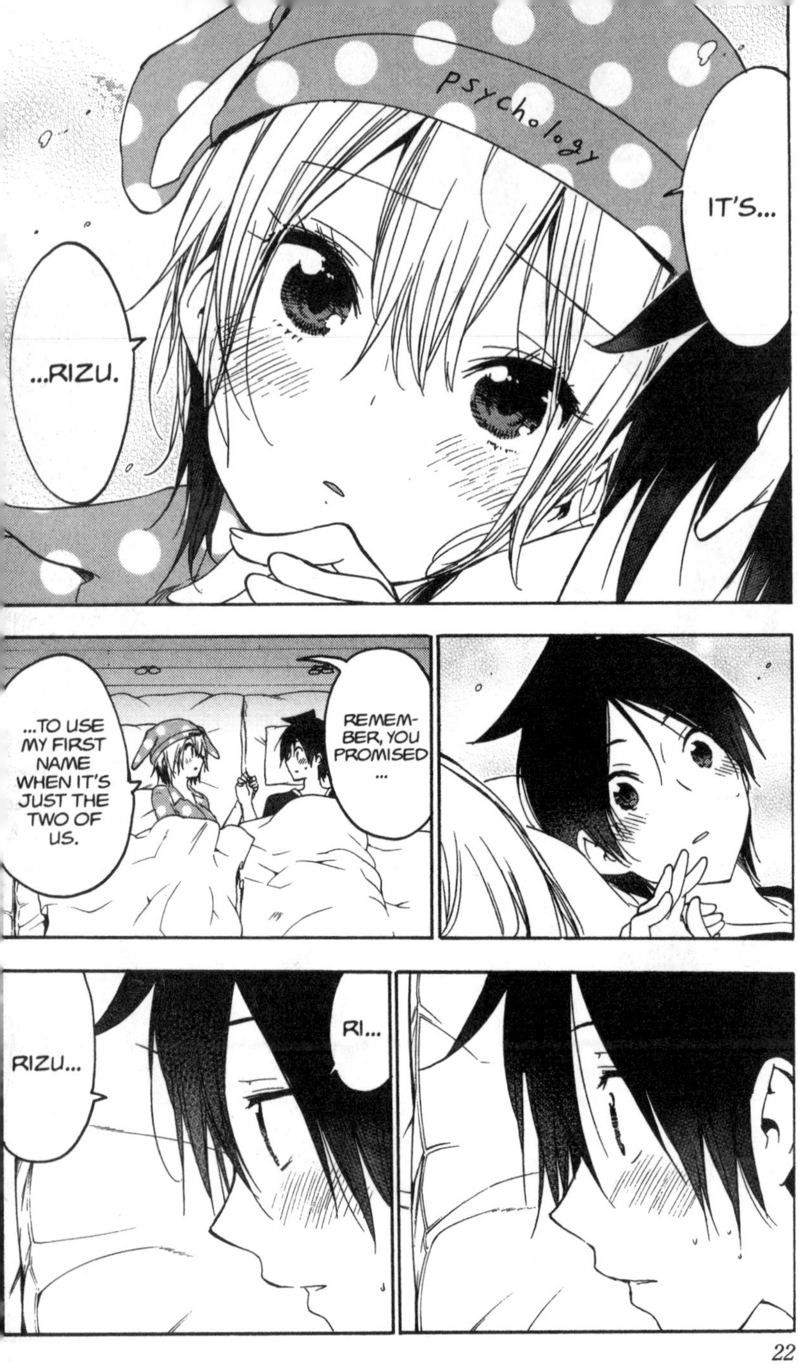
IT'S...
...RIZU.
REMEM-BER, YOU PROMISED...
...TO USE MY FIRST NAME WHEN IT'S JUST THE TWO OF US.
RI...
RIZU...

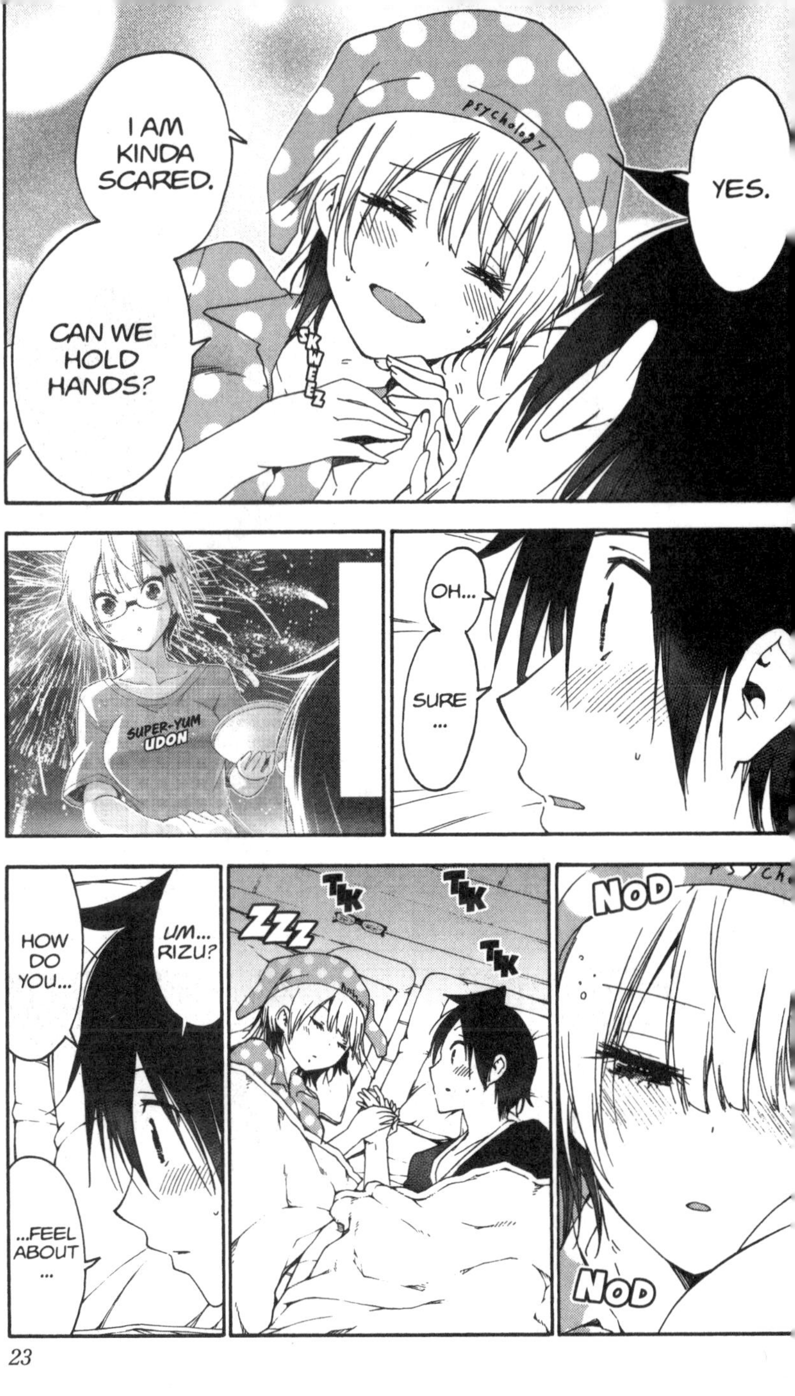
YES.
psychology
I AM KINDA SCARED.
SKWEEZ
CAN WE HOLD HANDS?
OH...
SURE ...
SUPER-YUM UDON
NOD
psych
NOD
TIK
TIK
TIK
ZZZ
UM... RIZU?
HOW DO YOU...
...FEEL ABOUT ...

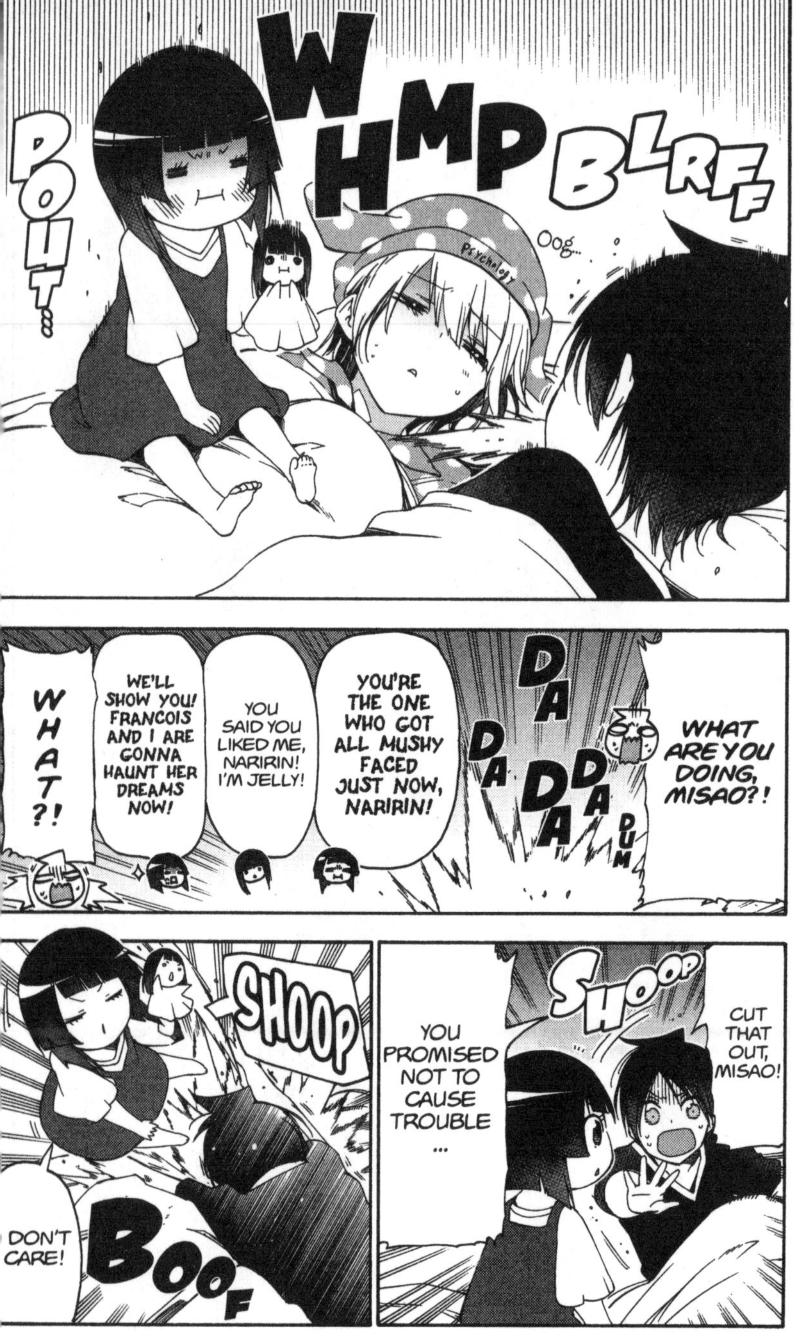
BLRFF
Oog...
WHMP
POUT...
WHAT ARE YOU DOING, MISAO?!
DADADADADA DUM
YOU'RE THE ONE WHO GOT ALL MUSHY FACED JUST NOW, NARIRIN!
YOU SAID YOU LIKED ME, NARIRIN! I'M JELLY!
WE'LL SHOW YOU! FRANCOIS AND I ARE GONNA HAUNT HER DREAMS NOW!
WHAT?!
SHOOP
CUT THAT OUT, MISAO!
YOU PROMISED NOT TO CAUSE TROUBLE ...
SHOOP
DON'T CARE!
BOOF

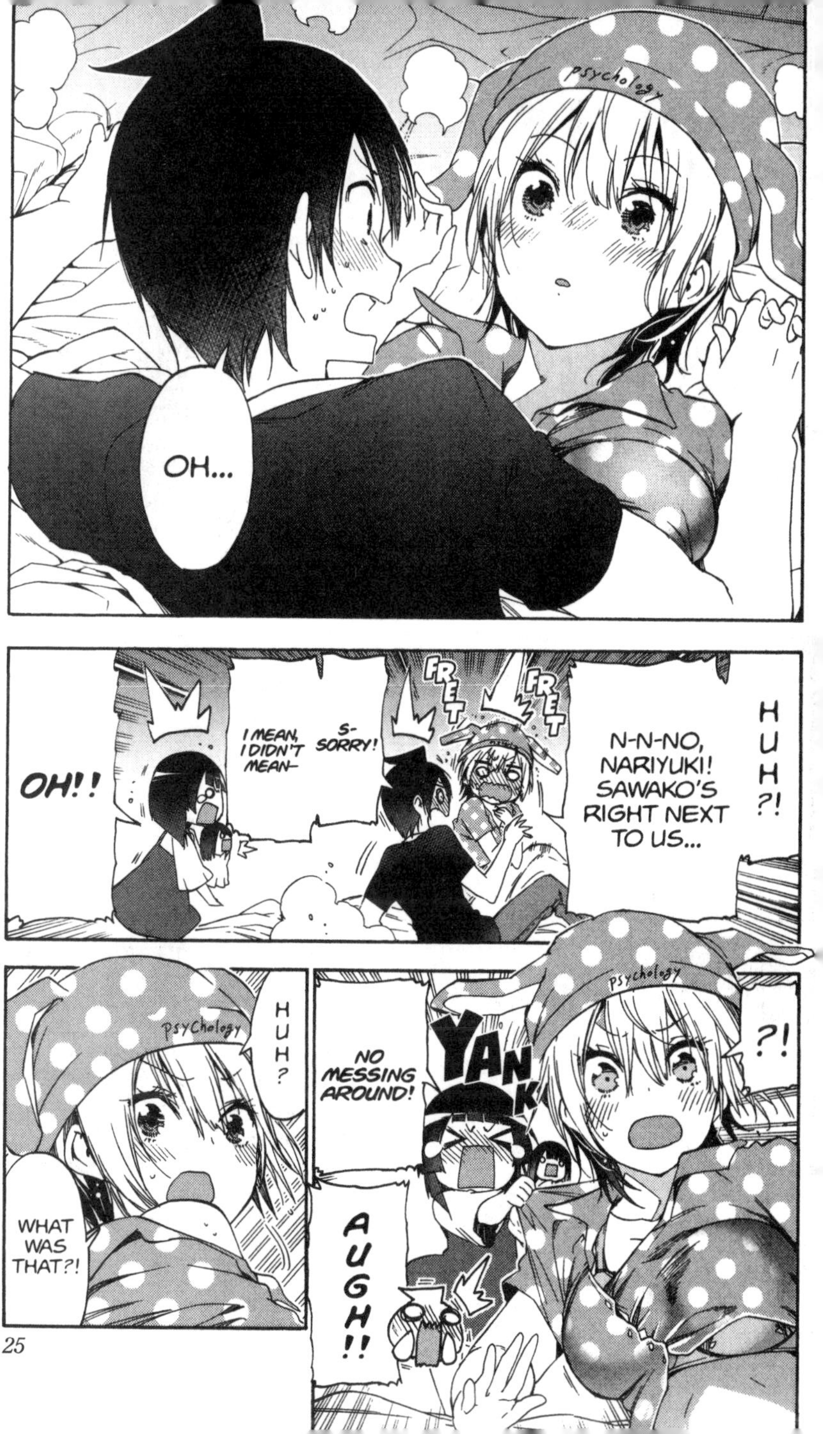

OH...
HUH?!
N-N-NO, NARIYUKI! SAWAKO'S RIGHT NEXT TO US...
FRET
FRET
S-SORRY!
I MEAN, I DIDN'T MEAN—
OH!!
?!
YANK
NO MESSING AROUND!
AUGH!!
HUH?
WHAT WAS THAT?!

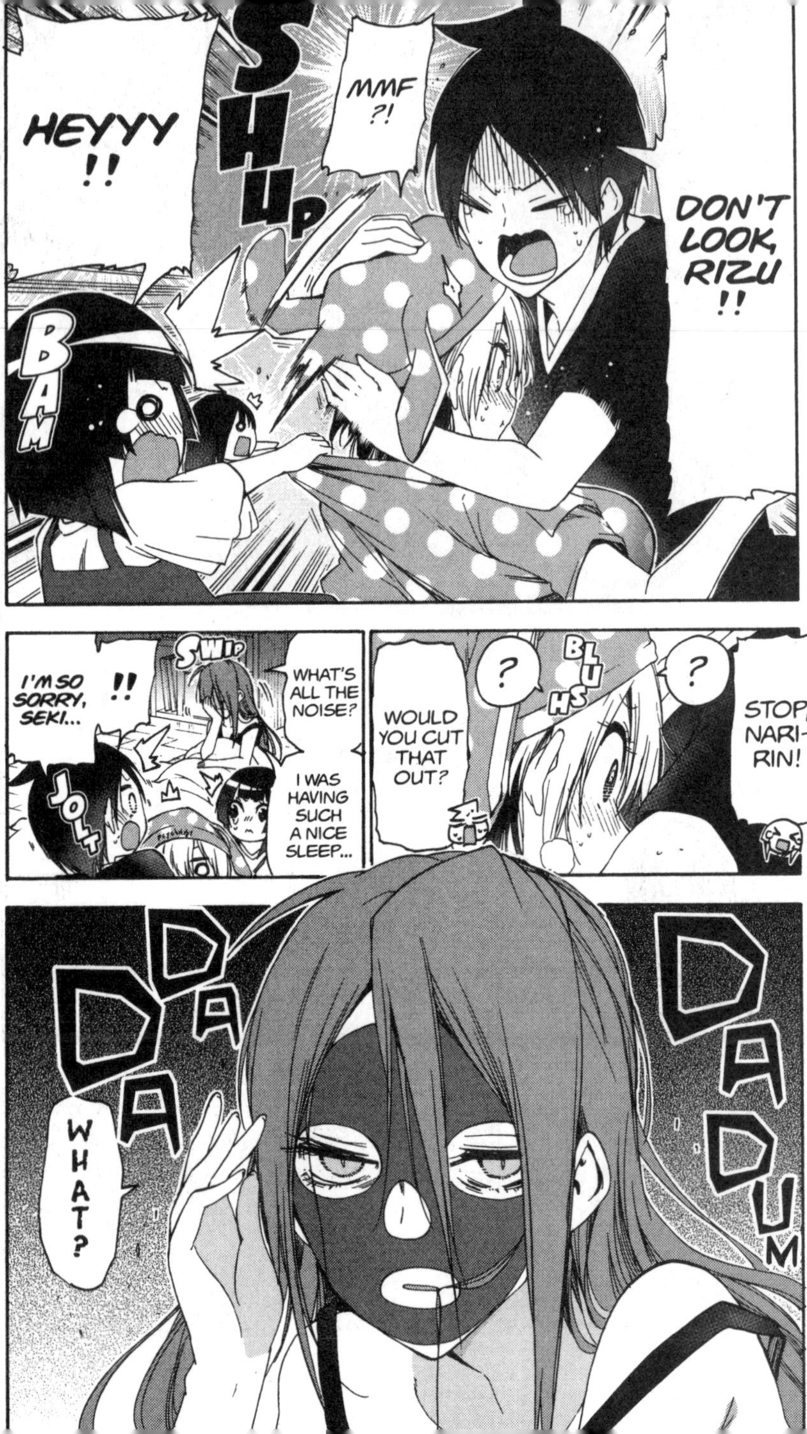
DON'T LOOK, RIZU!!
MMF ?!
SHUP
HEYYY !!
BAM
STOP, NARI-RIN!
?
BLUSH
?
WOULD YOU CUT THAT OUT?
WHAT'S ALL THE NOISE?
SWIP
!!
I'M SO SORRY, SEKI...
I WAS HAVING SUCH A NICE SLEEP...
JOLT
DADUM
DADA
WHAT?

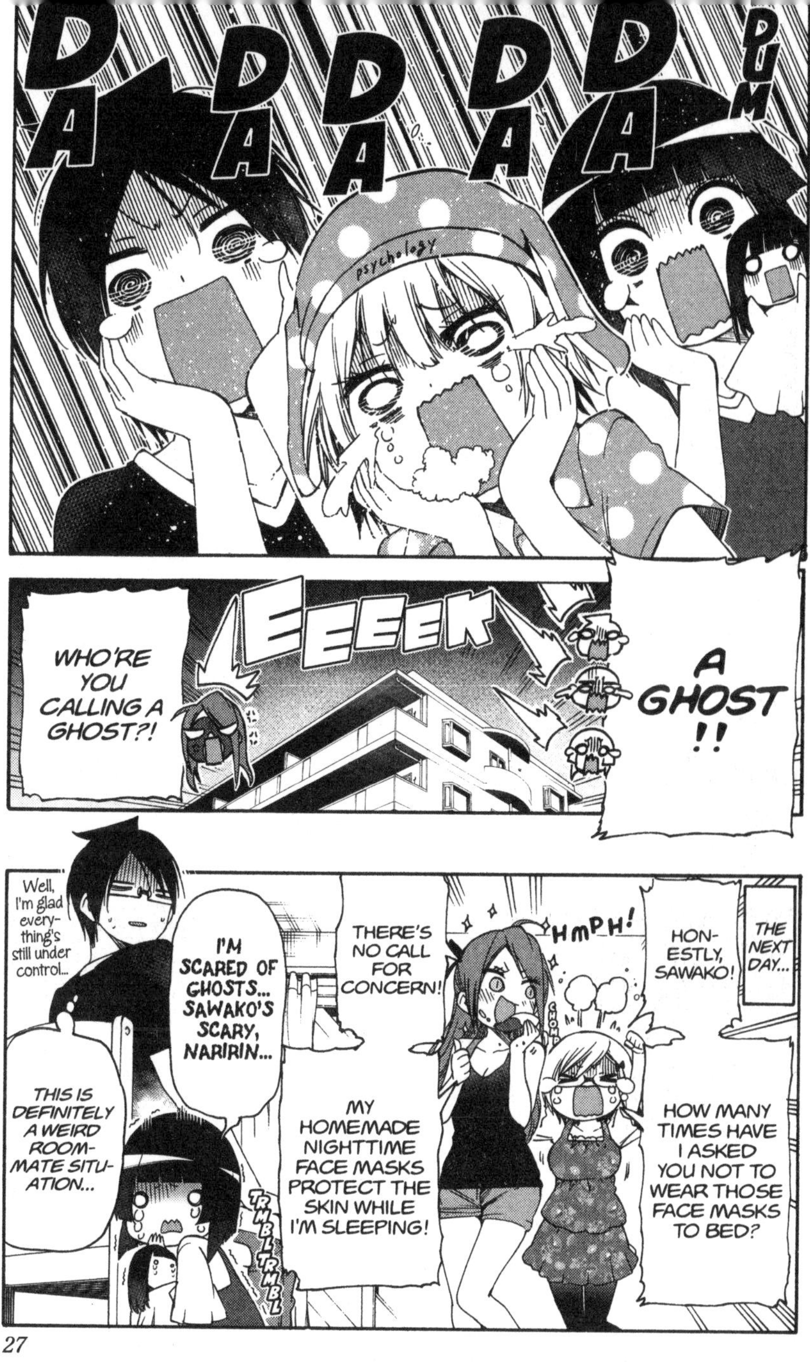
DA DA DA DA DA DUM
A GHOST!!
EEEEK
WHO'RE YOU CALLING A GHOST?!
THE NEXT DAY...
HON-ESTLY, SAWAKO!
HOW MANY TIMES HAVE I ASKED YOU NOT TO WEAR THOSE FACE MASKS TO BED?
HMPH!
THERE'S NO CALL FOR CONCERN!
MY HOMEMADE NIGHTTIME FACE MASKS PROTECT THE SKIN WHILE I'M SLEEPING!
I'M SCARED OF GHOSTS... SAWAKO'S SCARY, NARIRIN...
TRMBL TRMBL
THIS IS DEFINITELY A WEIRD ROOM-MATE SITU-ATION...
Well, I'm glad every-thing's still under control...

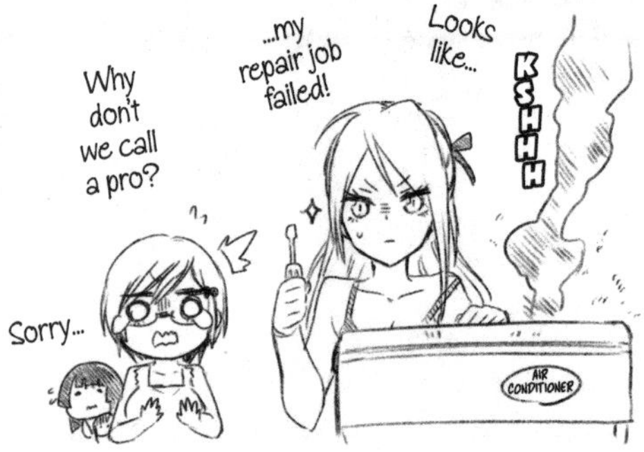
Looks like...
KSHHH
...my repair job failed!
Why don't we call a pro?
AIR CONDITIONER
Sorry...

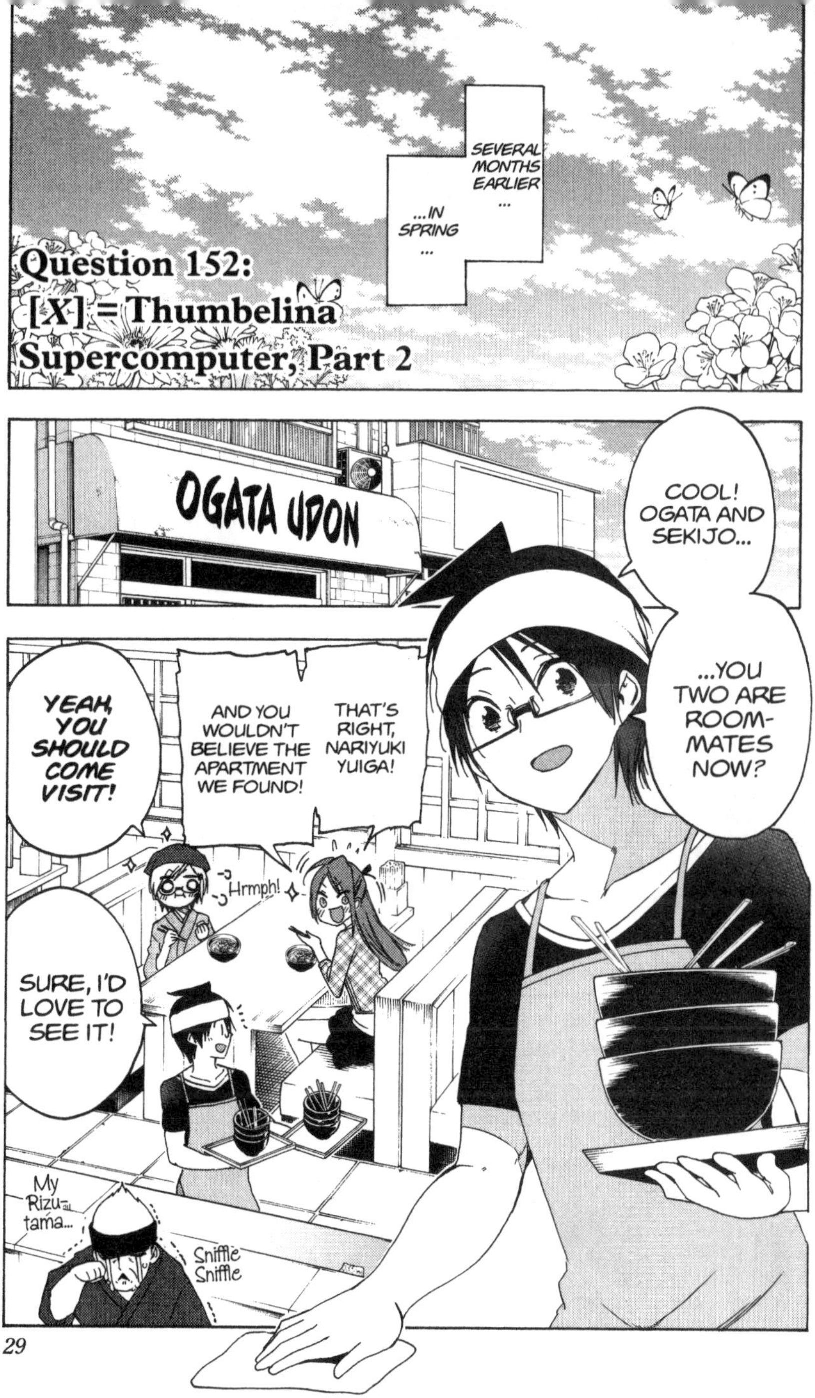
SEVERAL MONTHS EARLIER...
...IN SPRING...
Question 152: [X] = Thumbelina Supercomputer, Part 2
COOL! OGATA AND SEKIJO...
OGATA UDON
...YOU TWO ARE ROOM-MATES NOW?
THAT'S RIGHT, NARIYUKI YUIGA!
AND YOU WOULDN'T BELIEVE THE APARTMENT WE FOUND!
YEAH, YOU SHOULD COME VISIT!
Hrmph!
SURE, I'D LOVE TO SEE IT!
My Rizu-tama...
Sniffle Sniffle

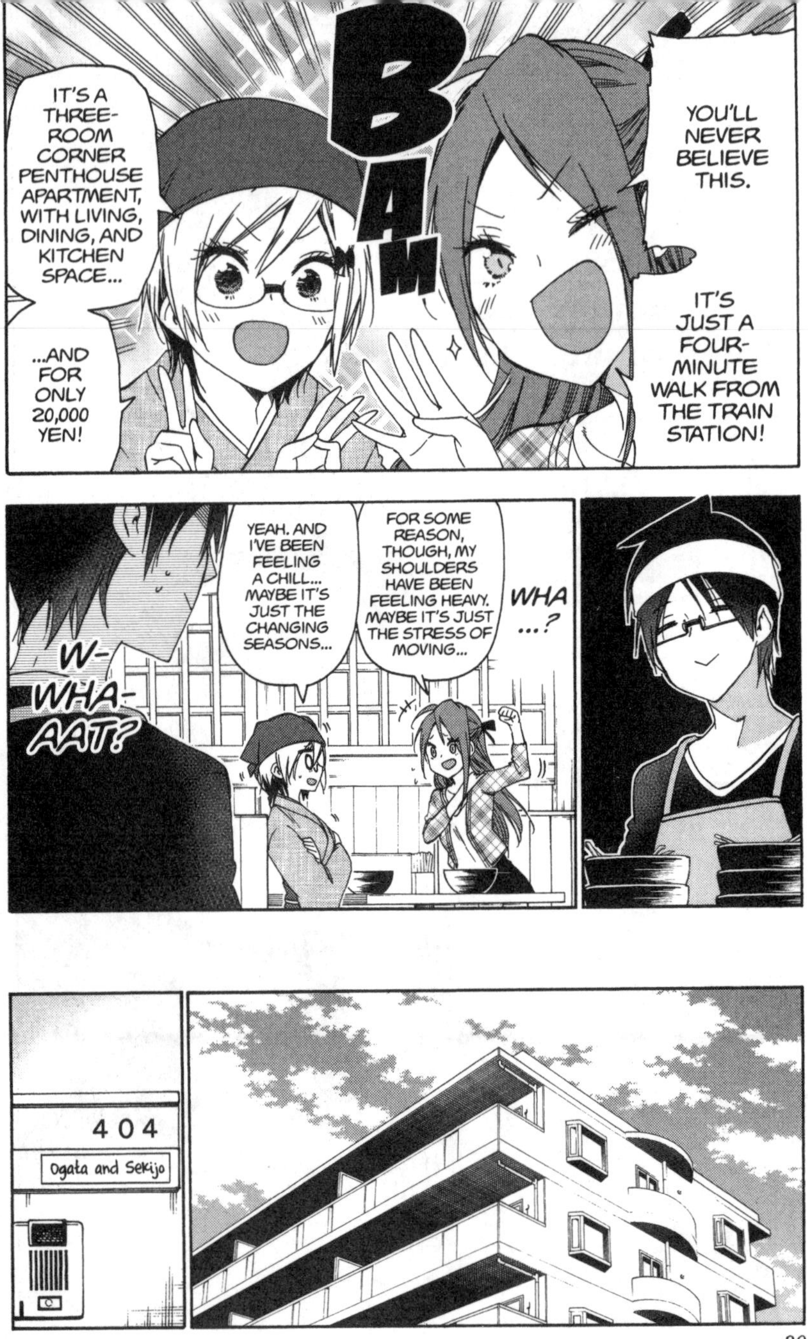
YOU'LL NEVER BELIEVE THIS.
IT'S JUST A FOUR-MINUTE WALK FROM THE TRAIN STATION!
BAM
IT'S A THREE-ROOM CORNER PENTHOUSE APARTMENT, WITH LIVING, DINING, AND KITCHEN SPACE...
...AND FOR ONLY 20,000 YEN!
WHA ...?
FOR SOME REASON, THOUGH, MY SHOULDERS HAVE BEEN FEELING HEAVY. MAYBE IT'S JUST THE STRESS OF MOVING...
YEAH. AND I'VE BEEN FEELING A CHILL... MAYBE IT'S JUST THE CHANGING SEASONS...
W-WHA-AAT?
404
Ogata and Sekijo

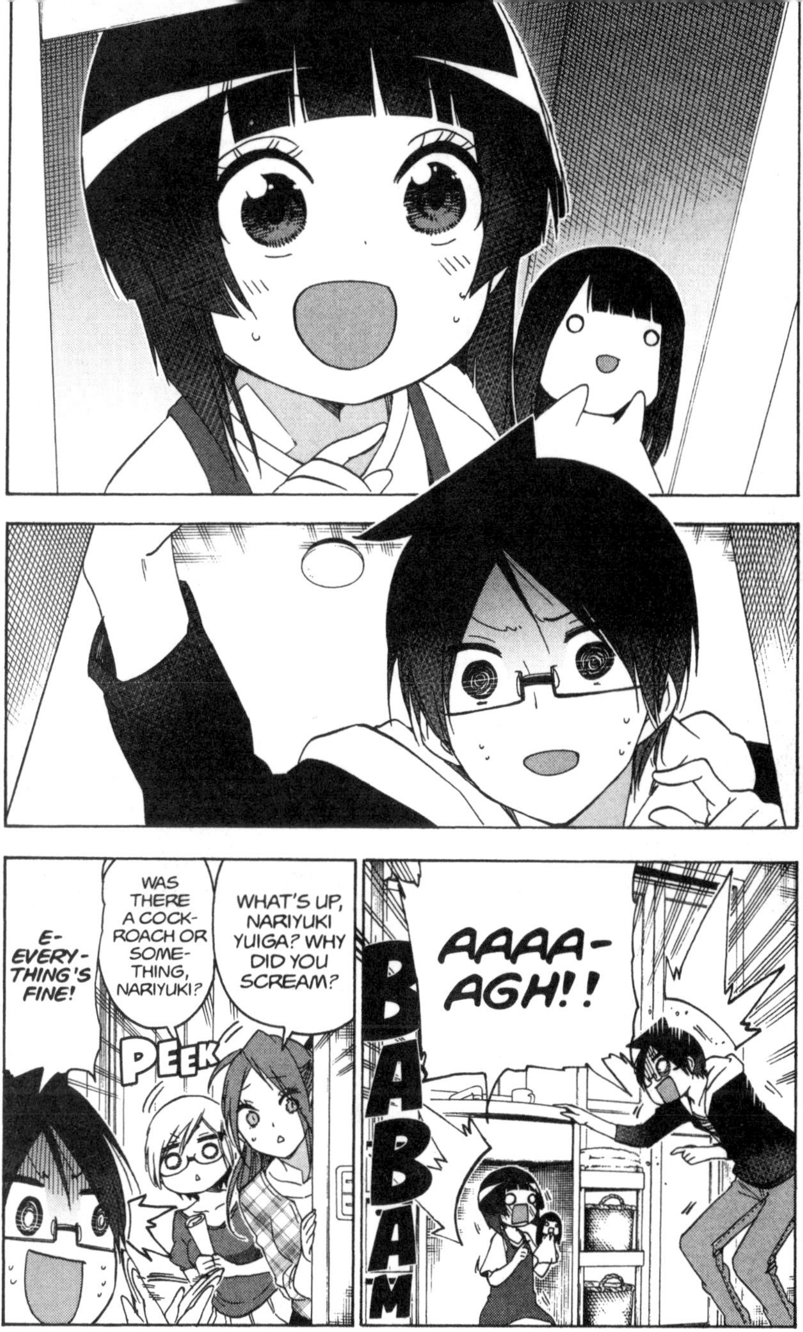
AAAA-AGH!!
BABAM
WHAT'S UP, NARIYUKI YUIGA? WHY DID YOU SCREAM?
WAS THERE A COCKROACH OR SOMETHING, NARIYUKI?
PEEK
E-EVERYTHING'S FINE!

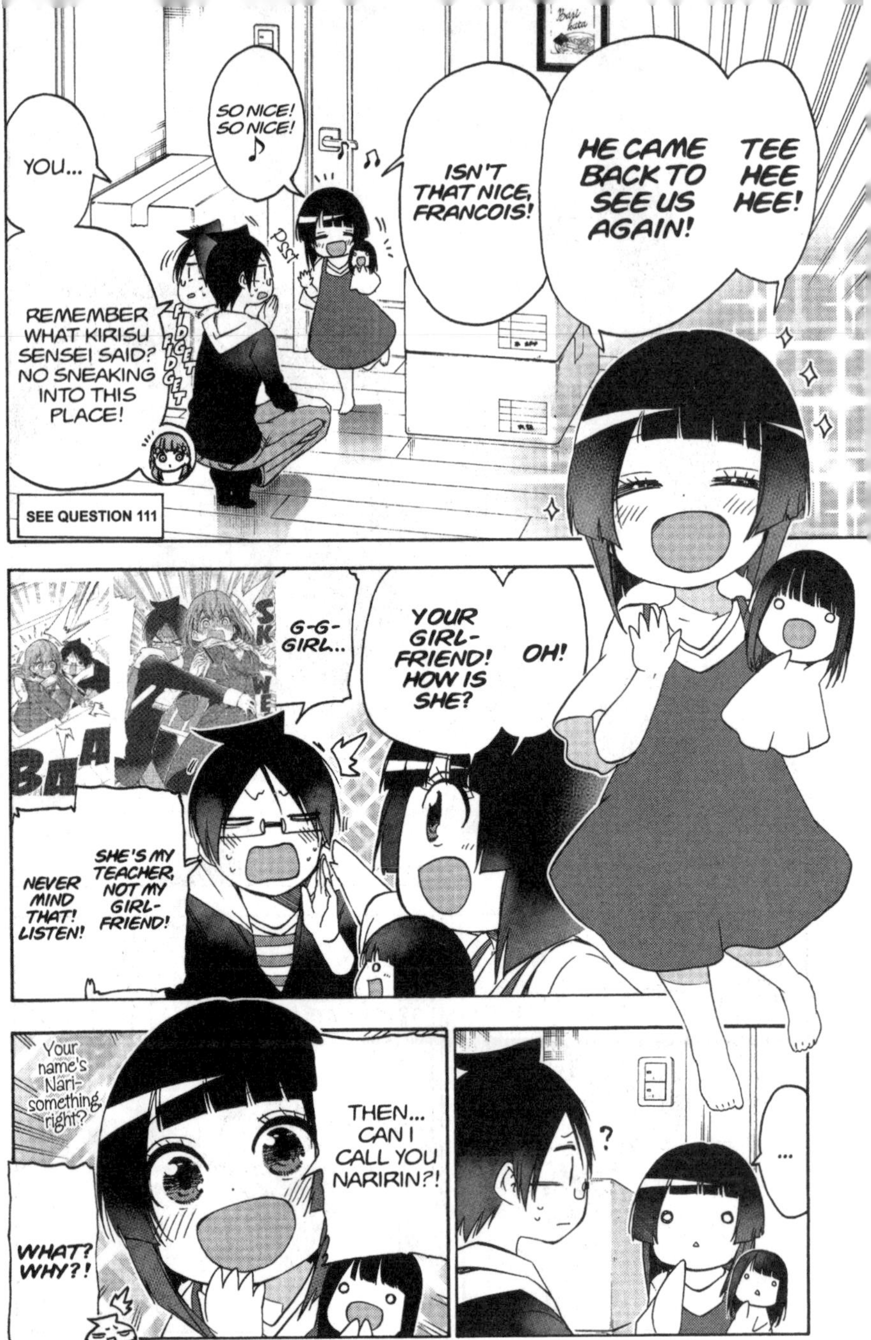
TEE HEE HEE!
HE CAME BACK TO SEE US AGAIN!
ISN'T THAT NICE, FRANCOIS!
SO NICE! SO NICE! ♪
PSST
FIDGET FIDGET
YOU... REMEMBER WHAT KIRISU SENSEI SAID? NO SNEAKING INTO THIS PLACE!
SEE QUESTION 111
OH!
YOUR GIRL-FRIEND! HOW IS SHE?
G-G-GIRL...
SHE'S MY TEACHER, NOT MY GIRL-FRIEND!
NEVER MIND THAT! LISTEN!
...
?
THEN... CAN I CALL YOU NARIRIN?!
Your name's Nari-something, right?
WHAT? WHY?!

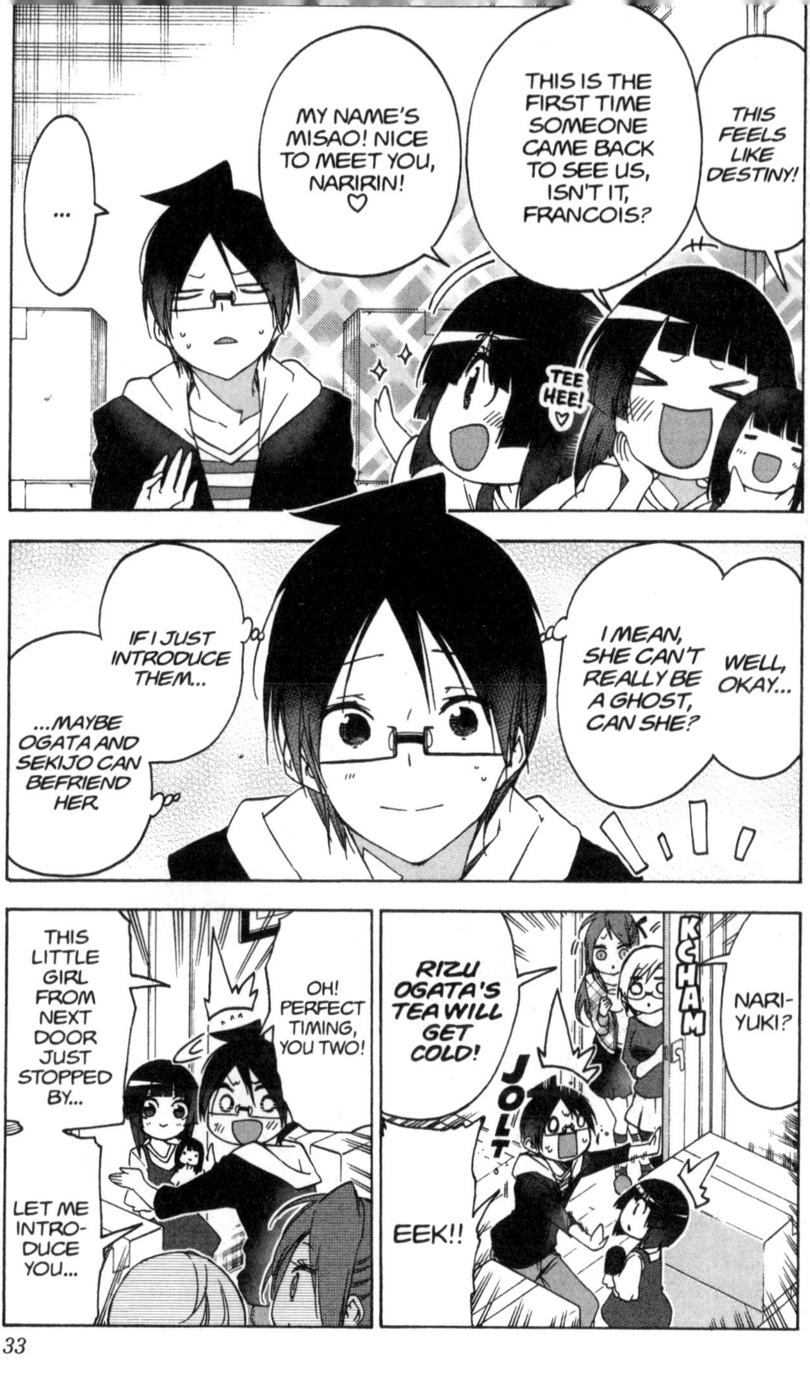
THIS FEELS LIKE DESTINY!
THIS IS THE FIRST TIME SOMEONE CAME BACK TO SEE US, ISN'T IT, FRANCOIS?
TEE HEE! ♡
MY NAME'S MISAO! NICE TO MEET YOU, NARIRIN! ♡
...
WELL, OKAY...
I MEAN, SHE CAN'T REALLY BE A GHOST, CAN SHE?
IF I JUST INTRODUCE THEM...
...MAYBE OGATA AND SEKIJO CAN BEFRIEND HER
NARI-YUKI?
KCHAM
RIZU OGATA'S TEA WILL GET COLD!
JOLT
EEK!!
OH! PERFECT TIMING, YOU TWO!
THIS LITTLE GIRL FROM NEXT DOOR JUST STOPPED BY...
LET ME INTRO-DUCE YOU...

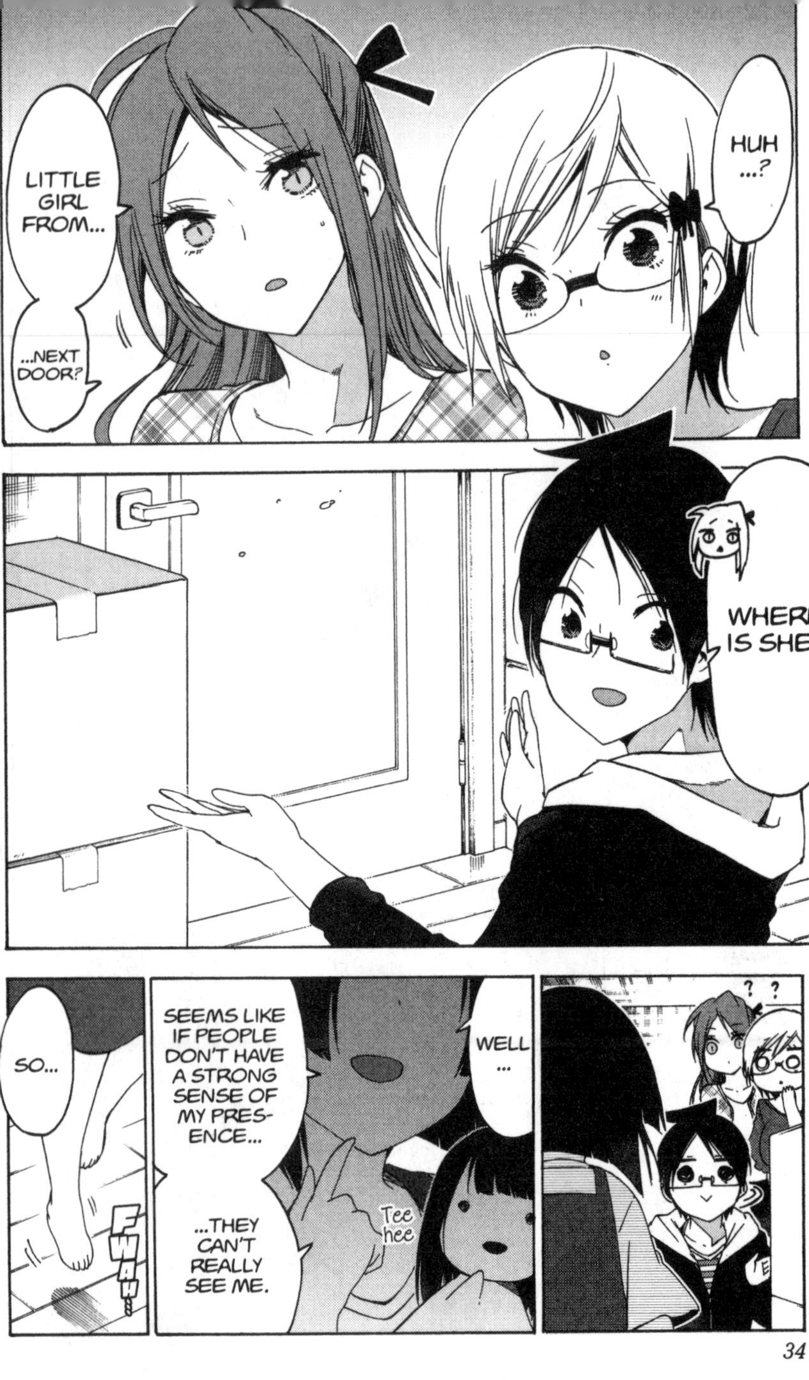
HUH ...?
LITTLE GIRL FROM...
...NEXT DOOR?
WHERE IS SHE?
? ?
WELL ...
SEEMS LIKE IF PEOPLE DON'T HAVE A STRONG SENSE OF MY PRES-ENCE...
Tee hee
...THEY CAN'T REALLY SEE ME.
SO...
FWAH

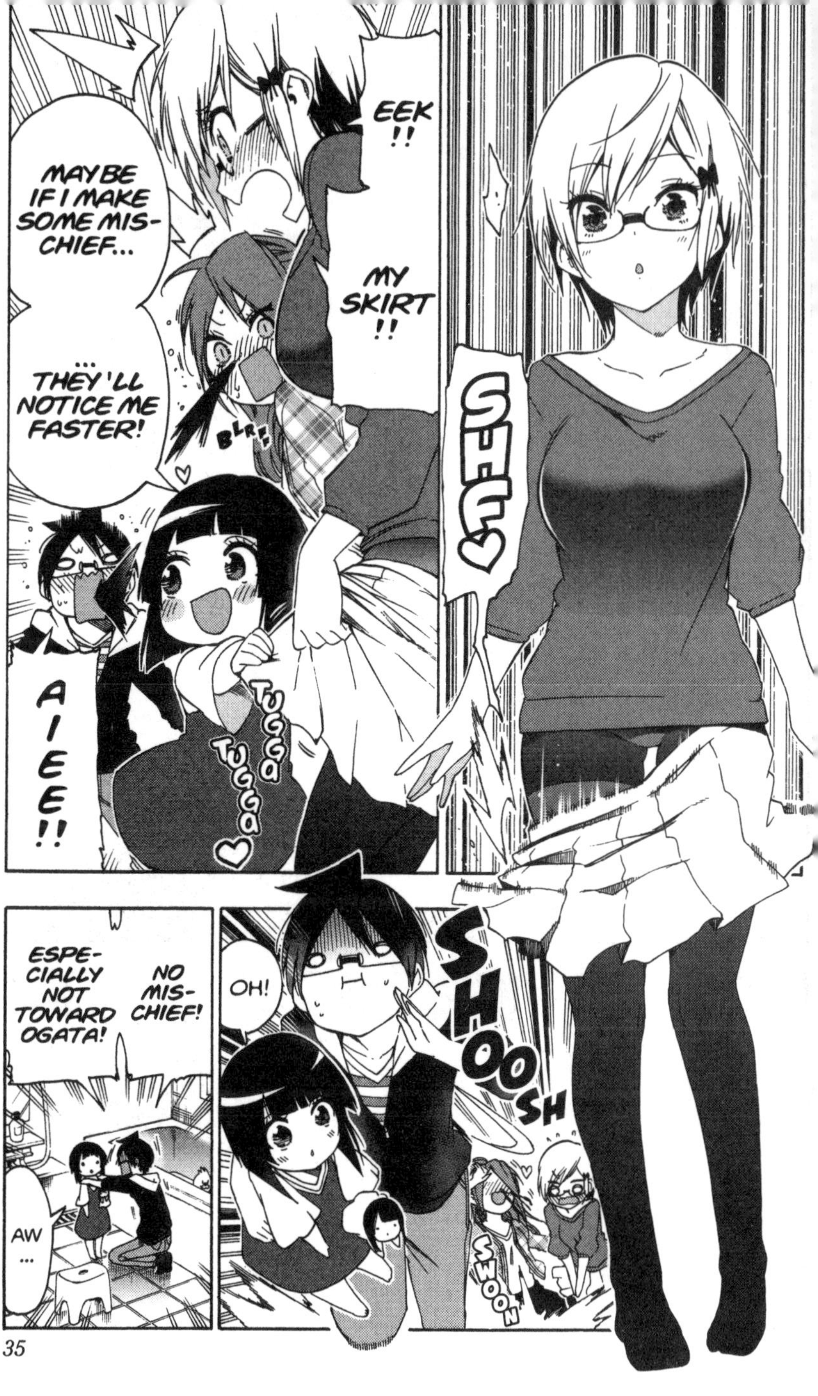
SHF♥
EEK!!
MY SKIRT!!
MAYBE IF I MAKE SOME MIS-CHIEF...
...THEY'LL NOTICE ME FASTER!
TUGGA TUGGA♥
AIEEE!!
SHOOSH
OH!
SWOON
NO MIS-CHIEF!
ESPE-CIALLY NOT TOWARD OGATA!
AW...

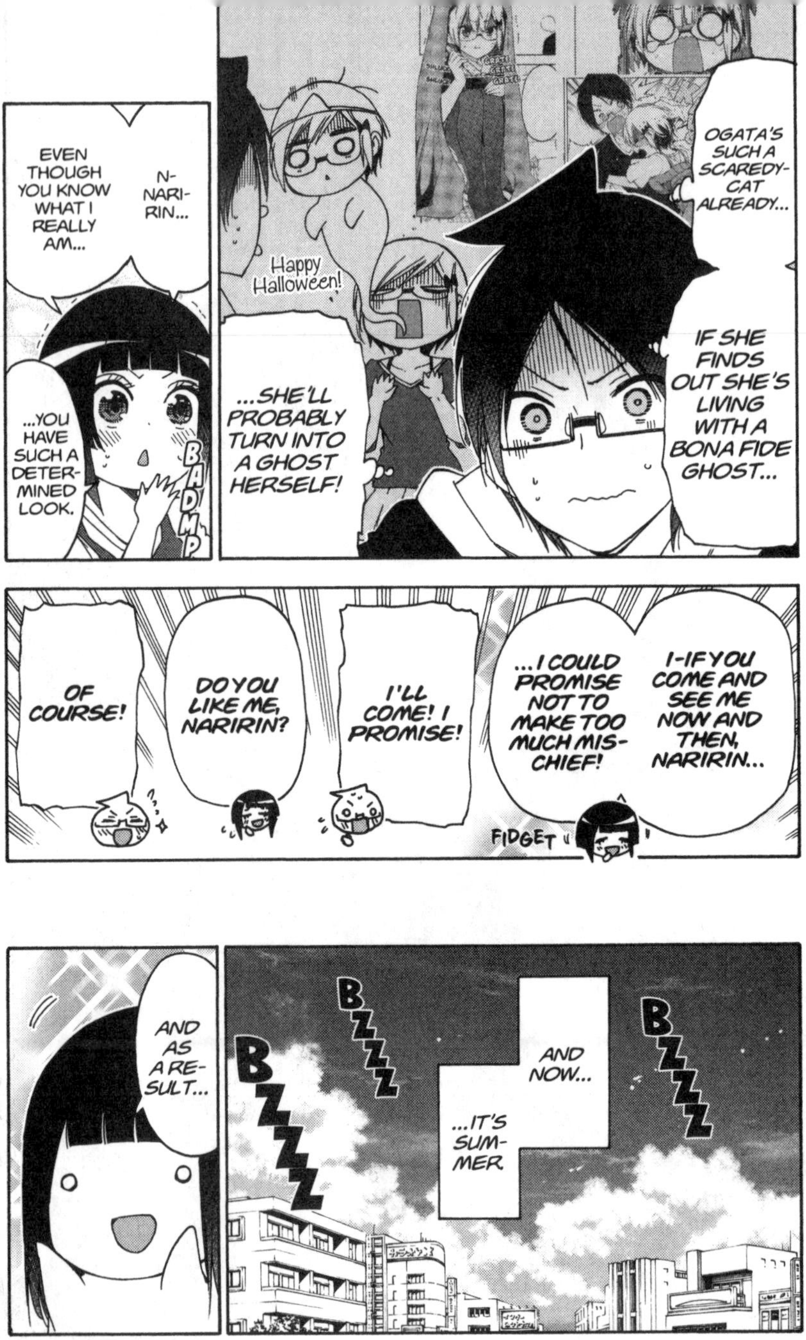
OGATA'S SUCH A SCAREDY-CAT ALREADY...
IF SHE FINDS OUT SHE'S LIVING WITH A BONA FIDE GHOST...
...SHE'LL PROBABLY TURN INTO A GHOST HERSELF!
Happy Halloween!
N-NARI-RIN...
EVEN THOUGH YOU KNOW WHAT I REALLY AM...
...YOU HAVE SUCH A DETER-MINED LOOK.
BADMP
I-IF YOU COME AND SEE ME NOW AND THEN, NARIRIN...
...I COULD PROMISE NOT TO MAKE TOO MUCH MIS-CHIEF!
FIDGET
I'LL COME! I PROMISE!
DO YOU LIKE ME, NARIRIN?
OF COURSE!
BZZZZ
AND NOW...
...IT'S SUM-MER.
BZZZZ
BZZZ
AND AS A RE-SULT...

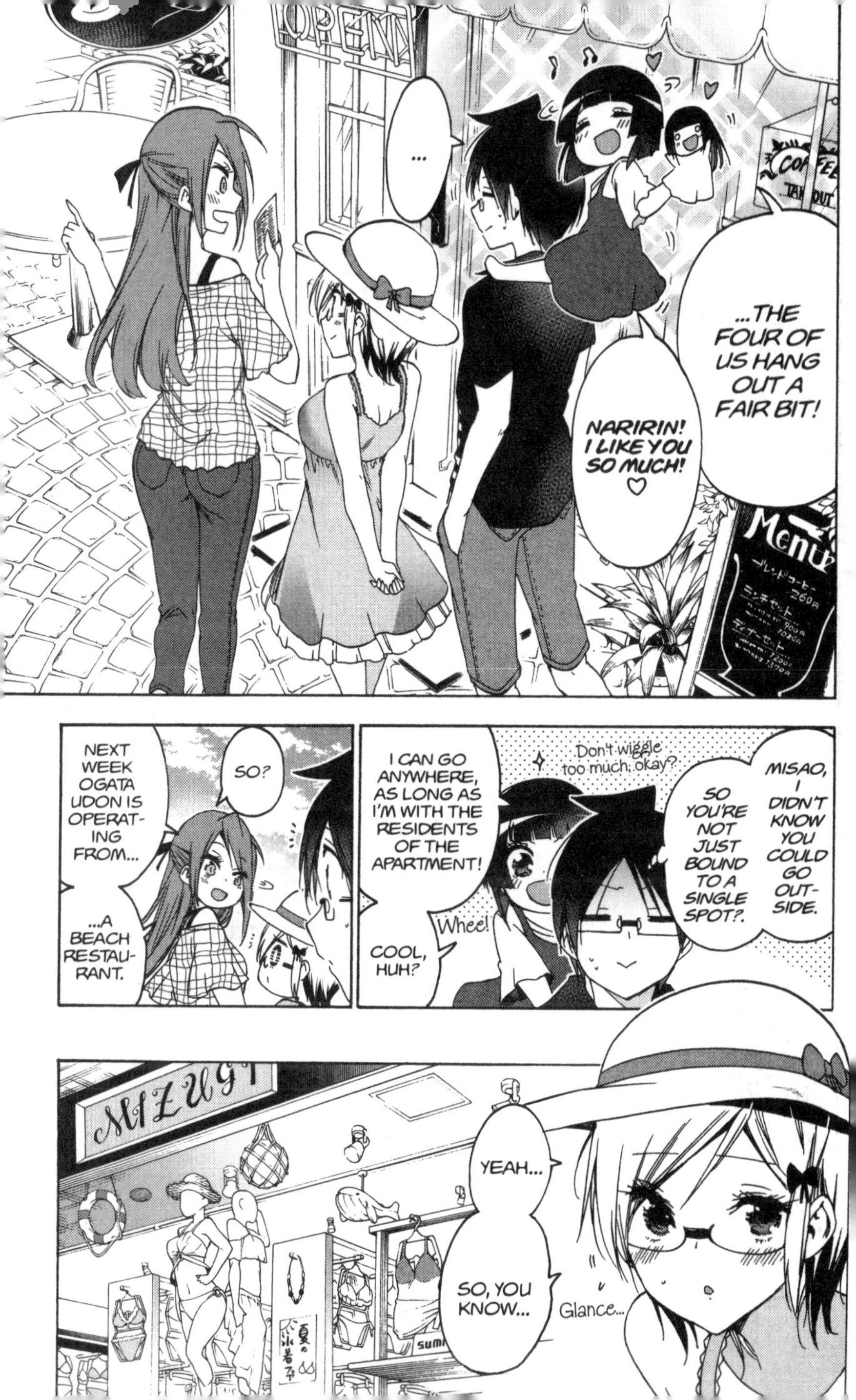
...THE FOUR OF US HANG OUT A FAIR BIT!
NARIRIN! I LIKE YOU SO MUCH! ♡
...
OPEN
COFFEE TAKE OUT
Menu
MISAO, I DIDN'T KNOW YOU COULD GO OUTSIDE.
SO YOU'RE NOT JUST BOUND TO A SINGLE SPOT?.
Don't wiggle too much, okay?
I CAN GO ANYWHERE, AS LONG AS I'M WITH THE RESIDENTS OF THE APARTMENT!
Whee!
COOL, HUH?
SO?
NEXT WEEK OGATA UDON IS OPERATING FROM...
...A BEACH RESTAURANT.
YEAH...
SO, YOU KNOW...
Glance...
MIZUGI

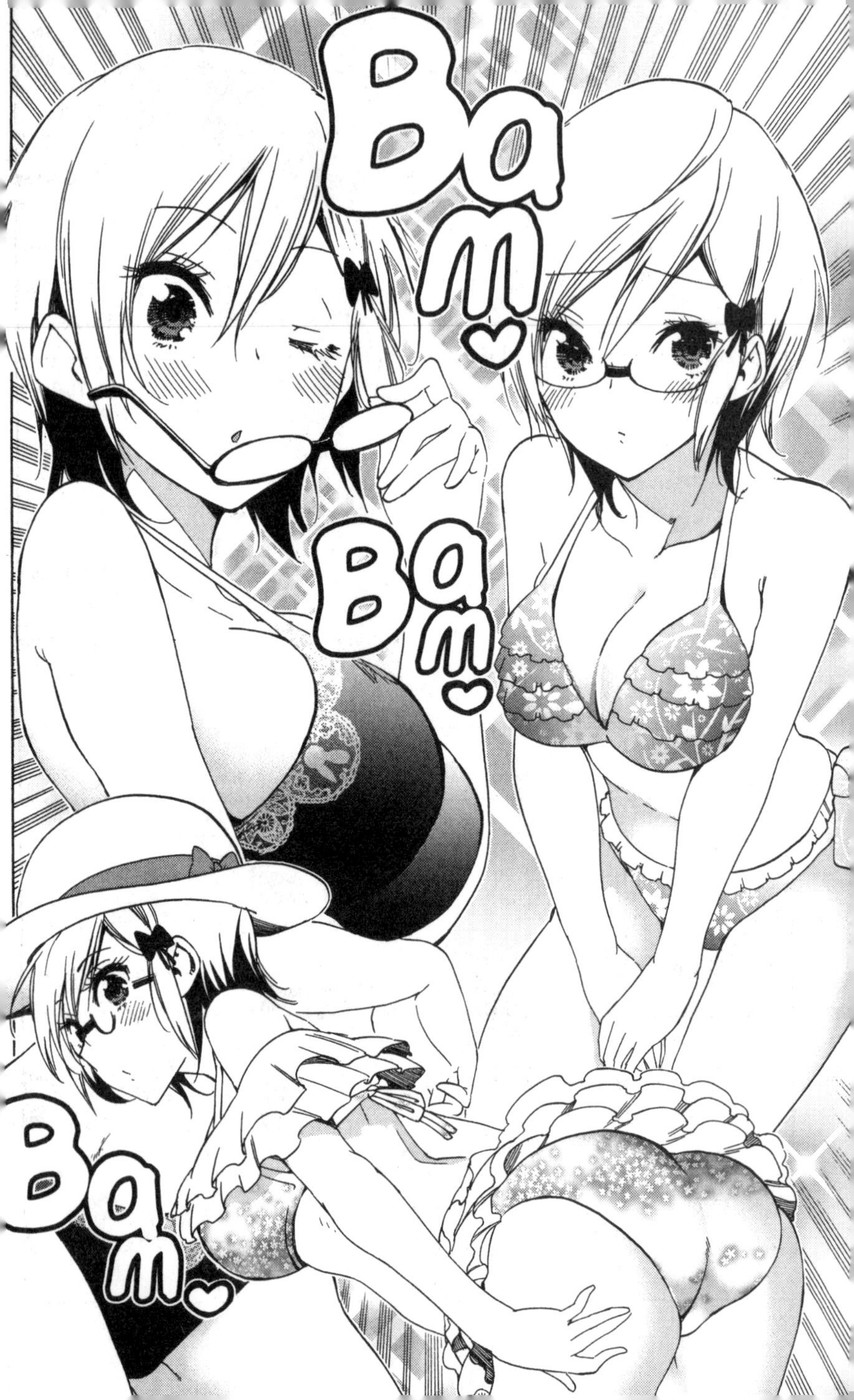

Bam♥
Bam♥
Bam.♥

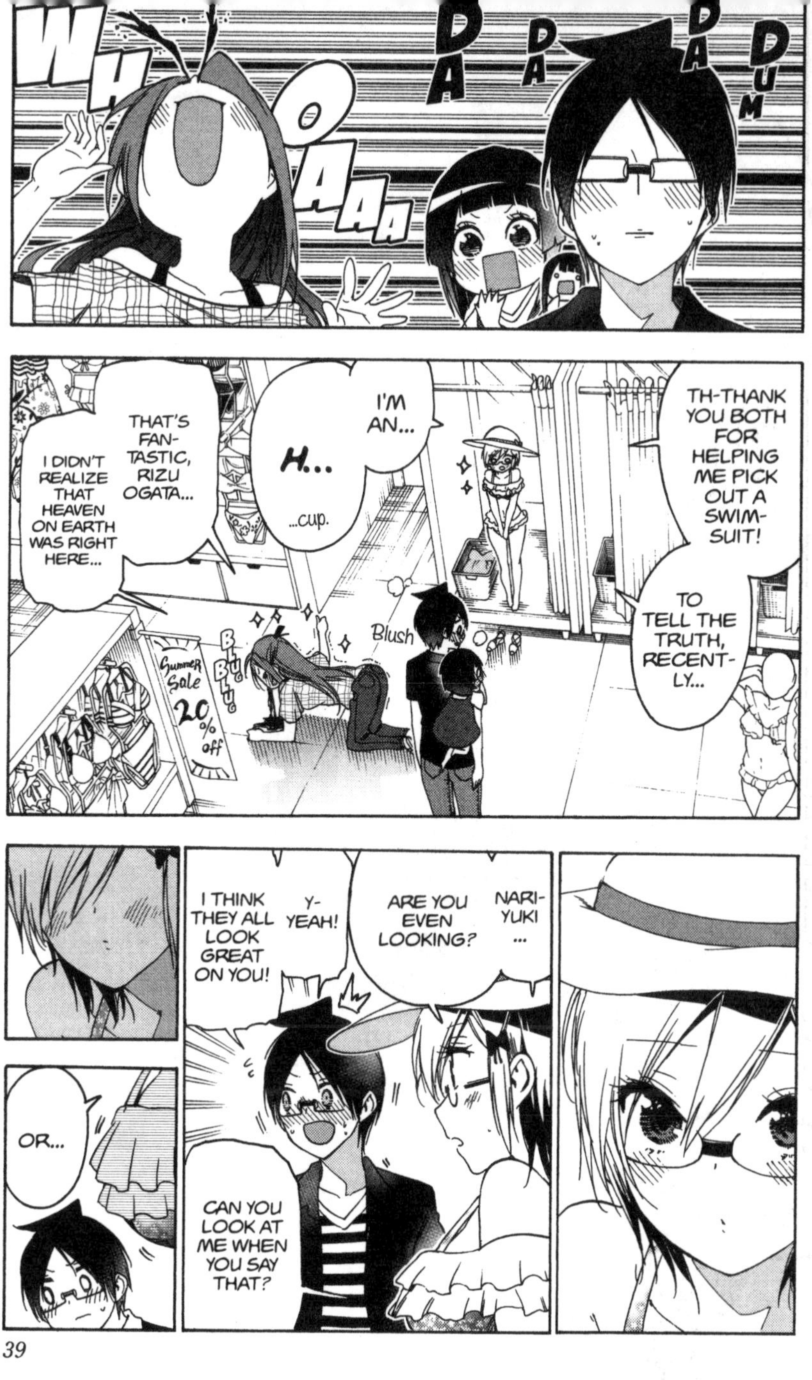

DA DA DA DUM
WHOOAAAA
TH-THANK YOU BOTH FOR HELPING ME PICK OUT A SWIMSUIT!
TO TELL THE TRUTH, RECENTLY...
Blush
I'M AN...
H... ...cup.
BLUG BLUG
THAT'S FANTASTIC, RIZU OGATA...
I DIDN'T REALIZE THAT HEAVEN ON EARTH WAS RIGHT HERE...
Summer Sale 20% off
NARIYUKI...
ARE YOU EVEN LOOKING?
Y-YEAH!
I THINK THEY ALL LOOK GREAT ON YOU!
CAN YOU LOOK AT ME WHEN YOU SAY THAT?
OR...

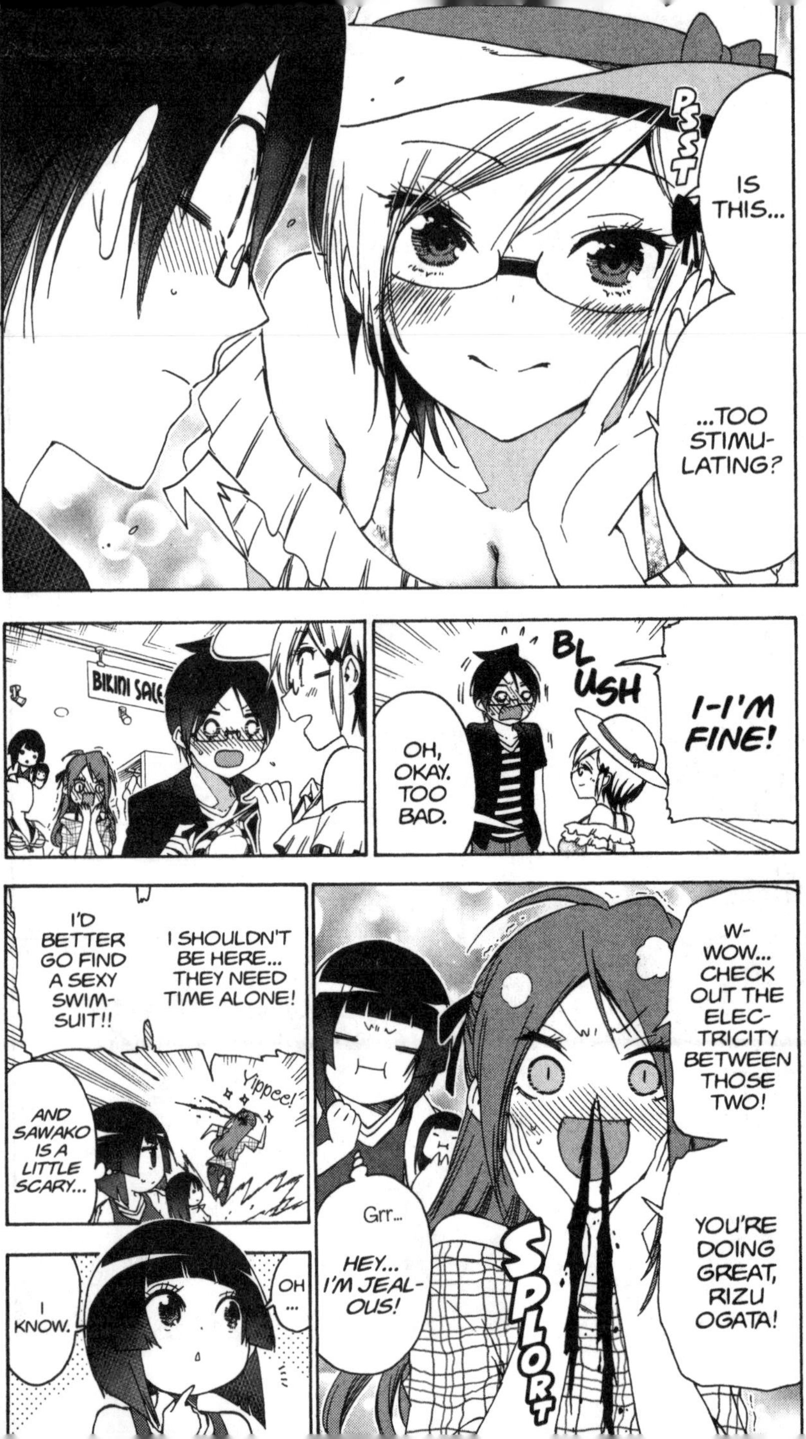
PSSST
IS THIS...
...TOO STIMU-LATING?
BLUSH
I-I'M FINE!
OH, OKAY. TOO BAD.
BIKINI SALE
W-WOW... CHECK OUT THE ELEC-TRICITY BETWEEN THOSE TWO!
YOU'RE DOING GREAT, RIZU OGATA!
SPLORT
Grr...
HEY... I'M JEAL-OUS!
I SHOULDN'T BE HERE... THEY NEED TIME ALONE!
I'D BETTER GO FIND A SEXY SWIM-SUIT!!
Yippee!
AND SAWAKO IS A LITTLE SCARY...
OH ...
I KNOW.

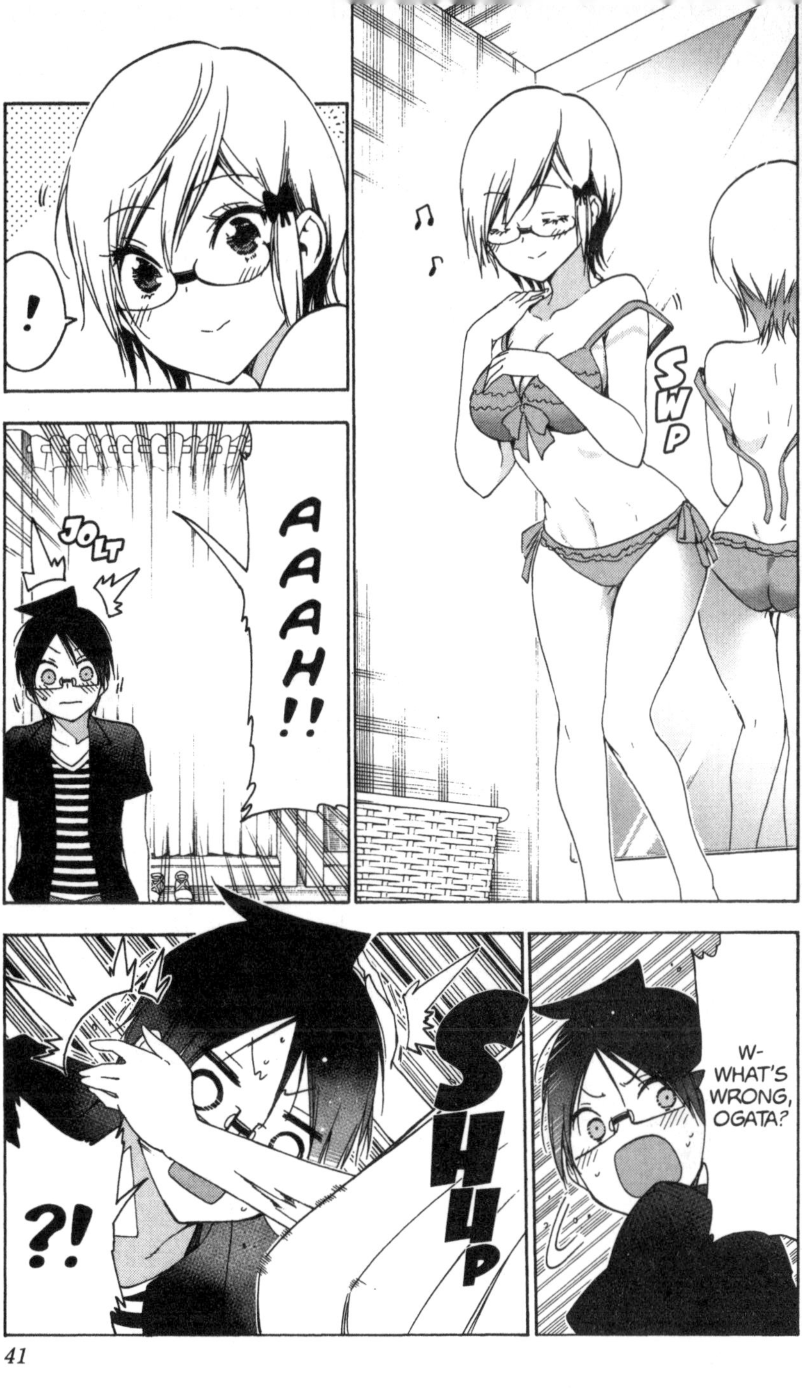
SWP
!
AAAAH!!
JOLT
W-WHAT'S WRONG, OGATA?
SHUP
?!

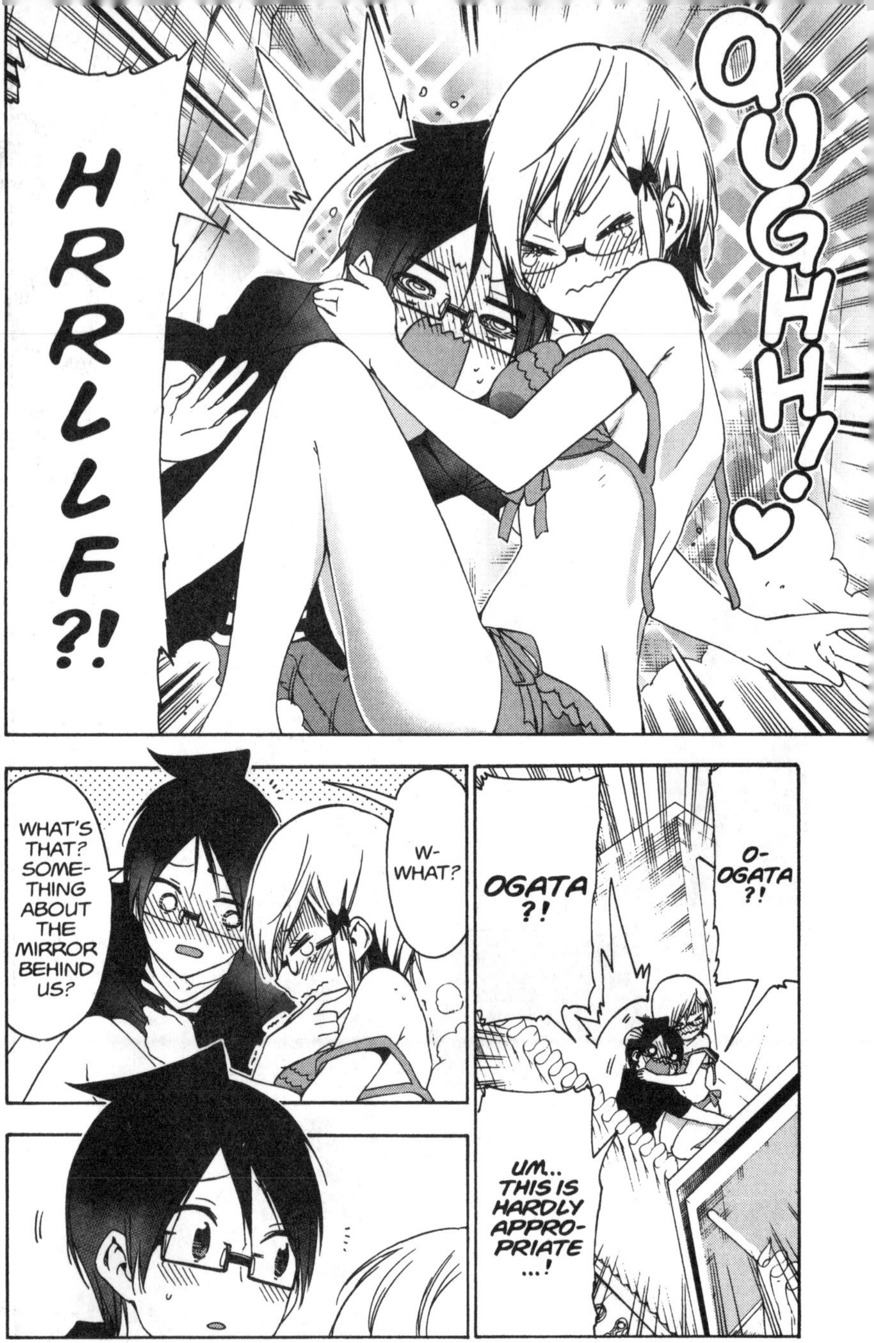
AUGHH!♥
HRRLLF?!
O-OGATA?!
OGATA?!
UM... THIS IS HARDLY APPROPRIATE...!
W-WHAT?
WHAT'S THAT? SOMETHING ABOUT THE MIRROR BEHIND US?

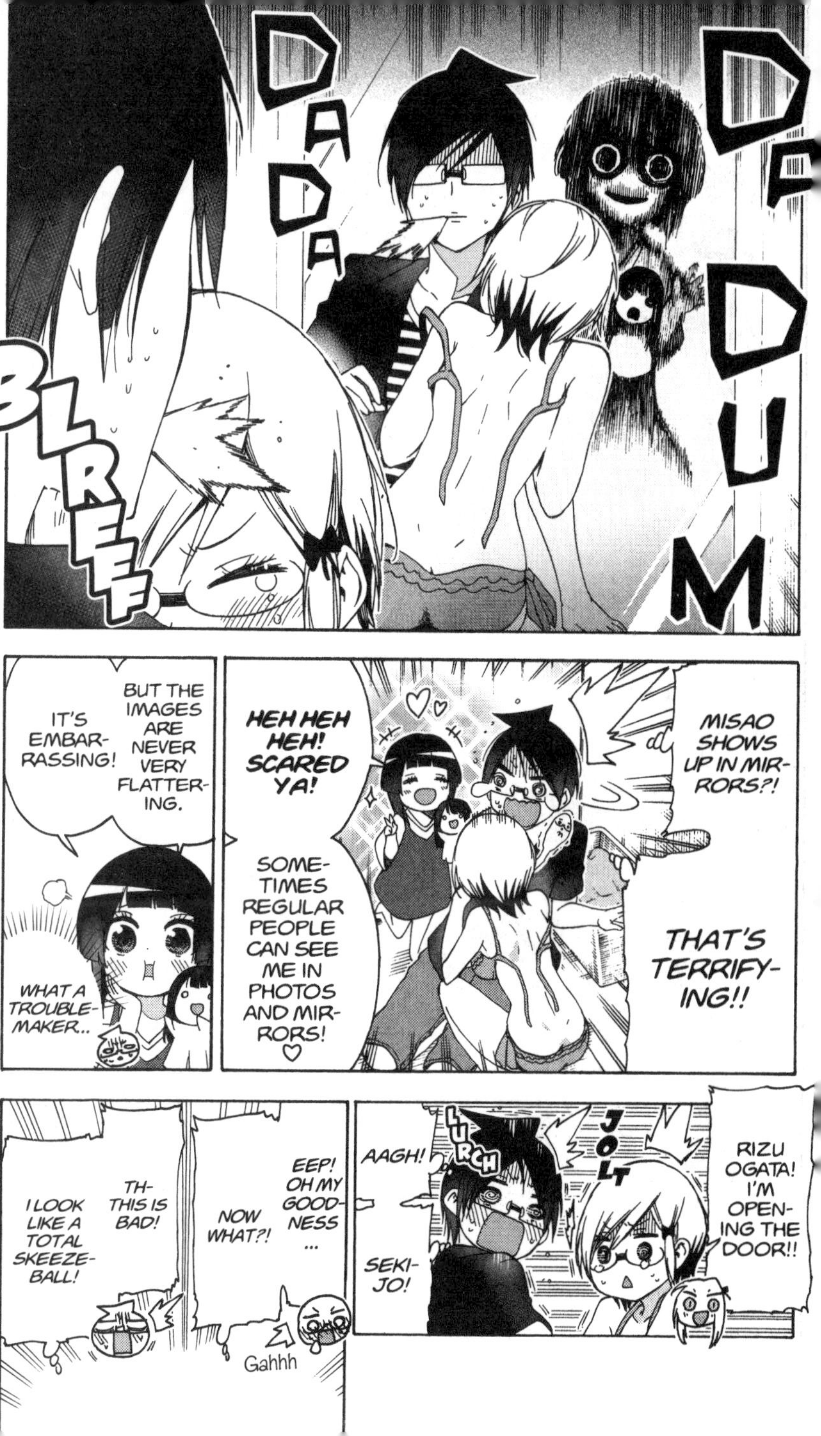
DA DUM
DA DA DA
BLREEF
MISAO SHOWS UP IN MIRRORS?!
THAT'S TERRIFYING!!
HEH HEH HEH! SCARED YA!
SOMETIMES REGULAR PEOPLE CAN SEE ME IN PHOTOS AND MIRRORS! ♡
BUT THE IMAGES ARE NEVER VERY FLATTERING.
IT'S EMBARRASSING!
WHAT A TROUBLEMAKER...
RIZU OGATA! I'M OPENING THE DOOR!!
JOLT
LURCH
AAGH!
SEKIJO!
EEP! OH MY GOODNESS...
NOW WHAT?!
Gahhh
TH-THIS IS BAD!
I LOOK LIKE A TOTAL SKEEZEBALL!

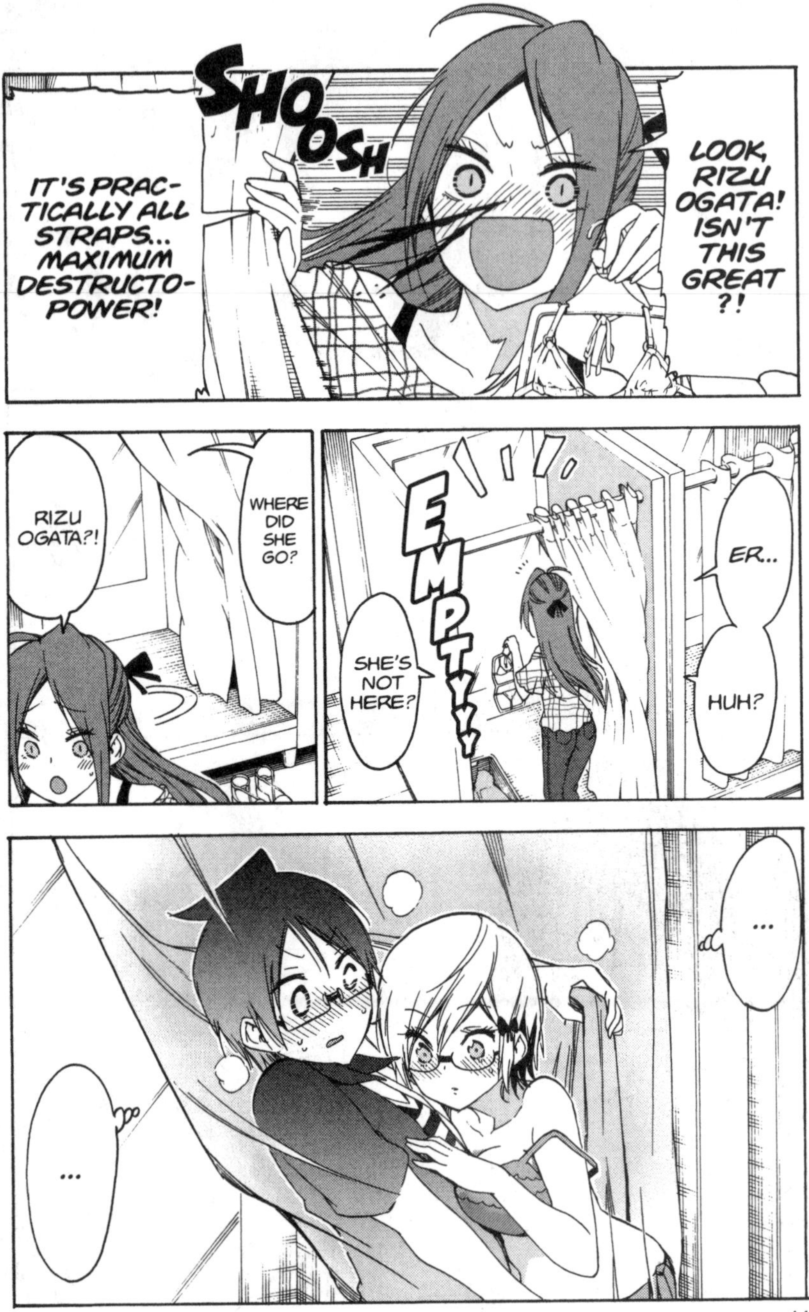

LOOK, RIZU OGATA! ISN'T THIS GREAT?!
SHOOSH
IT'S PRACTICALLY ALL STRAPS... MAXIMUM DESTRUCTO-POWER!
ER...
HUH?
EMPTYYY
SHE'S NOT HERE?
WHERE DID SHE GO?
RIZU OGATA?!
...
...

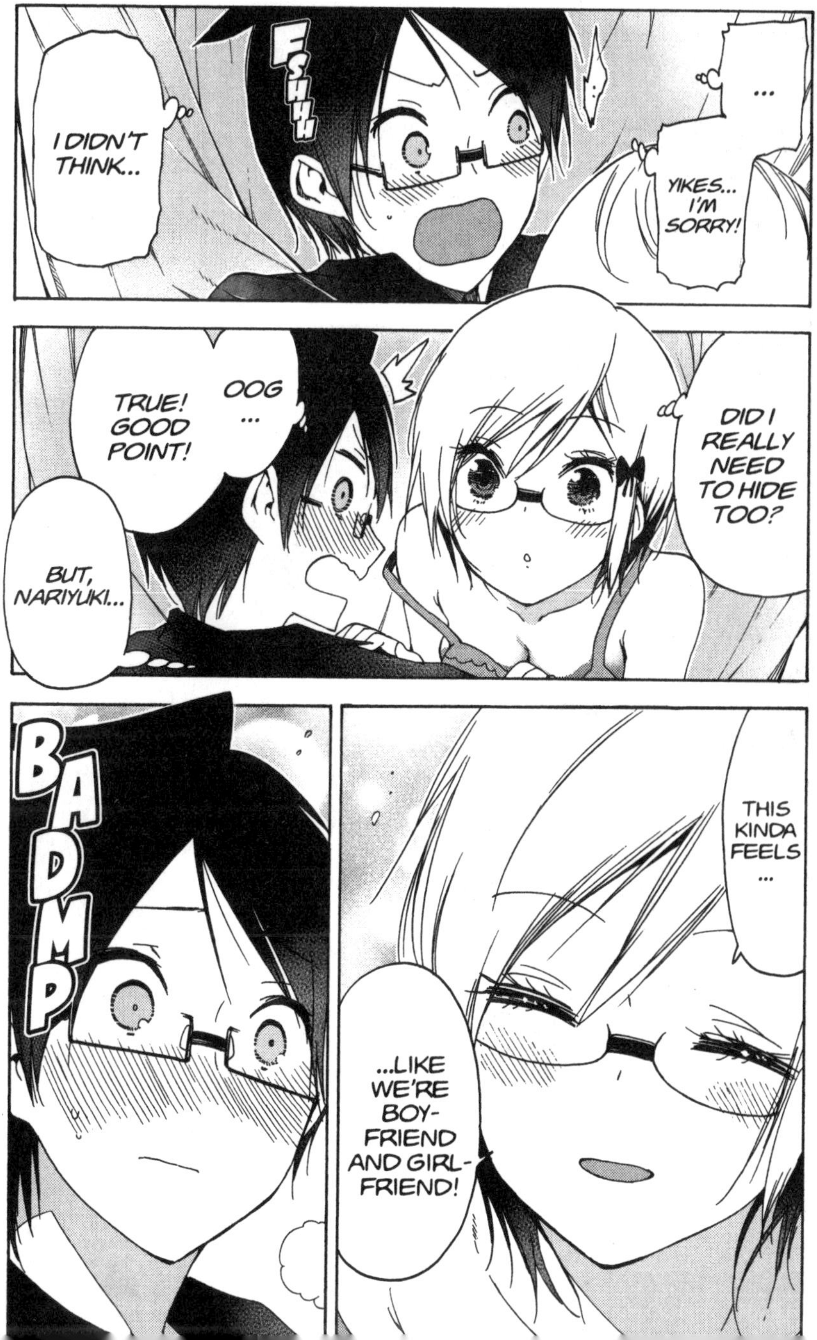
...
YIKES... I'M SORRY!
FSHHH
I DIDN'T THINK...
DID I REALLY NEED TO HIDE TOO?
OOG ...
TRUE! GOOD POINT!
BUT, NARIYUKI...
THIS KINDA FEELS ...
...LIKE WE'RE BOY-FRIEND AND GIRL-FRIEND!
BADMP

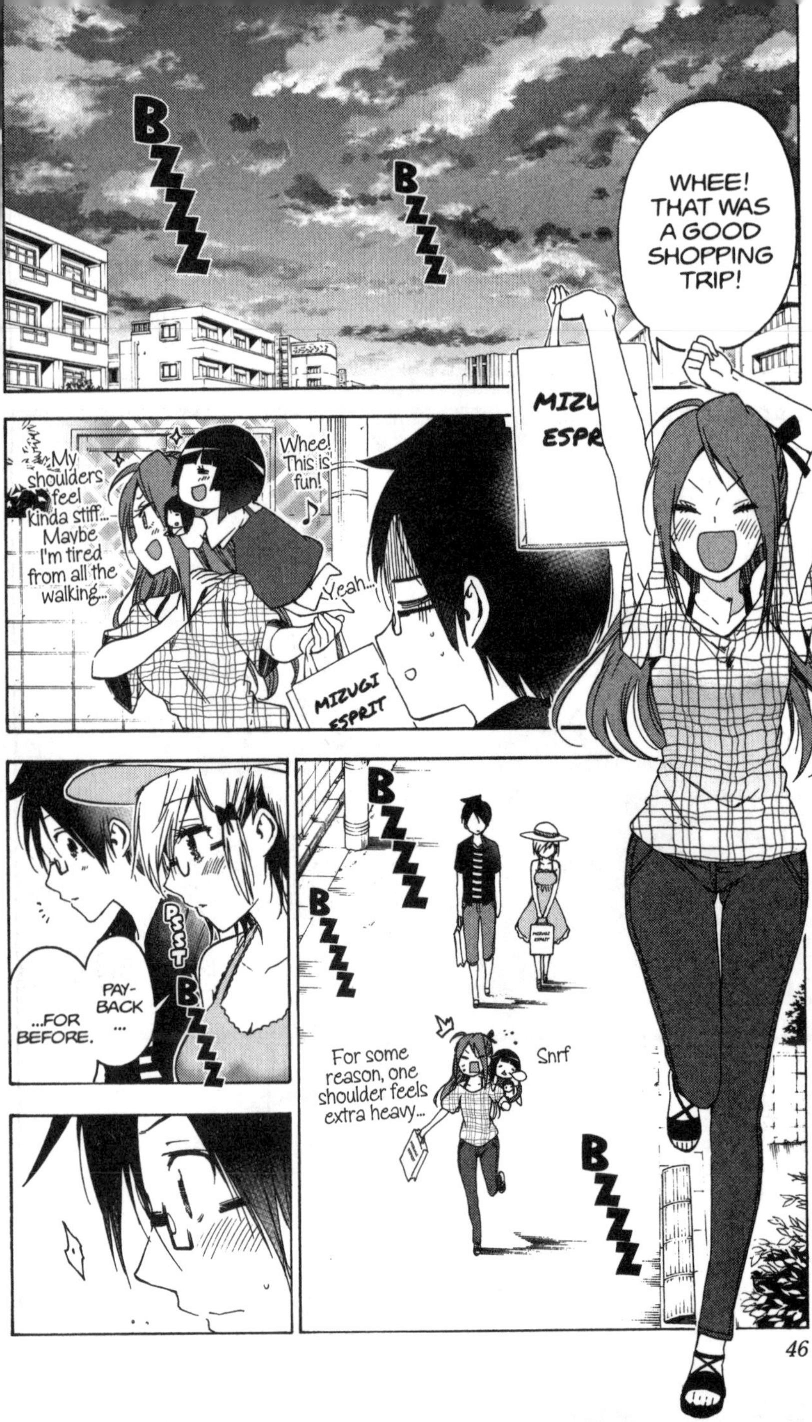
WHEE! THAT WAS A GOOD SHOPPING TRIP!
BZZZ
BZZZZ
Whee! This is fun! ♪
My shoulders feel kinda stiff... Maybe I'm tired from all the walking...
Yeah...
MIZUGI ESPRIT
BZZZZ
BZZZZ
MIZUGI ESPRIT
Snrf
For some reason, one shoulder feels extra heavy...
BZZZZ
PSST
BZZZ
PAY-BACK...
...FOR BEFORE.

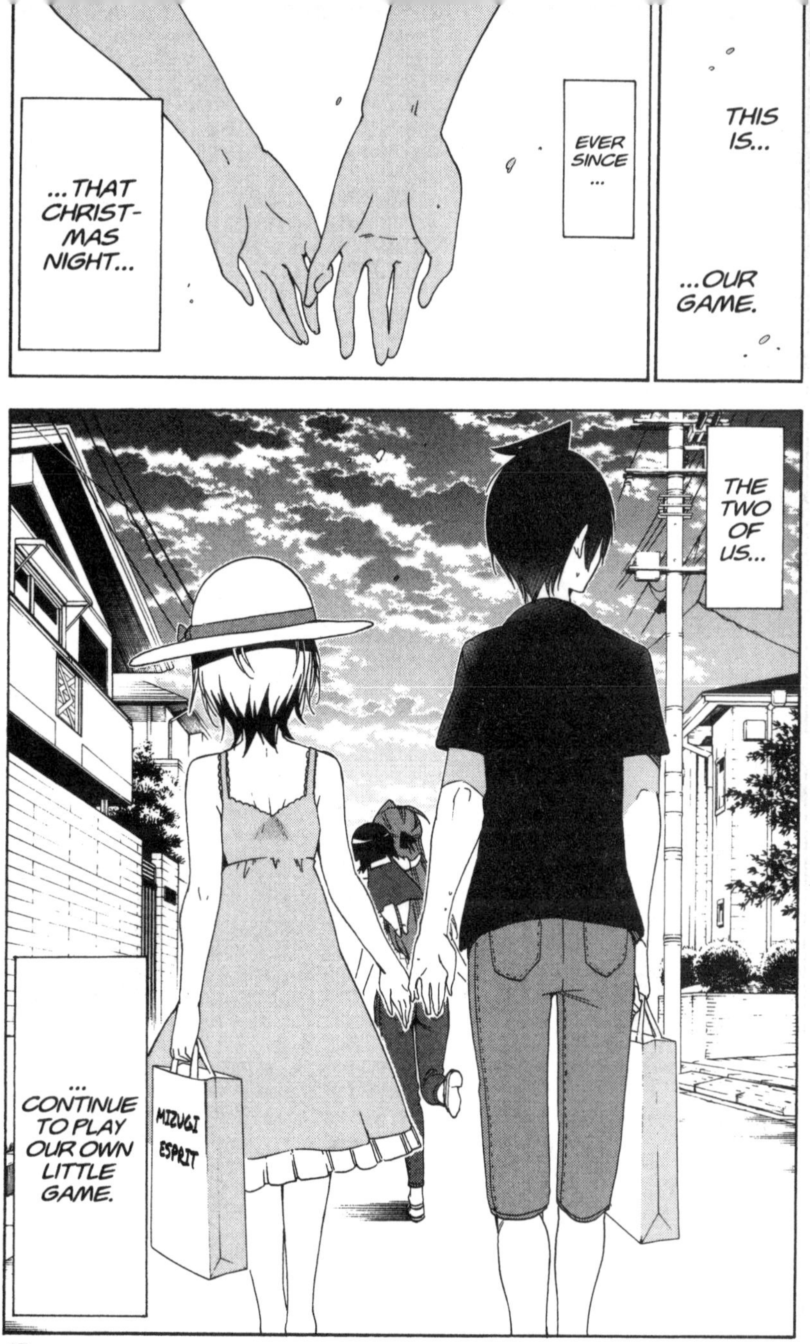
THIS IS...
...OUR GAME.
EVER SINCE ...
...THAT CHRIST-MAS NIGHT...
THE TWO OF US...
MIZUGI ESPRIT
... CONTINUE TO PLAY OUR OWN LITTLE GAME.

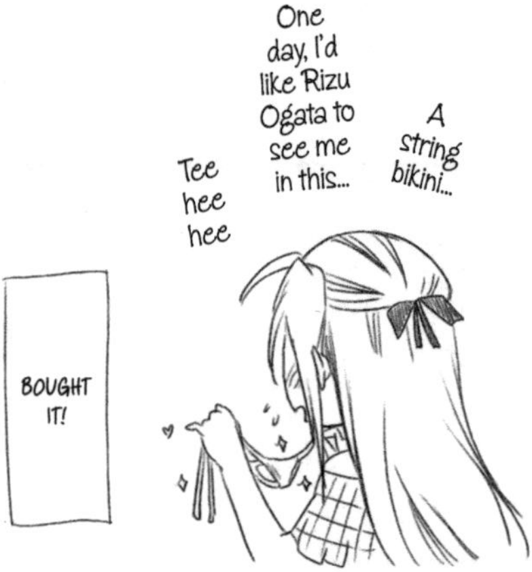
A string bikini...
One day, I'd like Rizu Ogata to see me in this...
Tee hee hee
BOUGHT IT!

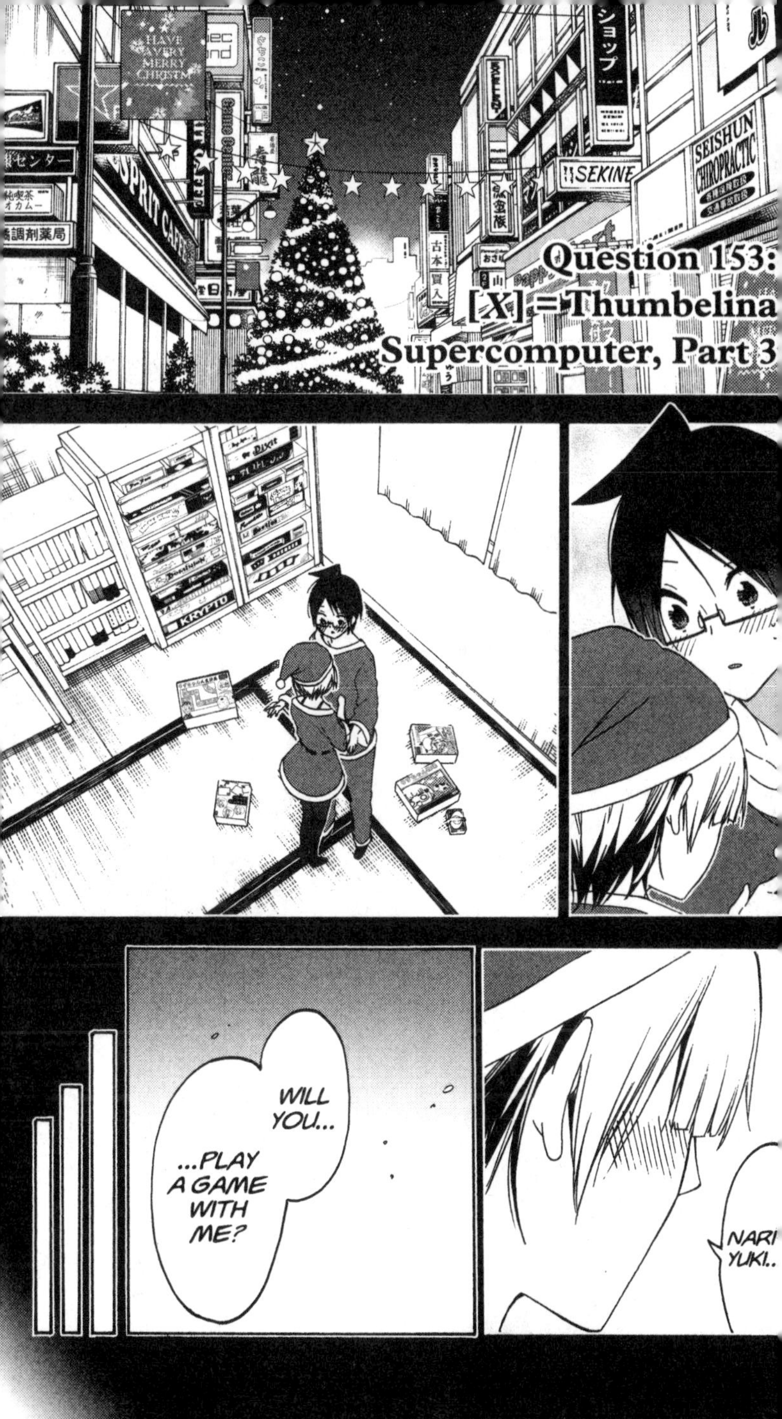
Question 153:
[X] = Thumbelina
Supercomputer, Part 3
NARI
YUKI..
WILL
YOU...
...PLAY
A GAME
WITH
ME?

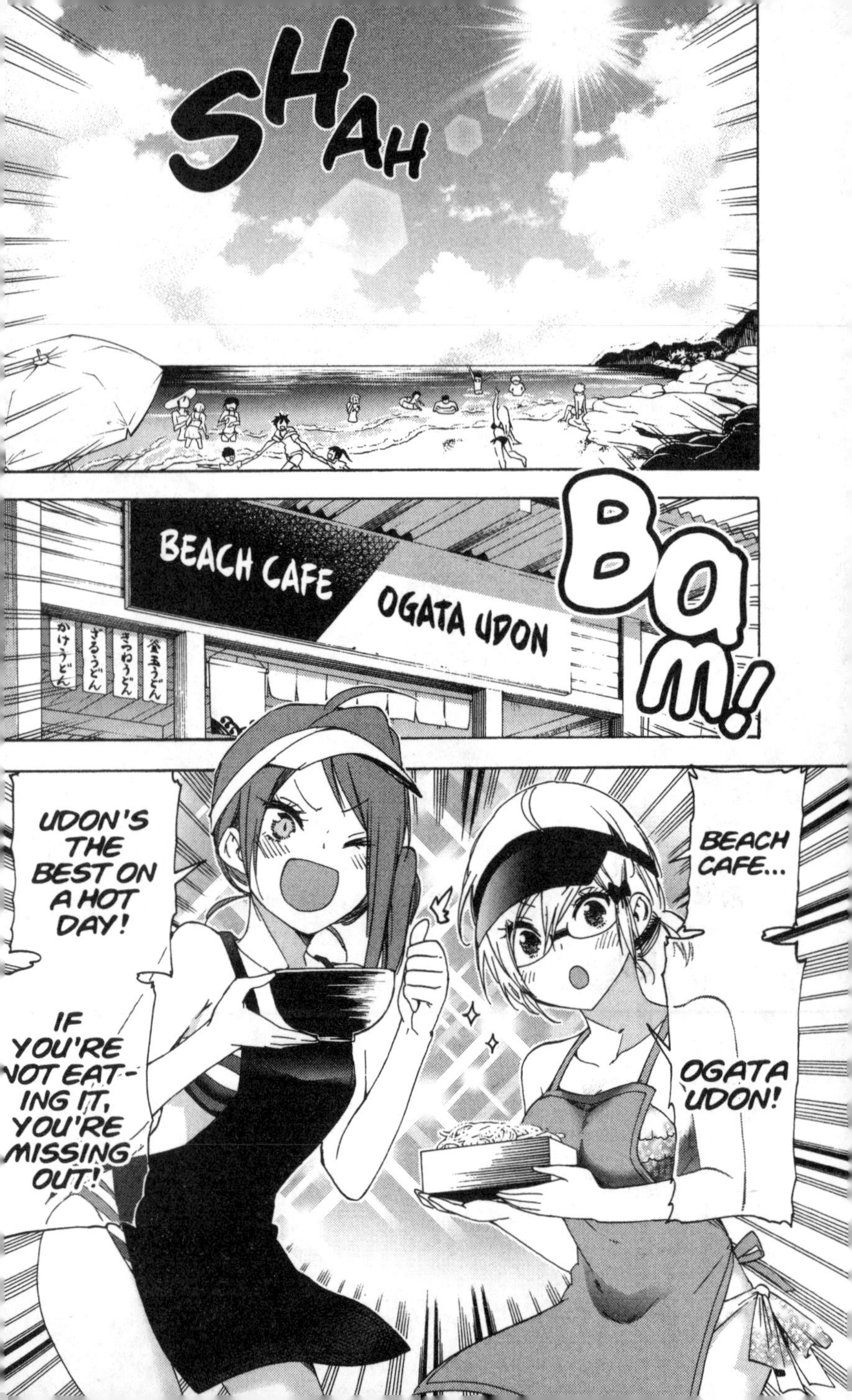
SHAH
BEACH CAFE
OGATA UDON
釜玉うどん
きつねうどん
ざるうどん
かけうどん
Bam!
BEACH CAFE...
OGATA UDON!
UDON'S THE BEST ON A HOT DAY!
IF YOU'RE NOT EATING IT, YOU'RE MISSING OUT!

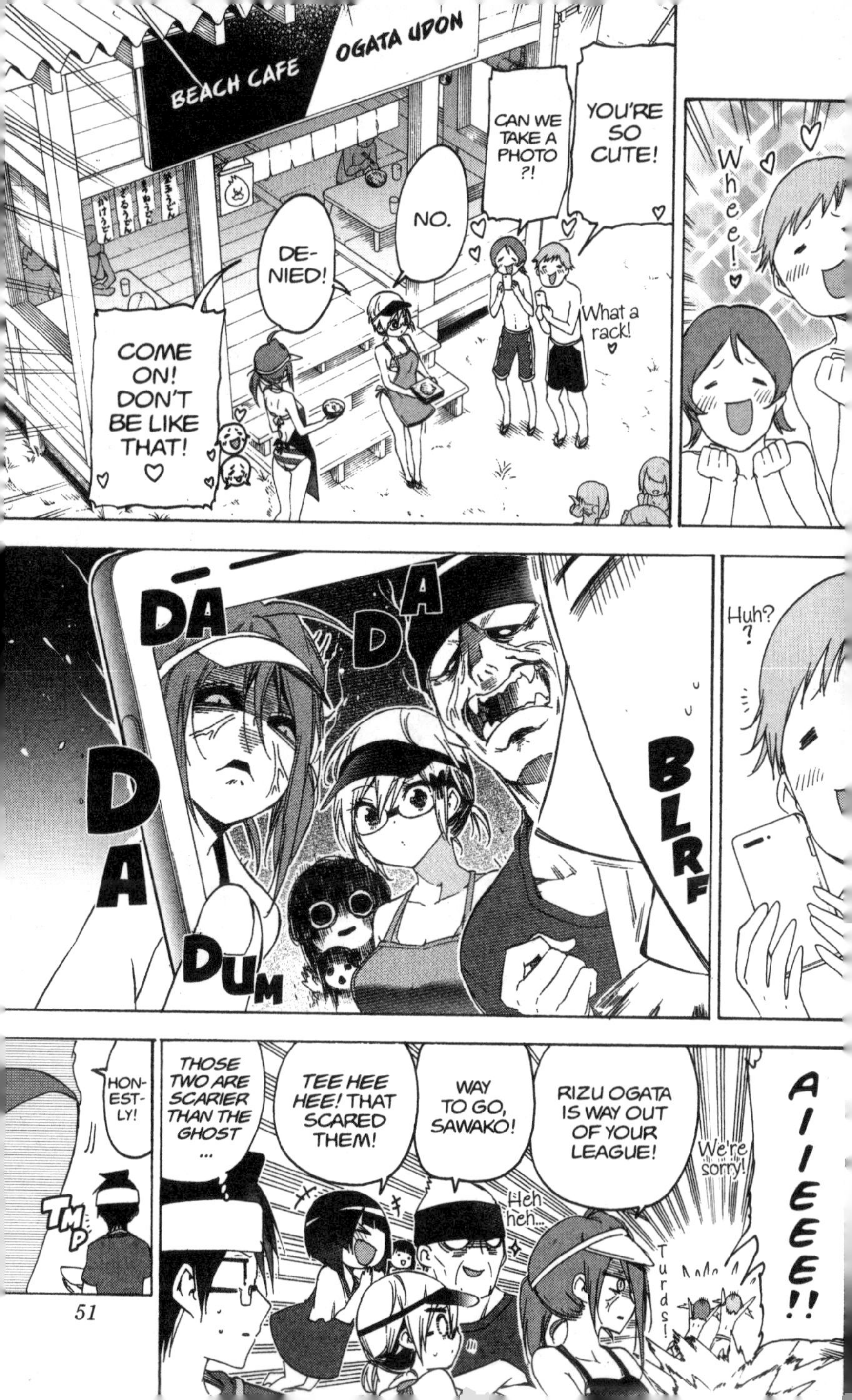
Whee!
OGATA UDON
BEACH CAFE
YOU'RE SO CUTE!
CAN WE TAKE A PHOTO?!
What a rack!
NO.
DE-NIED!
COME ON! DON'T BE LIKE THAT!
Huh?
DA
DA
BLRF
DA
DUM
AIIEEE!!
We're sorry!
RIZU OGATA IS WAY OUT OF YOUR LEAGUE!
Turds!
Heh heh...
WAY TO GO, SAWAKO!
TEE HEE HEE! THAT SCARED THEM!
THOSE TWO ARE SCARIER THAN THE GHOST...
HON-EST-LY!
TMP

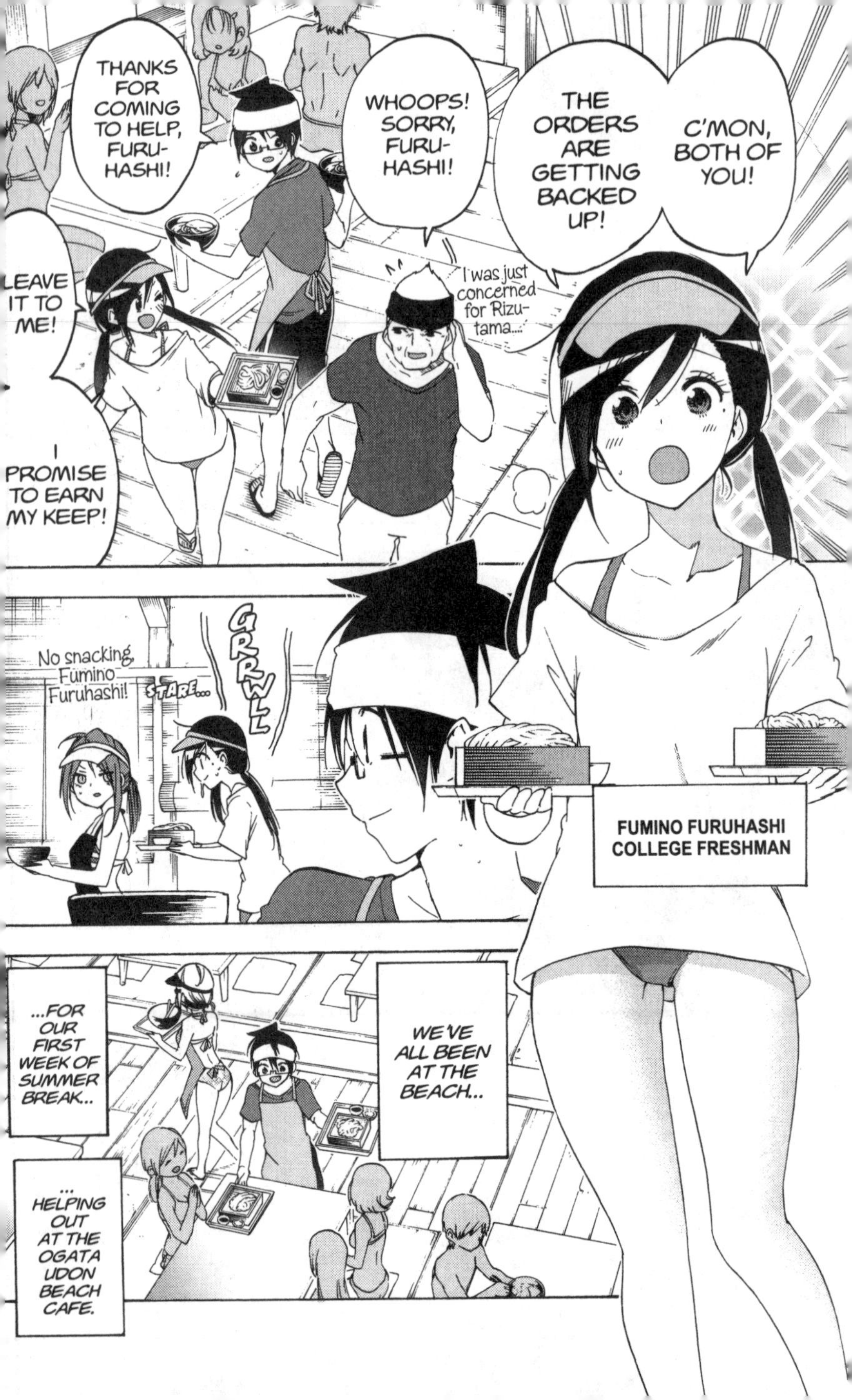
C'MON, BOTH OF YOU!
THE ORDERS ARE GETTING BACKED UP!
I was just concerned for Rizutama...
WHOOPS! SORRY, FURUHASHI!
THANKS FOR COMING TO HELP, FURUHASHI!
LEAVE IT TO ME!
I PROMISE TO EARN MY KEEP!
FUMINO FURUHASHI
COLLEGE FRESHMAN
GRRWLL
STARE...
No snacking, Fumino Furuhashi!
WE'VE ALL BEEN AT THE BEACH...
...FOR OUR FIRST WEEK OF SUMMER BREAK...
...HELPING OUT AT THE OGATA UDON BEACH CAFE.

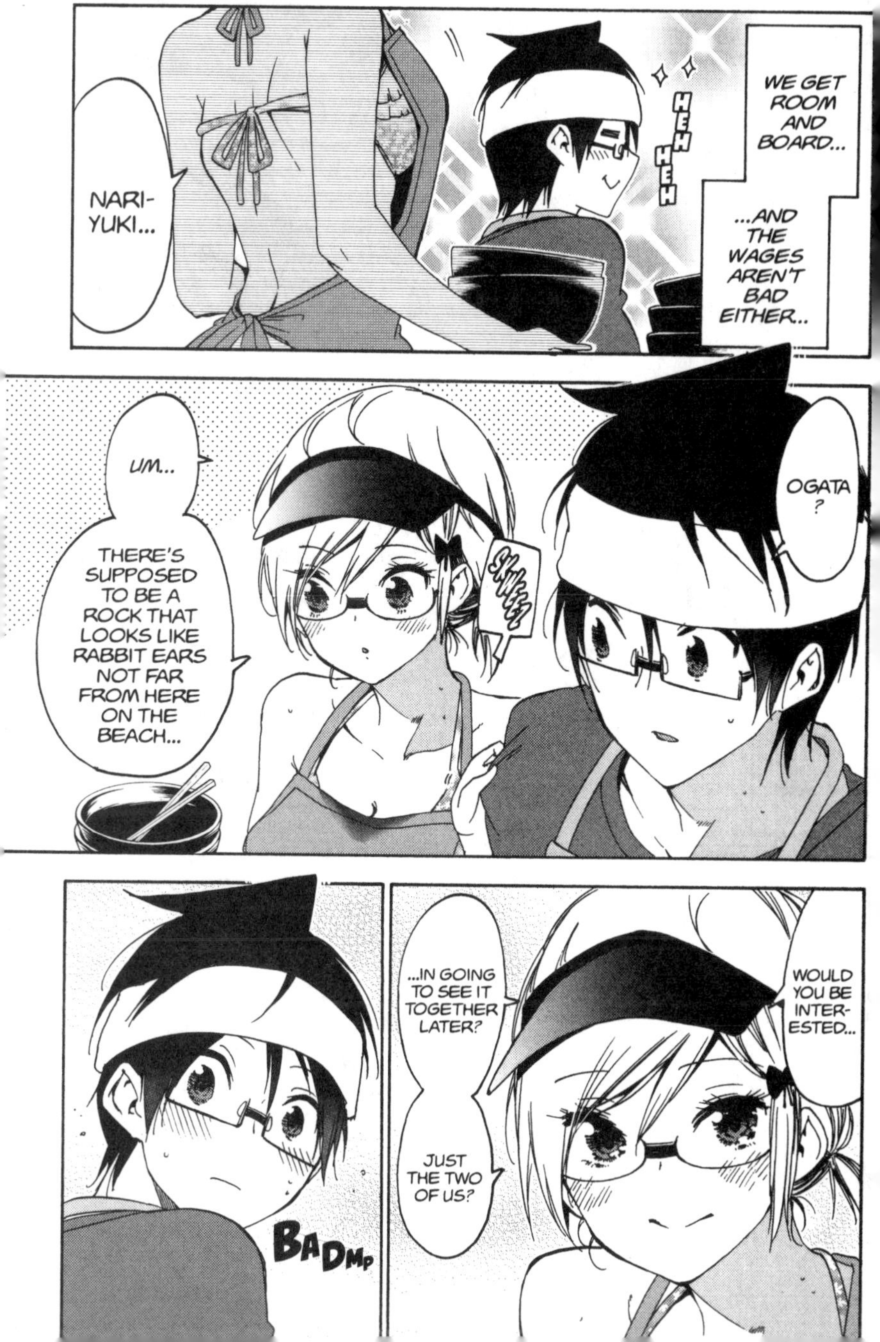

WE GET ROOM AND BOARD...
...AND THE WAGES AREN'T BAD EITHER...
HEH HEH
NARI-YUKI...
OGATA?
SKWEEZ
UM...
THERE'S SUPPOSED TO BE A ROCK THAT LOOKS LIKE RABBIT EARS NOT FAR FROM HERE ON THE BEACH...
WOULD YOU BE INTER-ESTED...
...IN GOING TO SEE IT TOGETHER LATER?
JUST THE TWO OF US?
BADMP

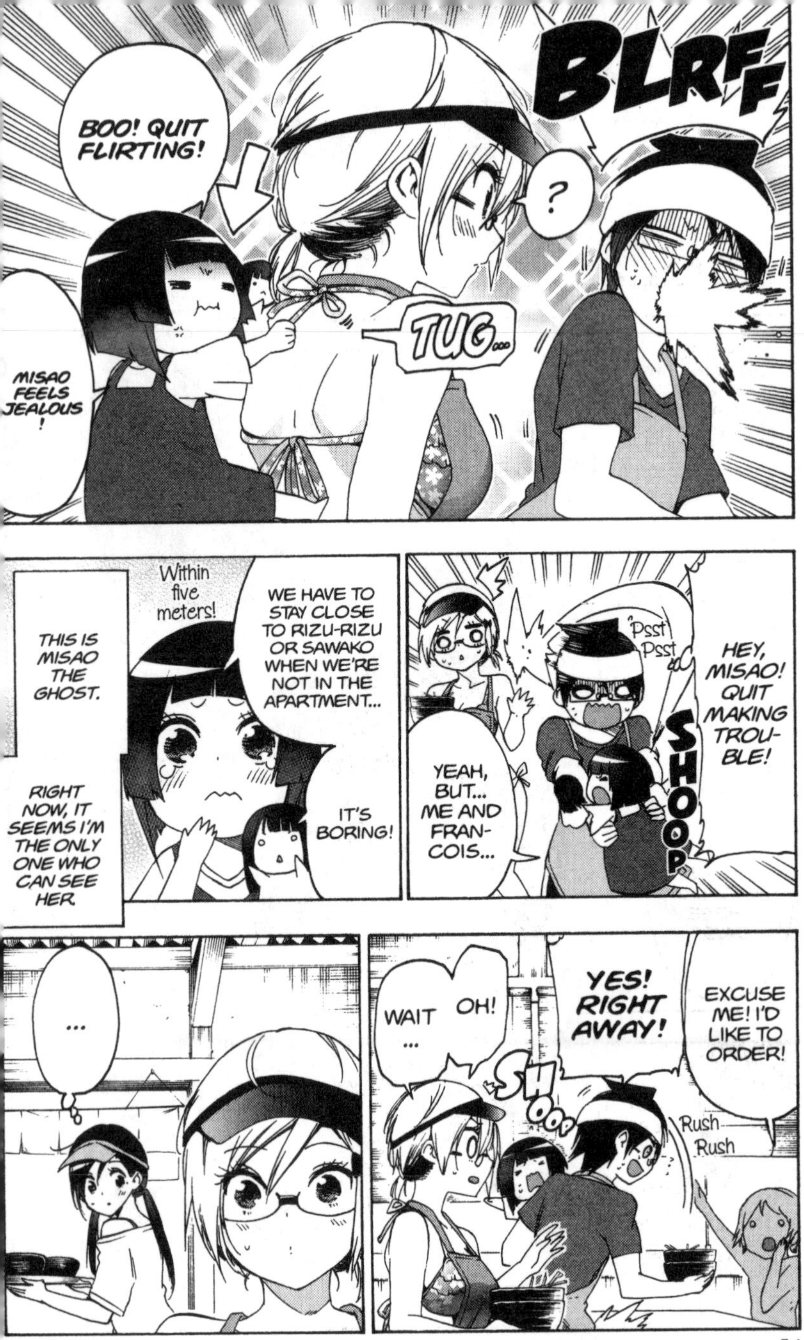
BLRFFF
?
BOO! QUIT FLIRTING!
TUG...
MISAO FEELS JEALOUS!
HEY, MISAO! QUIT MAKING TROUBLE!
Psst Psst
SHOOOP
YEAH, BUT... ME AND FRANCOIS...
WE HAVE TO STAY CLOSE TO RIZU-RIZU OR SAWAKO WHEN WE'RE NOT IN THE APARTMENT...
Within five meters!
IT'S BORING!
THIS IS MISAO THE GHOST.
RIGHT NOW, IT SEEMS I'M THE ONLY ONE WHO CAN SEE HER.
EXCUSE ME! I'D LIKE TO ORDER!
YES! RIGHT AWAY!
OH!
WAIT...
SHOOOP
Rush Rush
...

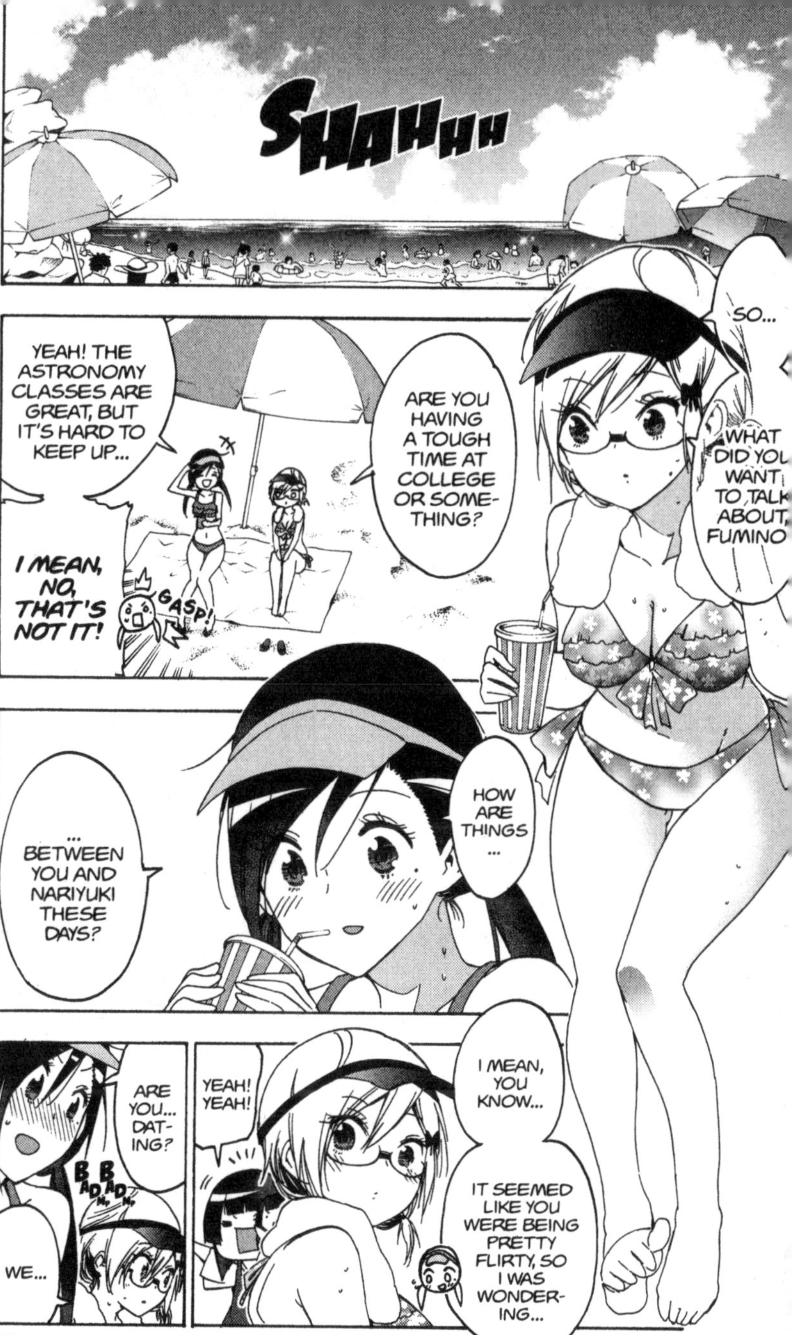
SHAHHH
SO... WHAT DID YOU WANT TO TALK ABOUT, FUMINO?
ARE YOU HAVING A TOUGH TIME AT COLLEGE OR SOME-THING?
YEAH! THE ASTRONOMY CLASSES ARE GREAT, BUT IT'S HARD TO KEEP UP...
I MEAN, NO, THAT'S NOT IT!
GASP!
HOW ARE THINGS ...
... BETWEEN YOU AND NARIYUKI THESE DAYS?
I MEAN, YOU KNOW...
IT SEEMED LIKE YOU WERE BEING PRETTY FLIRTY, SO I WAS WONDER-ING...
YEAH! YEAH!
ARE YOU... DAT-ING?
WE...

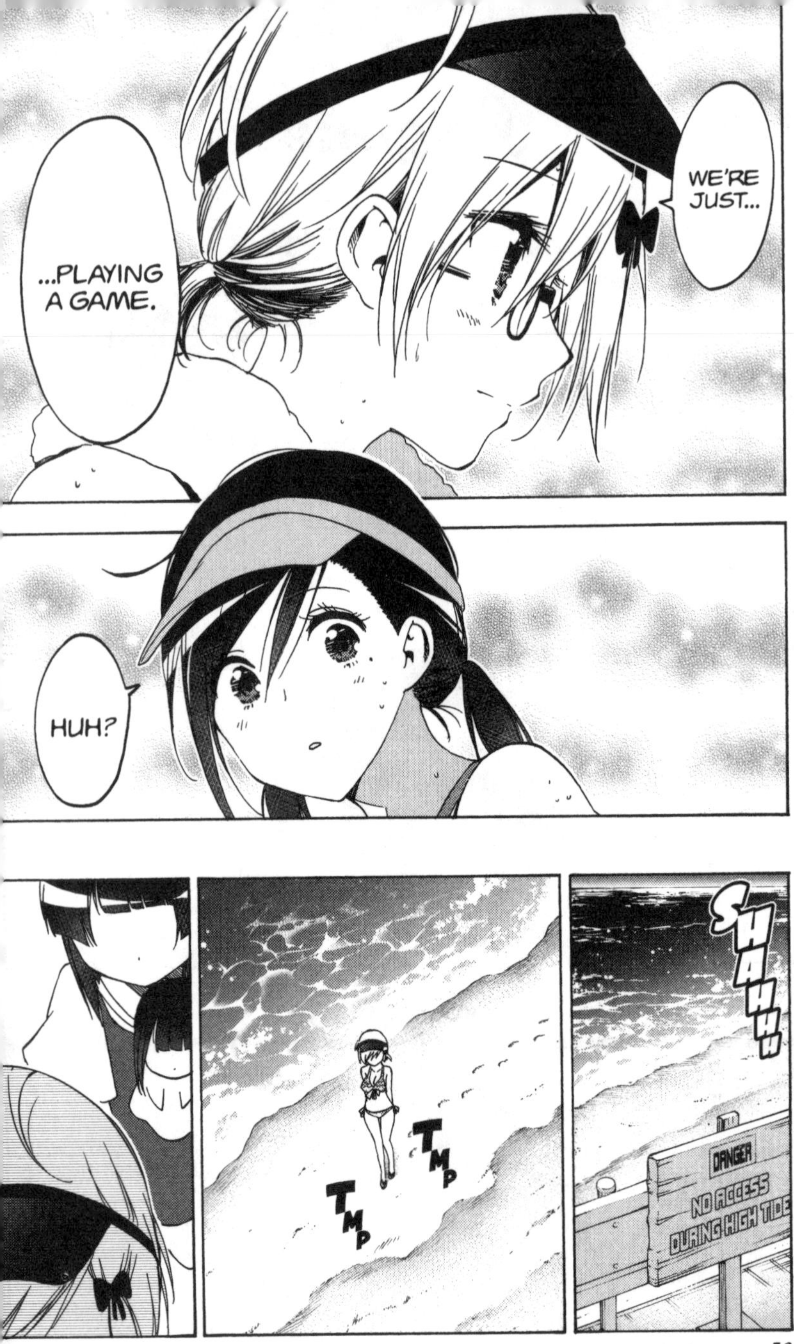
WE'RE JUST...
...PLAYING A GAME.
HUH?
SHAHHH
DANGER
NO ACCESS DURING HIGH TIDE
TMP
TMP

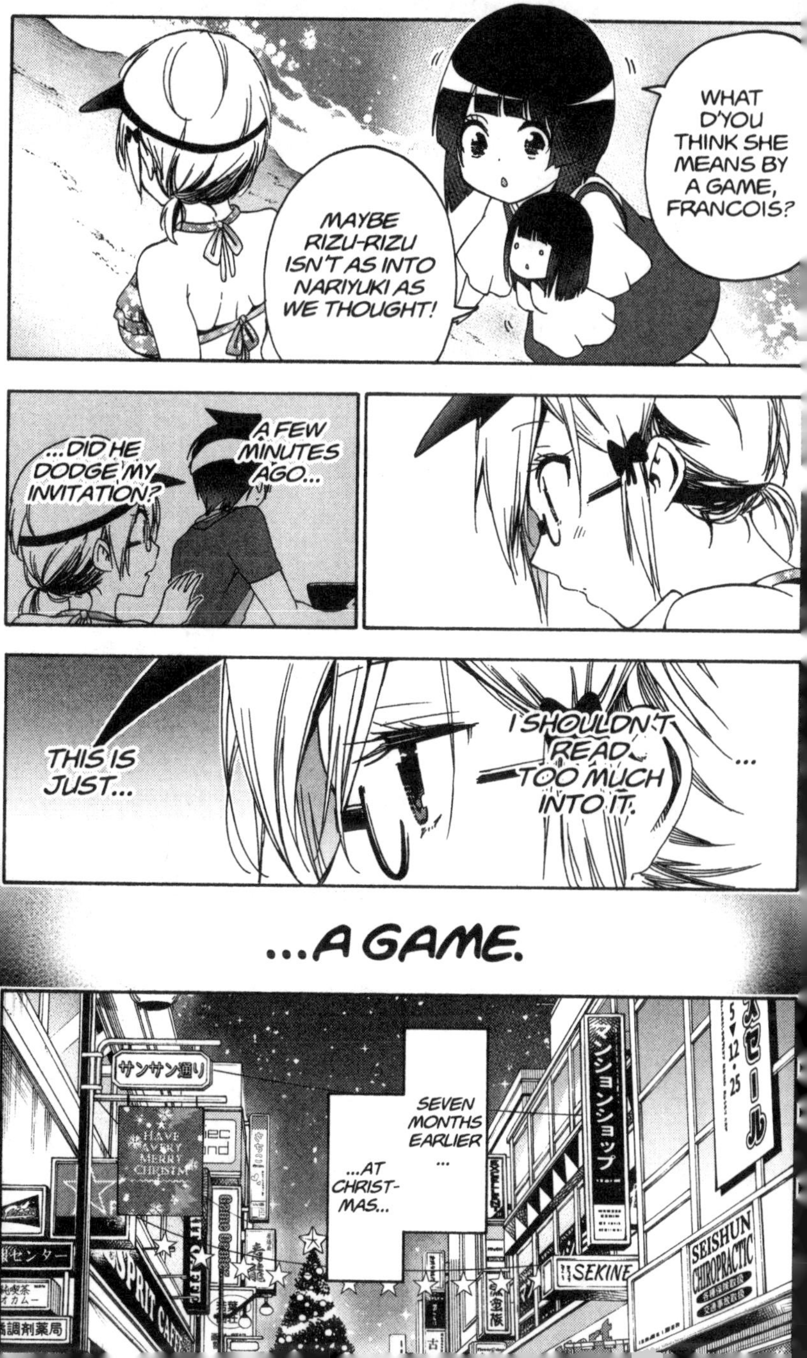
WHAT D'YOU THINK SHE MEANS BY A GAME, FRANCOIS?
MAYBE RIZU-RIZU ISN'T AS INTO NARIYUKI AS WE THOUGHT!
A FEW MINUTES AGO...
...DID HE DODGE MY INVITATION?
...
I SHOULDN'T READ TOO MUCH INTO IT.
THIS IS JUST...
...A GAME.
SEVEN MONTHS EARLIER...
...AT CHRISTMAS...
マンションショップ
SEISHUN CHIROPRACTIC
SEKINE
サンサン通り

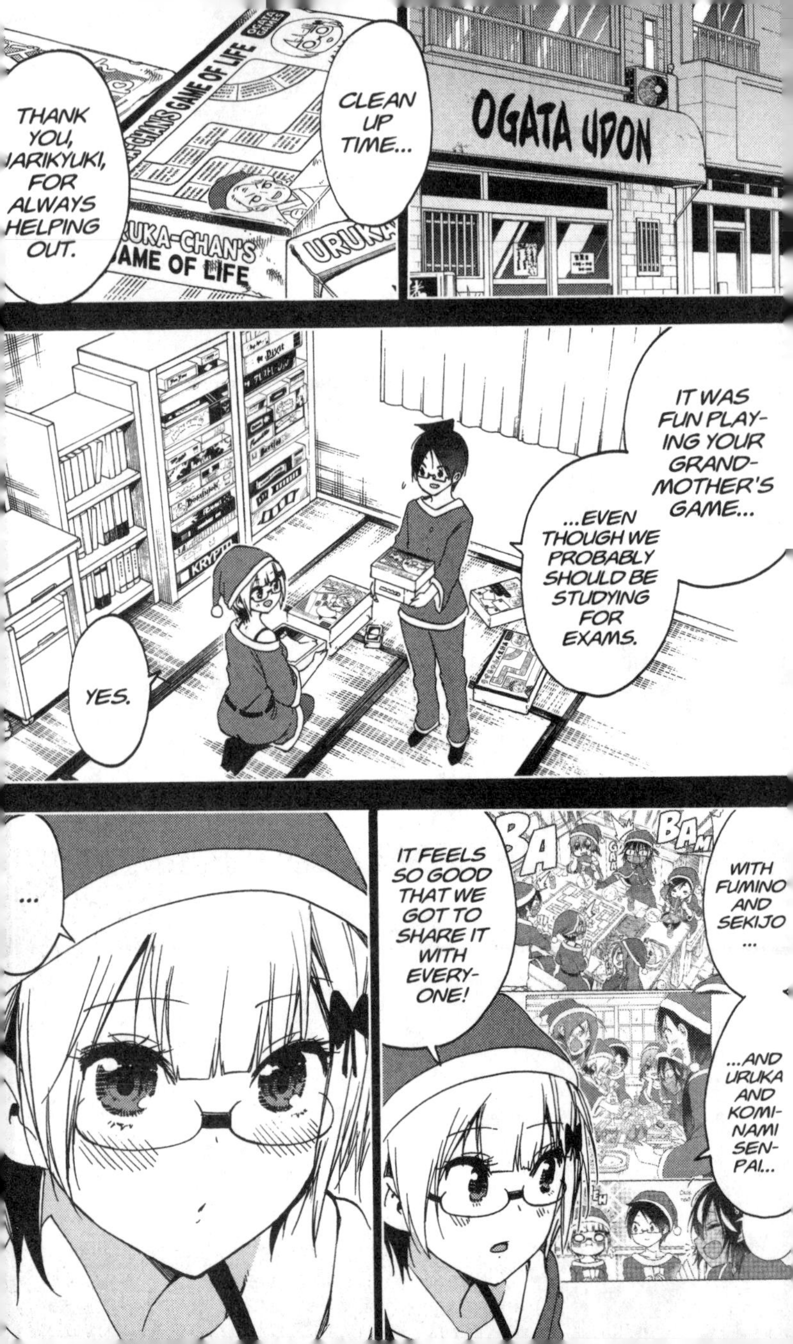
OGATA UDON
CLEAN UP TIME...
ARIKYUKI, FOR ALWAYS HELPING OUT.
URUKA-CHAN'S GAME OF LIFE
IT WAS FUN PLAYING YOUR GRANDMOTHER'S GAME...
...EVEN THOUGH WE PROBABLY SHOULD BE STUDYING FOR EXAMS.
YES.
BAM
BA
WITH FUMINO AND SEKIJO ...
...AND URUKA AND KOMINAMI SENPAI...
IT FEELS SO GOOD THAT WE GOT TO SHARE IT WITH EVERYONE!
...

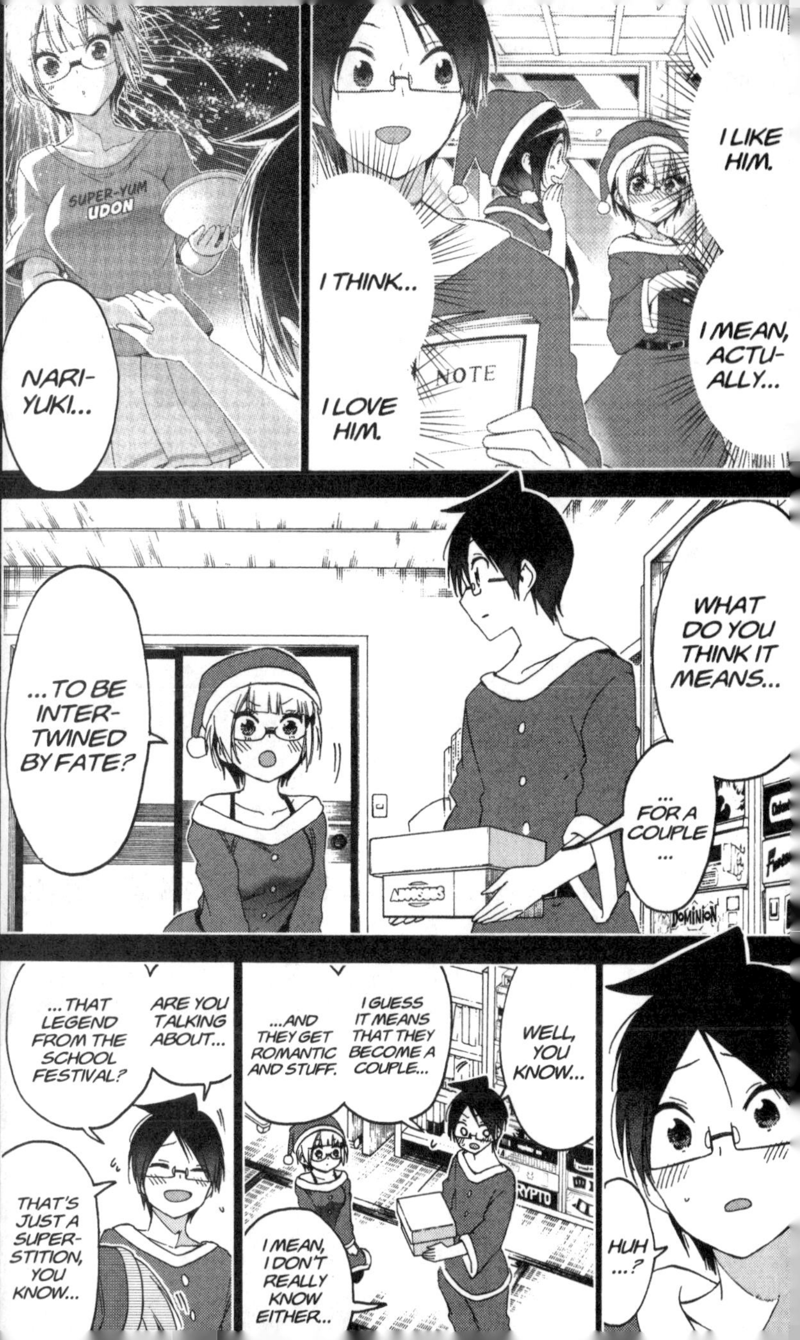
I LIKE HIM.
I MEAN, ACTUALLY...
I THINK...
I LOVE HIM.
NOTE
SUPER-YUM UDON
NARI-YUKI...
WHAT DO YOU THINK IT MEANS...
...FOR A COUPLE...
...TO BE INTER-TWINED BY FATE?
HUH...?
WELL, YOU KNOW...
I GUESS IT MEANS THAT THEY BECOME A COUPLE...
...AND THEY GET ROMANTIC AND STUFF.
I MEAN, I DON'T REALLY KNOW EITHER...
ARE YOU TALKING ABOUT...
...THAT LEGEND FROM THE SCHOOL FESTIVAL?
THAT'S JUST A SUPER-STITION, YOU KNOW...

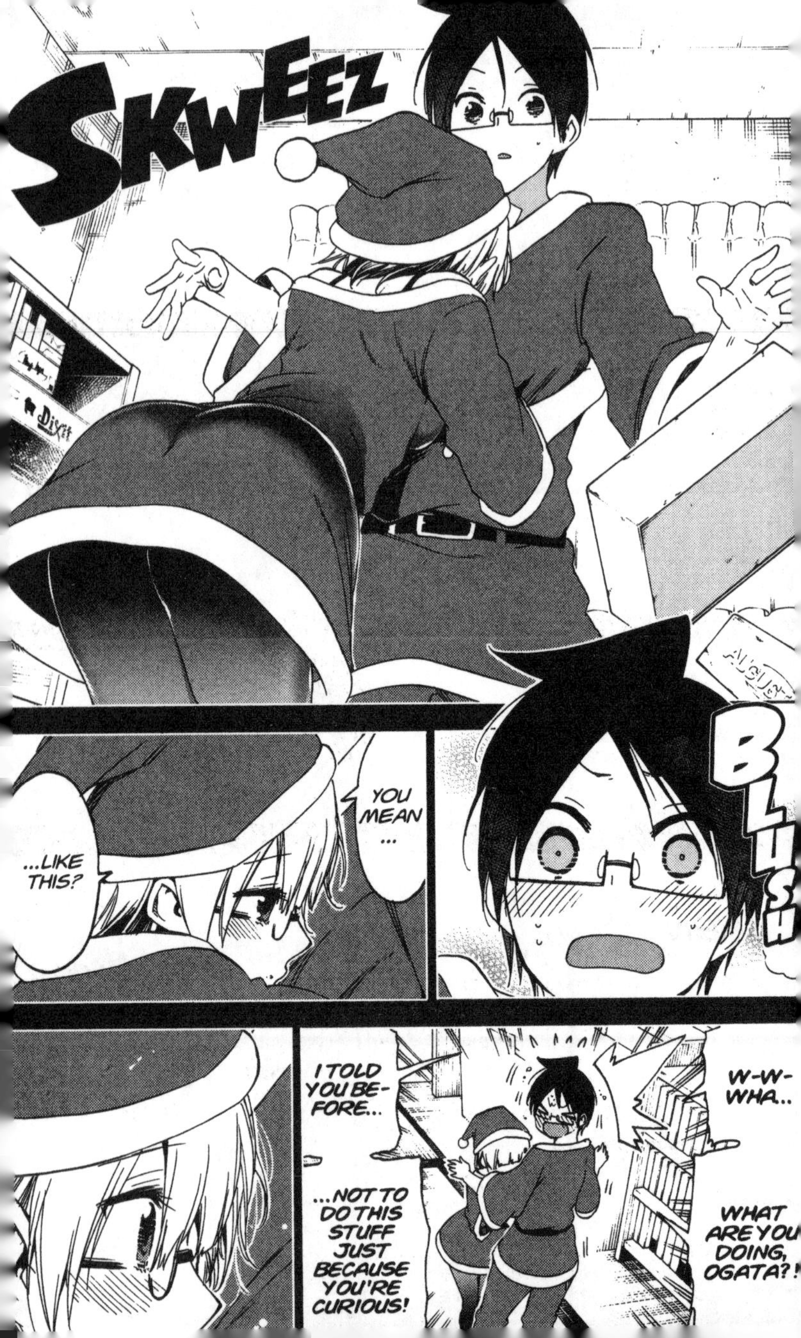
SKWEEZ
BLUSH
YOU MEAN ...
...LIKE THIS?
W-W-WHA...
WHAT ARE YOU DOING, OGATA?!
I TOLD YOU BEFORE...
...NOT TO DO THIS STUFF JUST BECAUSE YOU'RE CURIOUS!

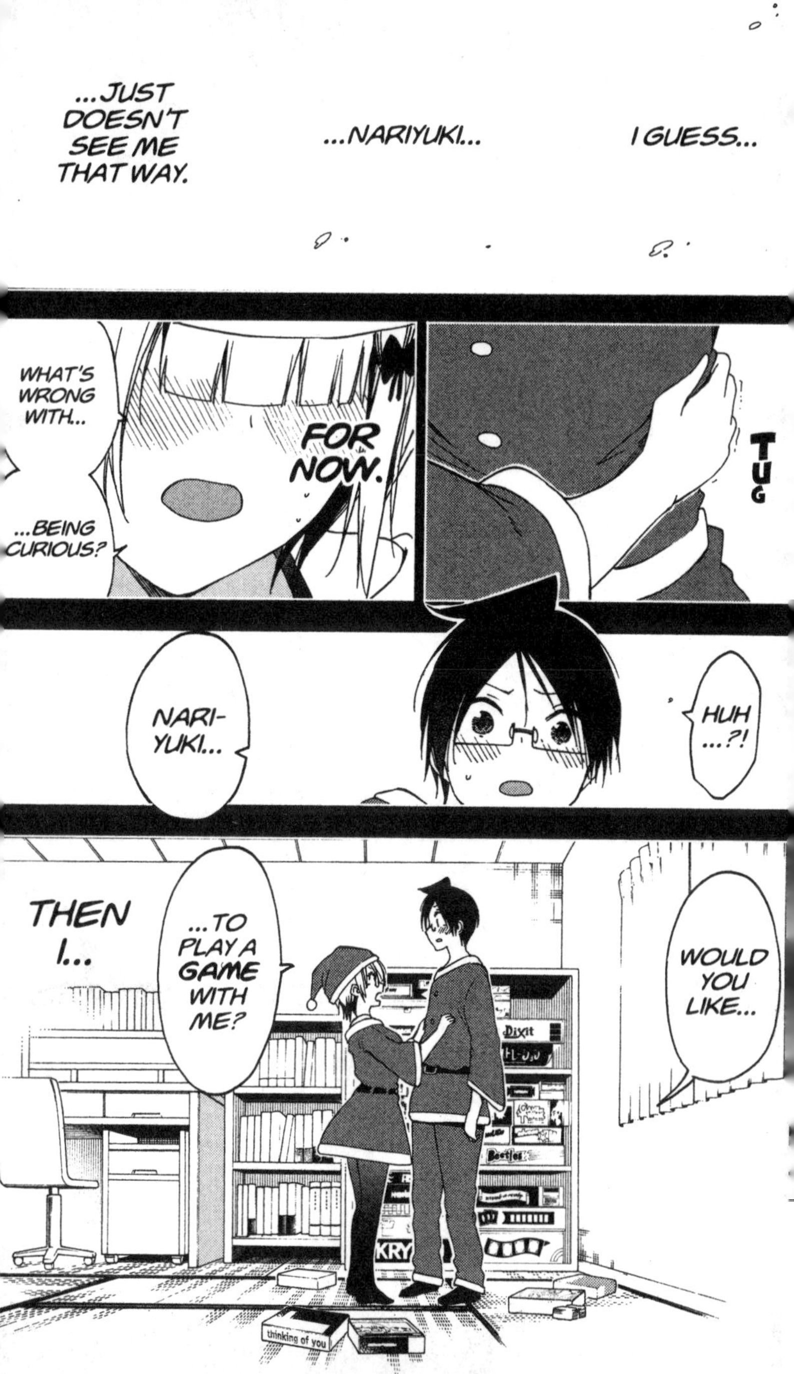
I GUESS...
...NARIYUKI...
...JUST DOESN'T SEE ME THAT WAY.
TUG
FOR NOW.
WHAT'S WRONG WITH...
...BEING CURIOUS?
HUH ...?!
NARI-YUKI...
WOULD YOU LIKE...
...TO PLAY A GAME WITH ME?
THEN I...
Dixit
Beetles
KRY
thinking of you

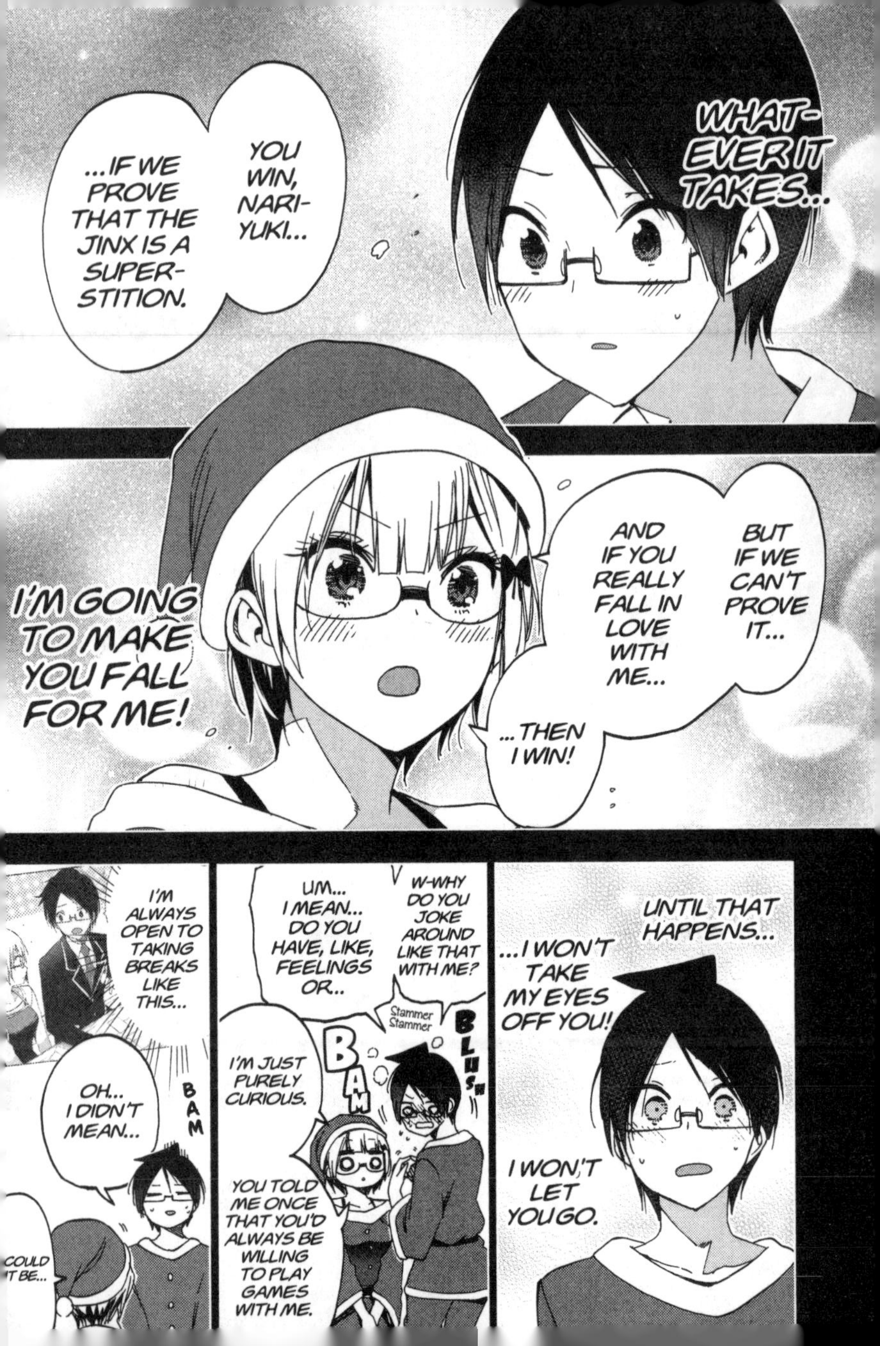
WHAT-EVER IT TAKES...
YOU WIN, NARI-YUKI...
...IF WE PROVE THAT THE JINX IS A SUPER-STITION.
BUT IF WE CAN'T PROVE IT...
AND IF YOU REALLY FALL IN LOVE WITH ME...
...THEN I WIN!
I'M GOING TO MAKE YOU FALL FOR ME!
UNTIL THAT HAPPENS...
...I WON'T TAKE MY EYES OFF YOU!
I WON'T LET YOU GO.
W-WHY DO YOU JOKE AROUND LIKE THAT WITH ME?
UM... I MEAN... DO YOU HAVE, LIKE, FEELINGS OR...
Stammer Stammer
BLUSH
BAM
I'M JUST PURELY CURIOUS.
YOU TOLD ME ONCE THAT YOU'D ALWAYS BE WILLING TO PLAY GAMES WITH ME.
I'M ALWAYS OPEN TO TAKING BREAKS LIKE THIS...
BAM
OH... I DIDN'T MEAN...
COULD IT BE...

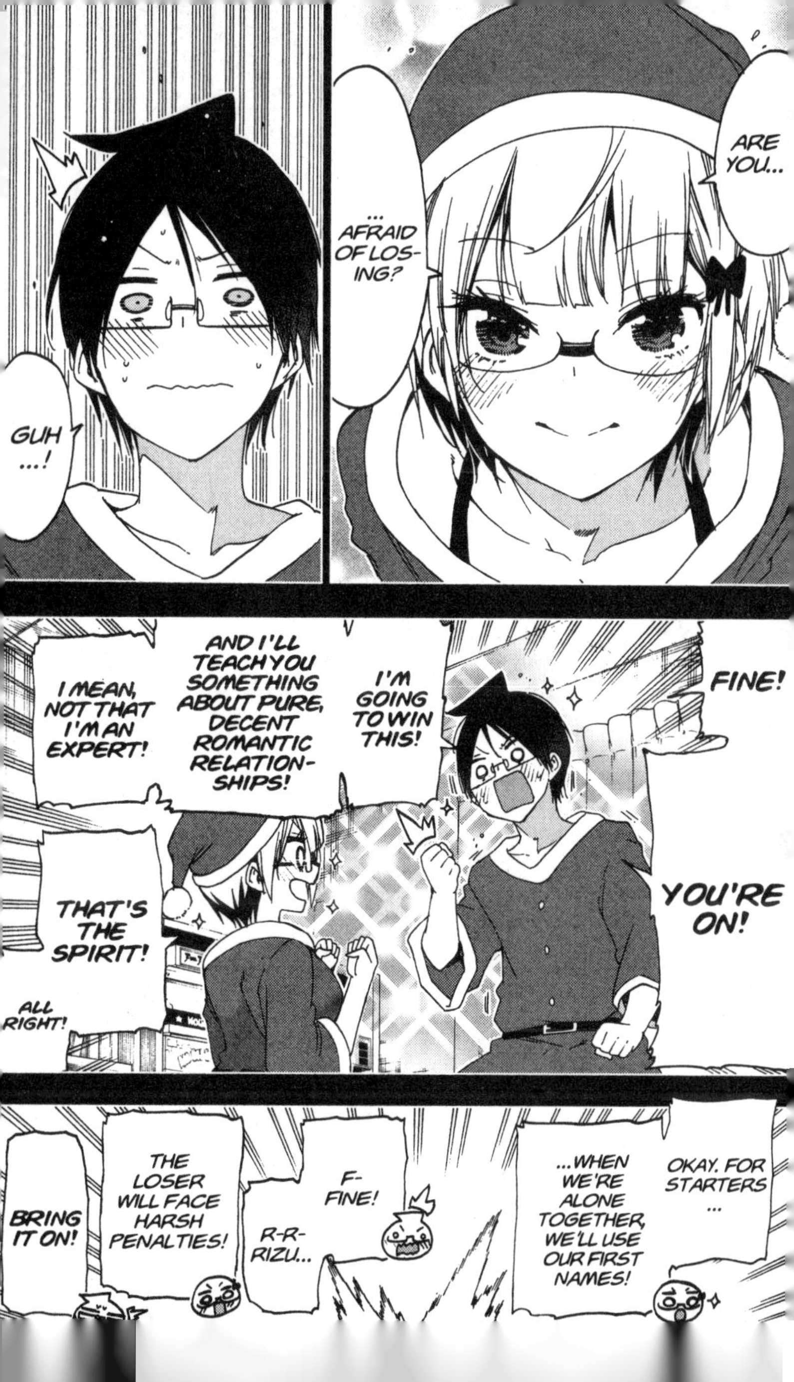
ARE YOU...
...AFRAID OF LOS-ING?
GUH ...!
FINE!
YOU'RE ON!
I'M GOING TO WIN THIS!
AND I'LL TEACH YOU SOMETHING ABOUT PURE, DECENT ROMANTIC RELATION-SHIPS!
I MEAN, NOT THAT I'M AN EXPERT!
THAT'S THE SPIRIT!
ALL RIGHT!
OKAY. FOR STARTERS ...
...WHEN WE'RE ALONE TOGETHER, WE'LL USE OUR FIRST NAMES!
F-FINE!
R-R-RIZU...
THE LOSER WILL FACE HARSH PENALTIES!
BRING IT ON!

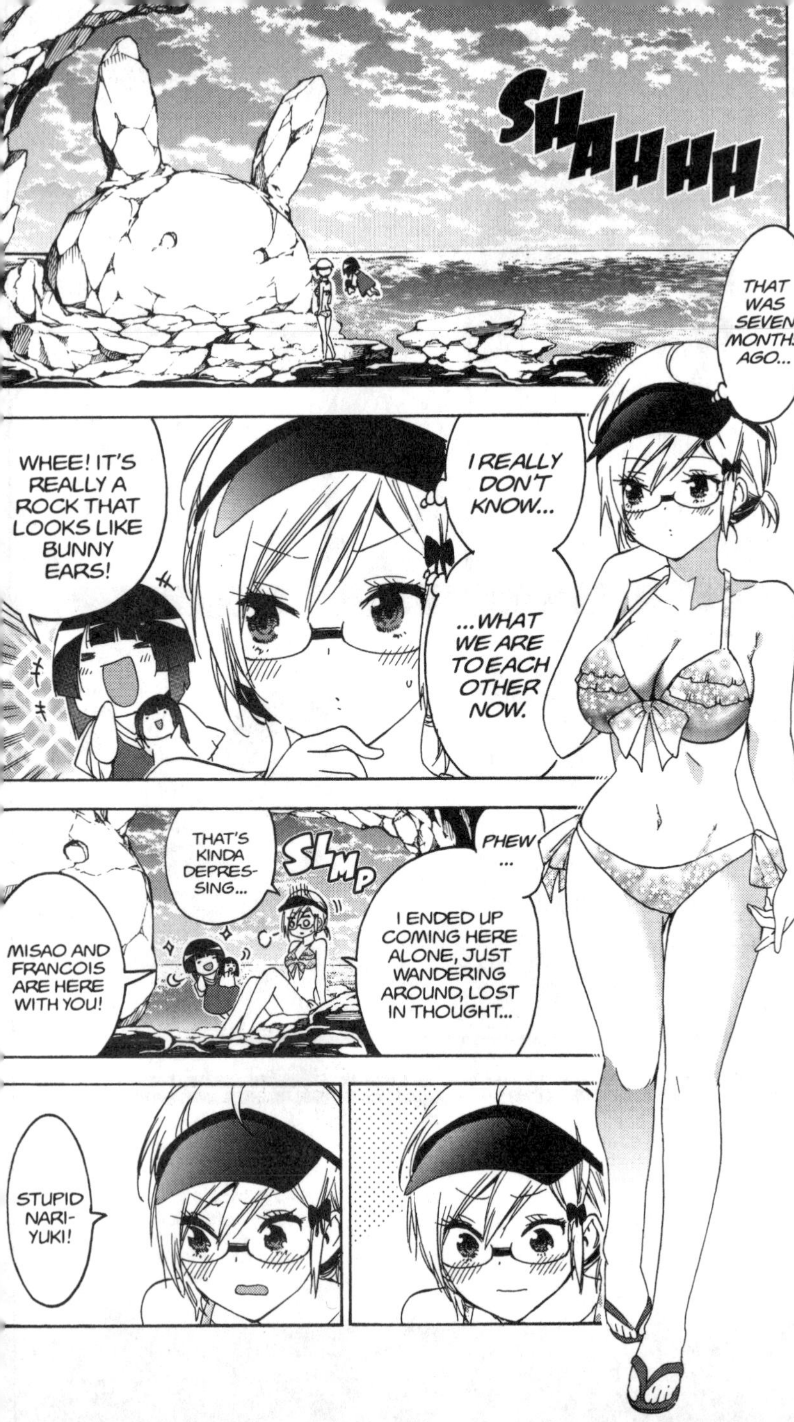
SHAHHH
THAT WAS SEVEN MONTHS AGO...
I REALLY DON'T KNOW...
...WHAT WE ARE TO EACH OTHER NOW.
WHEE! IT'S REALLY A ROCK THAT LOOKS LIKE BUNNY EARS!
PHEW...
I ENDED UP COMING HERE ALONE, JUST WANDERING AROUND, LOST IN THOUGHT...
SLMP
THAT'S KINDA DEPRES-SING...
MISAO AND FRANCOIS ARE HERE WITH YOU!
STUPID NARI-YUKI!

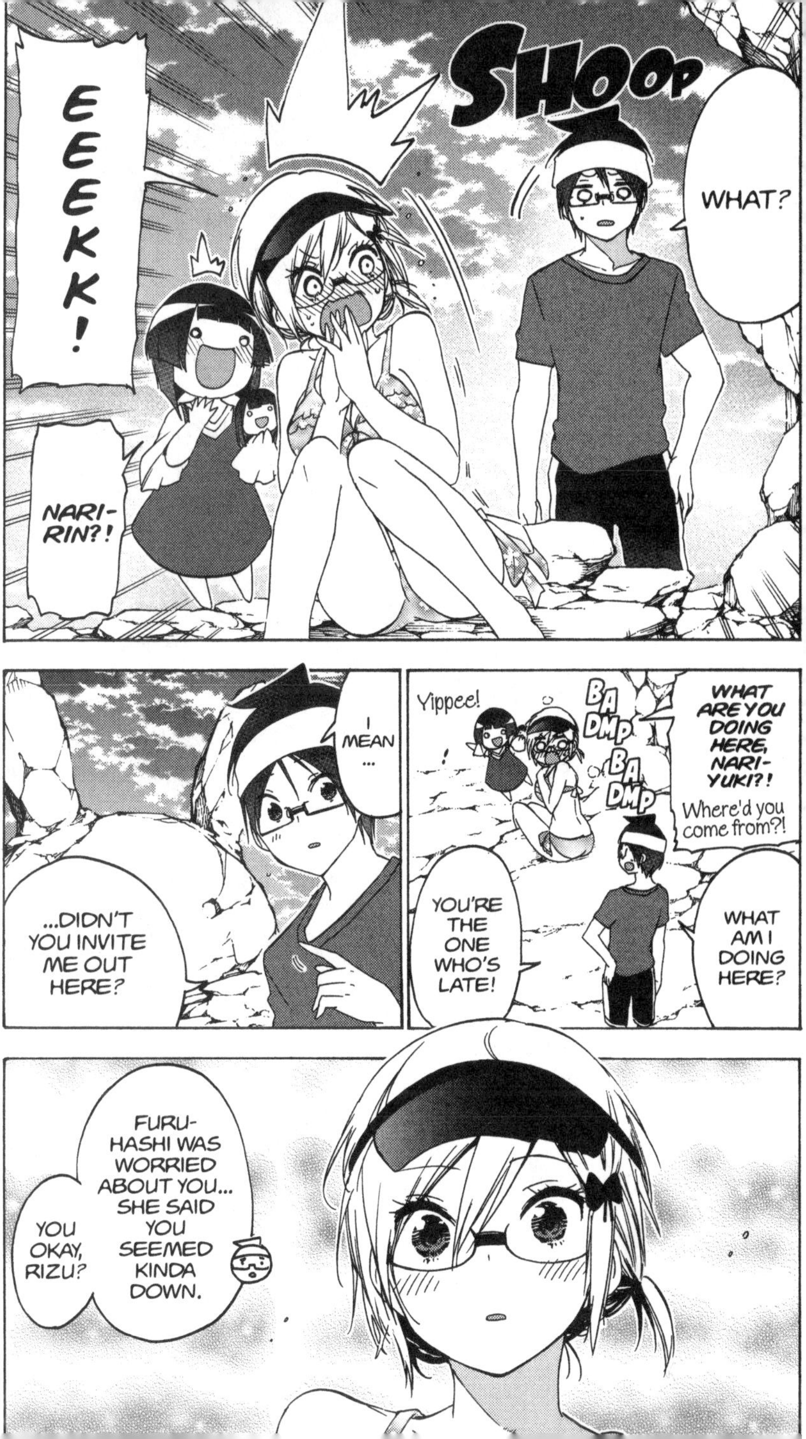
SHOOP
WHAT?
EEEEKK!
NARI-RIN?!
WHAT ARE YOU DOING HERE, NARI-YUKI?!
Where'd you come from?!
BA DMP BA DMP
Yippee!
WHAT AM I DOING HERE?
YOU'RE THE ONE WHO'S LATE!
I MEAN...
...DIDN'T YOU INVITE ME OUT HERE?
FURU-HASHI WAS WORRIED ABOUT YOU... SHE SAID YOU SEEMED KINDA DOWN.
YOU OKAY, RIZU?

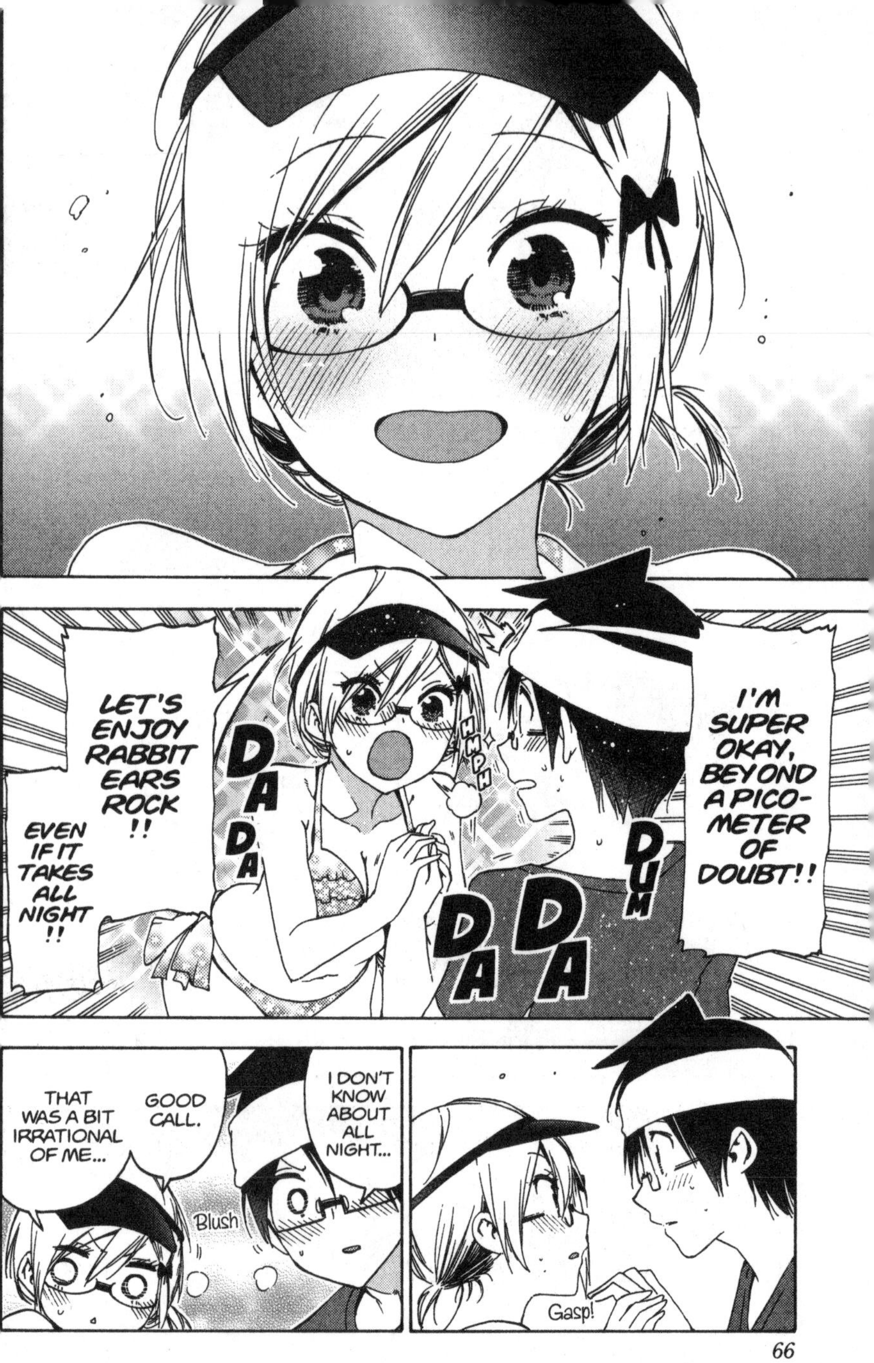
I'M SUPER OKAY, BEYOND A PICO-METER OF DOUBT!!
DUM
DA DA
HMPH
DA DA
LET'S ENJOY RABBIT EARS ROCK!!
EVEN IF IT TAKES ALL NIGHT!!
Gasp!
I DON'T KNOW ABOUT ALL NIGHT...
GOOD CALL.
THAT WAS A BIT IRRATIONAL OF ME...
Blush

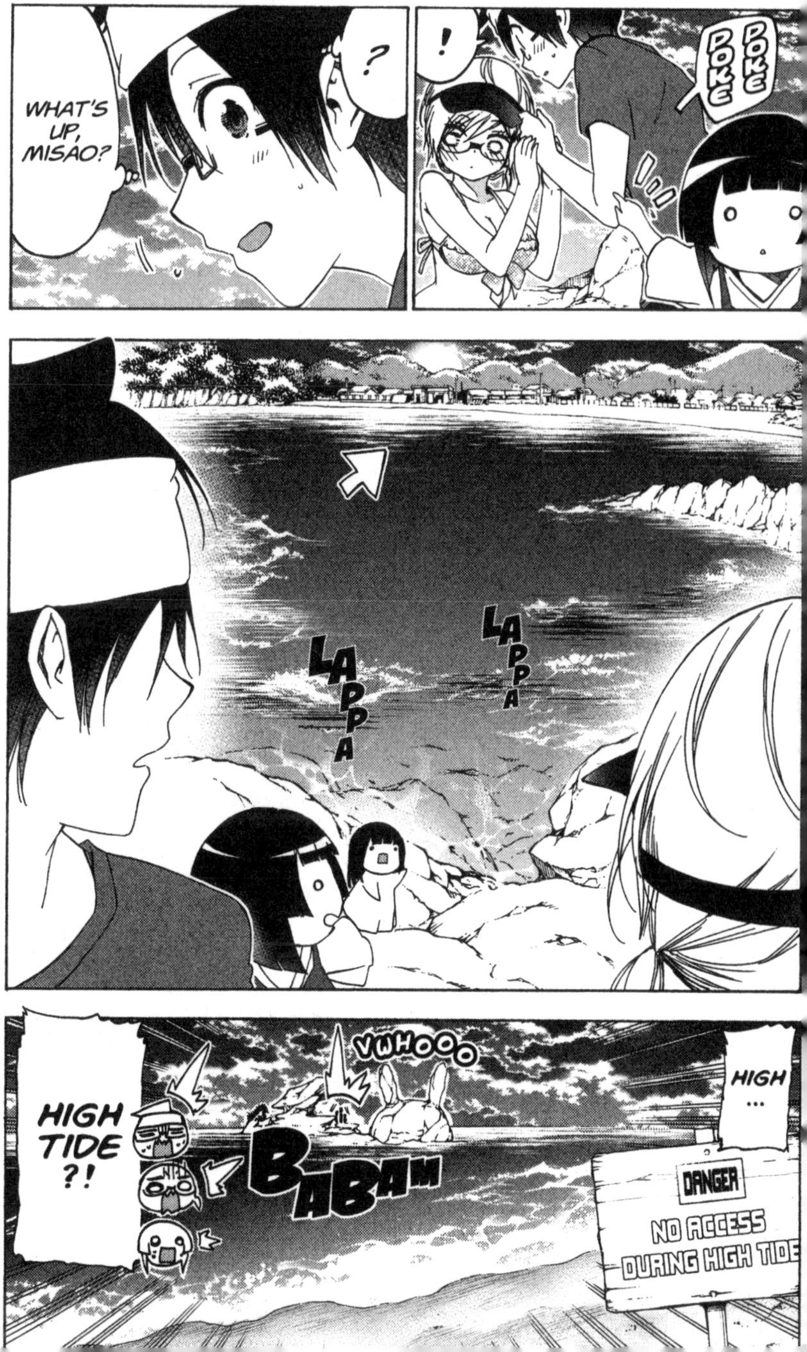
POKE POKE
!
!!
?
WHAT'S UP, MISAO?
LAPPA
LAPPA
HIGH ...
VWHOOOO
HIGH TIDE ?!
BABAM
DANGER
NO ACCESS DURING HIGH TIDE

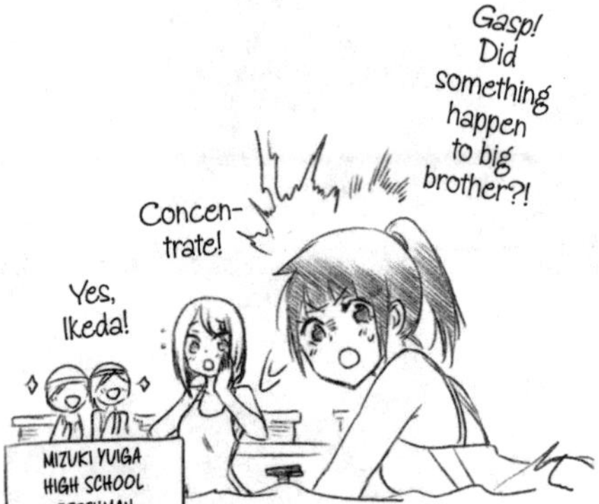
Gasp! Did something happen to big brother?!
Concen-trate!
Yes, Ikeda!
MIZUKI YUIGA HIGH SCHOOL FRESHMAN SWIM TEAM

Question 154: [X] = Thumbelina Supercomputer, Part 4

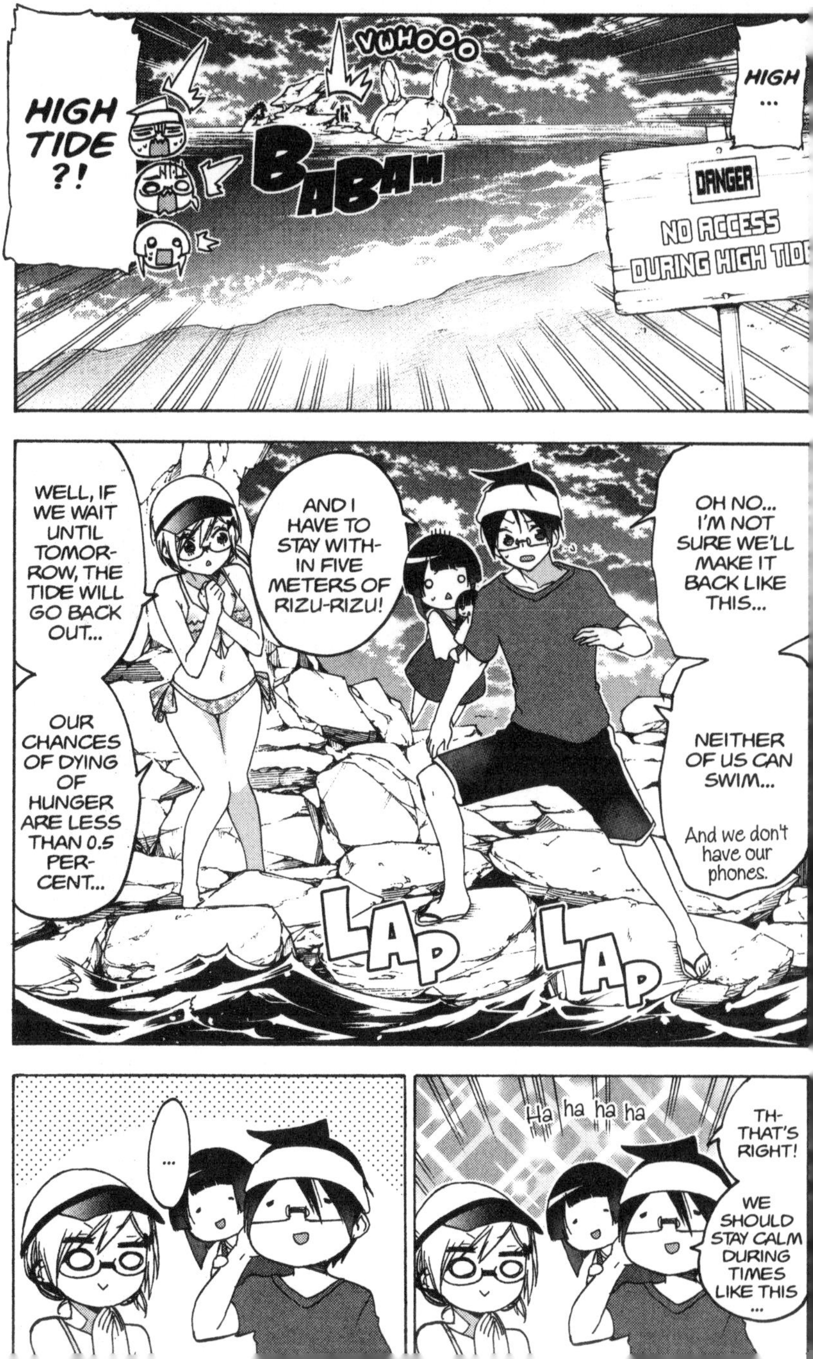
HIGH ...
DANGER
NO ACCESS
DURING HIGH TID
VWHOOO
BABAM
HIGH TIDE ?!
OH NO... I'M NOT SURE WE'LL MAKE IT BACK LIKE THIS...
NEITHER OF US CAN SWIM...
And we don't have our phones.
AND I HAVE TO STAY WITH-IN FIVE METERS OF RIZU-RIZU!
WELL, IF WE WAIT UNTIL TOMOR-ROW, THE TIDE WILL GO BACK OUT...
OUR CHANCES OF DYING OF HUNGER ARE LESS THAN 0.5 PER-CENT...
LAP
LAP
Ha ha ha ha
TH-THAT'S RIGHT!
WE SHOULD STAY CALM DURING TIMES LIKE THIS ...
...

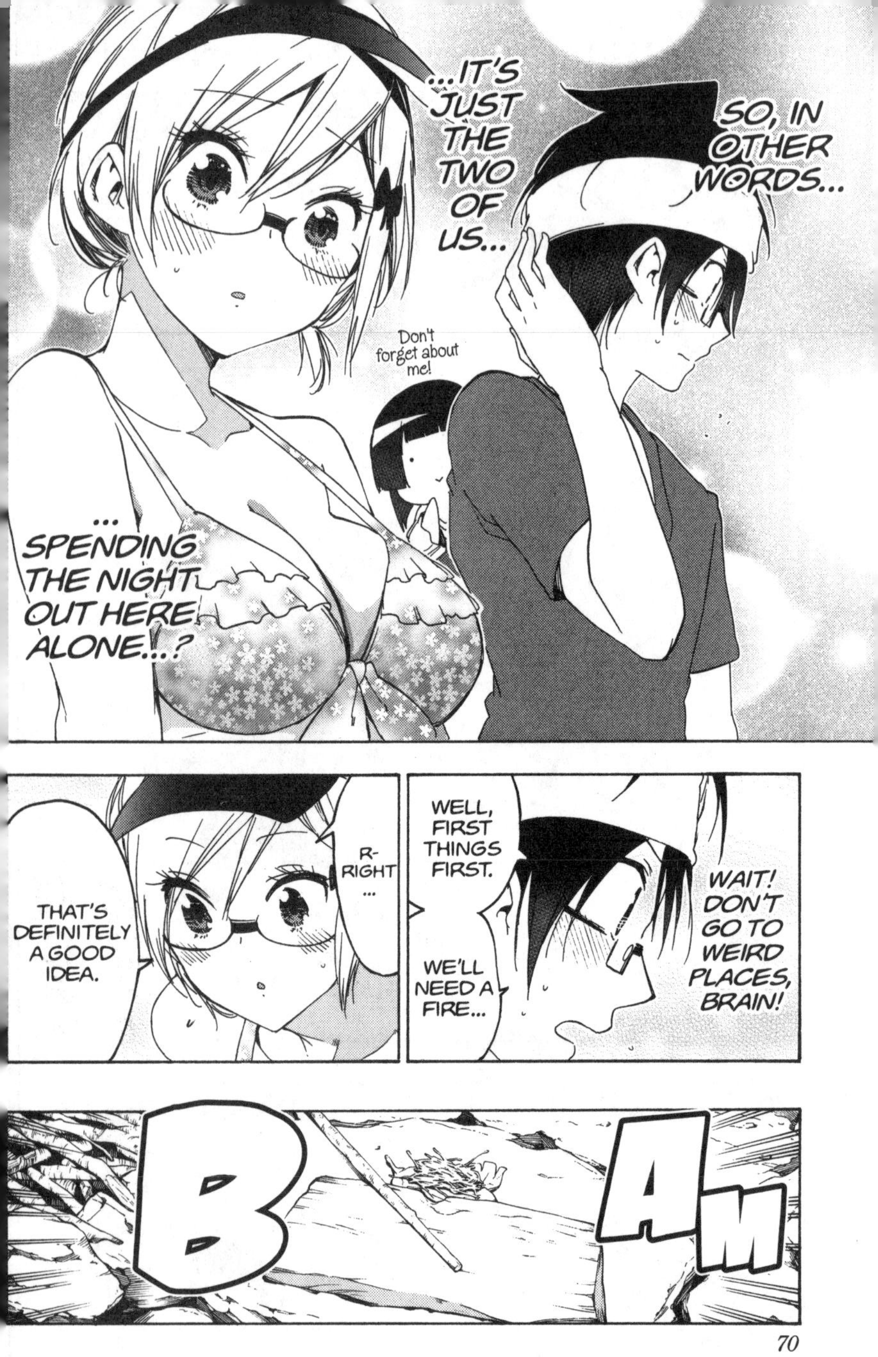
SO, IN OTHER WORDS...
...IT'S JUST THE TWO OF US...
Don't forget about me!
...SPENDING THE NIGHT OUT HERE ALONE...?
WAIT! DON'T GO TO WEIRD PLACES, BRAIN!
WELL, FIRST THINGS FIRST.
WE'LL NEED A FIRE...
R-RIGHT...
THAT'S DEFINITELY A GOOD IDEA.
BAM

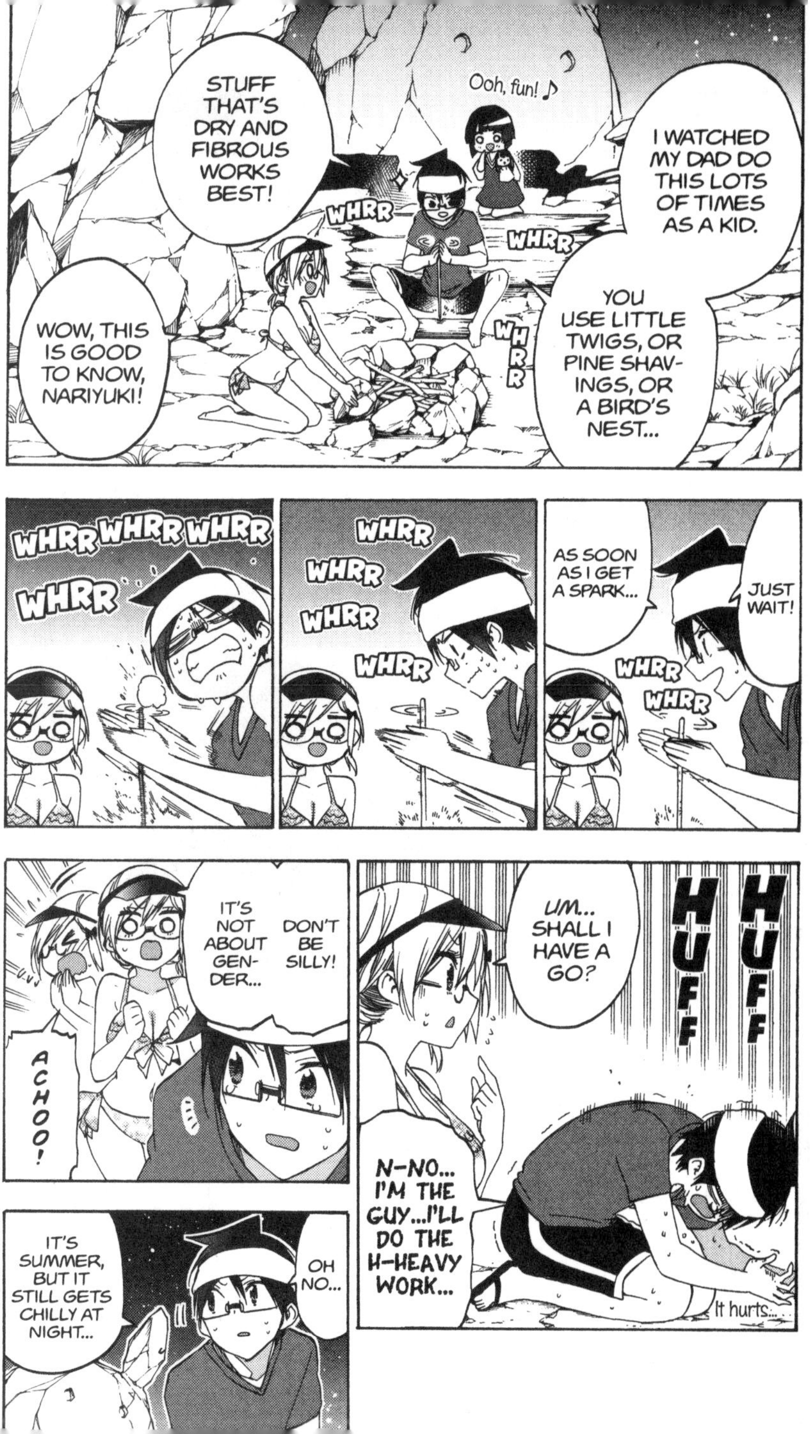
I WATCHED MY DAD DO THIS LOTS OF TIMES AS A KID.
Ooh, fun! ♪
YOU USE LITTLE TWIGS, OR PINE SHAVINGS, OR A BIRD'S NEST...
STUFF THAT'S DRY AND FIBROUS WORKS BEST!
WHRR
WHRR
WHRR
WOW, THIS IS GOOD TO KNOW, NARIYUKI!
JUST WAIT!
AS SOON AS I GET A SPARK...
WHRR
WHRR
WHRR
WHRR
WHRR
WHRR
WHRR WHRR WHRR
WHRR
HUFF
HUFF
UM... SHALL I HAVE A GO?
N-NO... I'M THE GUY...I'LL DO THE H-HEAVY WORK...
It hurts...
DON'T BE SILLY!
IT'S NOT ABOUT GENDER...
ACHOO!
OH NO...
IT'S SUMMER, BUT IT STILL GETS CHILLY AT NIGHT...

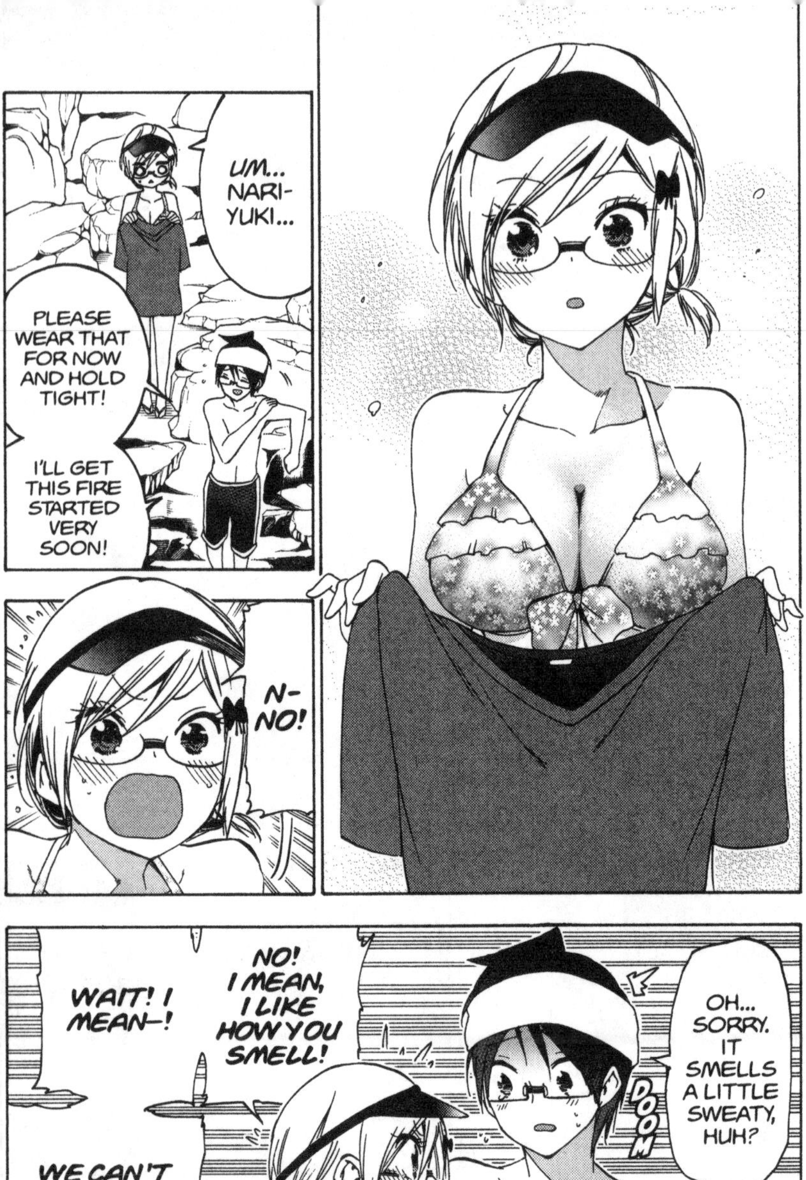
UM... NARI-YUKI...
PLEASE WEAR THAT FOR NOW AND HOLD TIGHT!
I'LL GET THIS FIRE STARTED VERY SOON!
N-NO!
OH... SORRY. IT SMELLS A LITTLE SWEATY, HUH?
DOOM
NO! I MEAN, I LIKE HOW YOU SMELL!
WAIT! I MEAN—!
WE CAN'T HAVE YOU GETTING SICK, NARIYUKI!

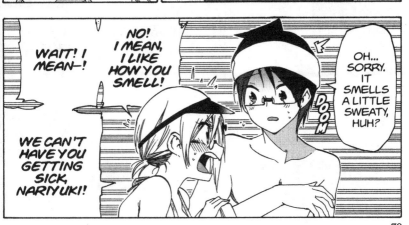

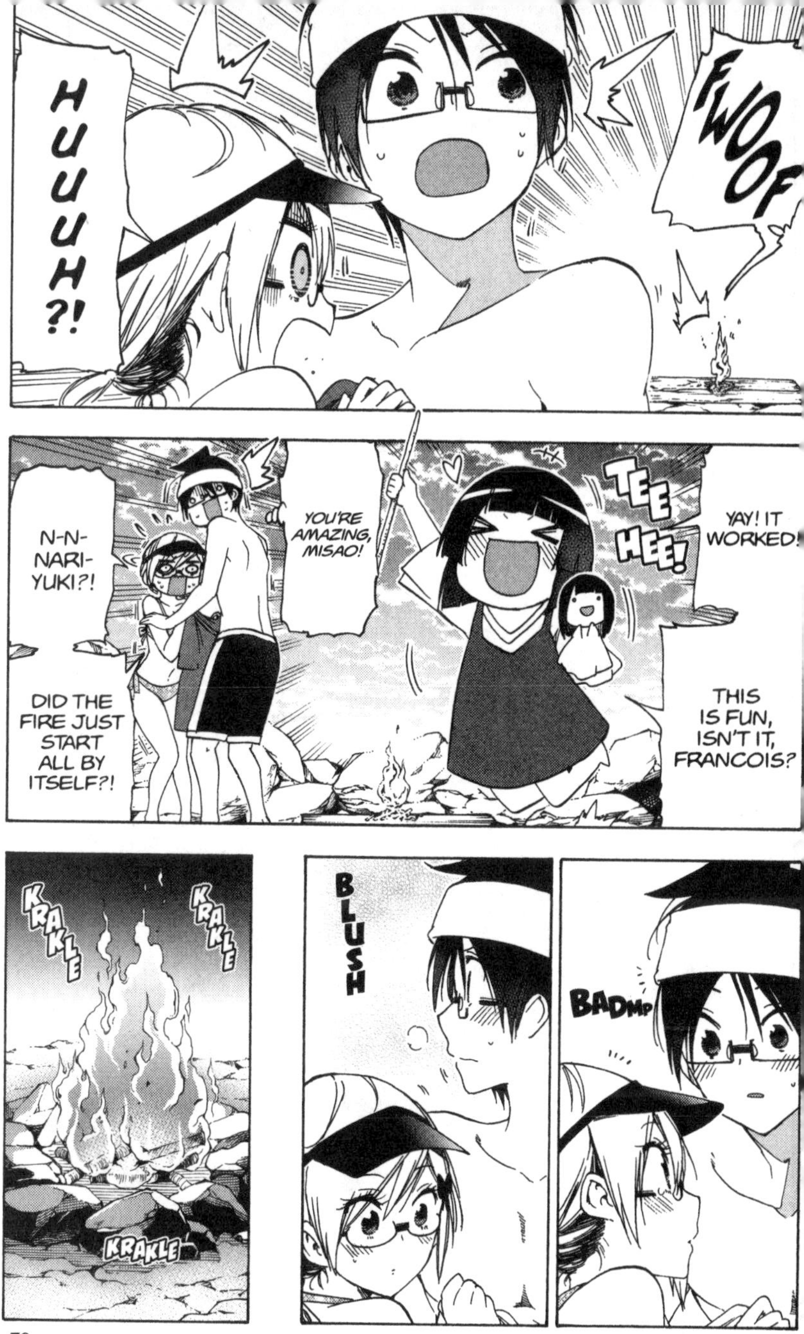
FWOOF
HUUUUH?!
YAY! IT WORKED!
TEE HEE!
THIS IS FUN, ISN'T IT, FRANCOIS?
YOU'RE AMAZING, MISAO!
N-N-NARI-YUKI?!
DID THE FIRE JUST START ALL BY ITSELF?!
BADMP
BLUSH
KRAKLE
KRAKLE
KRAKLE

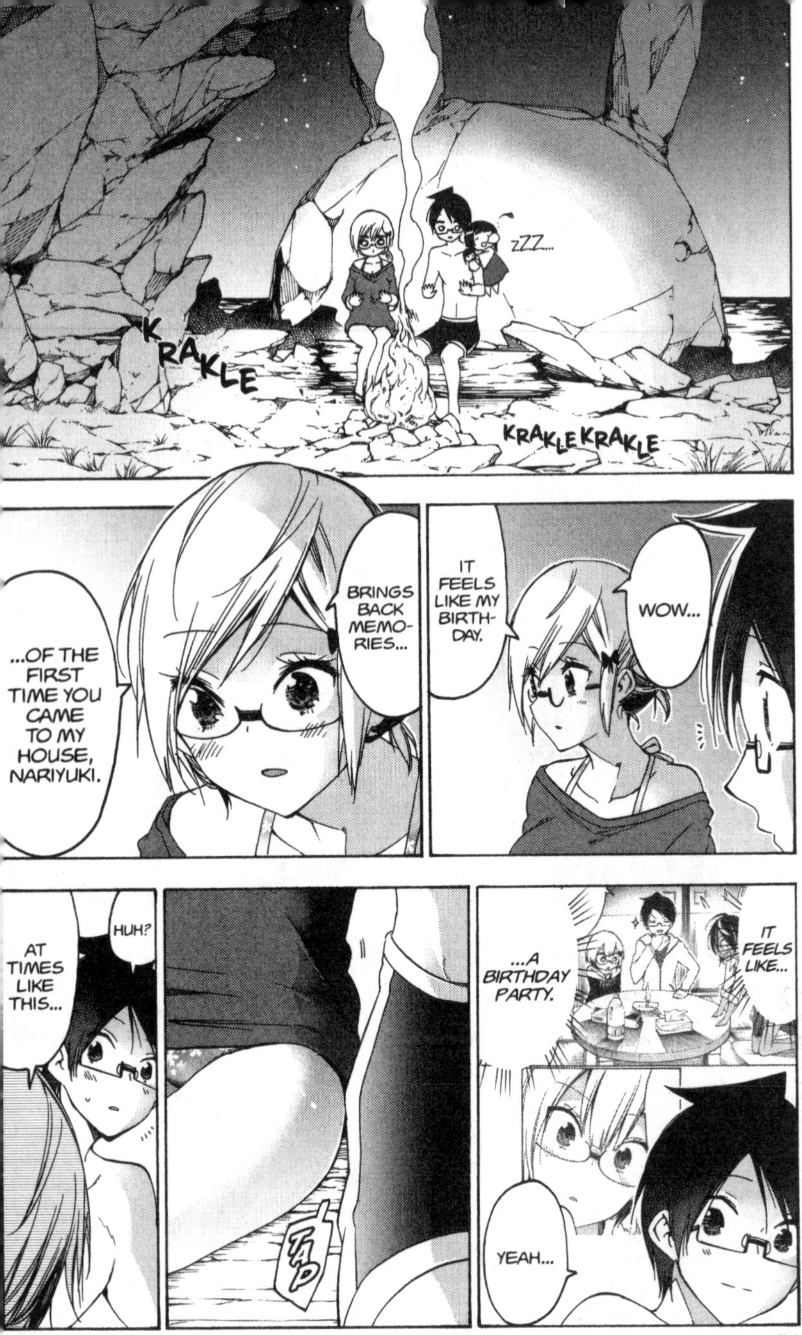
zZZ...
KRAKLE
KRAKLEKRAKLE
WOW...
IT FEELS LIKE MY BIRTH-DAY.
BRINGS BACK MEMO-RIES...
...OF THE FIRST TIME YOU CAME TO MY HOUSE, NARIYUKI.
IT FEELS LIKE...
...A BIRTHDAY PARTY.
YEAH...
TAP
HUH?
AT TIMES LIKE THIS...

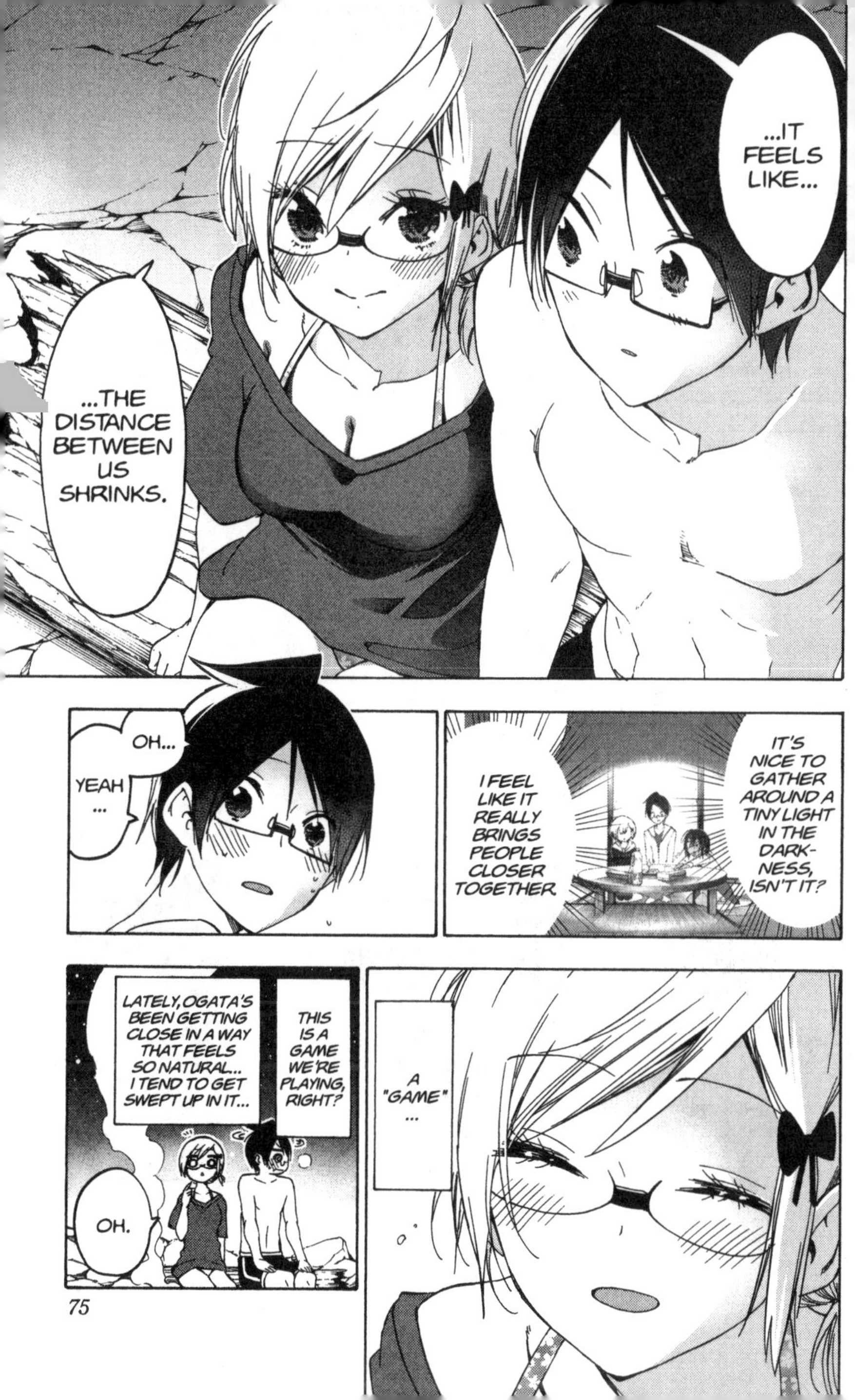
...IT FEELS LIKE...
...THE DISTANCE BETWEEN US SHRINKS.
IT'S NICE TO GATHER AROUND A TINY LIGHT IN THE DARKNESS, ISN'T IT?
I FEEL LIKE IT REALLY BRINGS PEOPLE CLOSER TOGETHER.
OH...
YEAH ...
A "GAME" ...
THIS IS A GAME WE'RE PLAYING, RIGHT?
LATELY, OGATA'S BEEN GETTING CLOSE IN A WAY THAT FEELS SO NATURAL... I TEND TO GET SWEPT UP IN IT...
OH.

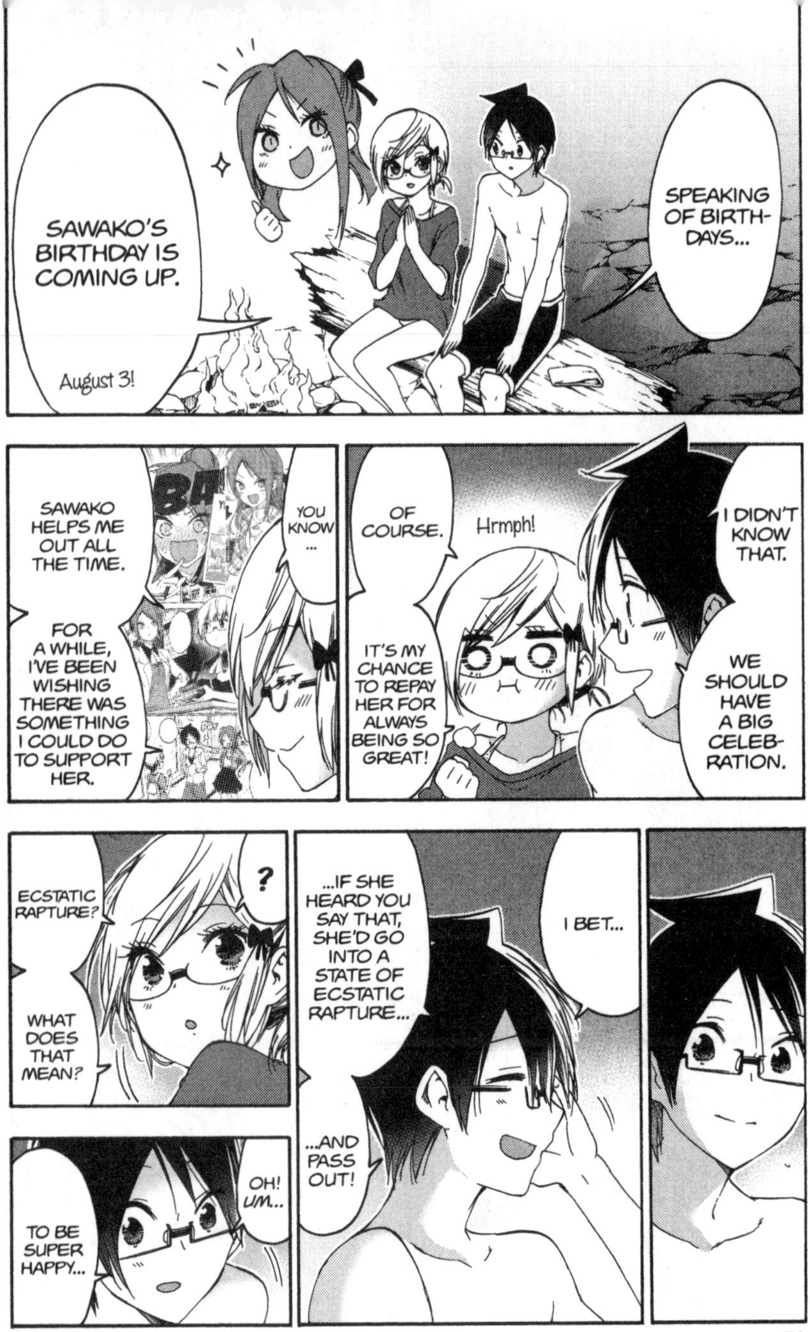
SPEAKING OF BIRTH-DAYS...
SAWAKO'S BIRTHDAY IS COMING UP.
August 3!
I DIDN'T KNOW THAT.
WE SHOULD HAVE A BIG CELEB-RATION.
Hrmph!
OF COURSE.
IT'S MY CHANCE TO REPAY HER FOR ALWAYS BEING SO GREAT!
YOU KNOW ...
SAWAKO HELPS ME OUT ALL THE TIME.
FOR A WHILE, I'VE BEEN WISHING THERE WAS SOMETHING I COULD DO TO SUPPORT HER.
I BET...
...IF SHE HEARD YOU SAY THAT, SHE'D GO INTO A STATE OF ECSTATIC RAPTURE...
...AND PASS OUT!
?
ECSTATIC RAPTURE?
WHAT DOES THAT MEAN?
OH! UM...
TO BE SUPER HAPPY...

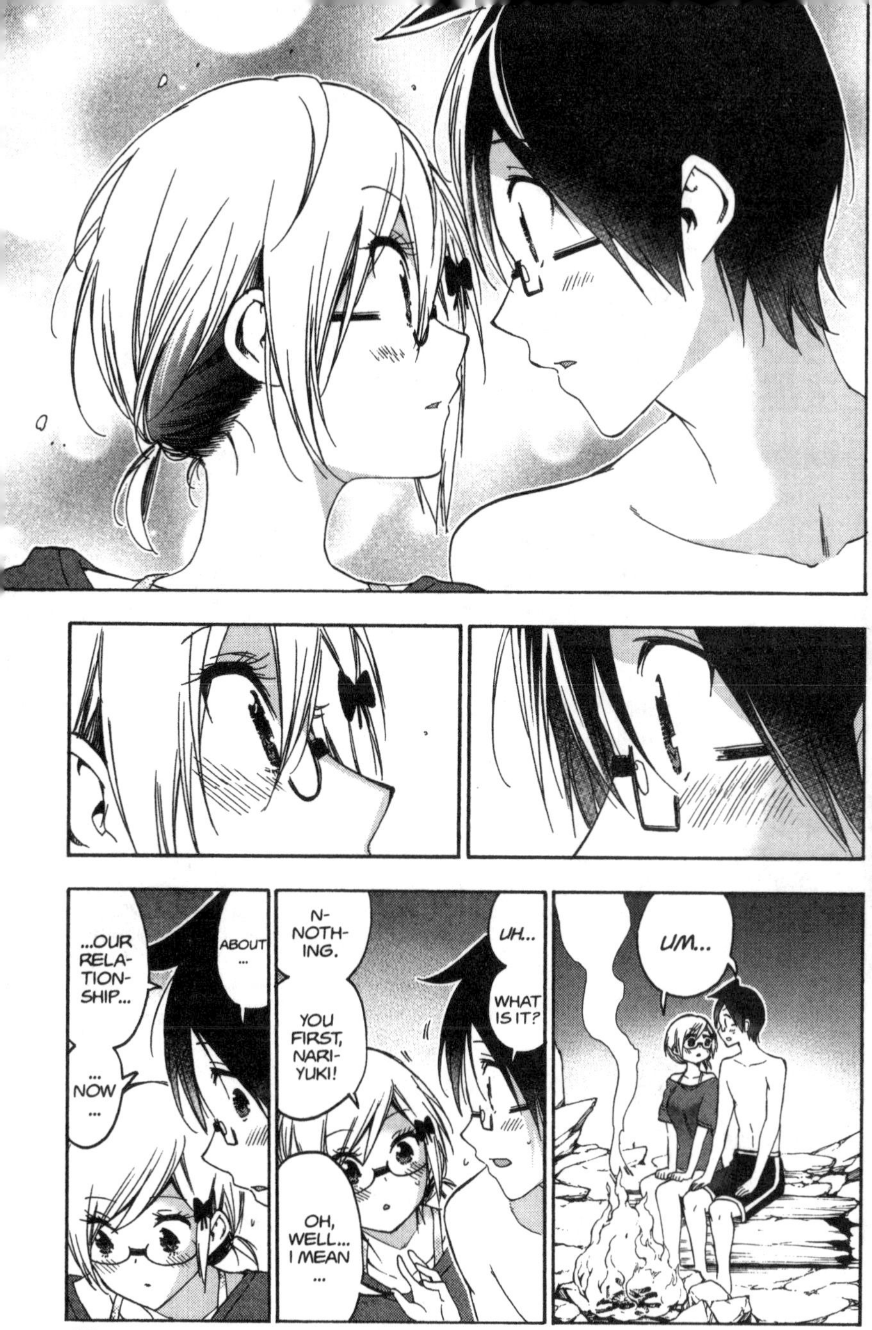
UM...
UH...
WHAT IS IT?
N-NOTHING.
YOU FIRST, NARIYUKI!
OH, WELL... I MEAN ...
ABOUT ...
...OUR RELATIONSHIP...
... NOW ...

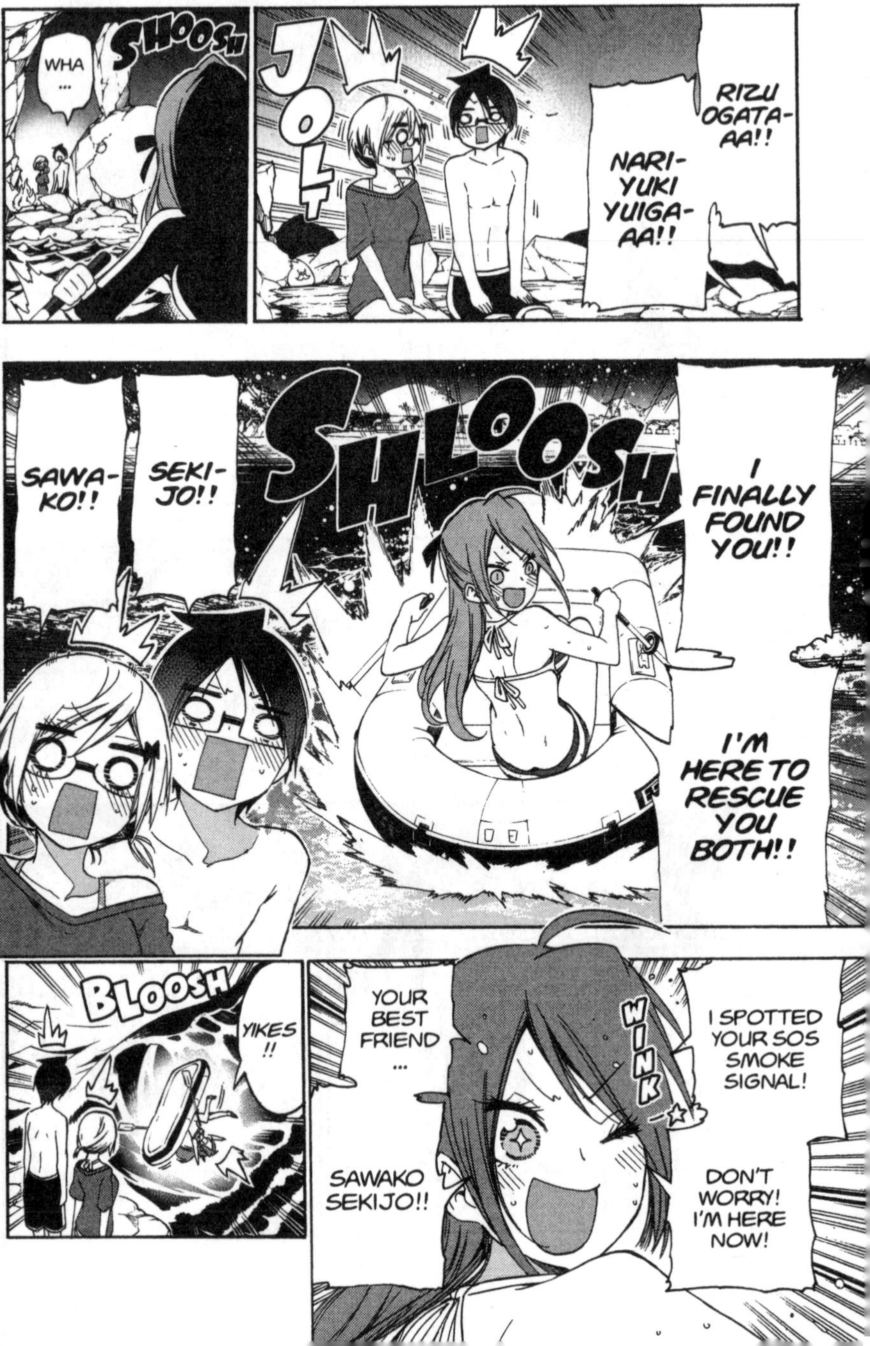
RIZU OGATAAA!!
NARI-YUKI YUIGAAA!!
JOLT
SHOOSH
WHA ...
I FINALLY FOUND YOU!!
I'M HERE TO RESCUE YOU BOTH!!
SHLOOSH
SEKI-JO!!
SAWA-KO!!
I SPOTTED YOUR SOS SMOKE SIGNAL!
WINK
DON'T WORRY! I'M HERE NOW!
YOUR BEST FRIEND ...
SAWAKO SEKIJO!!
BLOOSH
YIKES!!

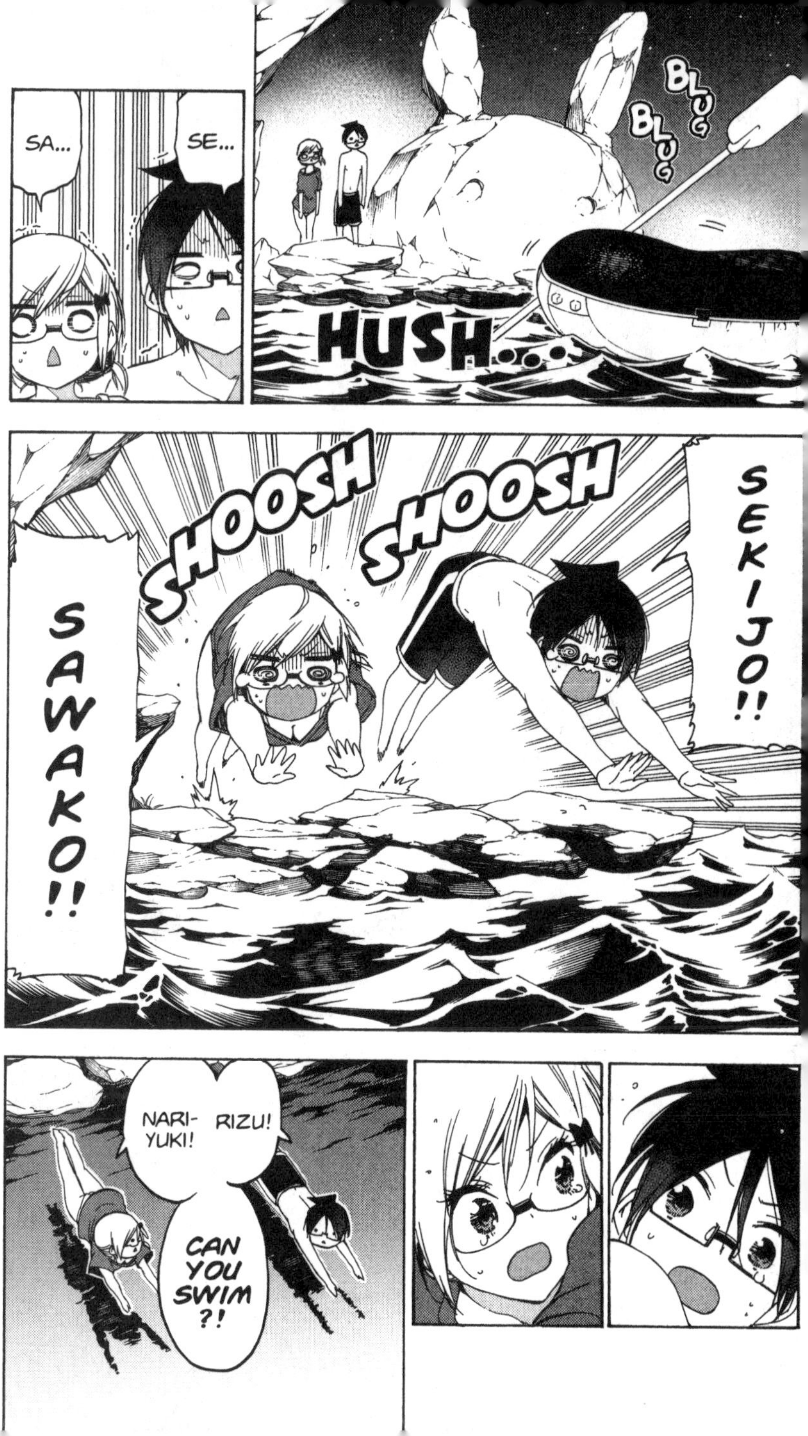
BLUG BLUG
HUSH...
SE...
SA...
SEKIJO!!
SHOOSH
SHOOSH
SAWAKO!!
RIZU!
NARI-YUKI!
CAN YOU SWIM?!

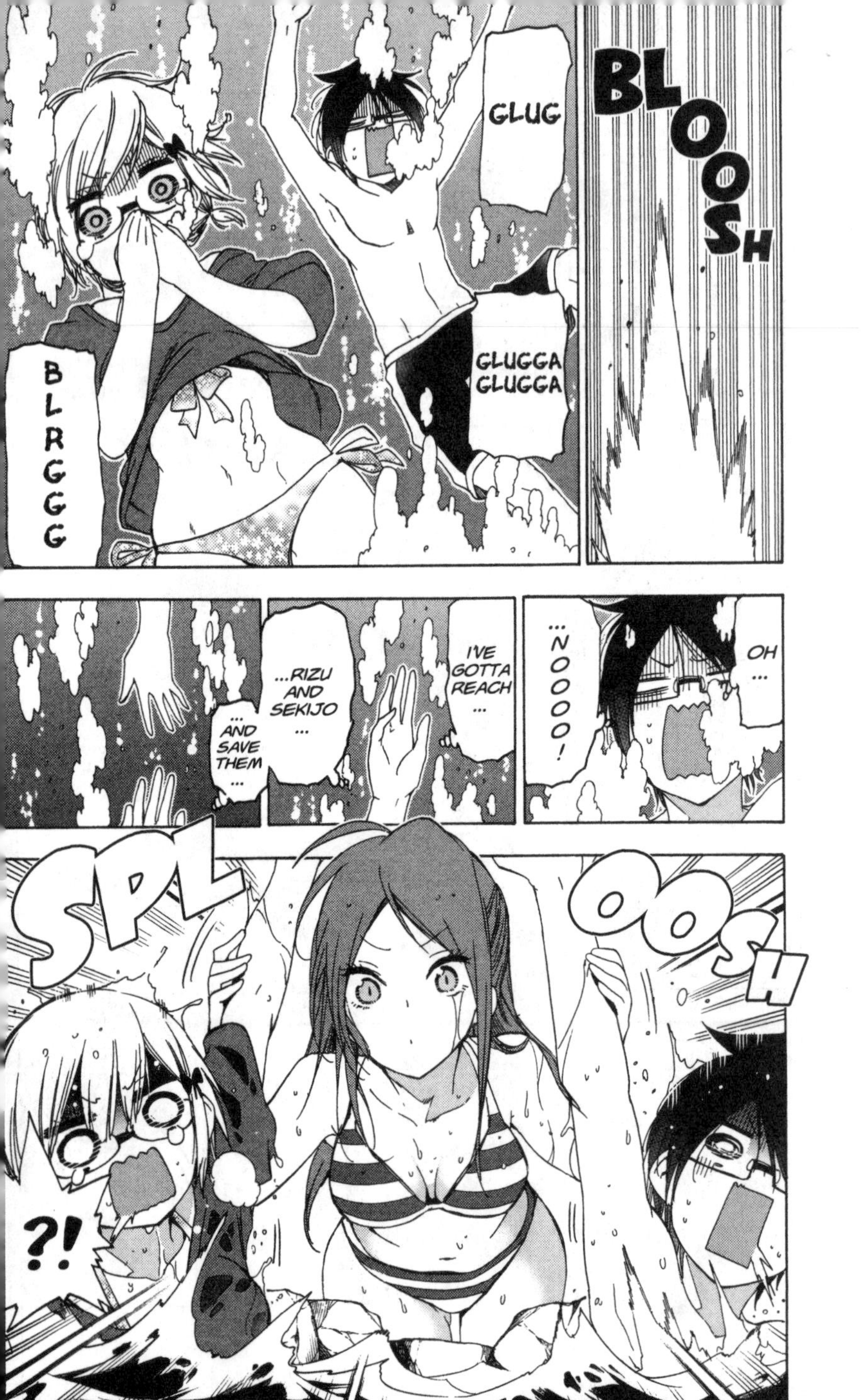
BLOOSH
GLUG
GLUGGA GLUGGA
BLRGGG
OH ...
...NOOOOO!
I'VE GOTTA REACH ...
...RIZU AND SEKIJO ...
... AND SAVE THEM ...
SPLOOSH
?!

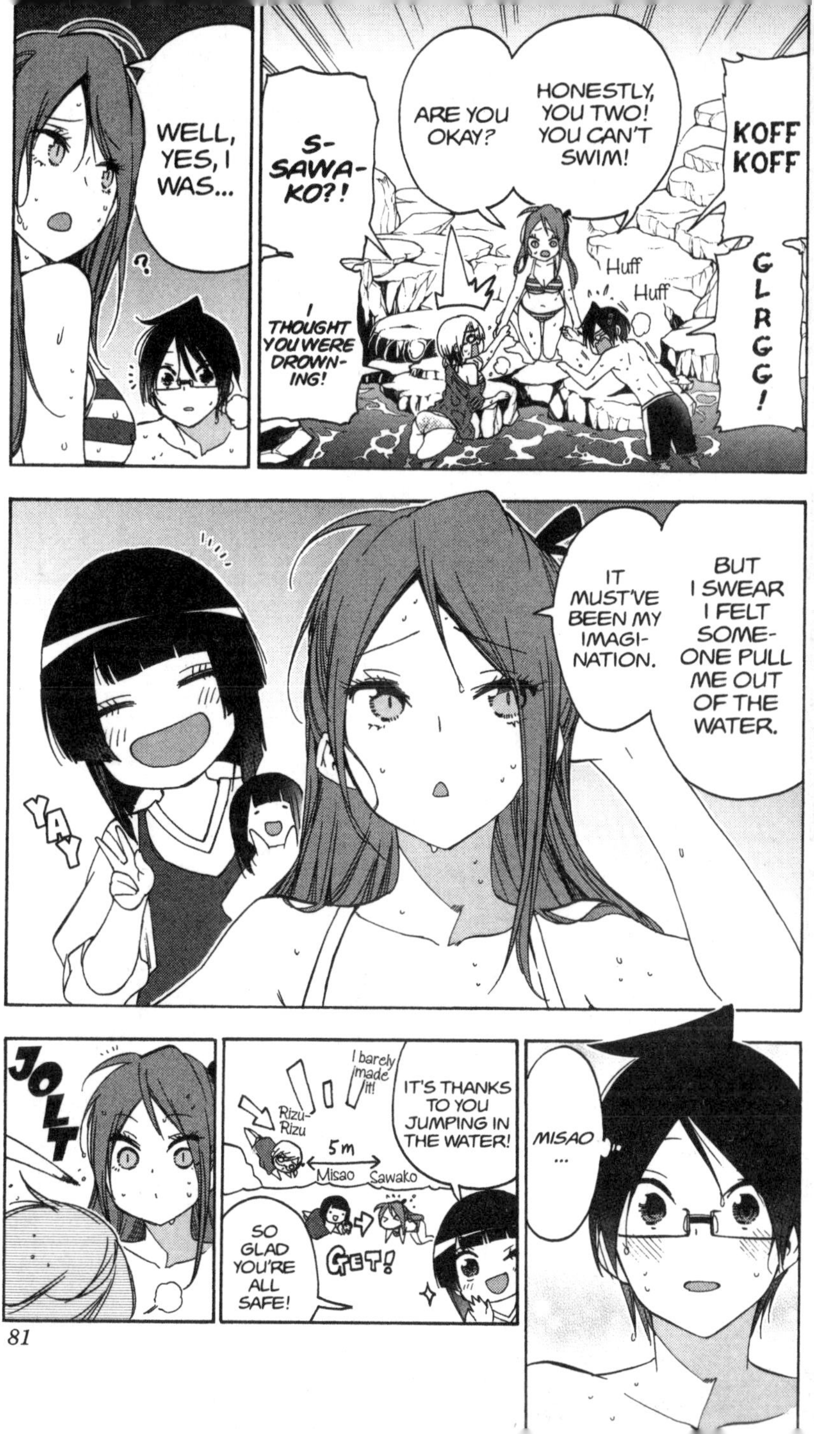
KOFF KOFF
GLRGG!
HONESTLY, YOU TWO! YOU CAN'T SWIM!
ARE YOU OKAY?
Huff
Huff
S-SAWAKO?!
I THOUGHT YOU WERE DROWNING!
WELL, YES, I WAS...
?
BUT I SWEAR I FELT SOMEONE PULL ME OUT OF THE WATER.
IT MUST'VE BEEN MY IMAGINATION.
YAY
MISAO...
IT'S THANKS TO YOU JUMPING IN THE WATER!
I barely made it!
Rizu-Rizu
5 m
Misao
Sawako
GET!
SO GLAD YOU'RE ALL SAFE!
JOLT

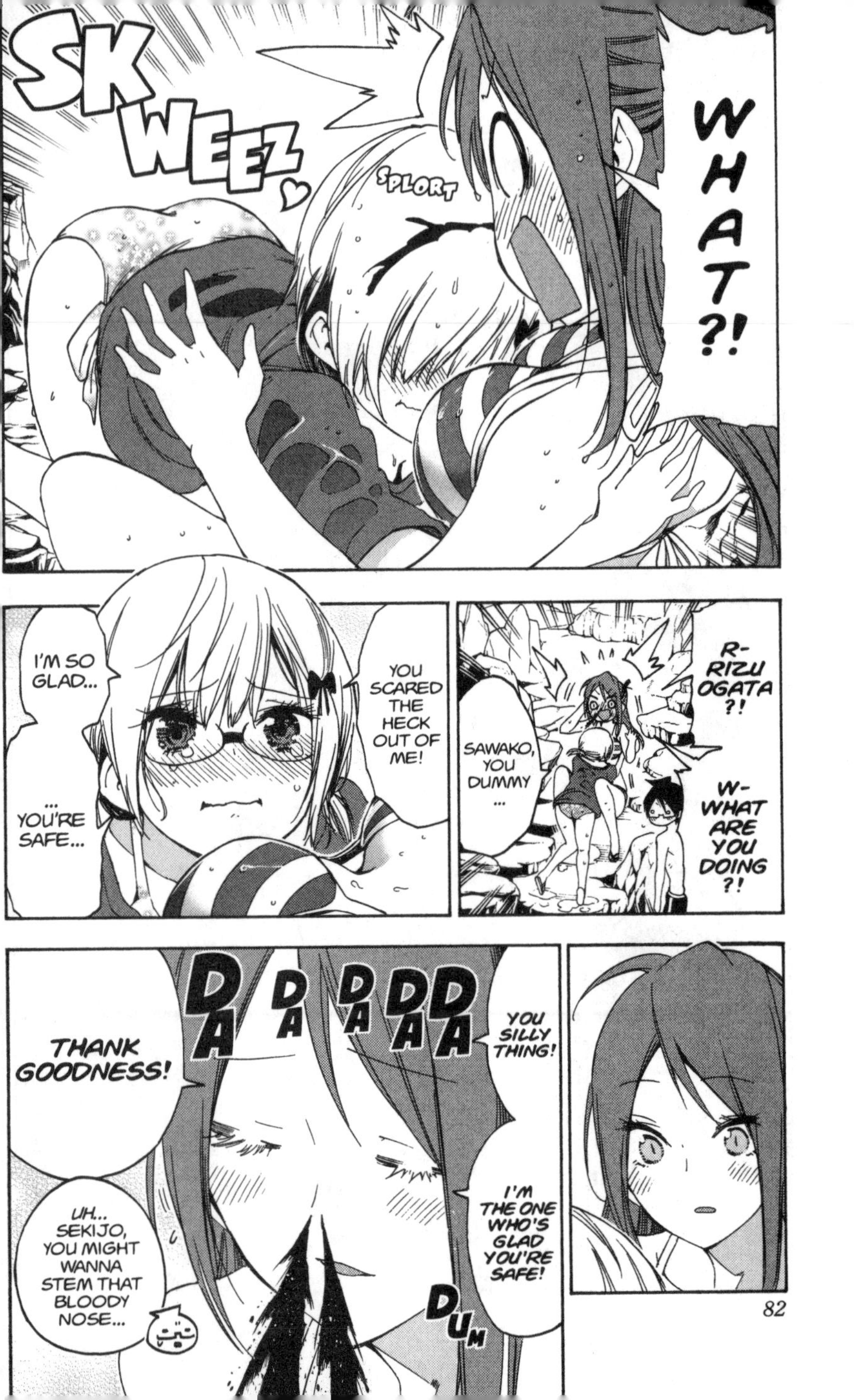
WHAT?!
SPLORT
SKWEEZ ♡
R-RIZU OGATA?!
W-WHAT ARE YOU DOING?!
SAWAKO, YOU DUMMY...
YOU SCARED THE HECK OUT OF ME!
I'M SO GLAD...
...YOU'RE SAFE...
DA DA DA DA DA
YOU SILLY THING!
THANK GOODNESS!
I'M THE ONE WHO'S GLAD YOU'RE SAFE!
UH... SEKIJO, YOU MIGHT WANNA STEM THAT BLOODY NOSE...
DUM

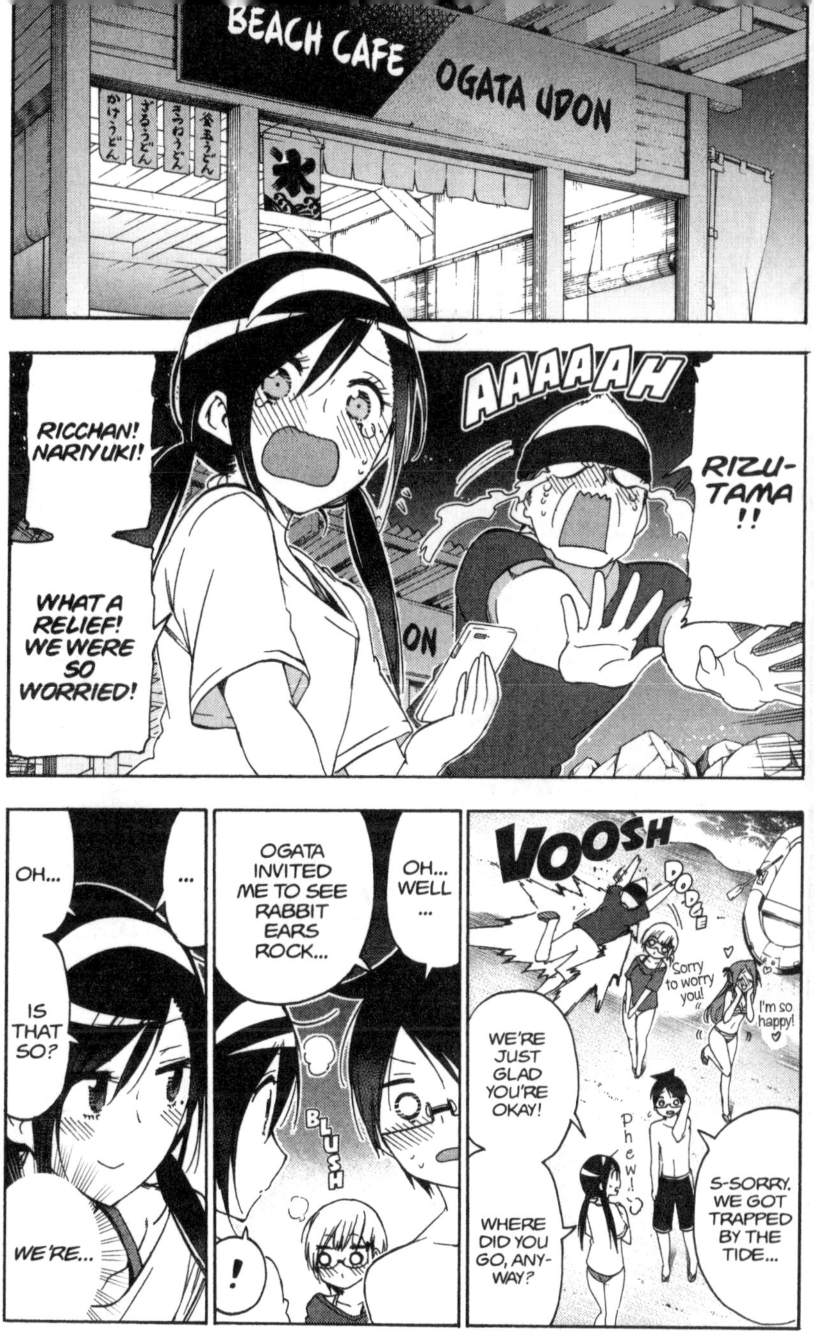
BEACH CAFE
OGATA UDON
釜玉うどん
きつねうどん
ざるうどん
かけうどん
氷
RIZU-TAMA!!
AAAAAH
RICCHAN! NARIYUKI!
WHAT A RELIEF! WE WERE SO WORRIED!
ON
VOOSH
DODGE
Sorry to worry you!
I'm so happy!
S-SORRY. WE GOT TRAPPED BY THE TIDE...
WE'RE JUST GLAD YOU'RE OKAY!
Phew!
WHERE DID YOU GO, ANYWAY?
OH... WELL...
OGATA INVITED ME TO SEE RABBIT EARS ROCK...
BLUSH
!
...
OH...
IS THAT SO?
WE'RE...

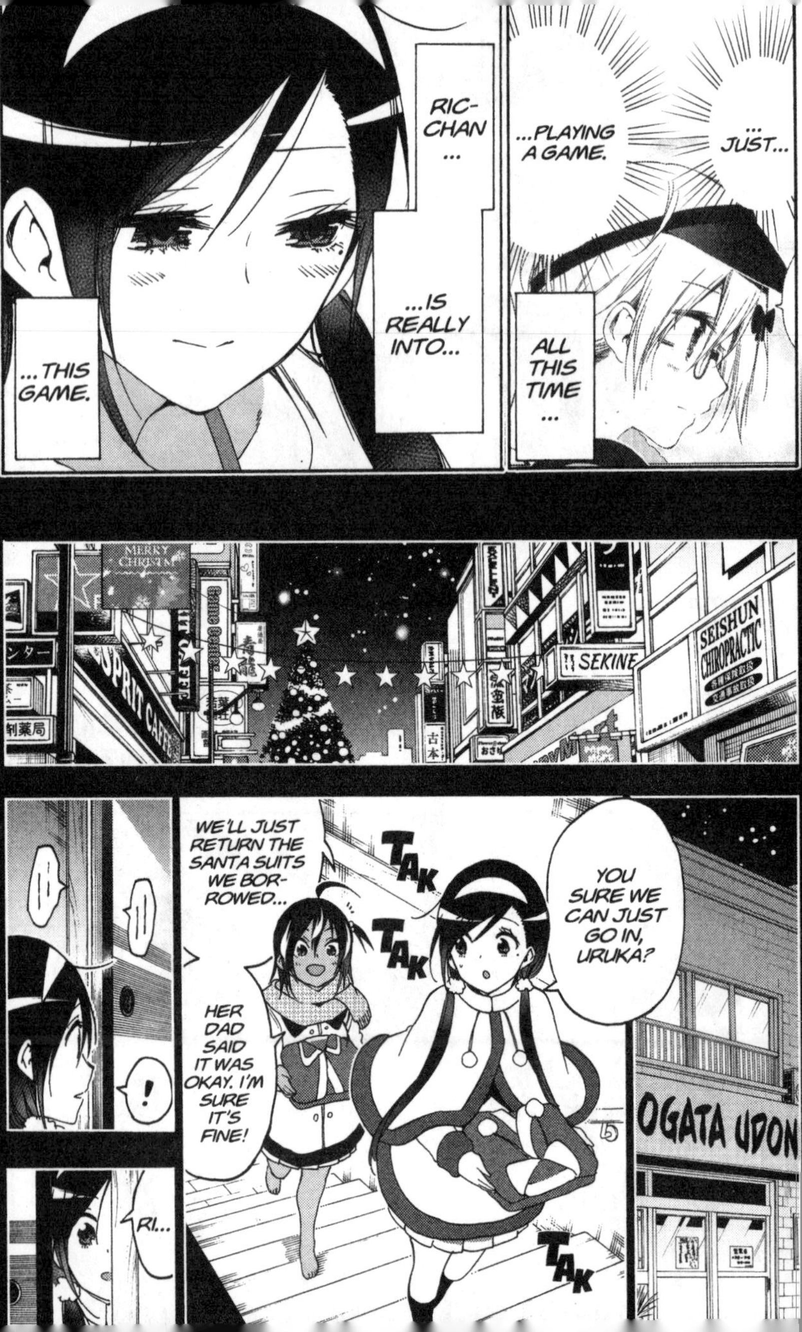
... JUST...
...PLAYING A GAME.
ALL THIS TIME ...
RIC-CHAN ...
...IS REALLY INTO...
...THIS GAME.
SEISHUN CHIROPRACTIC
SEKINE
YOU SURE WE CAN JUST GO IN, URUKA?
WE'LL JUST RETURN THE SANTA SUITS WE BOR-ROWED...
TAK
TAK
HER DAD SAID IT WAS OKAY. I'M SURE IT'S FINE!
TAK
OGATA UDON
!
RI...

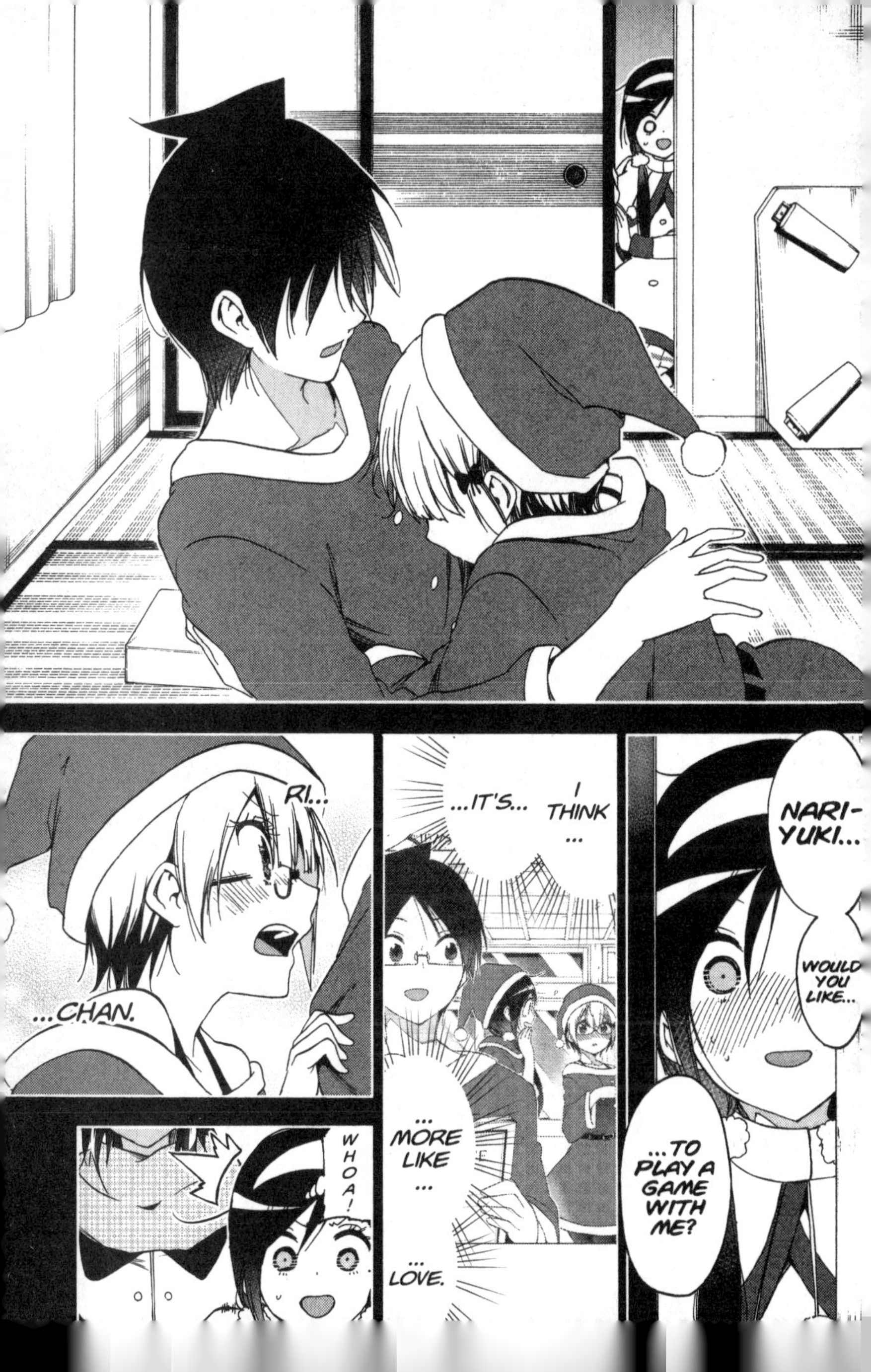
NARI-YUKI...
WOULD YOU LIKE...
...TO PLAY A GAME WITH ME?
I THINK ...
...IT'S...
... MORE LIKE ...
... LOVE.
RI...
...CHAN.
WHOA!

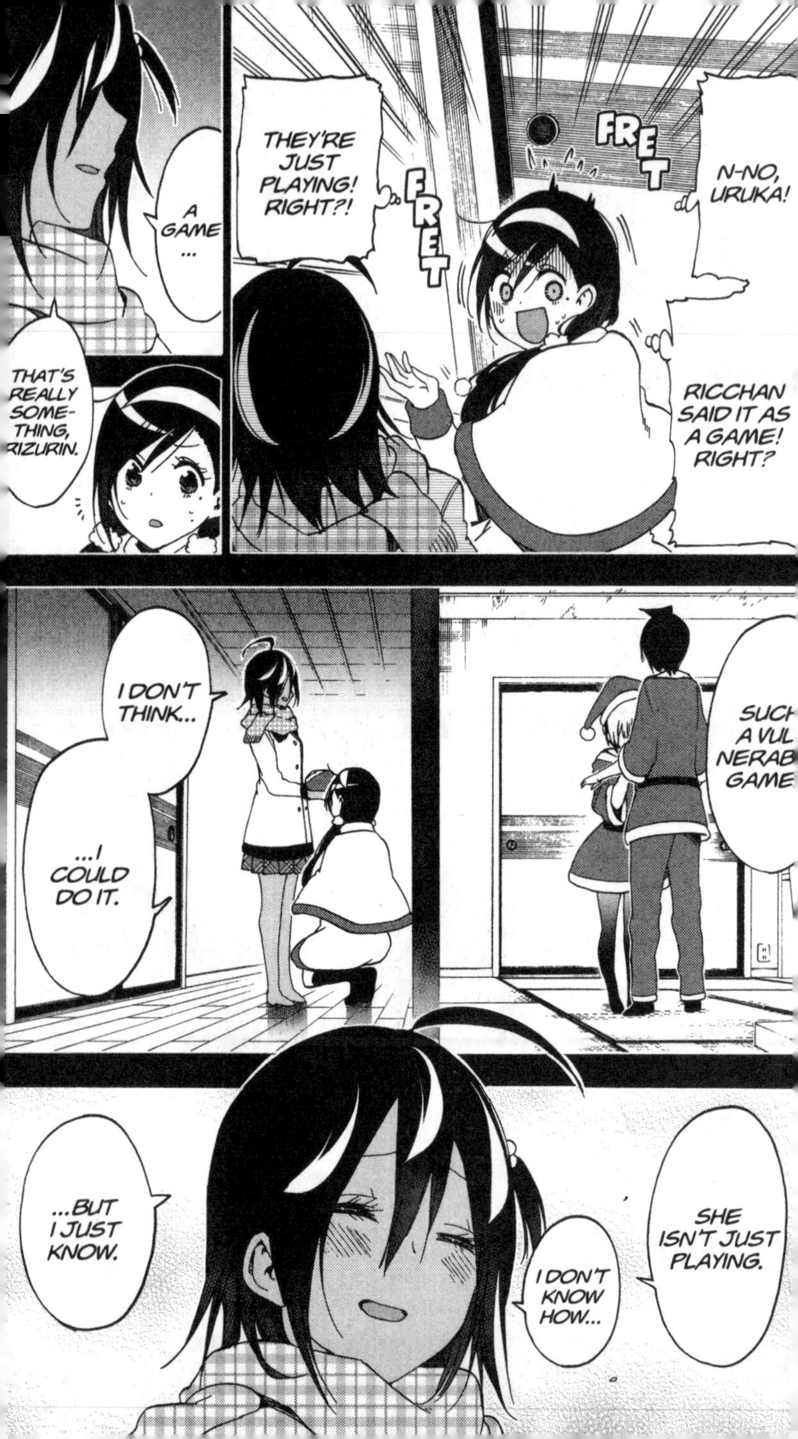

N-NO, URUKA!
FRET
RICCHAN SAID IT AS A GAME! RIGHT?
THEY'RE JUST PLAYING! RIGHT?!
FRET
A GAME...
THAT'S REALLY SOME-THING, RIZURIN.
SUCH A VUL NERAB GAME
I DON'T THINK...
...I COULD DO IT.
SHE ISN'T JUST PLAYING.
I DON'T KNOW HOW...
...BUT I JUST KNOW.

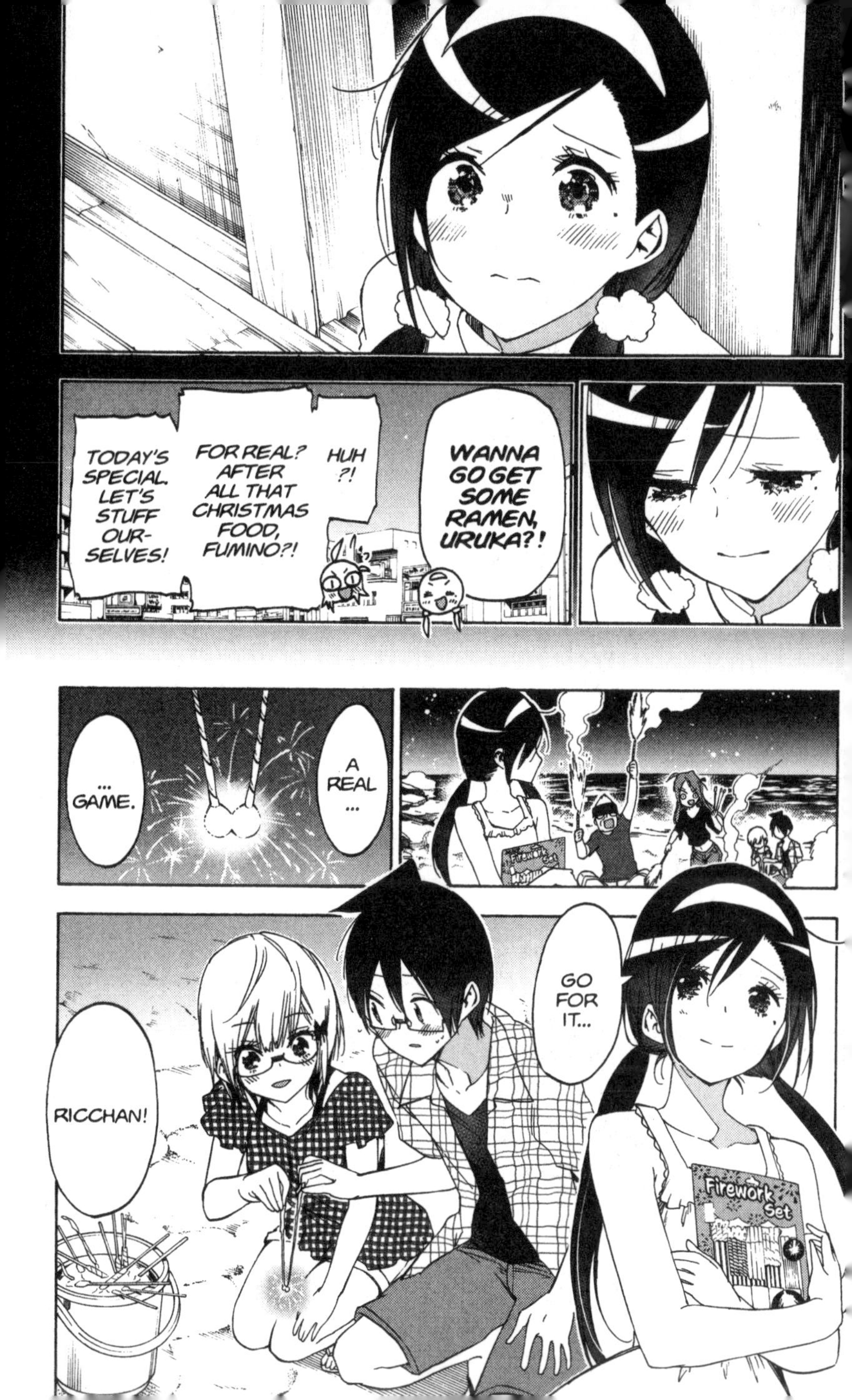
WANNA GO GET SOME RAMEN, URUKA?!
HUH ?!
FOR REAL? AFTER ALL THAT CHRISTMAS FOOD, FUMINO?!
TODAY'S SPECIAL. LET'S STUFF OUR-SELVES!
A REAL ...
... GAME.
GO FOR IT...
Firework Set
RICCHAN!

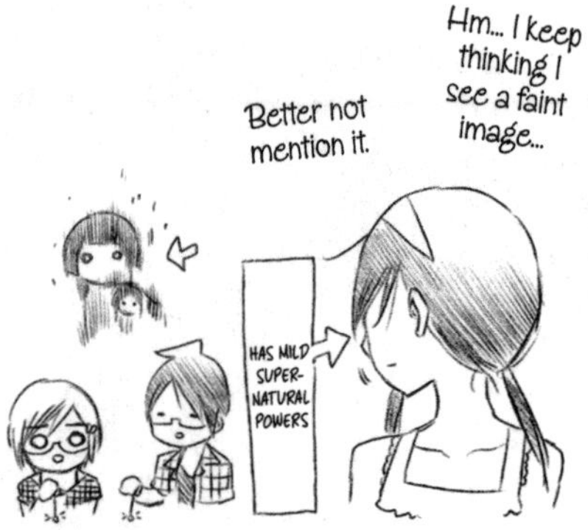
Hm... I keep thinking I see a faint image...
Better not mention it.
HAS MILD SUPER-NATURAL POWERS

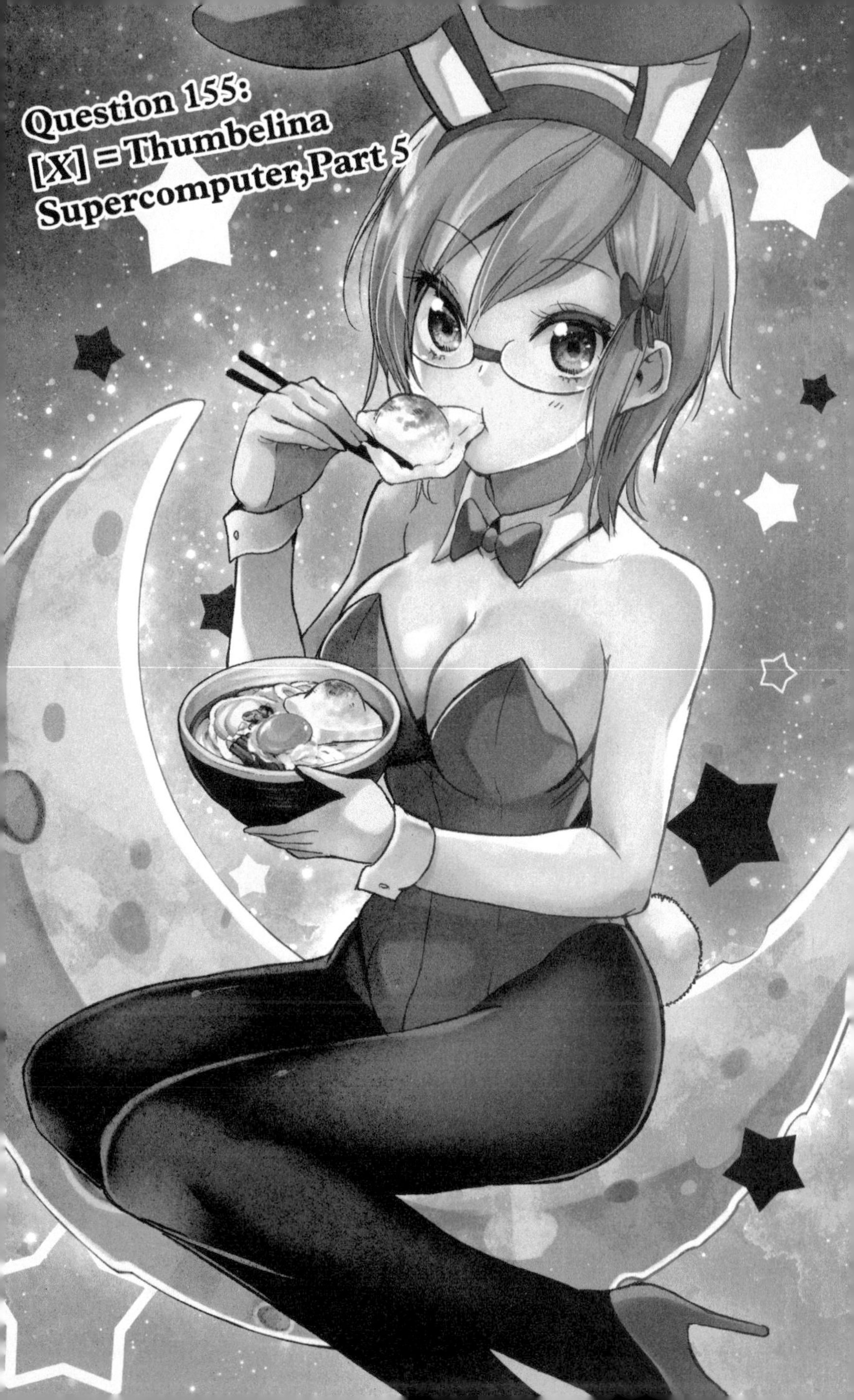
Question 155:
[X] = Thumbelina
Supercomputer, Part 5

[x] We +
Never ⁘
× Learn ×

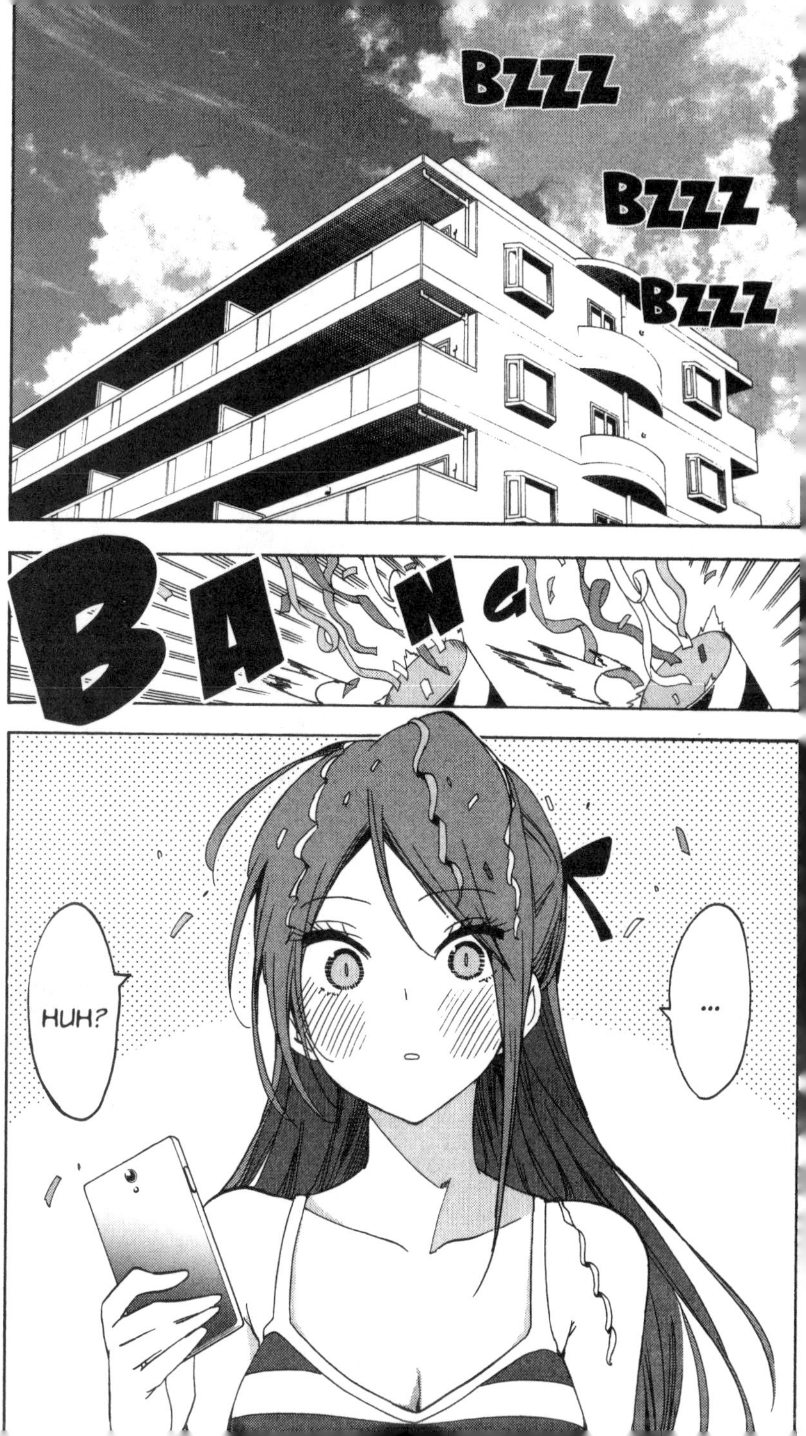
BZZZ
BZZZ
BZZZ
BANG
...
HUH?

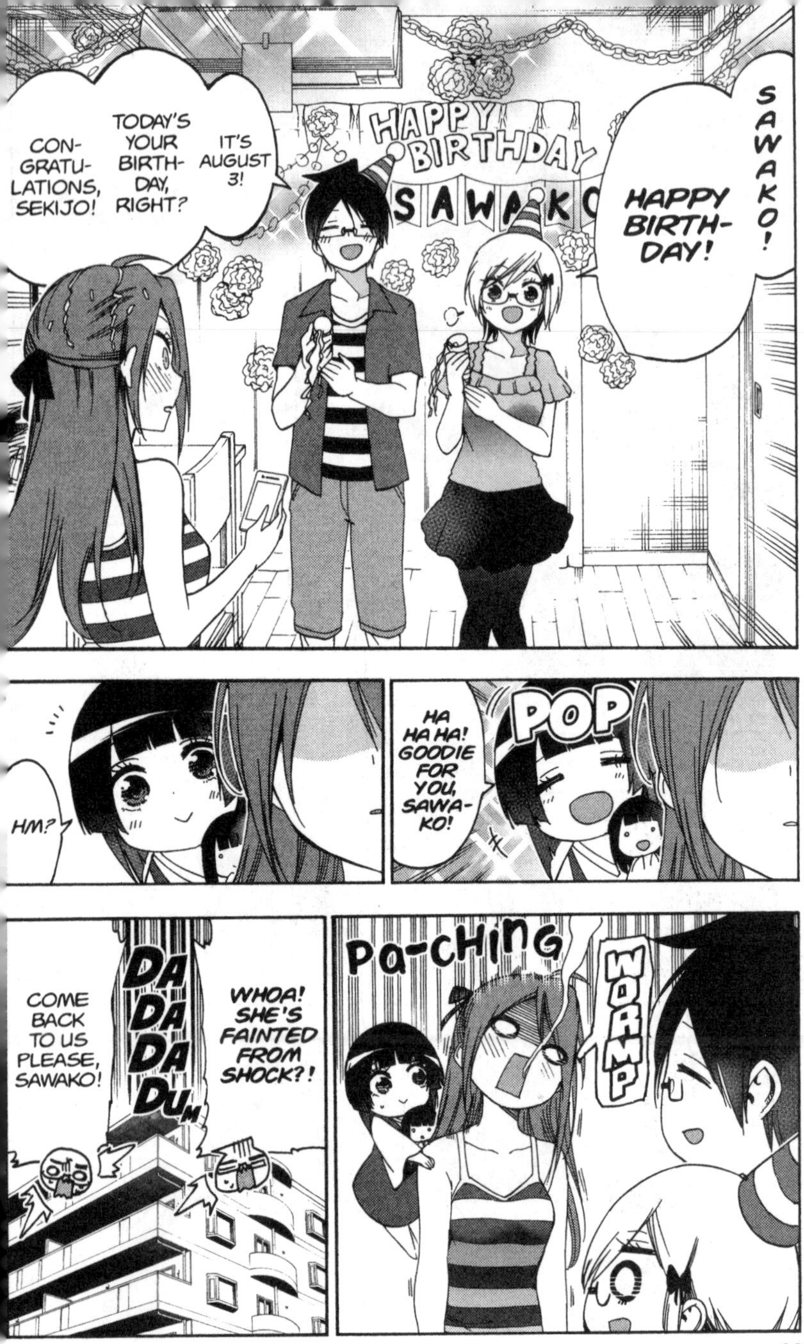
SAWAKO!
HAPPY BIRTHDAY!
HAPPY BIRTHDAY SAWAKO
IT'S AUGUST 3!
TODAY'S YOUR BIRTHDAY, RIGHT?
CONGRATULATIONS, SEKIJO!
POP
HA HA HA! GOODIE FOR YOU, SAWAKO!
HM?
WORMP
Pa-CHING
WHOA! SHE'S FAINTED FROM SHOCK?!
DA DA DA DA DUM
COME BACK TO US PLEASE, SAWAKO!

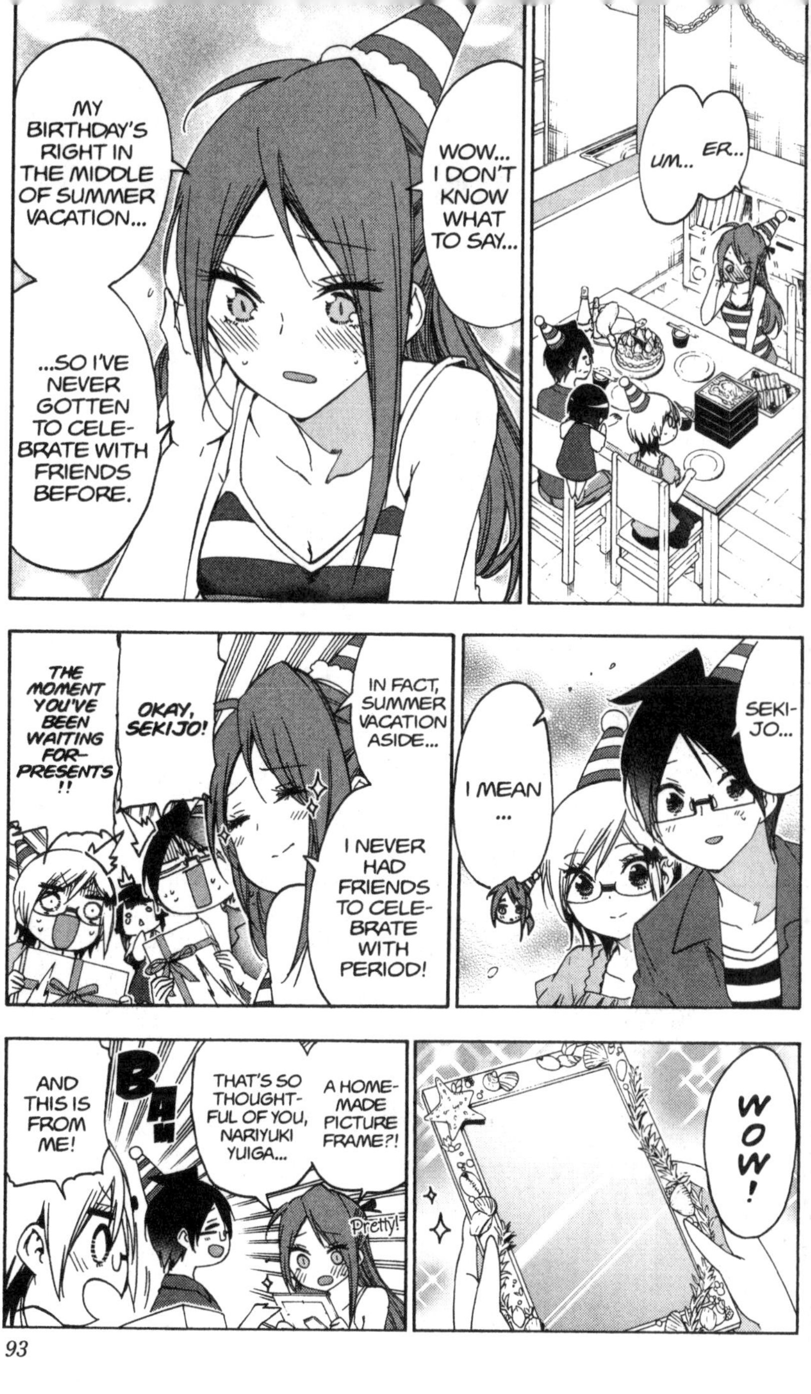
UM... ER...
WOW... I DON'T KNOW WHAT TO SAY...
MY BIRTHDAY'S RIGHT IN THE MIDDLE OF SUMMER VACATION...
...SO I'VE NEVER GOTTEN TO CELE-BRATE WITH FRIENDS BEFORE.
SEKI-JO...
I MEAN...
IN FACT, SUMMER VACATION ASIDE...
I NEVER HAD FRIENDS TO CELE-BRATE WITH PERIOD!
OKAY, SEKIJO!
THE MOMENT YOU'VE BEEN WAITING FOR—PRESENTS!!
WOW!
A HOME-MADE PICTURE FRAME?!
THAT'S SO THOUGHT-FUL OF YOU, NARIYUKI YUIGA...
BAM
AND THIS IS FROM ME!
Pretty!

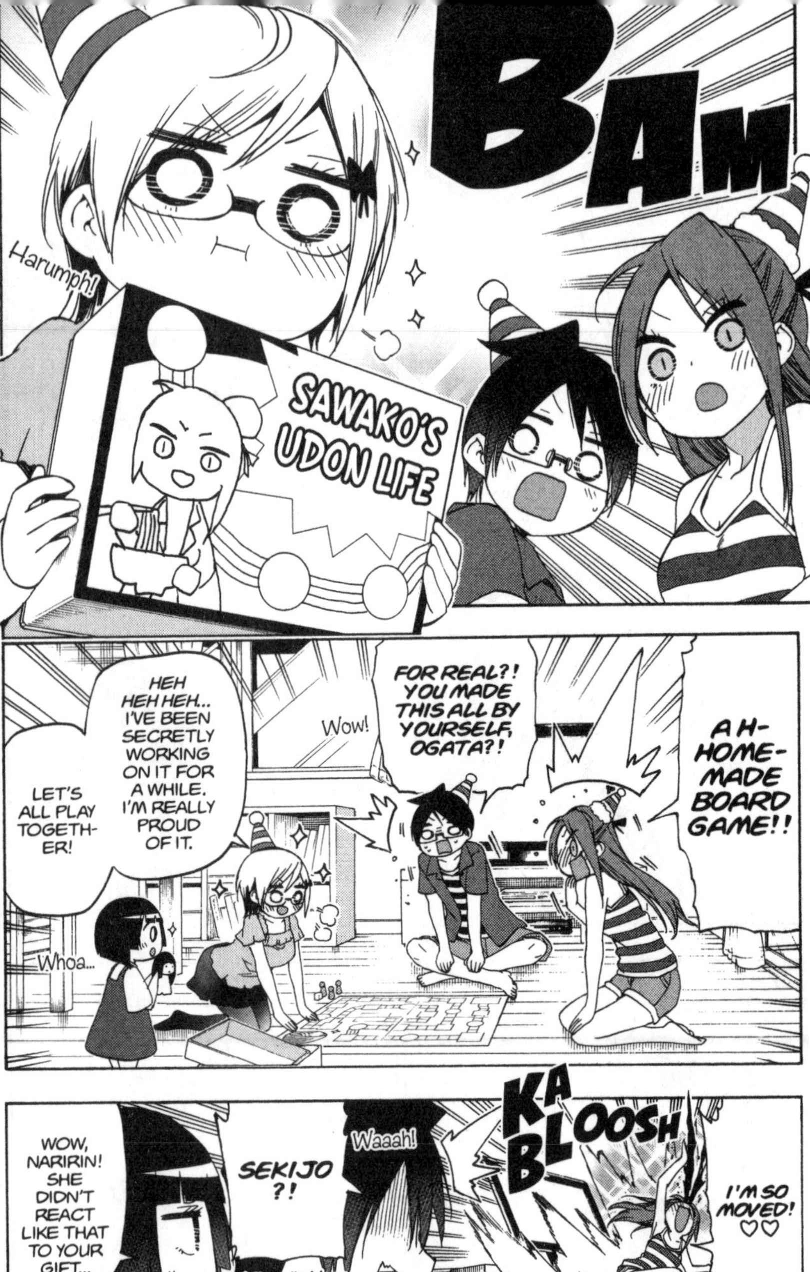
BAM
SAWAKO'S UDON LIFE
Harumph!
A H-HOME-MADE BOARD GAME!!
FOR REAL?! YOU MADE THIS ALL BY YOURSELF, OGATA?!
Wow!
HEH HEH HEH... I'VE BEEN SECRETLY WORKING ON IT FOR A WHILE. I'M REALLY PROUD OF IT.
LET'S ALL PLAY TOGETH-ER!
Whoa...
I'M SO MOVED! ♡♡
KA BLOOSH
Waaah!
SEKIJO?!
Literally blew her away!
WOW, NARIRIN! SHE DIDN'T REACT LIKE THAT TO YOUR GIFT...

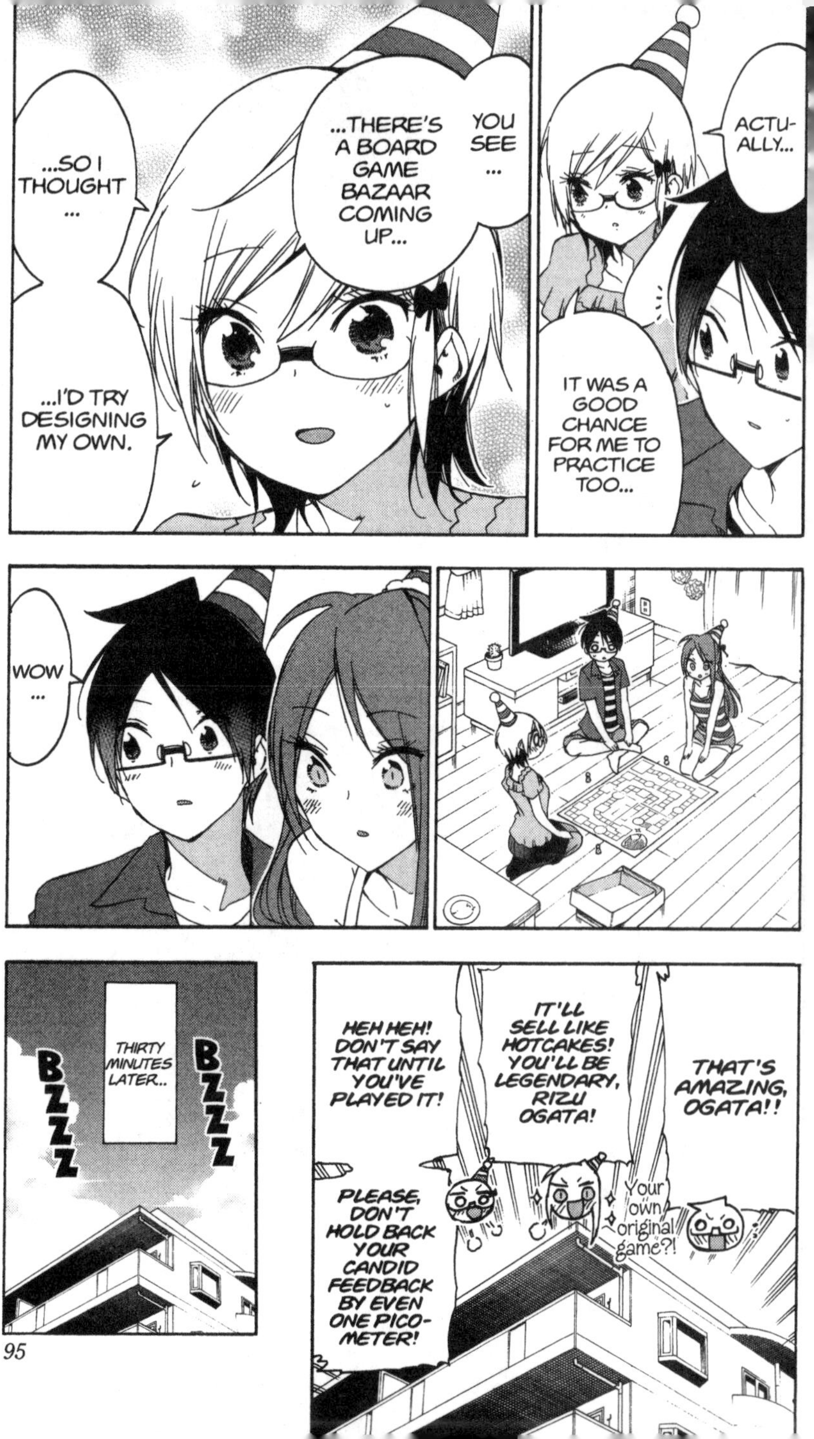
ACTU-ALLY...
IT WAS A GOOD CHANCE FOR ME TO PRACTICE TOO...
YOU SEE ...
...THERE'S A BOARD GAME BAZAAR COMING UP...
...SO I THOUGHT ...
...I'D TRY DESIGNING MY OWN.
WOW ...
THAT'S AMAZING, OGATA!!
IT'LL SELL LIKE HOTCAKES! YOU'LL BE LEGENDARY, RIZU OGATA!
HEH HEH! DON'T SAY THAT UNTIL YOU'VE PLAYED IT!
Your own original game?!
PLEASE, DON'T HOLD BACK YOUR CANDID FEEDBACK BY EVEN ONE PICO-METER!
BZZZ
THIRTY MINUTES LATER...
BZZZ

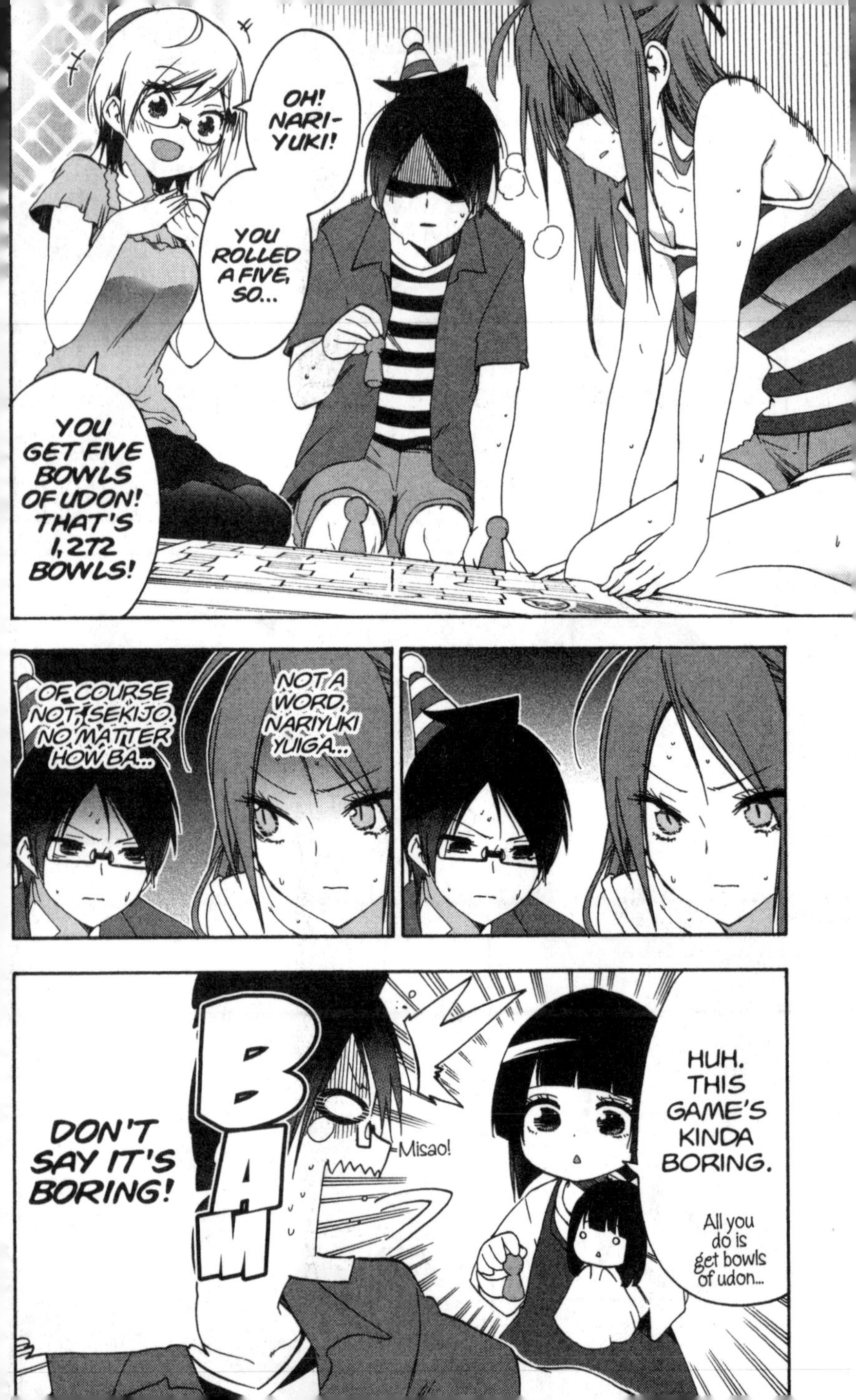
OH! NARI-YUKI!
YOU ROLLED A FIVE, SO...
YOU GET FIVE BOWLS OF UDON! THAT'S 1,272 BOWLS!
NOT A WORD, NARIYUKI YUIGA...
OF COURSE NOT, SEKIJO. NO MATTER HOW BA...
HUH. THIS GAME'S KINDA BORING.
All you do is get bowls of udon...
Misao!
BAM
DON'T SAY IT'S BORING!

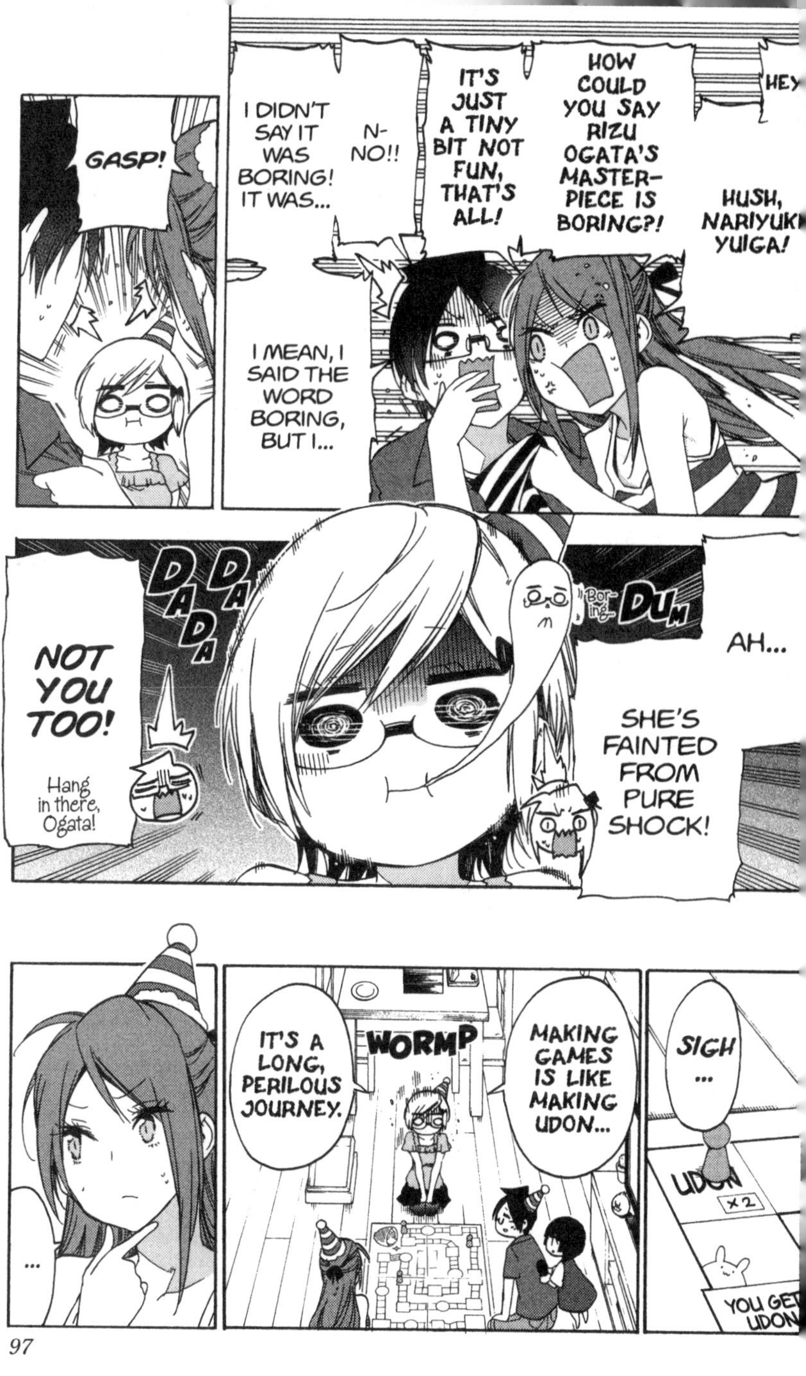
HEY
HUSH, NARIYUK YUIGA!
HOW COULD YOU SAY RIZU OGATA'S MASTERPIECE IS BORING?!
IT'S JUST A TINY BIT NOT FUN, THAT'S ALL!
N-NO!!
I DIDN'T SAY IT WAS BORING! IT WAS...
I MEAN, I SAID THE WORD BORING, BUT I...
GASP!
AH...
SHE'S FAINTED FROM PURE SHOCK!
DUM
Boring...
DA DA DA DA
NOT YOU TOO!
Hang in there, Ogata!
SIGH...
UDON
×2
YOU GET UDON
MAKING GAMES IS LIKE MAKING UDON...
WORMP
IT'S A LONG, PERILOUS JOURNEY.
...

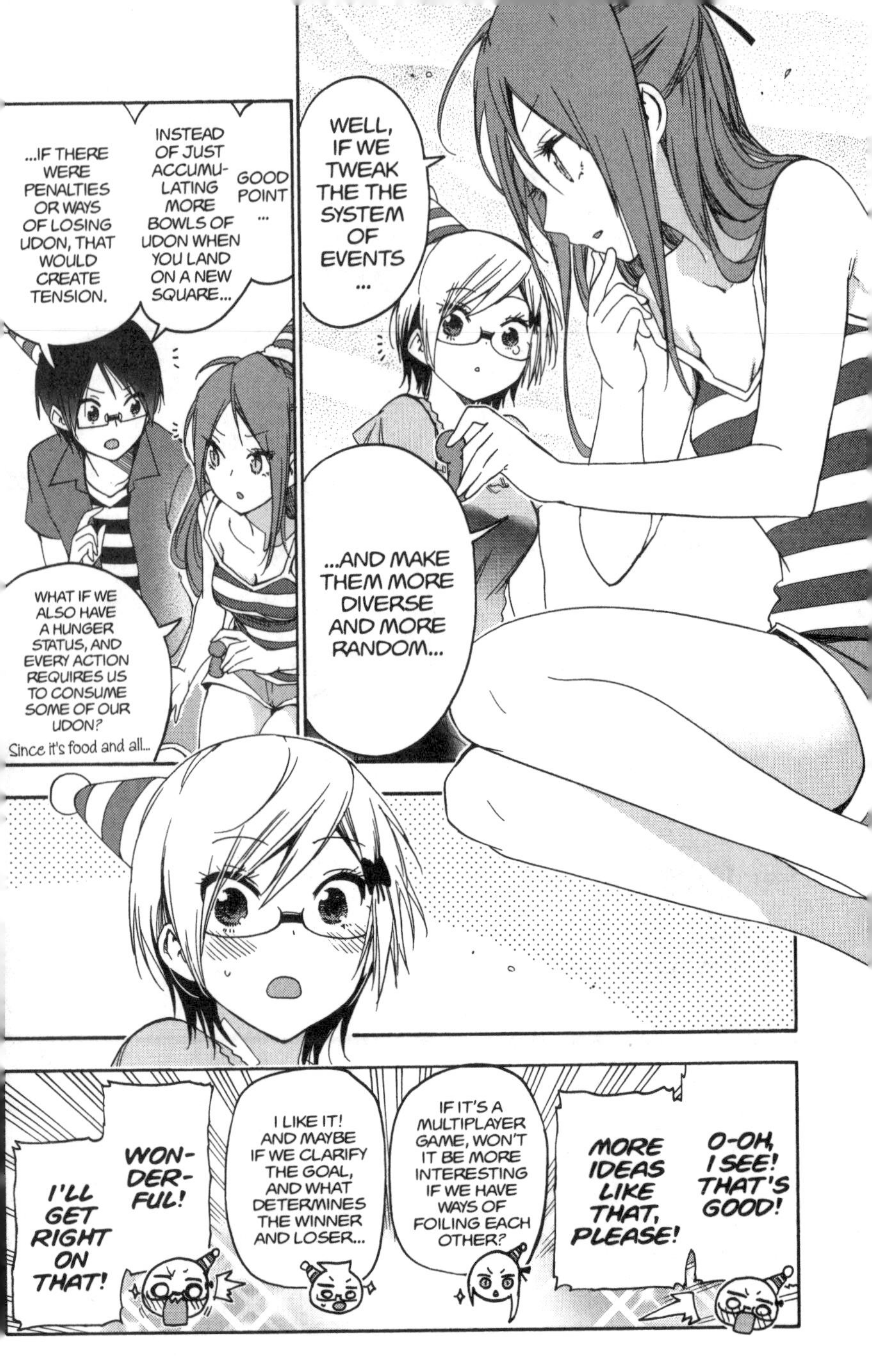
WELL, IF WE TWEAK THE THE SYSTEM OF EVENTS...
...AND MAKE THEM MORE DIVERSE AND MORE RANDOM...
GOOD POINT...
INSTEAD OF JUST ACCUMULATING MORE BOWLS OF UDON WHEN YOU LAND ON A NEW SQUARE...
...IF THERE WERE PENALTIES OR WAYS OF LOSING UDON, THAT WOULD CREATE TENSION.
WHAT IF WE ALSO HAVE A HUNGER STATUS, AND EVERY ACTION REQUIRES US TO CONSUME SOME OF OUR UDON?
Since it's food and all...
O-OH, I SEE! THAT'S GOOD!
MORE IDEAS LIKE THAT, PLEASE!
IF IT'S A MULTIPLAYER GAME, WON'T IT BE MORE INTERESTING IF WE HAVE WAYS OF FOILING EACH OTHER?
I LIKE IT! AND MAYBE IF WE CLARIFY THE GOAL, AND WHAT DETERMINES THE WINNER AND LOSER...
WONDERFUL!
I'LL GET RIGHT ON THAT!

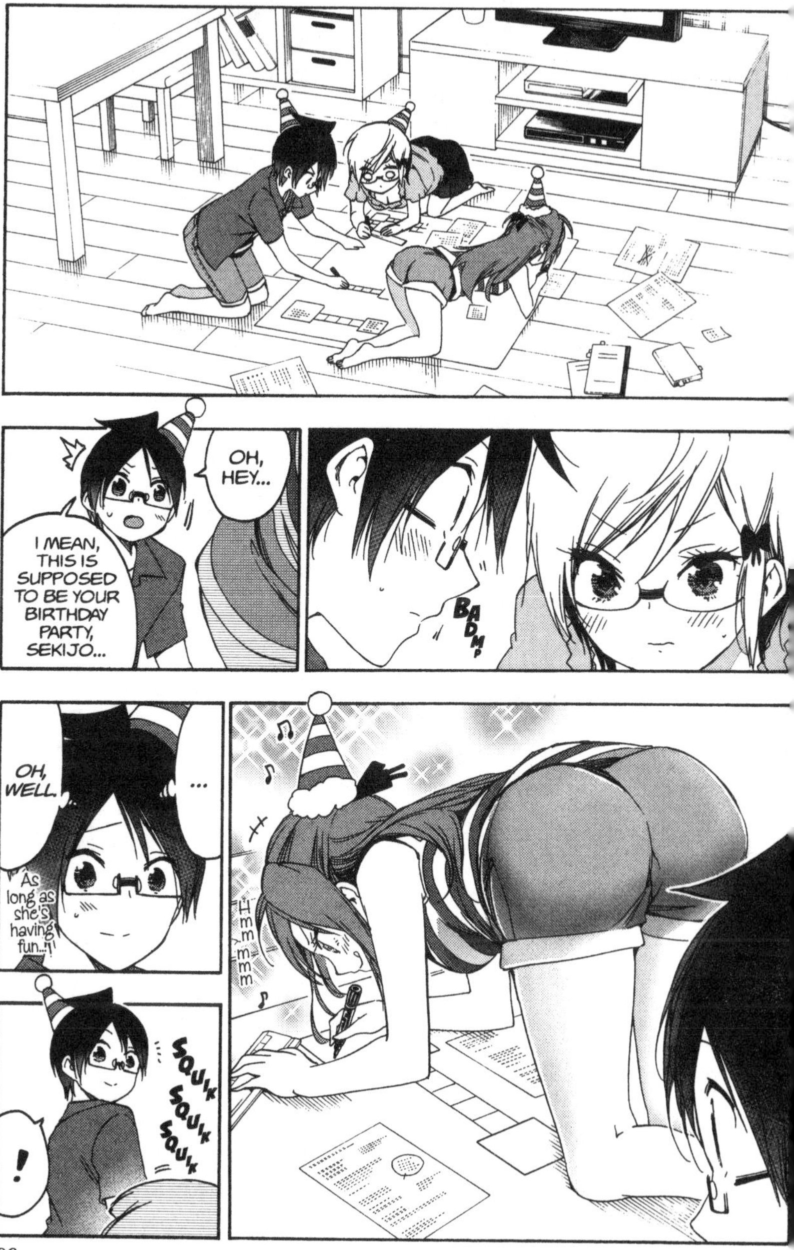
BADMP
OH, HEY...
I MEAN, THIS IS SUPPOSED TO BE YOUR BIRTHDAY PARTY, SEKIJO...
Hmm mmm mmm
...
OH, WELL.
As long as she's having fun...!
SQUIK SQUIK SQUIK
!

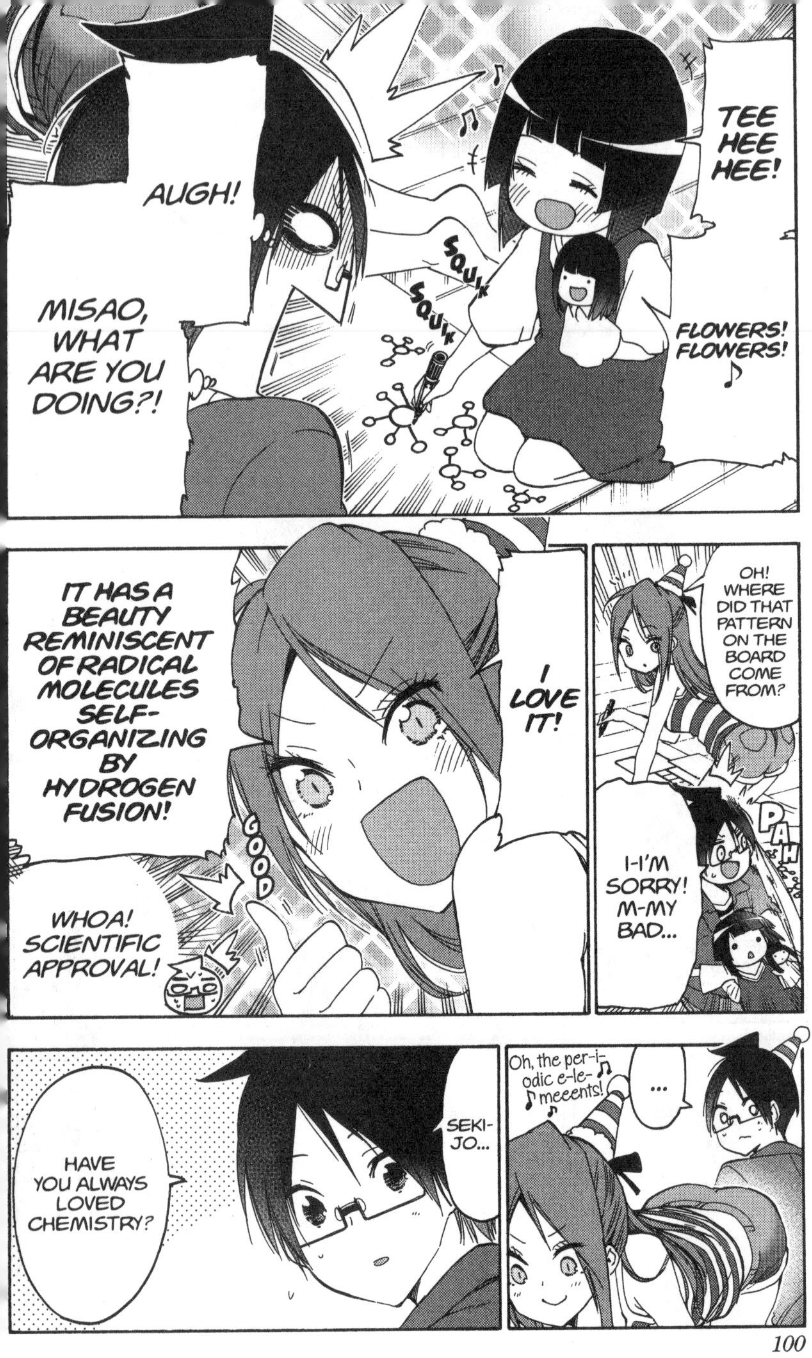
TEE HEE HEE!
FLOWERS! FLOWERS! ♪
SQUIK
SQUIK
AUGH!
MISAO, WHAT ARE YOU DOING?!
OH! WHERE DID THAT PATTERN ON THE BOARD COME FROM?
PAH
I-I'M SORRY! M-MY BAD...
I LOVE IT!
IT HAS A BEAUTY REMINISCENT OF RADICAL MOLECULES SELF-ORGANIZING BY HYDROGEN FUSION!
GOOD
WHOA! SCIENTIFIC APPROVAL!
...
Oh, the per-i-odic e-le-♪ meeents! ♪
SEKI-JO...
HAVE YOU ALWAYS LOVED CHEMISTRY?

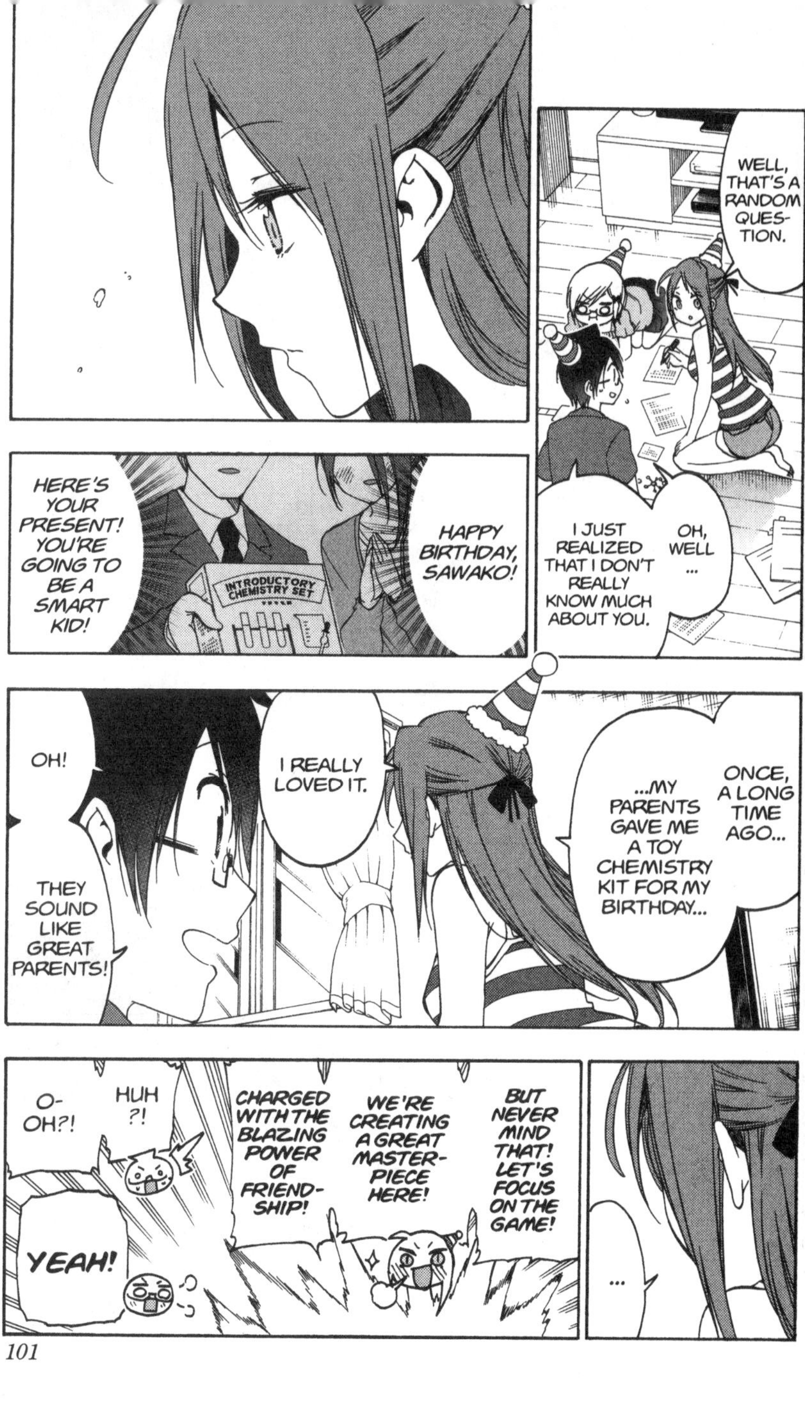
WELL, THAT'S A RANDOM QUESTION.
OH, WELL ...
I JUST REALIZED THAT I DON'T REALLY KNOW MUCH ABOUT YOU.
HAPPY BIRTHDAY, SAWAKO!
HERE'S YOUR PRESENT! YOU'RE GOING TO BE A SMART KID!
INTRODUCTORY CHEMISTRY SET
ONCE, A LONG TIME AGO...
...MY PARENTS GAVE ME A TOY CHEMISTRY KIT FOR MY BIRTHDAY...
I REALLY LOVED IT.
OH!
THEY SOUND LIKE GREAT PARENTS!
...
BUT NEVER MIND THAT! LET'S FOCUS ON THE GAME!
WE'RE CREATING A GREAT MASTERPIECE HERE!
CHARGED WITH THE BLAZING POWER OF FRIENDSHIP!
HUH?!
O-OH?!
YEAH!

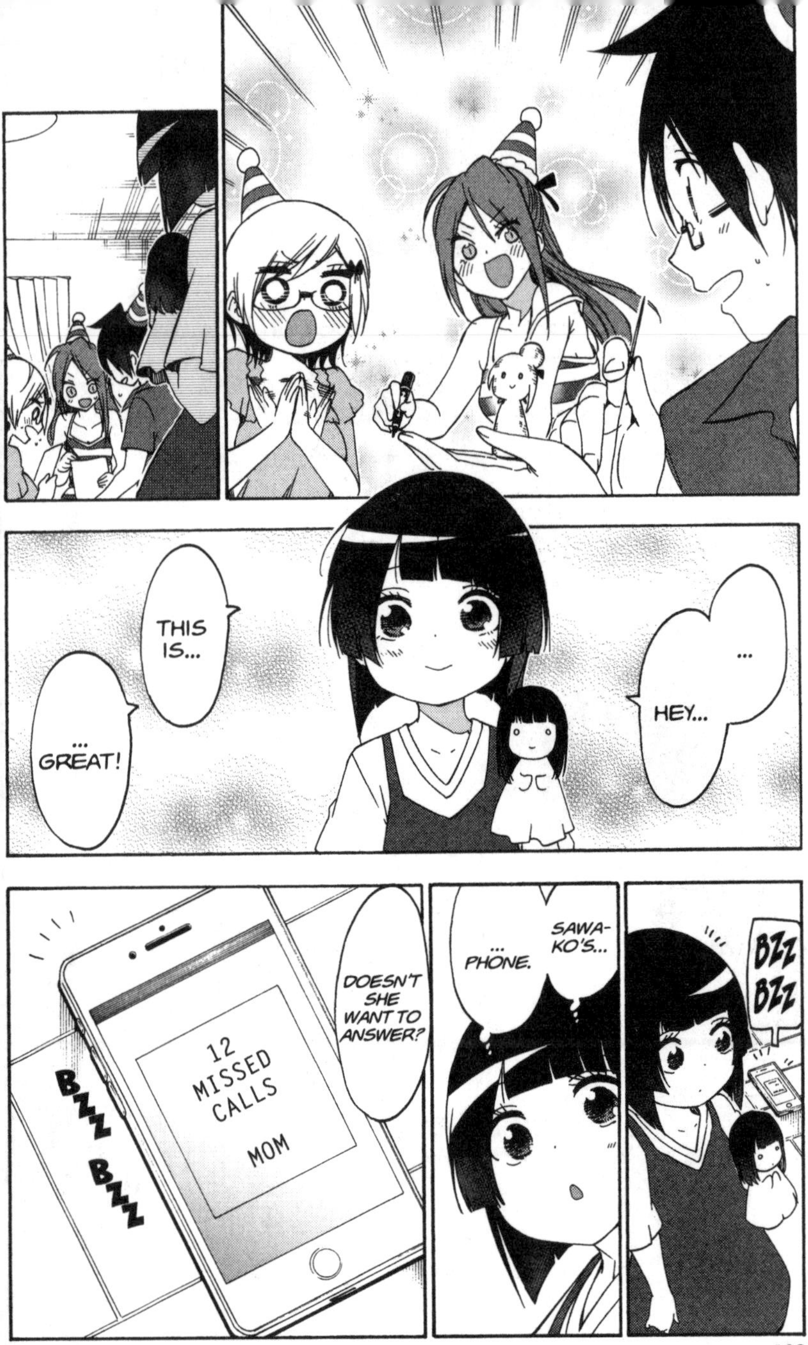
... HEY...
THIS IS...
... GREAT!
BZZ BZZ
SAWAKO'S...
... PHONE.
DOESN'T SHE WANT TO ANSWER?
12 MISSED CALLS MOM
BZZ BZZ

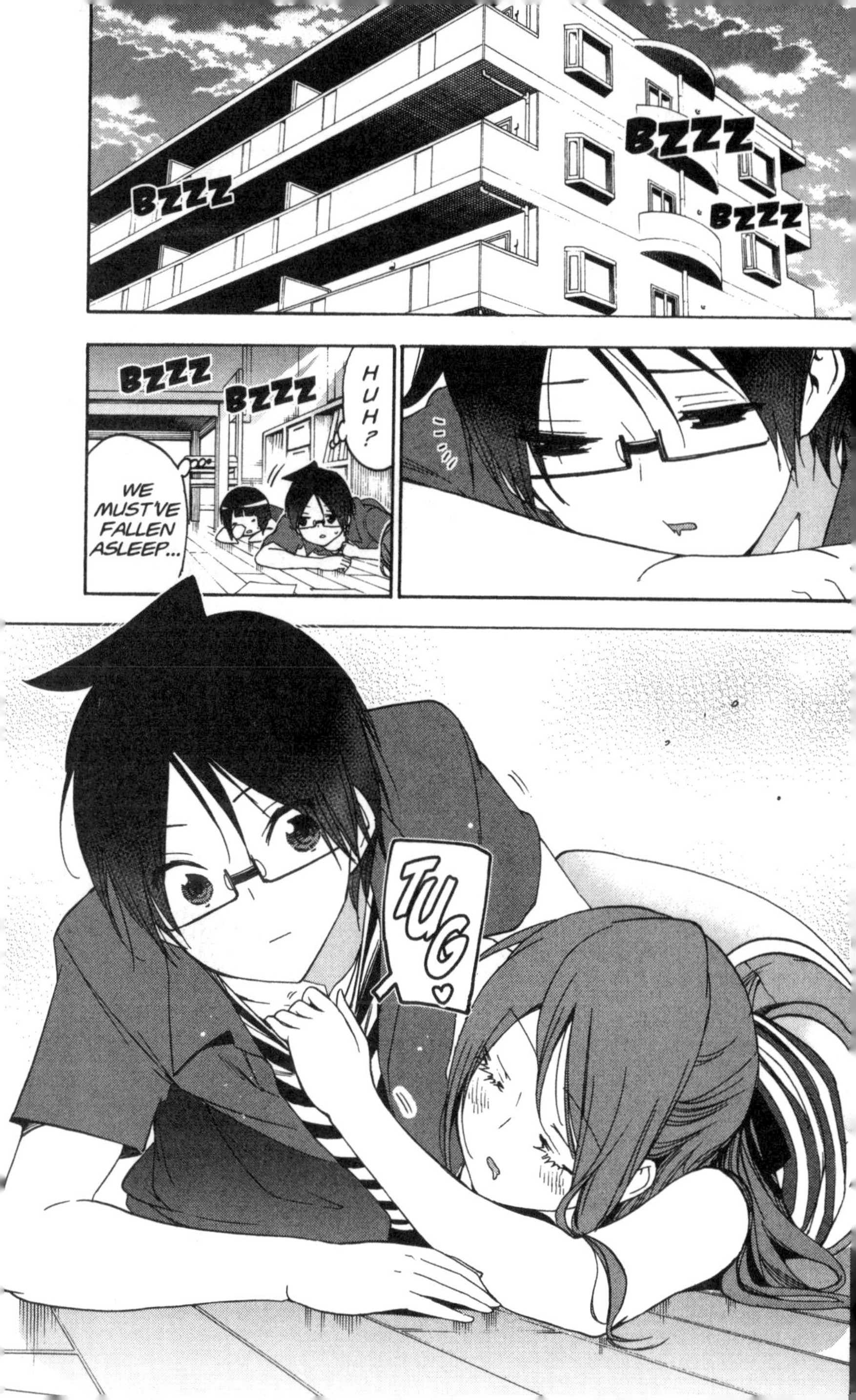
BZZZ
BZZZ
BZZZ
BZZZ
BZZZ
HUH?
WE MUST'VE FALLEN ASLEEP...
TUG ♥

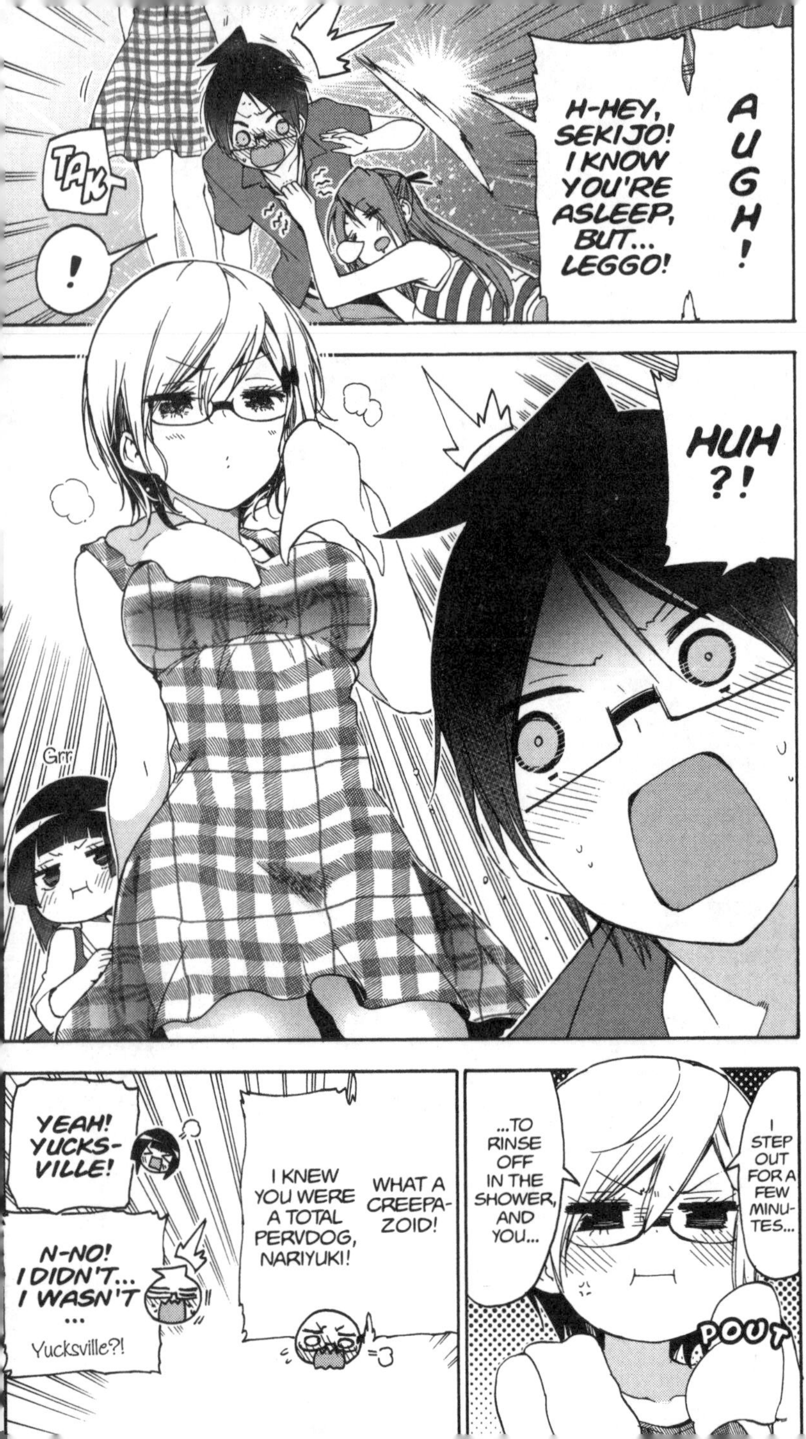
AUGH!
H-HEY, SEKIJO! I KNOW YOU'RE ASLEEP, BUT... LEGGO!
TAK
!
HUH ?!
Grr
I STEP OUT FOR A FEW MINUTES...
...TO RINSE OFF IN THE SHOWER, AND YOU...
POUT
WHAT A CREEPAZOID!
I KNEW YOU WERE A TOTAL PERVDOG, NARIYUKI!
YEAH! YUCKSVILLE!
N-NO! I DIDN'T... I WASN'T ...
Yucksville?!

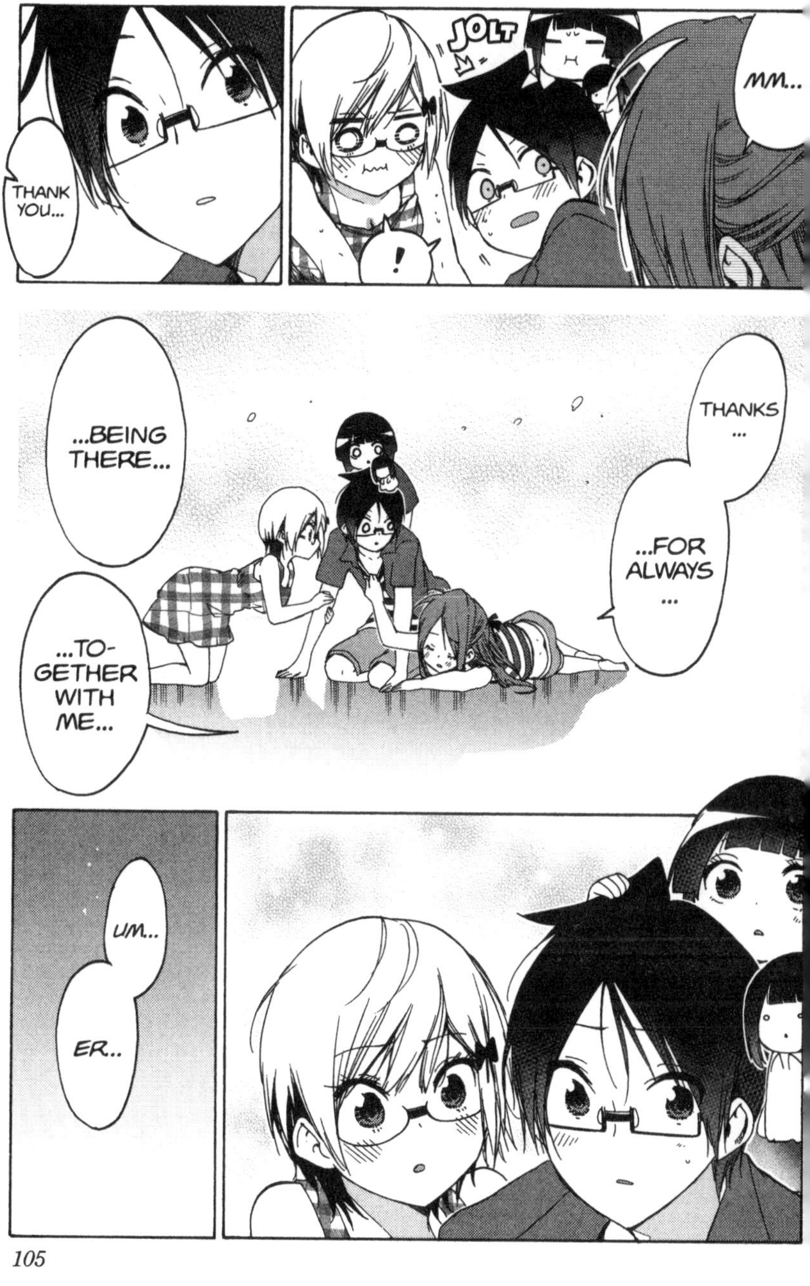
MM...
JOLT
!
THANK YOU...
THANKS ...
...FOR ALWAYS ...
...BEING THERE...
...TO-GETHER WITH ME...
UM...
ER...

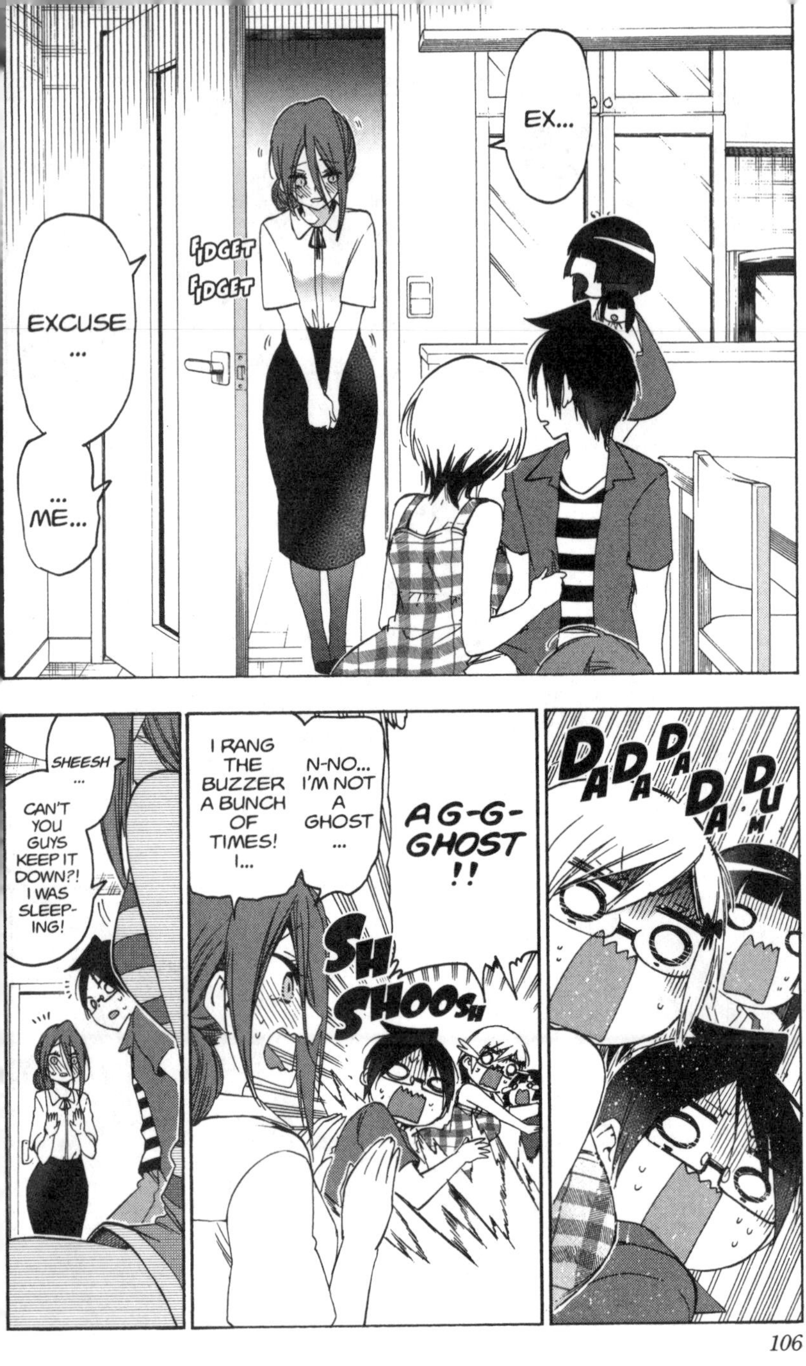
EX...
FIDGET FIDGET
EXCUSE ...
... ME...
DADADADADUM
A G-G-GHOST!!
SH SHOOSH
N-NO... I'M NOT A GHOST ...
I RANG THE BUZZER A BUNCH OF TIMES! I...
SHEESH ...
CAN'T YOU GUYS KEEP IT DOWN?! I WAS SLEEP-ING!

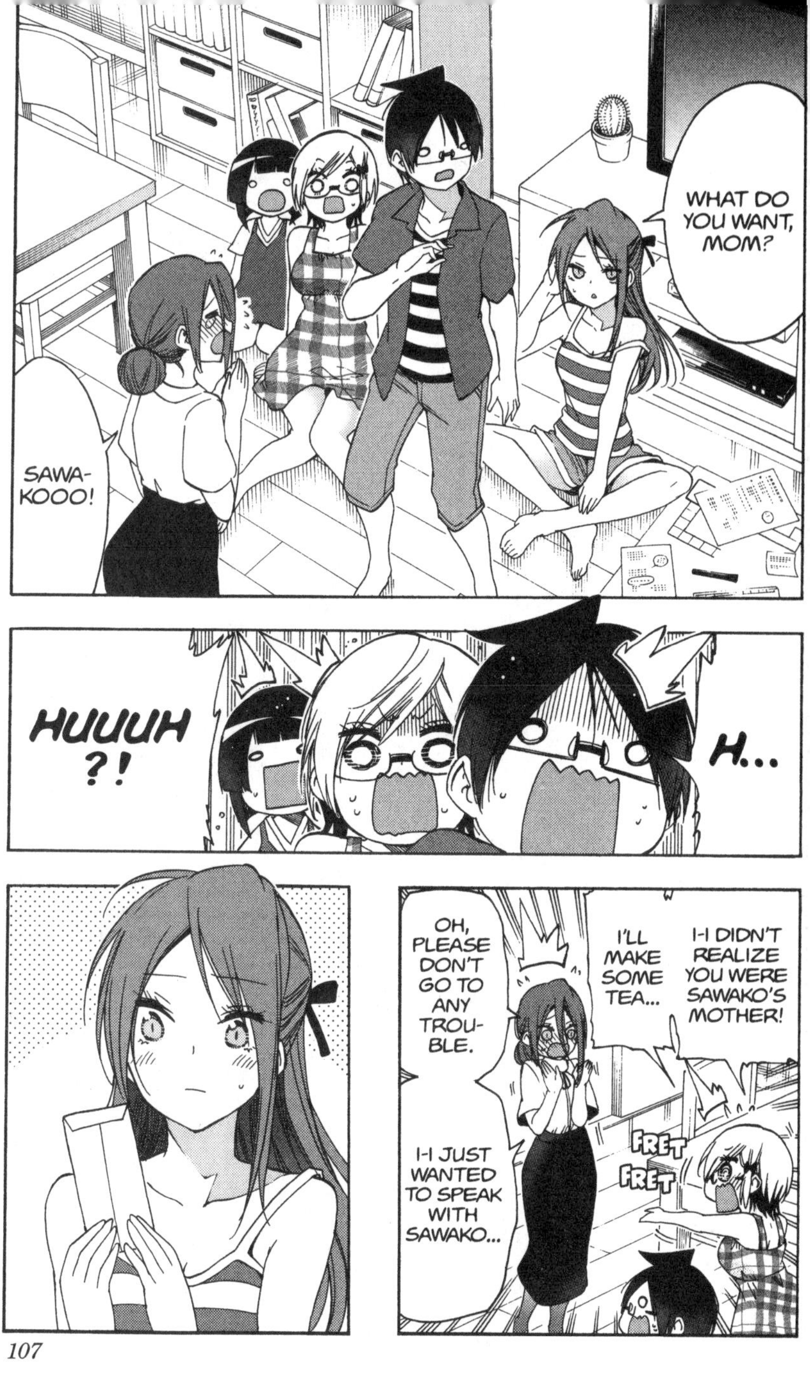
WHAT DO YOU WANT, MOM?
SAWA-KOOO!
H...
HUUUH ?!
I-I DIDN'T REALIZE YOU WERE SAWAKO'S MOTHER!
I'LL MAKE SOME TEA...
OH, PLEASE DON'T GO TO ANY TROU-BLE.
FRET FRET
I-I JUST WANTED TO SPEAK WITH SAWAKO...

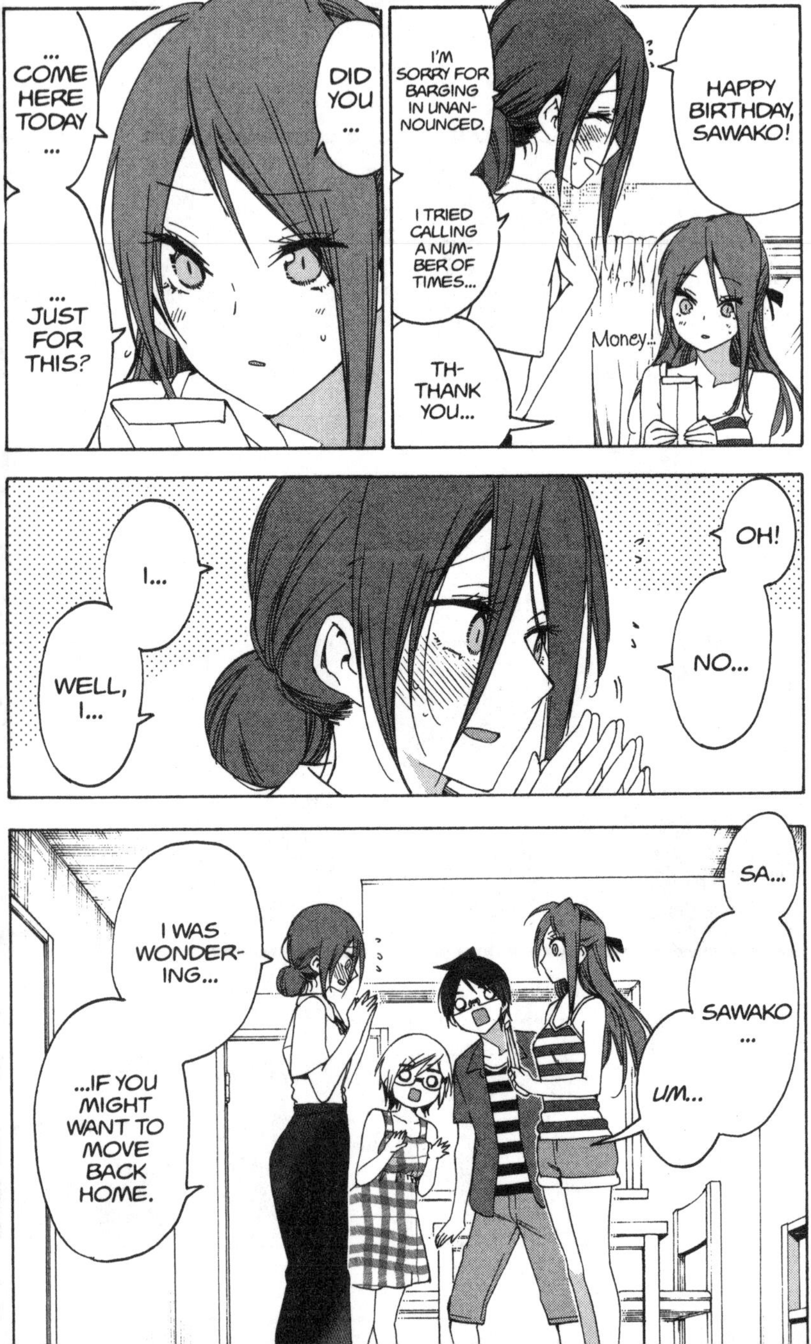
HAPPY BIRTHDAY, SAWAKO!
I'M SORRY FOR BARGING IN UNAN-NOUNCED.
I TRIED CALLING A NUM-BER OF TIMES...
Money...
TH-THANK YOU...
DID YOU ...
... COME HERE TODAY ...
... JUST FOR THIS?
OH!
NO...
I...
WELL, I...
SA...
SAWAKO ...
UM...
I WAS WONDER-ING...
...IF YOU MIGHT WANT TO MOVE BACK HOME.

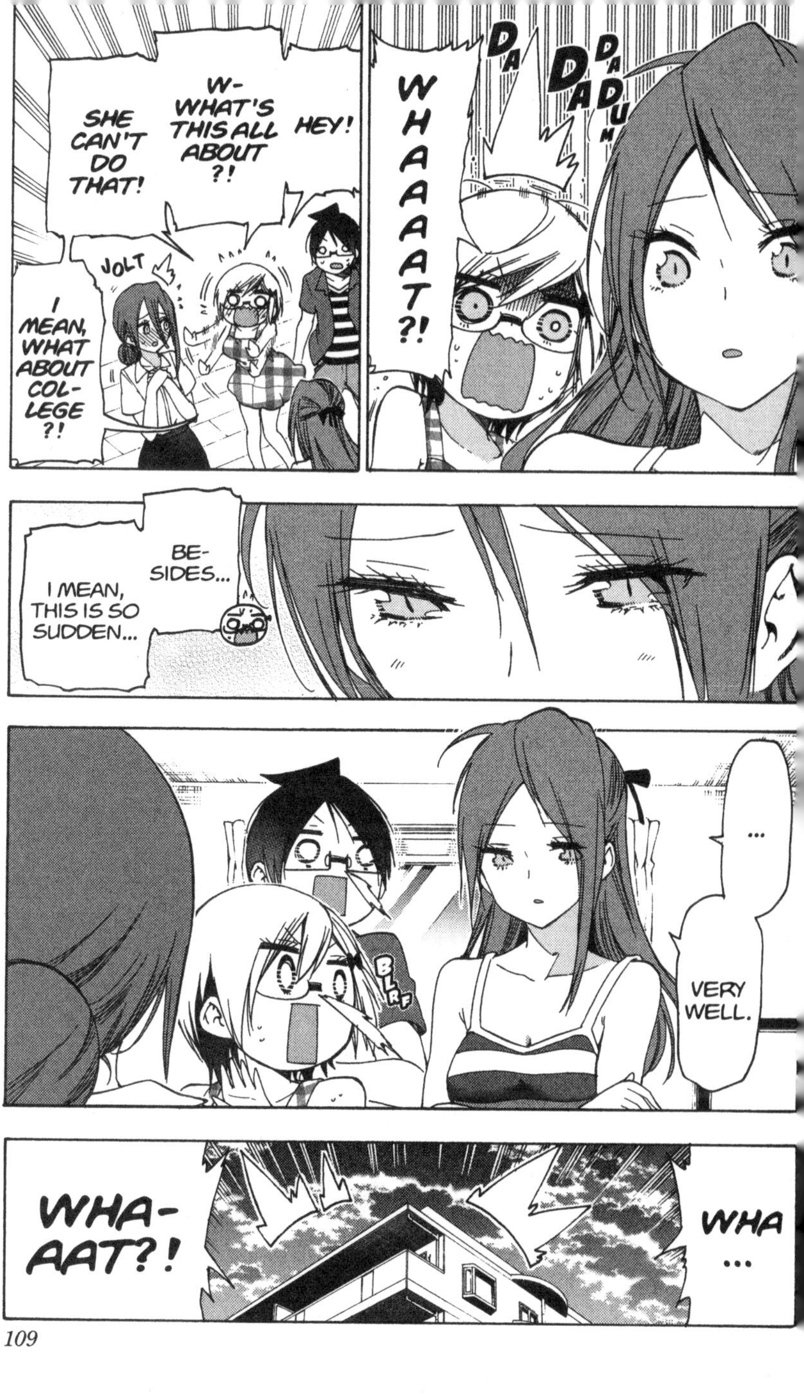
DA
DA
DADADUM
WHAAAAAT?!
HEY!
W-WHAT'S THIS ALL ABOUT?!
SHE CAN'T DO THAT!
JOLT
I MEAN, WHAT ABOUT COL-LEGE?!
BE-SIDES...
I MEAN, THIS IS SO SUDDEN...
...
VERY WELL.
BLRF
WHA...
WHA-AAT?!

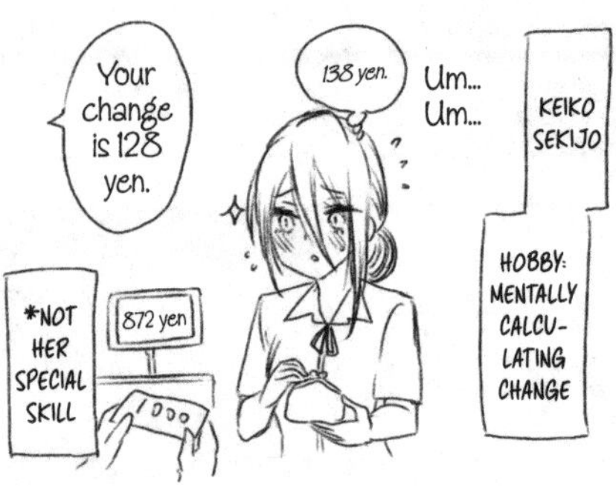
KEIKO SEKIJO
HOBBY: MENTALLY CALCU-LATING CHANGE
Um... Um...
138 yen.
Your change is 128 yen.
872 yen
1000
*NOT HER SPECIAL SKILL

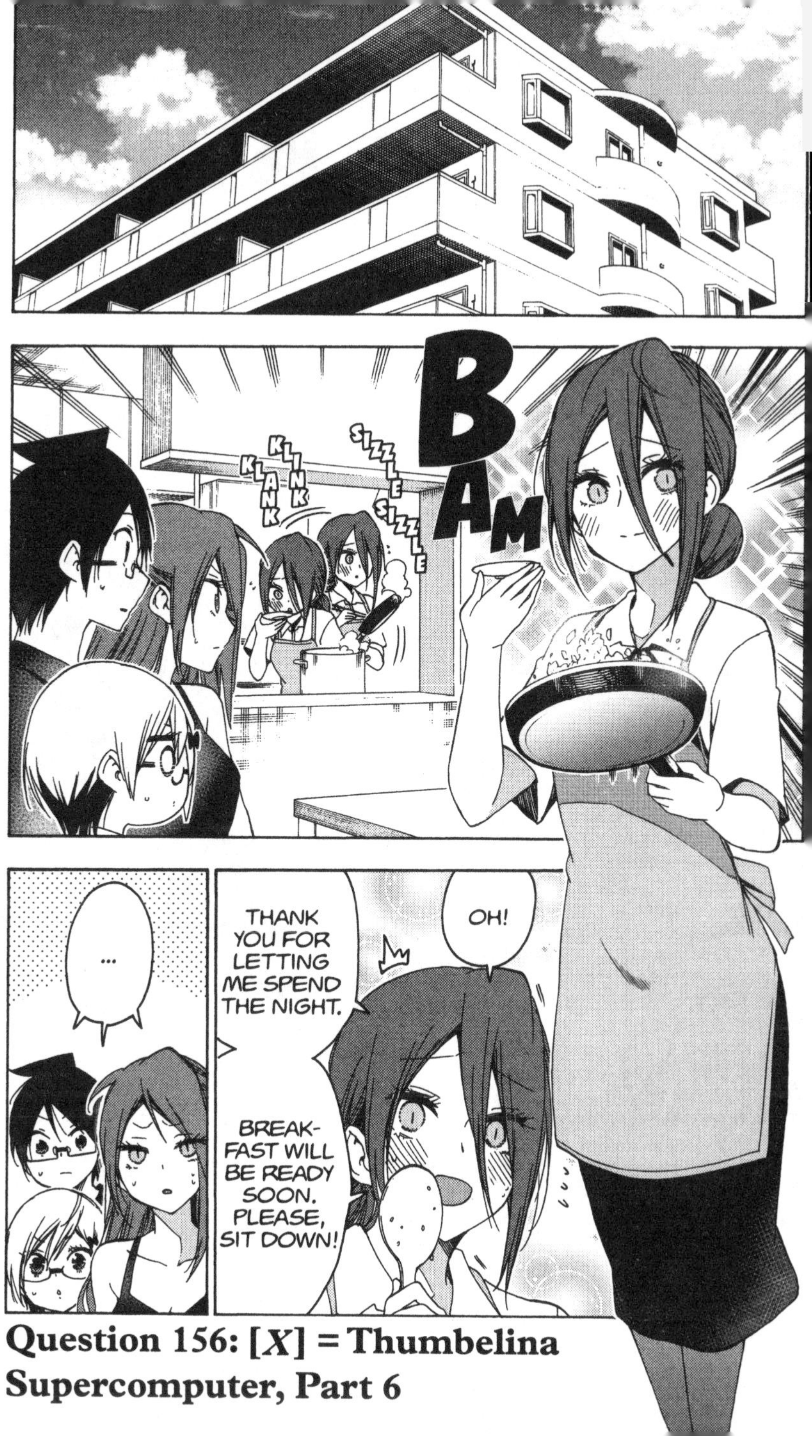
BAM
SIZZLE SIZZLE
KLINK
KLANK
OH!
THANK YOU FOR LETTING ME SPEND THE NIGHT.
BREAK-FAST WILL BE READY SOON. PLEASE, SIT DOWN!
...

Question 156: [*X*] = Thumbelina Supercomputer, Part 6

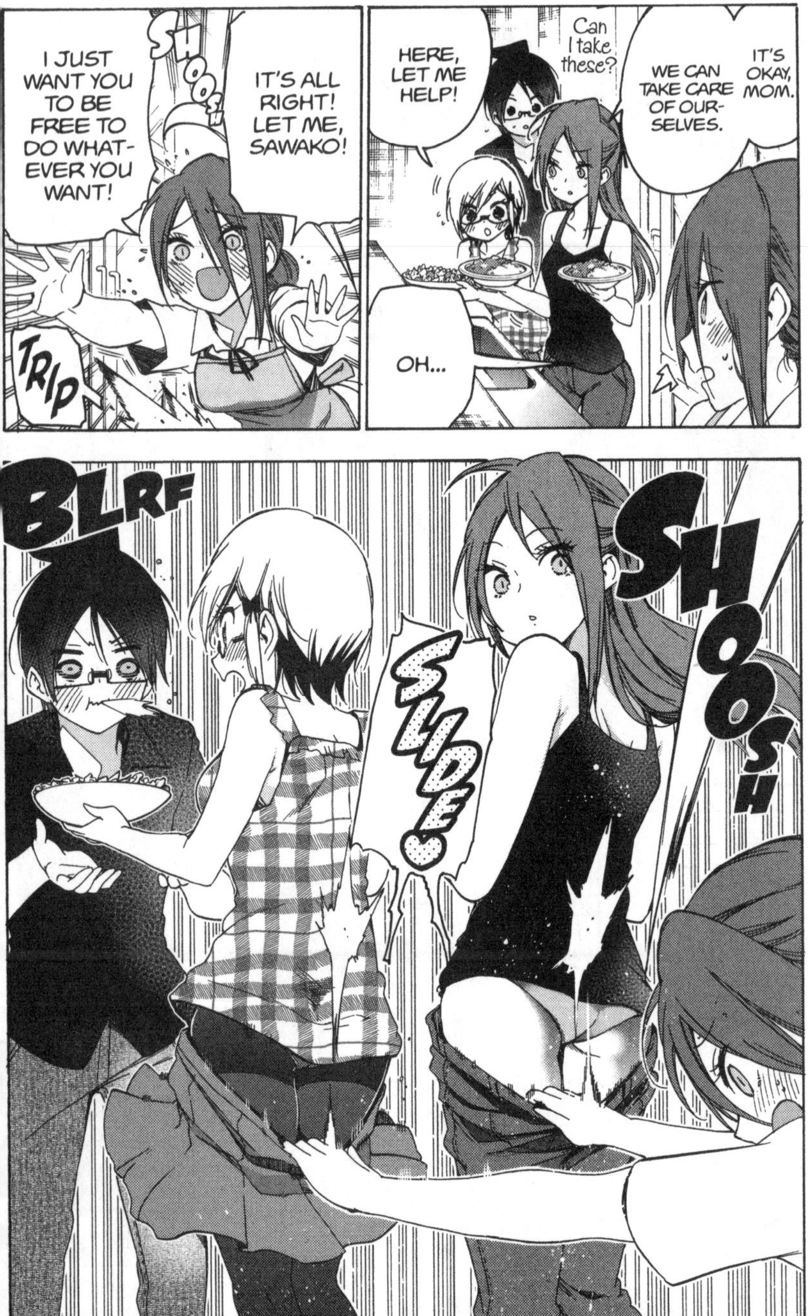
IT'S OKAY, MOM.
WE CAN TAKE CARE OF OUR-SELVES.
Can I take these?
HERE, LET ME HELP!
OH...
IT'S ALL RIGHT! LET ME, SAWAKO!
SHOOSH
I JUST WANT YOU TO BE FREE TO DO WHAT-EVER YOU WANT!
TRIP
SHOOSH
SLIDE!
BLRF

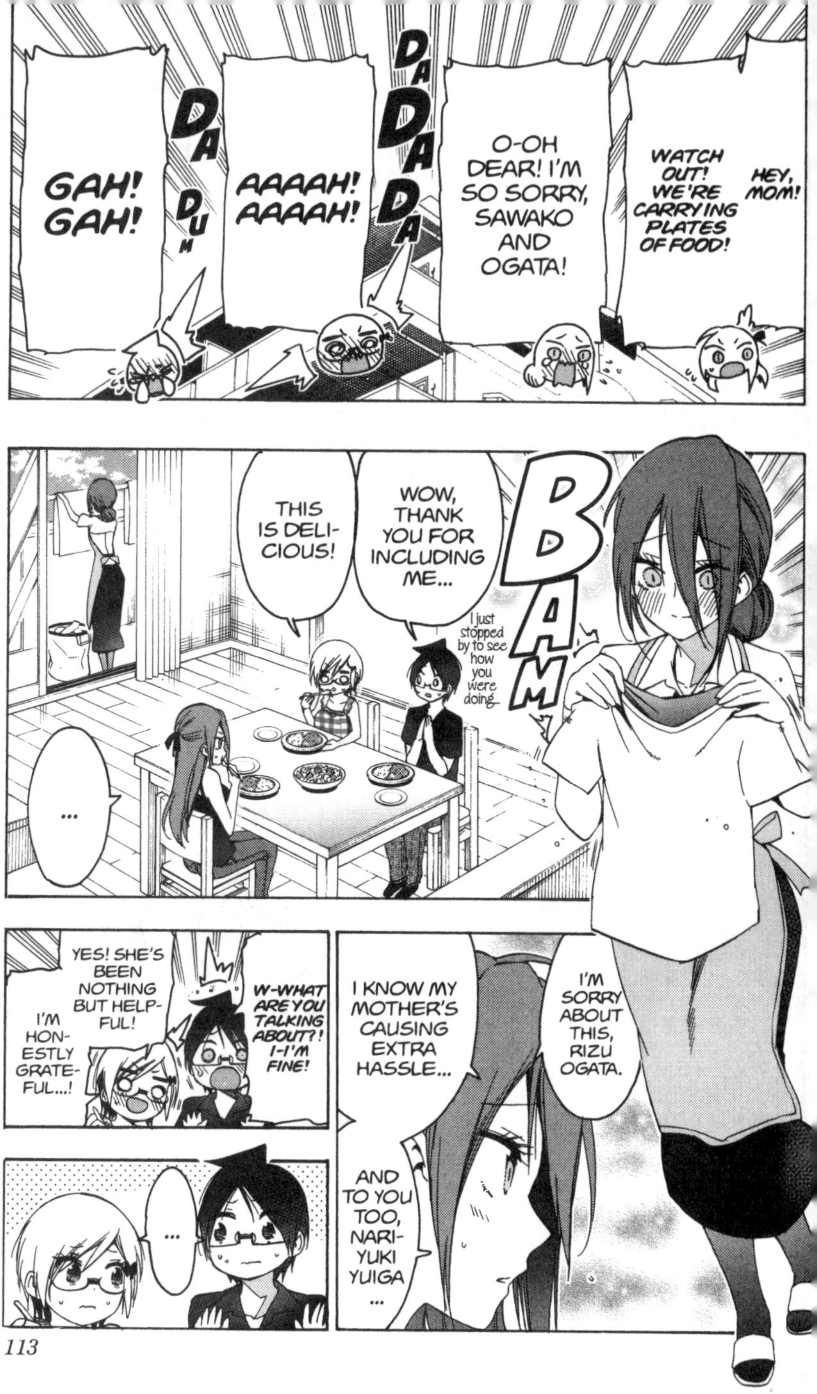
HEY, MOM!
WATCH OUT! WE'RE CARRYING PLATES OF FOOD!
O-OH DEAR! I'M SO SORRY, SAWAKO AND OGATA!
DADADADA
AAAAH! AAAAH!
DA DUM
GAH! GAH!
BAM
WOW, THANK YOU FOR INCLUDING ME...
I just stopped by to see how you were doing...
THIS IS DELICIOUS!
...
I'M SORRY ABOUT THIS, RIZU OGATA.
I KNOW MY MOTHER'S CAUSING EXTRA HASSLE...
AND TO YOU TOO, NARIYUKI YUIGA...
W-WHAT ARE YOU TALKING ABOUT?! I-I'M FINE!
YES! SHE'S BEEN NOTHING BUT HELPFUL!
I'M HONESTLY GRATEFUL...!
...

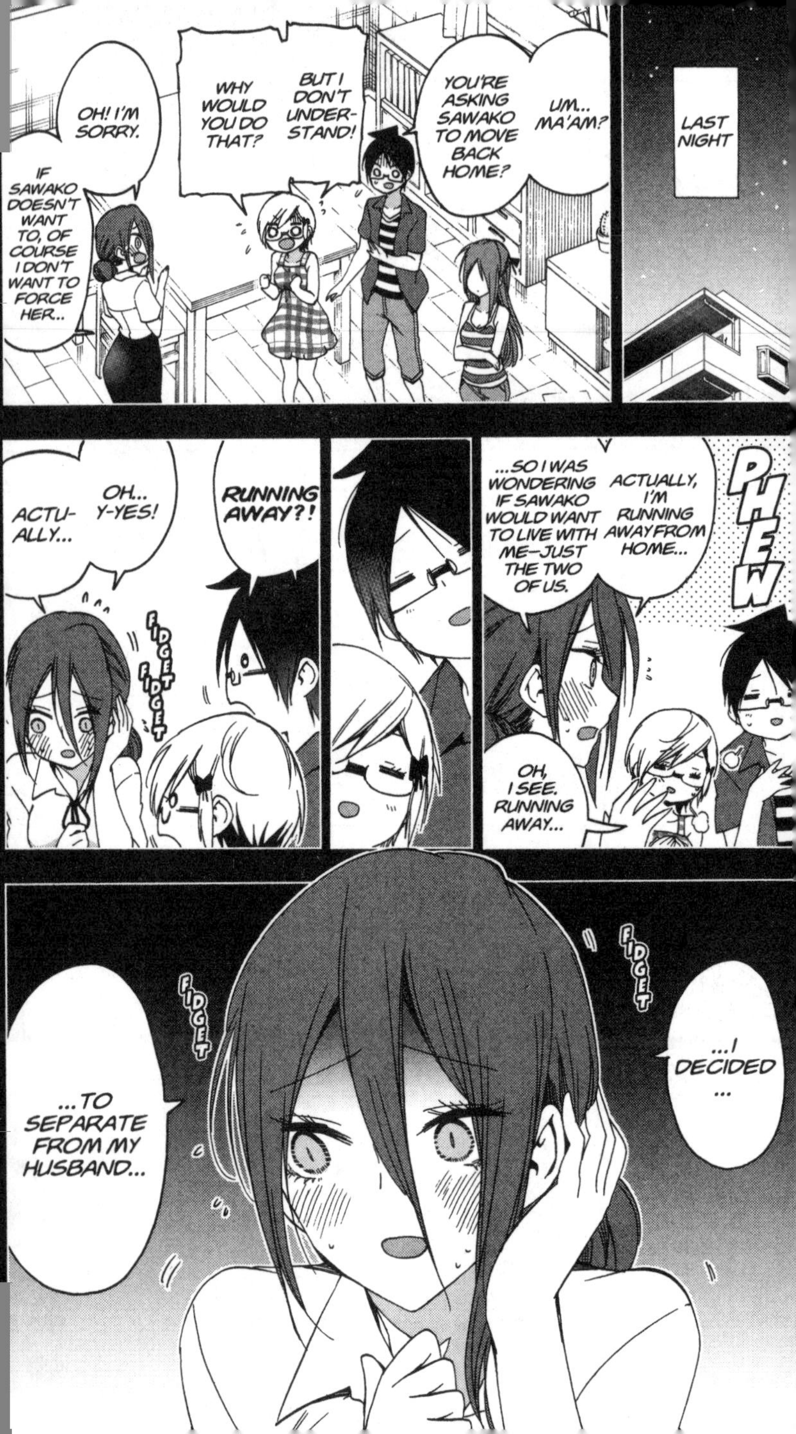
LAST NIGHT
UM.. MA'AM?
YOU'RE ASKING SAWAKO TO MOVE BACK HOME?
BUT I DON'T UNDER-STAND!
WHY WOULD YOU DO THAT?
OH! I'M SORRY.
IF SAWAKO DOESN'T WANT TO, OF COURSE I DON'T WANT TO FORCE HER...
PHEW
ACTUALLY, I'M RUNNING AWAY FROM HOME...
...SO I WAS WONDERING IF SAWAKO WOULD WANT TO LIVE WITH ME—JUST THE TWO OF US.
OH, I SEE. RUNNING AWAY...
RUNNING AWAY?!
OH... Y-YES!
ACTU-ALLY...
FIDGET FIDGET
FIDGET
...I DECIDED ...
FIDGET
...TO SEPARATE FROM MY HUSBAND...

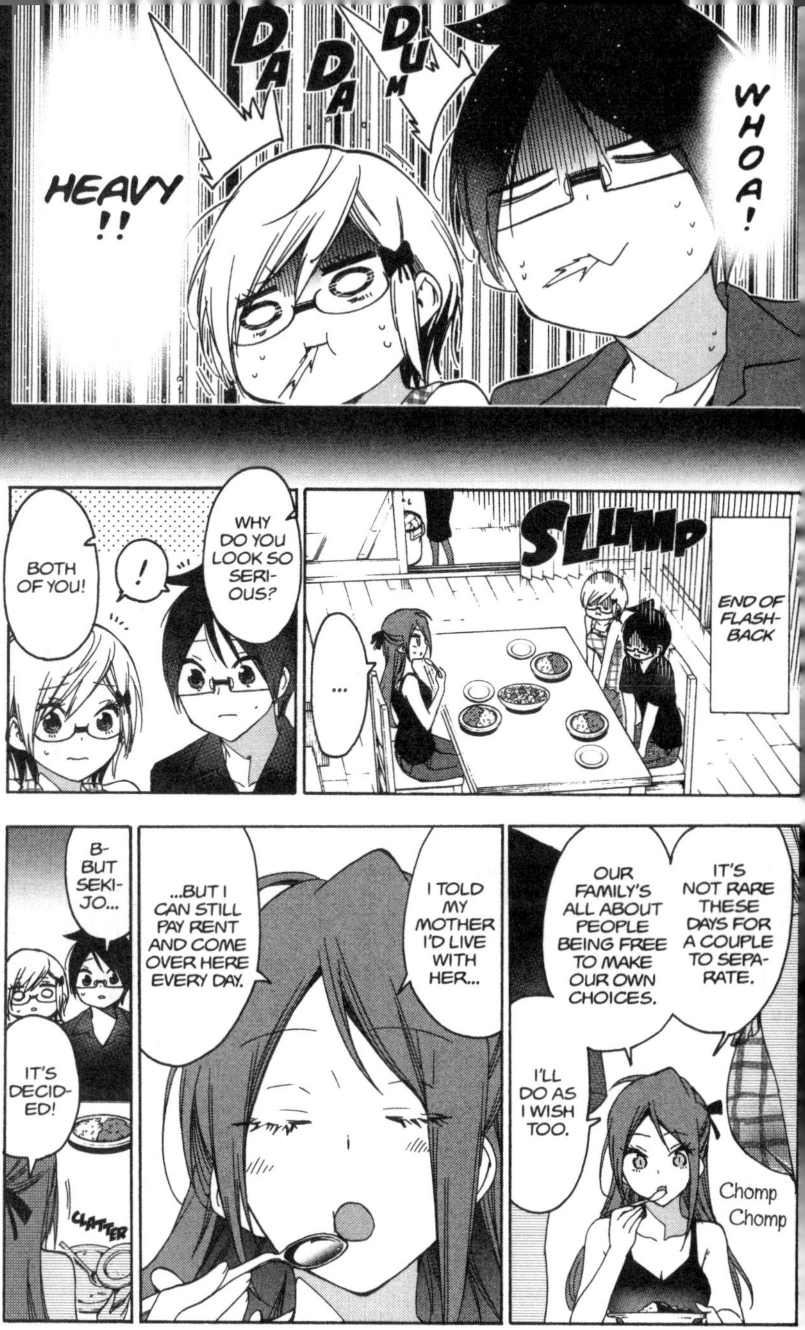
WHOA!
DA DA DUM
HEAVY!!
END OF FLASHBACK
SLUMP
...
WHY DO YOU LOOK SO SERIOUS?
!
BOTH OF YOU!
IT'S NOT RARE THESE DAYS FOR A COUPLE TO SEPARATE.
OUR FAMILY'S ALL ABOUT PEOPLE BEING FREE TO MAKE OUR OWN CHOICES.
I'LL DO AS I WISH TOO.
Chomp Chomp
I TOLD MY MOTHER I'D LIVE WITH HER...
...BUT I CAN STILL PAY RENT AND COME OVER HERE EVERY DAY.
B-BUT SEKIJO...
IT'S DECIDED!
CLATTER

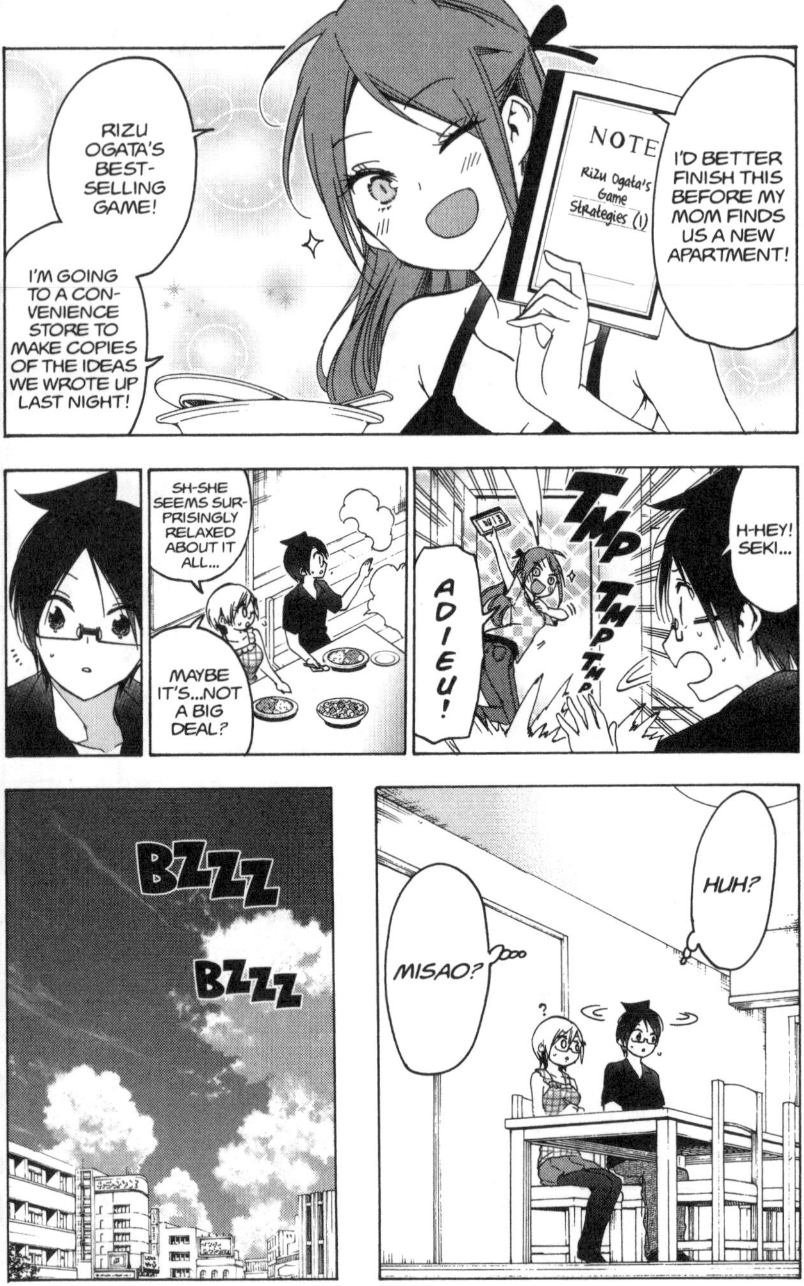
I'D BETTER FINISH THIS BEFORE MY MOM FINDS US A NEW APARTMENT!
NOTE
Rizu Ogata's Game Strategies (1)
RIZU OGATA'S BEST-SELLING GAME!
I'M GOING TO A CONVENIENCE STORE TO MAKE COPIES OF THE IDEAS WE WROTE UP LAST NIGHT!
H-HEY! SEKI...
TMP TMP TMP TMP
ADIEU!
SH-SHE SEEMS SURPRISINGLY RELAXED ABOUT IT ALL...
MAYBE IT'S...NOT A BIG DEAL?
HUH?
MISAO?
BZZZ
BZZZ

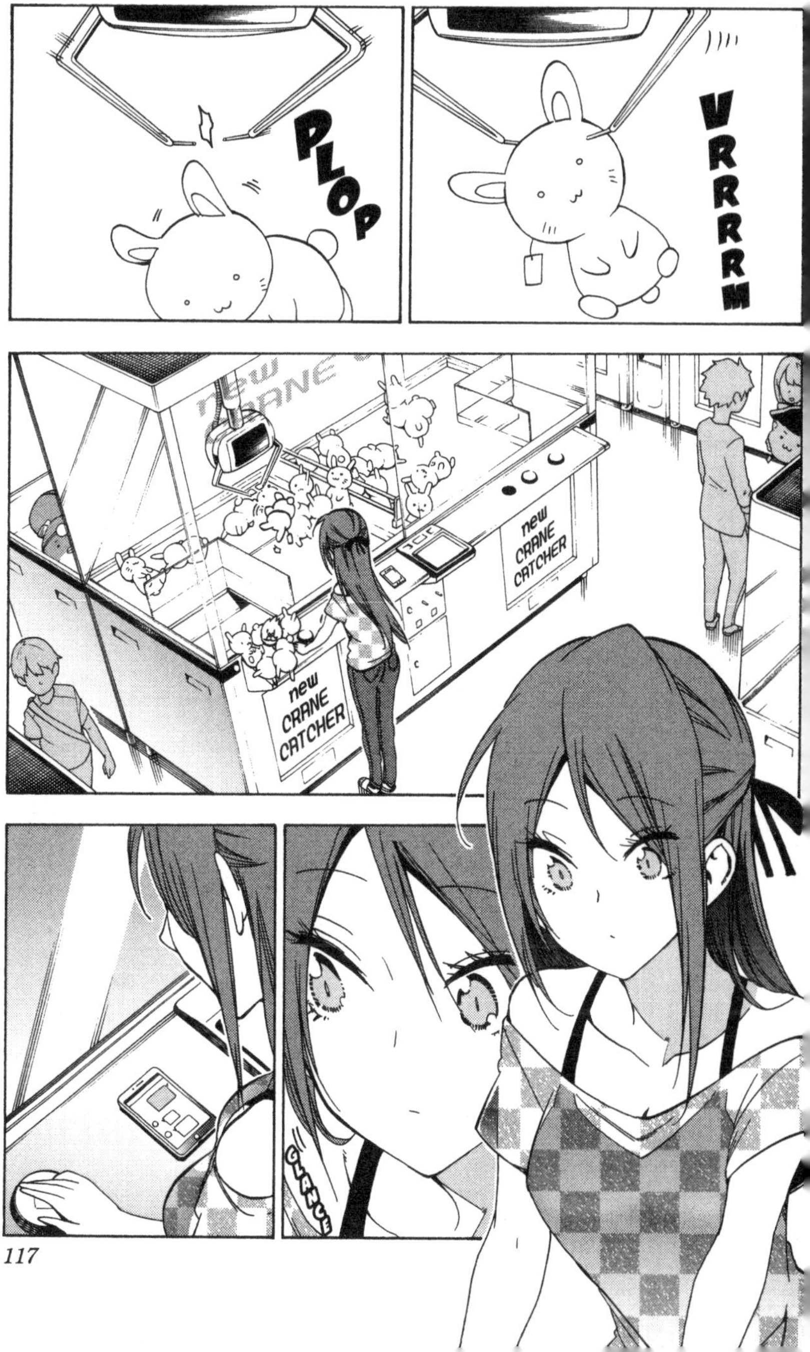
VRRRRM
PLOP
new CRANE CATCHER
new CRANE CATCHER
GLANCE

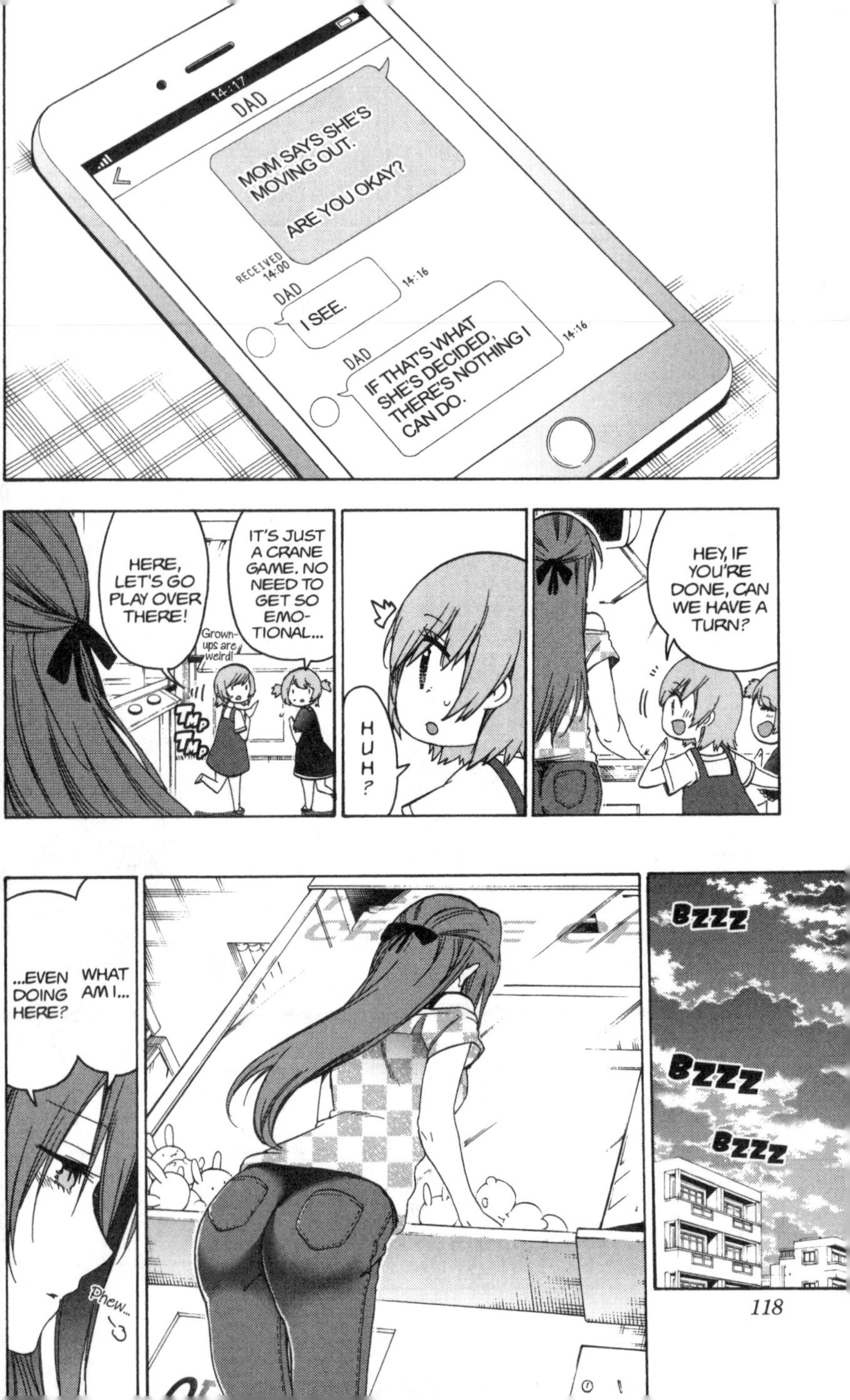
14:17
DAD
MOM SAYS SHE'S MOVING OUT.
ARE YOU OKAY?
RECEIVED 14:00
DAD
I SEE.
14:16
DAD
IF THAT'S WHAT SHE'S DECIDED, THERE'S NOTHING I CAN DO.
14:16
HEY, IF YOU'RE DONE, CAN WE HAVE A TURN?
HUH?
IT'S JUST A CRANE GAME. NO NEED TO GET SO EMOTIONAL...
HERE, LET'S GO PLAY OVER THERE!
Grown-ups are weird!
TMP TMP
BZZZ
BZZZ
BZZZ
WHAT AM I...
...EVEN DOING HERE?
Phew...

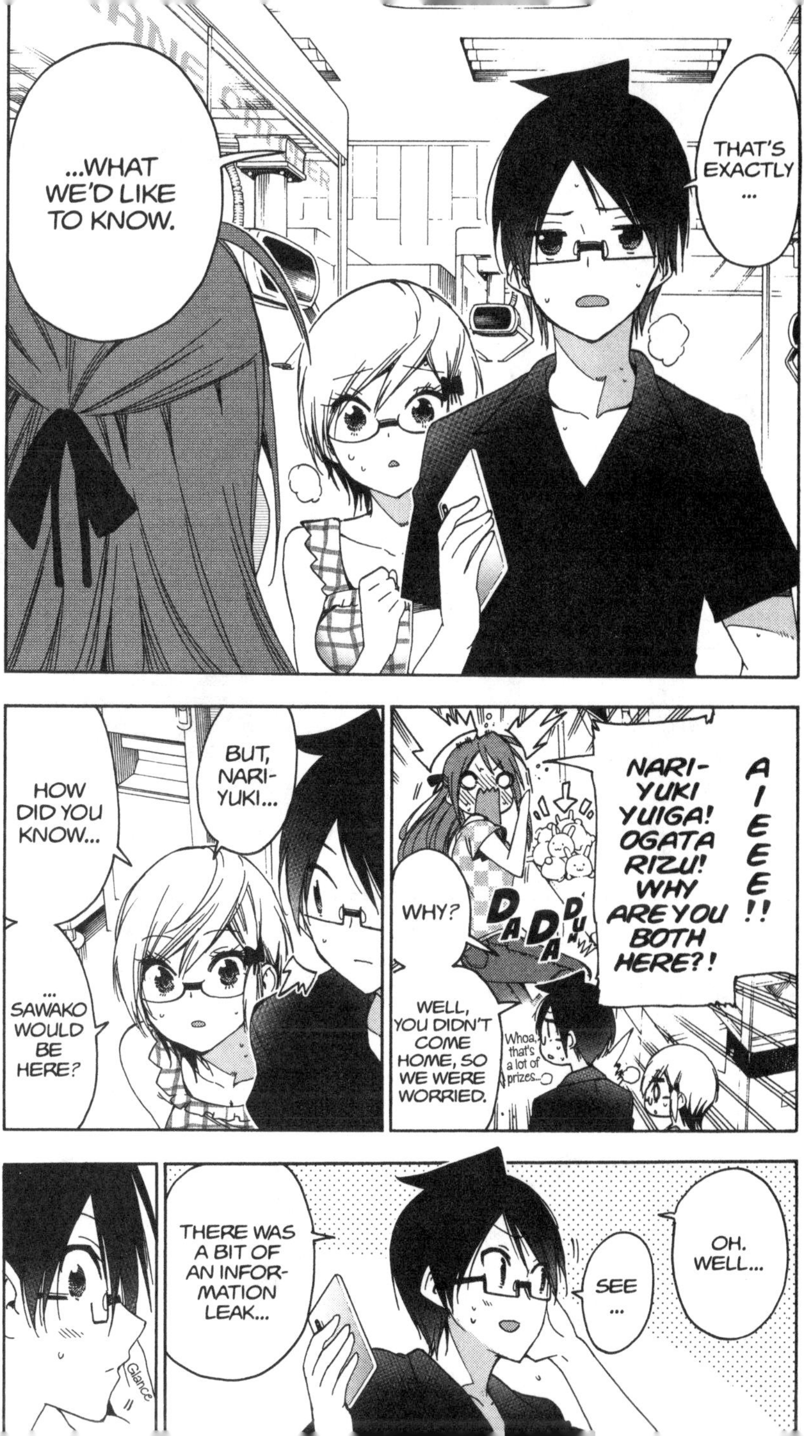
THAT'S EXACTLY ...
...WHAT WE'D LIKE TO KNOW.
AIEEEE!!
NARI-YUKI YUIGA! OGATA RIZU! WHY ARE YOU BOTH HERE?!
DADADUN
WHY?
WELL, YOU DIDN'T COME HOME, SO WE WERE WORRIED.
Whoa, that's a lot of prizes...
BUT, NARI-YUKI...
HOW DID YOU KNOW...
...SAWAKO WOULD BE HERE?
OH. WELL...
SEE ...
THERE WAS A BIT OF AN INFORMATION LEAK...
Glance

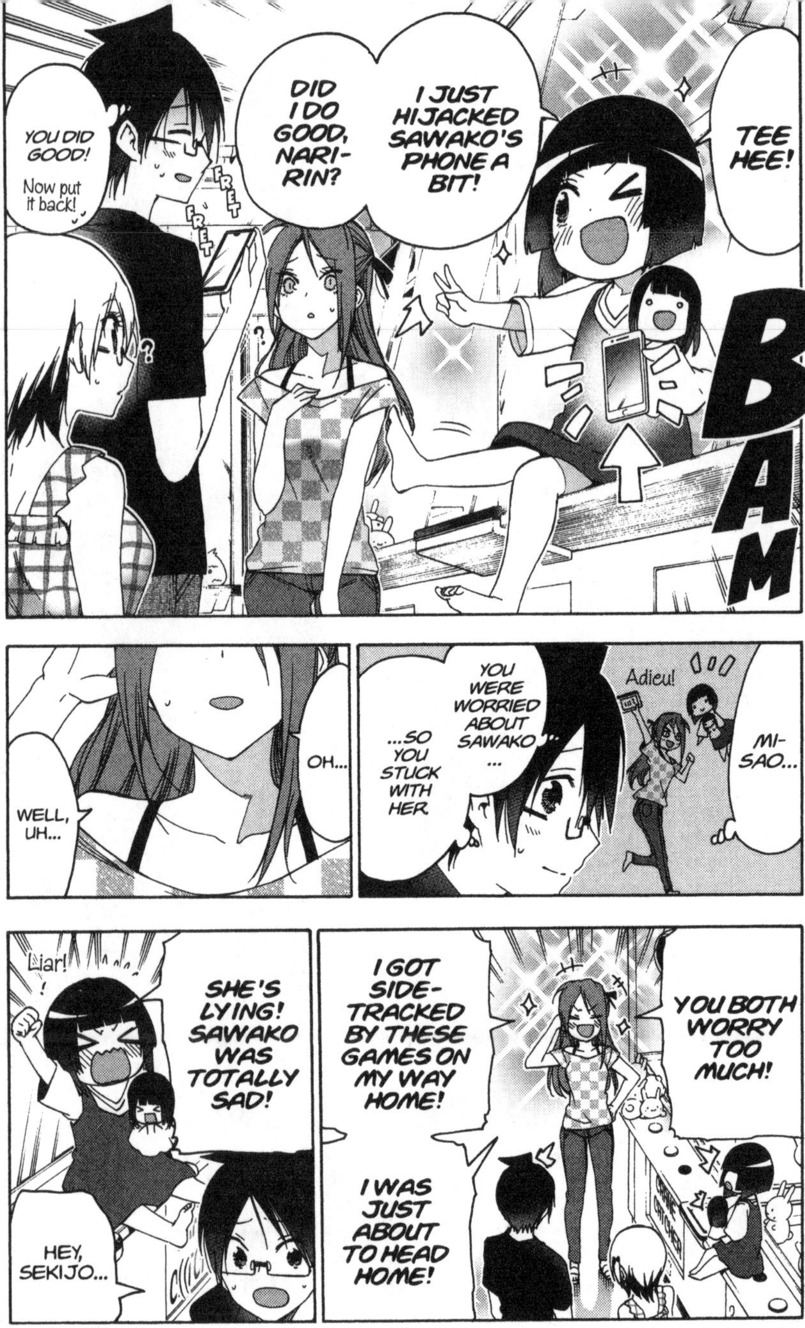
TEE HEE!
BAM
I JUST HIJACKED SAWAKO'S PHONE A BIT!
DID I DO GOOD, NARI-RIN?
FRET FRET
YOU DID GOOD! Now put it back!
MI-SAO...
Adieu!
YOU WERE WORRIED ABOUT SAWAKO...
...SO YOU STUCK WITH HER.
OH...
WELL, UH...
YOU BOTH WORRY TOO MUCH!
I GOT SIDE-TRACKED BY THESE GAMES ON MY WAY HOME!
I WAS JUST ABOUT TO HEAD HOME!
CRANE CATCHER
SHE'S LYING! SAWAKO WAS TOTALLY SAD!
Liar!
HEY, SEKIJO...

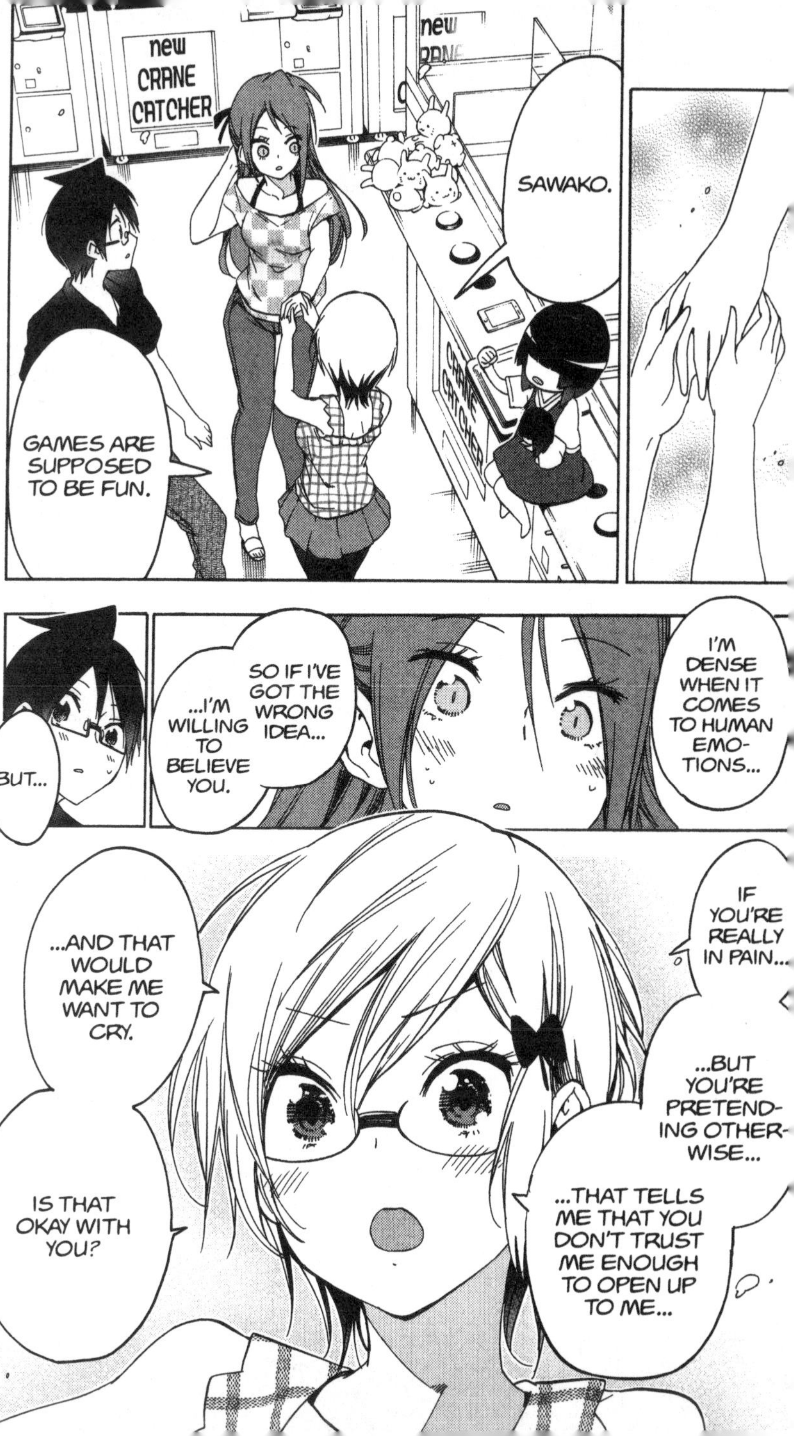
SAWAKO.
new
new CRANE CATCHER
CRANE CATCHER
GAMES ARE SUPPOSED TO BE FUN.
I'M DENSE WHEN IT COMES TO HUMAN EMO-TIONS...
SO IF I'VE GOT THE WRONG IDEA...
...I'M WILLING TO BELIEVE YOU.
BUT...
IF YOU'RE REALLY IN PAIN...
...BUT YOU'RE PRETEND-ING OTHER-WISE...
...THAT TELLS ME THAT YOU DON'T TRUST ME ENOUGH TO OPEN UP TO ME...
...AND THAT WOULD MAKE ME WANT TO CRY.
IS THAT OKAY WITH YOU?

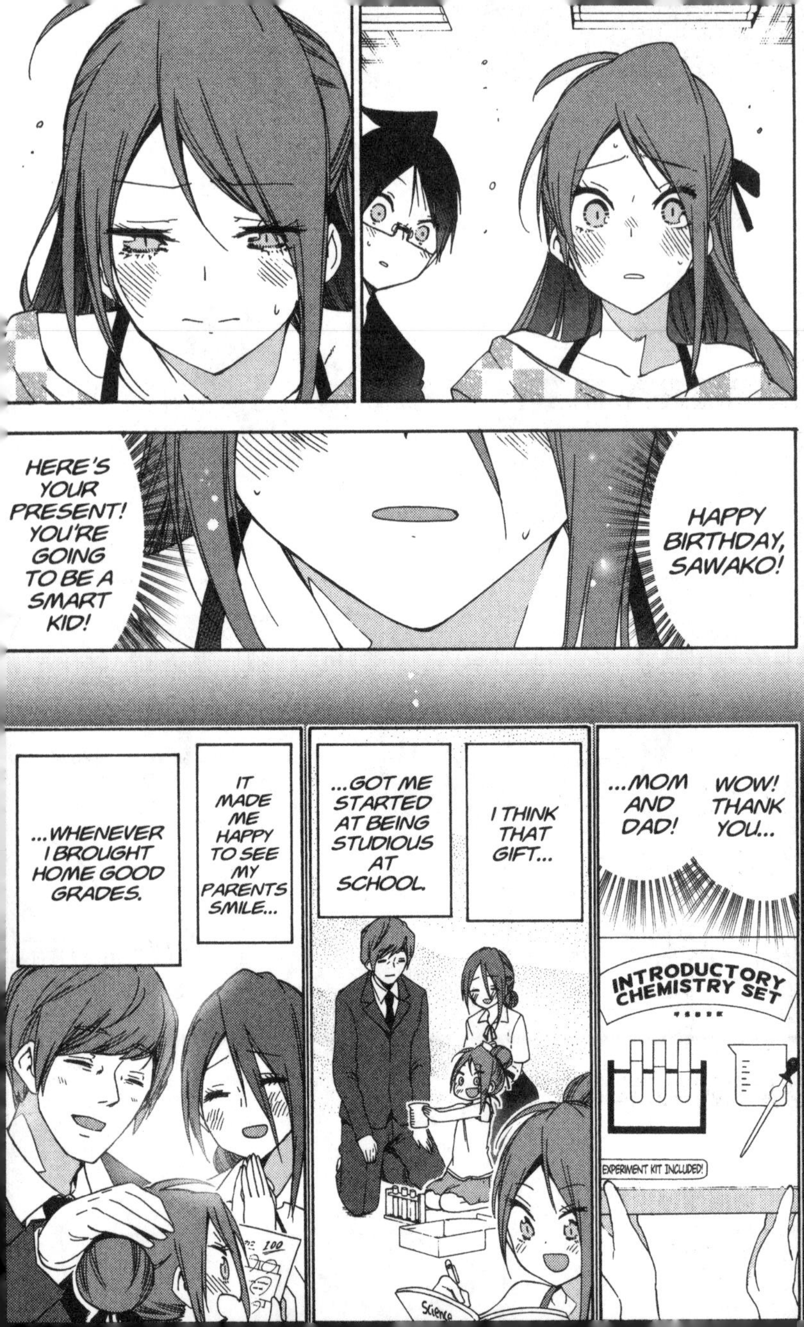
HAPPY BIRTHDAY, SAWAKO!
HERE'S YOUR PRESENT! YOU'RE GOING TO BE A SMART KID!
WOW! THANK YOU...
...MOM AND DAD!
INTRODUCTORY CHEMISTRY SET
EXPERIMENT KIT INCLUDED!
I THINK THAT GIFT...
...GOT ME STARTED AT BEING STUDIOUS AT SCHOOL.
Science
IT MADE ME HAPPY TO SEE MY PARENTS SMILE...
...WHENEVER I BROUGHT HOME GOOD GRADES.
100

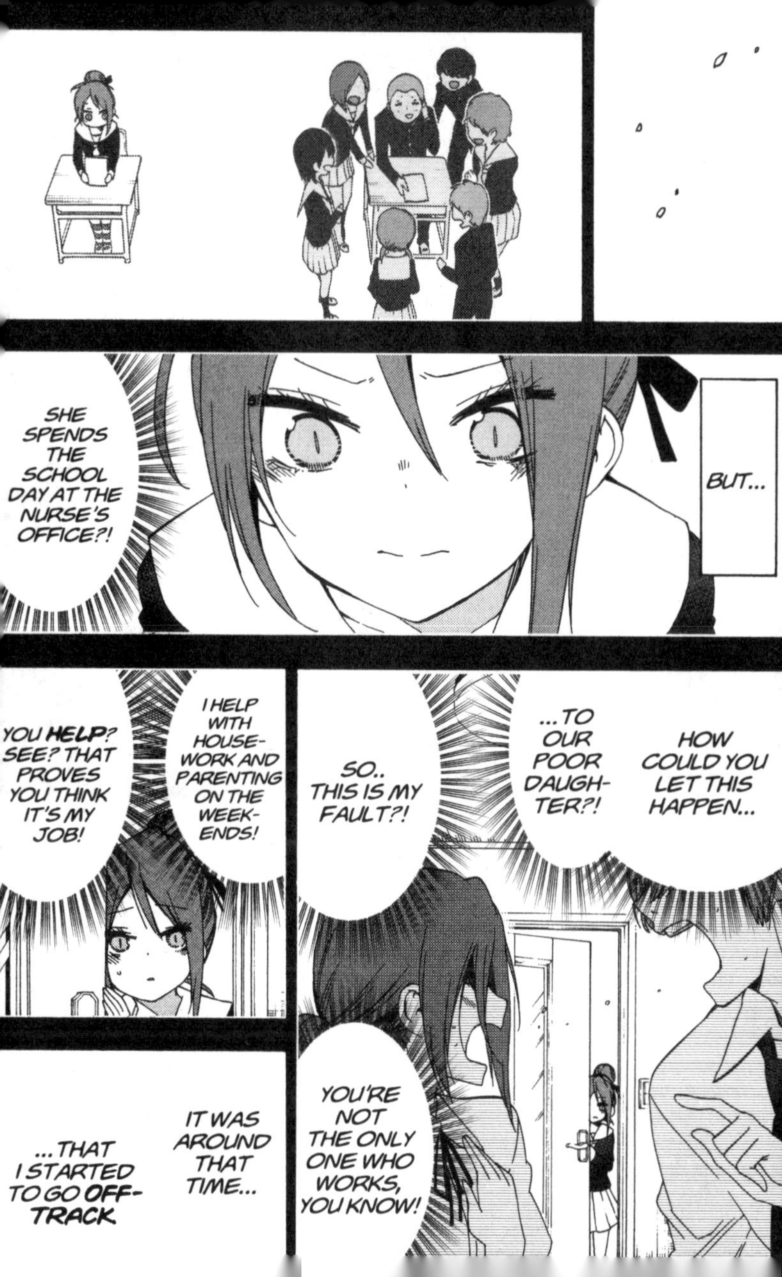
BUT...
SHE SPENDS THE SCHOOL DAY AT THE NURSE'S OFFICE?!
HOW COULD YOU LET THIS HAPPEN...
...TO OUR POOR DAUGHTER?!
SO.. THIS IS MY FAULT?!
YOU'RE NOT THE ONLY ONE WHO WORKS, YOU KNOW!
I HELP WITH HOUSE-WORK AND PARENTING ON THE WEEK-ENDS!
YOU HELP? SEE? THAT PROVES YOU THINK IT'S MY JOB!
IT WAS AROUND THAT TIME...
...THAT I STARTED TO GO OFF-TRACK

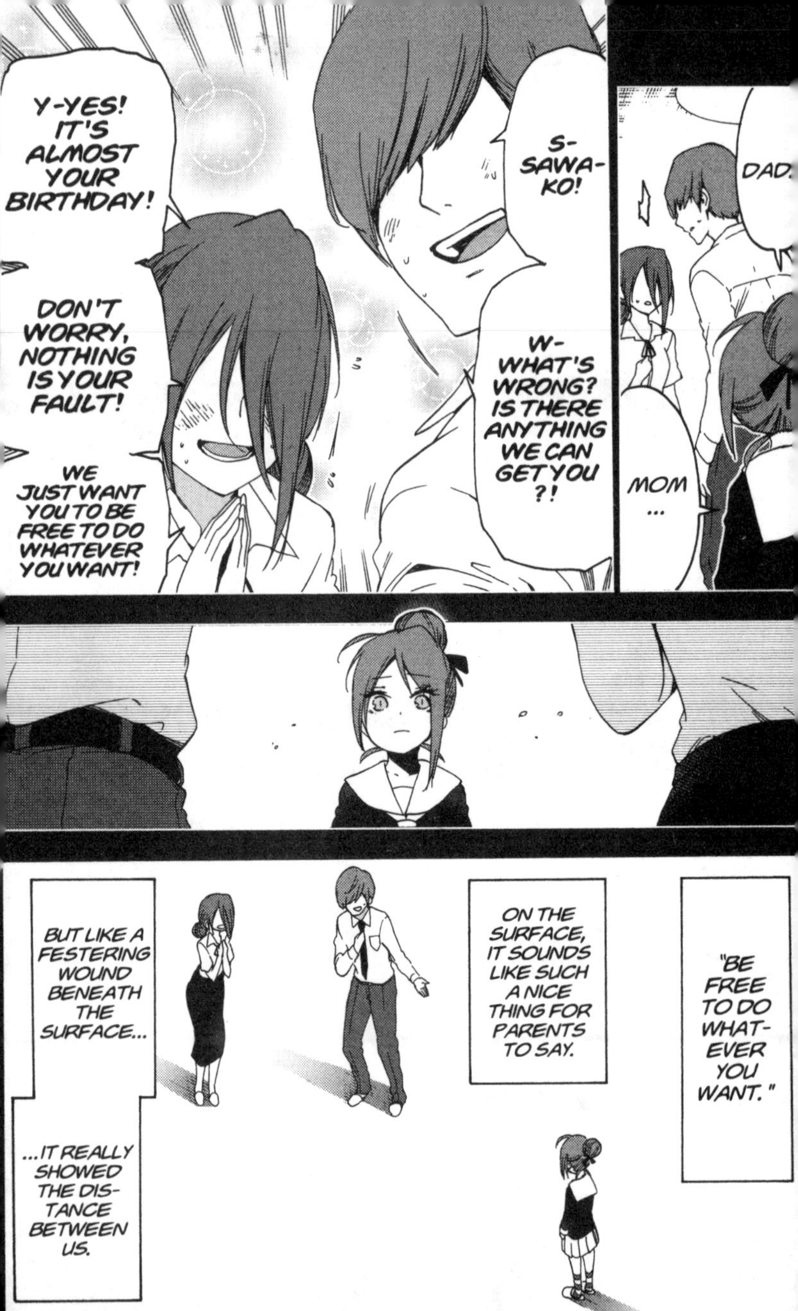
DAD.
MOM ...
S-SAWAKO!
W-WHAT'S WRONG? IS THERE ANYTHING WE CAN GET YOU?!
Y-YES! IT'S ALMOST YOUR BIRTHDAY!
DON'T WORRY, NOTHING IS YOUR FAULT!
WE JUST WANT YOU TO BE FREE TO DO WHATEVER YOU WANT!
"BE FREE TO DO WHAT-EVER YOU WANT."
ON THE SURFACE, IT SOUNDS LIKE SUCH A NICE THING FOR PARENTS TO SAY.
BUT LIKE A FESTERING WOUND BENEATH THE SURFACE...
...IT REALLY SHOWED THE DIS-TANCE BETWEEN US.

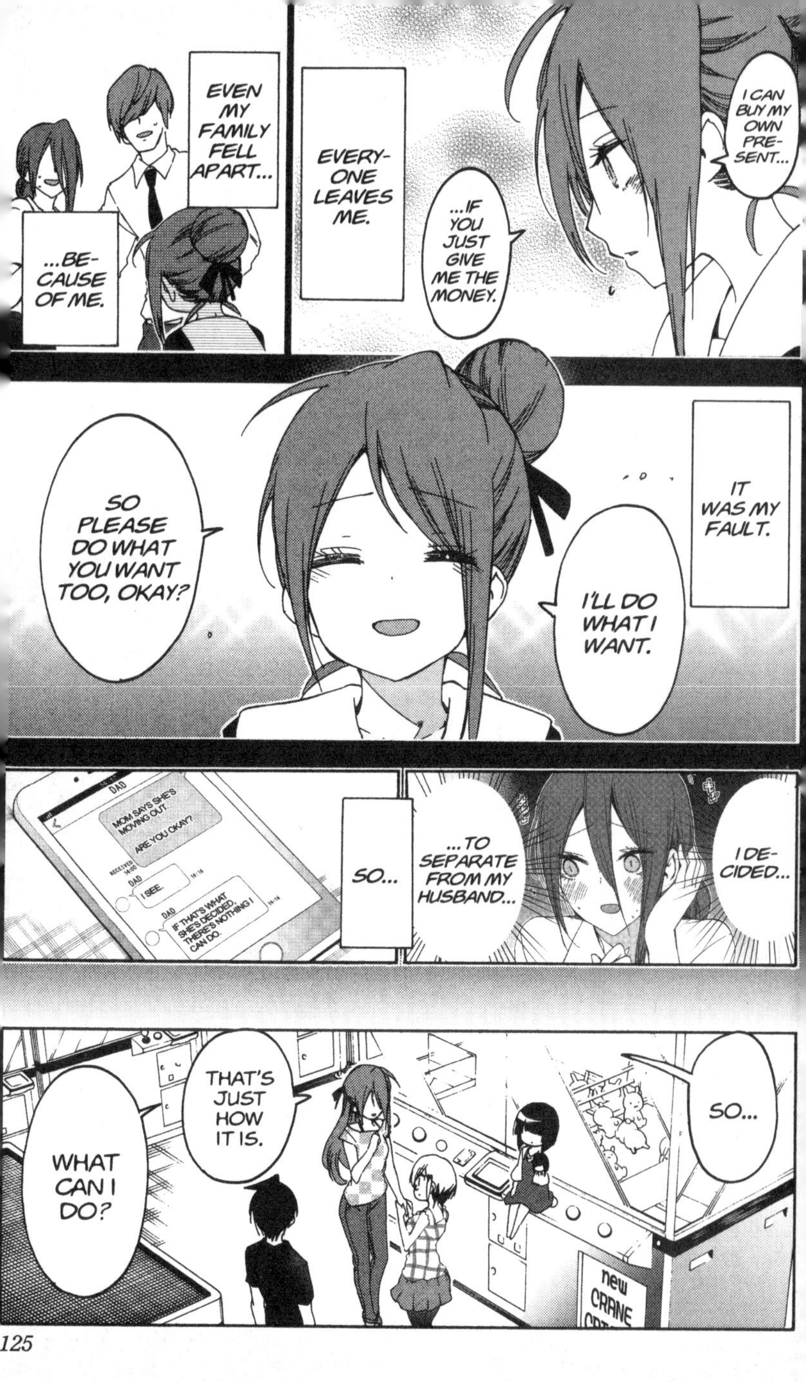
I CAN BUY MY OWN PRESENT...
...IF YOU JUST GIVE ME THE MONEY.
EVERYONE LEAVES ME.
EVEN MY FAMILY FELL APART...
...BECAUSE OF ME.
IT WAS MY FAULT.
I'LL DO WHAT I WANT.
SO PLEASE DO WHAT YOU WANT TOO, OKAY?
I DECIDED...
...TO SEPARATE FROM MY HUSBAND...
SO...
DAD
MOM SAYS SHE'S MOVING OUT.
ARE YOU OKAY?
I SEE.
IF THAT'S WHAT SHE'S DECIDED, THERE'S NOTHING I CAN DO.
SO...
THAT'S JUST HOW IT IS.
WHAT CAN I DO?
new CRANE

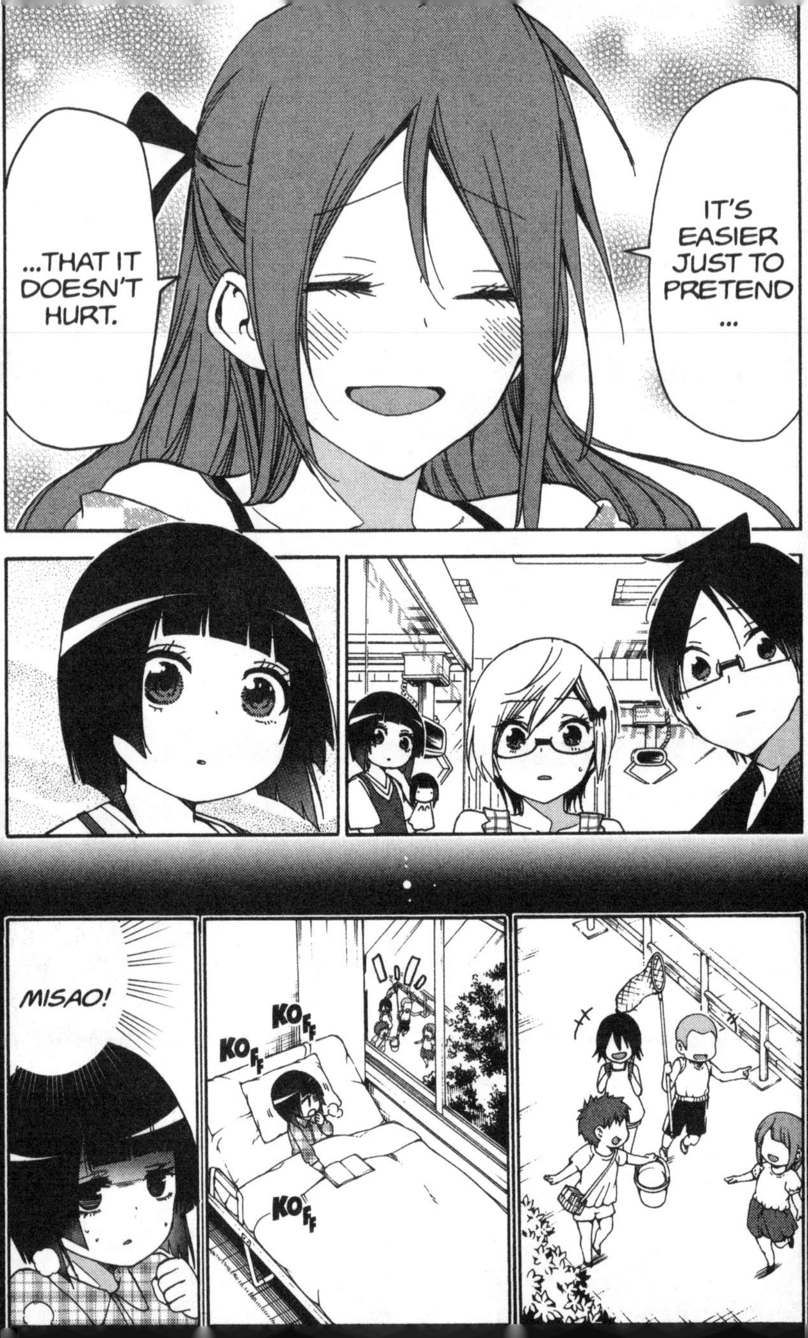
IT'S EASIER JUST TO PRETEND ...
...THAT IT DOESN'T HURT.
KOFF
KOFF
KOFF
MISAO!

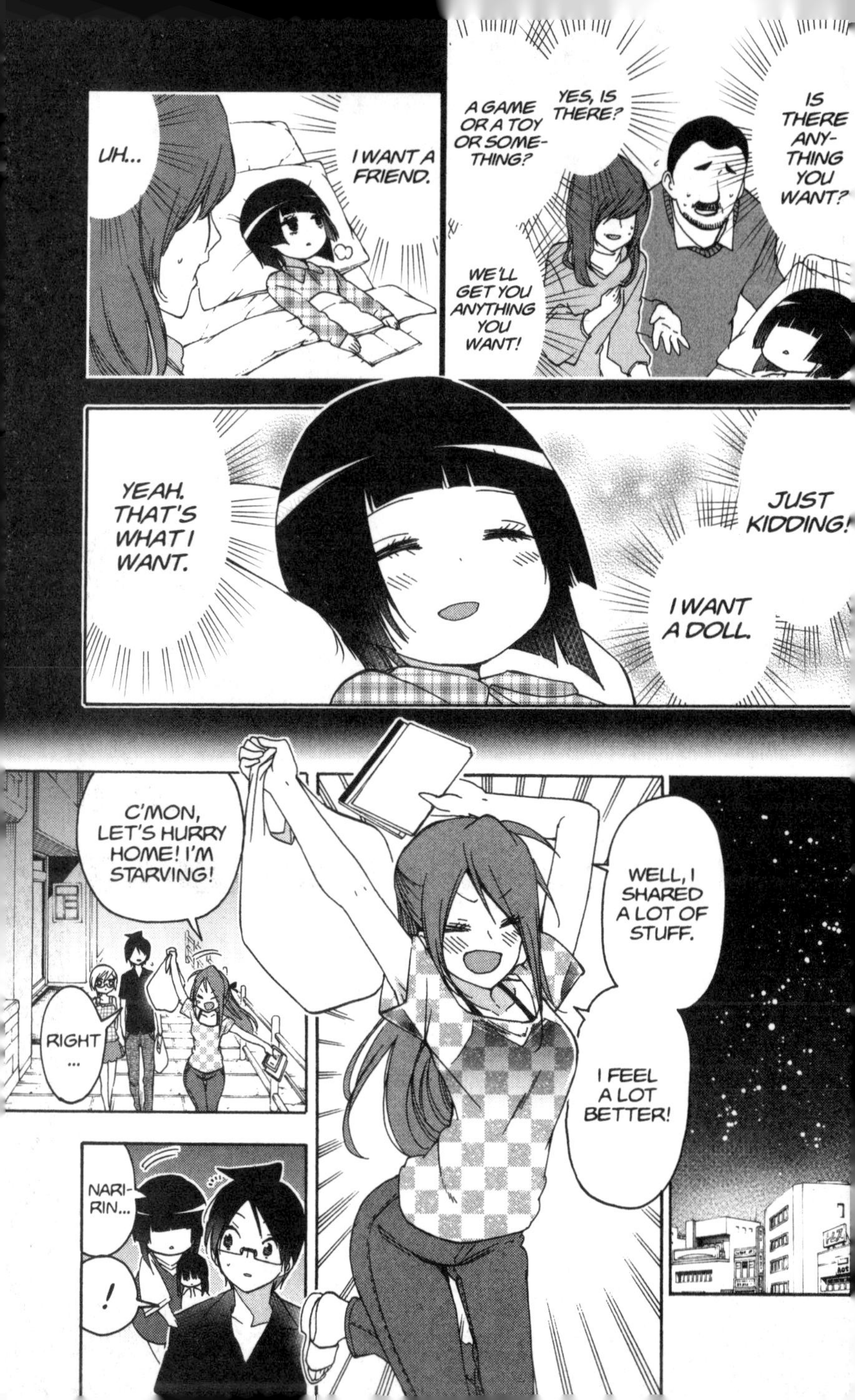
IS THERE ANYTHING YOU WANT?
YES, IS THERE?
A GAME OR A TOY OR SOMETHING?
WE'LL GET YOU ANYTHING YOU WANT!
I WANT A FRIEND.
UH...
JUST KIDDING!
I WANT A DOLL.
YEAH. THAT'S WHAT I WANT.
WELL, I SHARED A LOT OF STUFF.
I FEEL A LOT BETTER!
C'MON, LET'S HURRY HOME! I'M STARVING!
RIGHT ...
NARI-RIN...
!

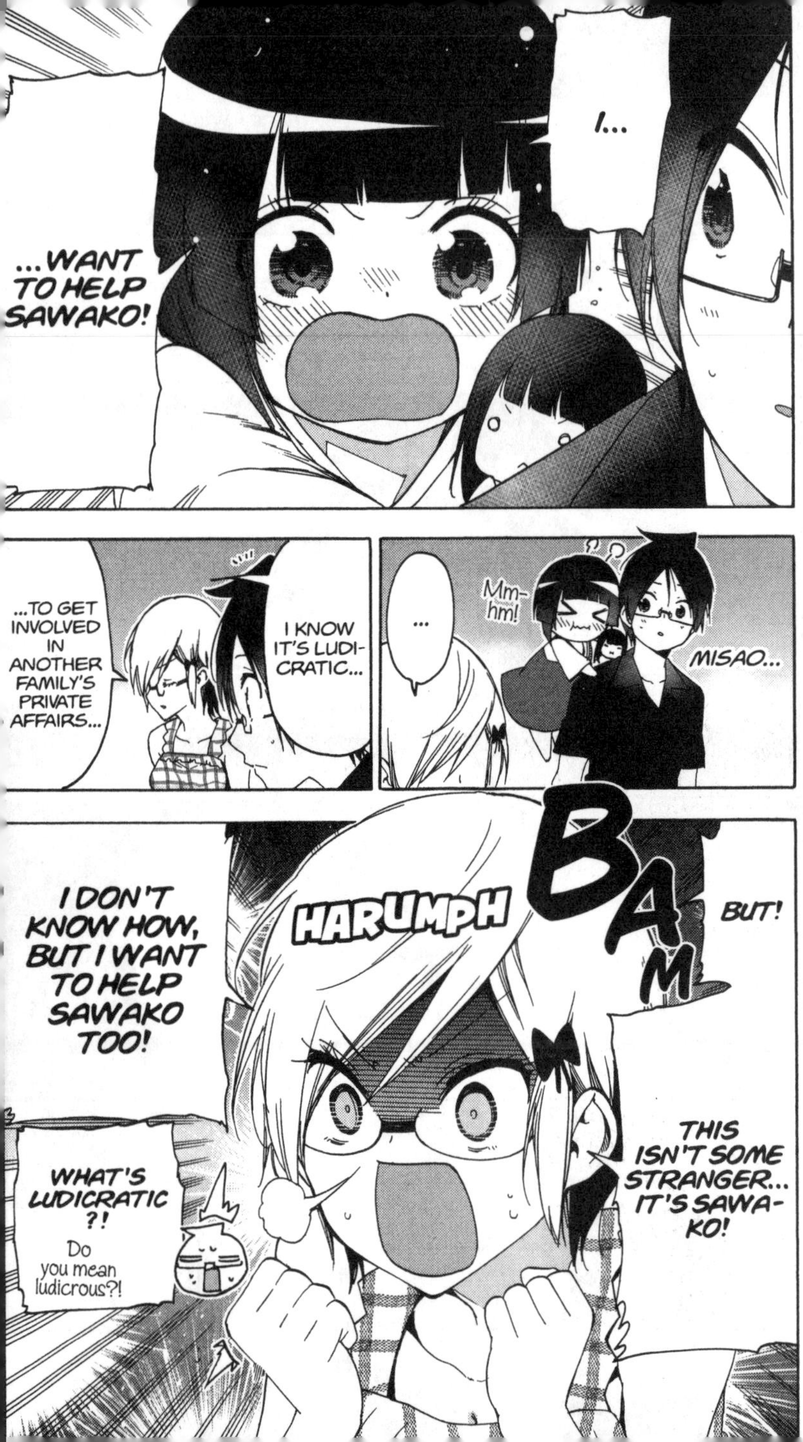
I...
...WANT TO HELP SAWAKO!
Mm-hm!
MISAO...
...
I KNOW IT'S LUDICRATIC...
...TO GET INVOLVED IN ANOTHER FAMILY'S PRIVATE AFFAIRS...
BUT!
BAM
HARUMPH
THIS ISN'T SOME STRANGER... IT'S SAWAKO!
I DON'T KNOW HOW, BUT I WANT TO HELP SAWAKO TOO!
WHAT'S LUDICRATIC?!
Do you mean ludicrous?!

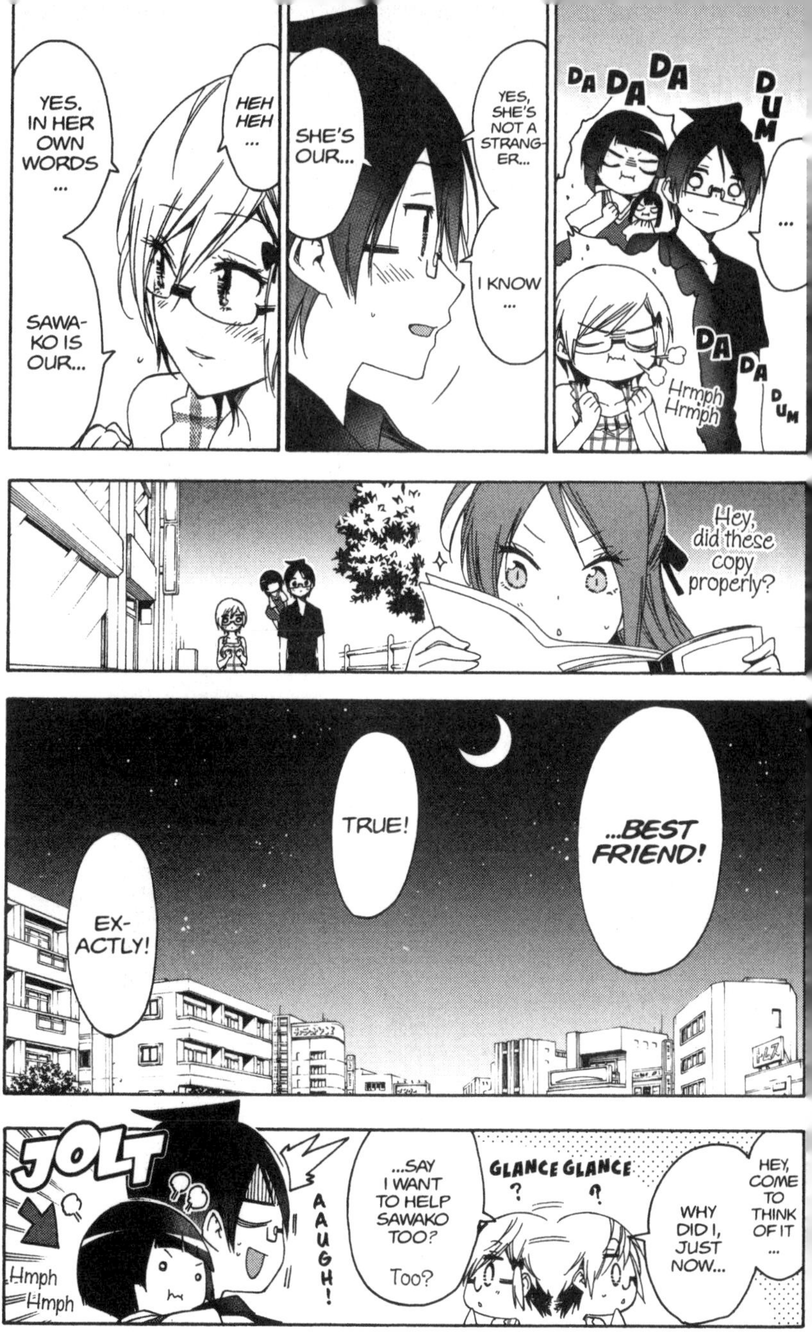
DA DA DA
DUM
...
DA DA DUM
Hrmph Hrmph
YES, SHE'S NOT A STRANGER...
I KNOW...
SHE'S OUR...
HEH HEH...
YES. IN HER OWN WORDS...
SAWAKO IS OUR...
Hey, did these copy properly?
...BEST FRIEND!
TRUE!
EX-ACTLY!
HEY, COME TO THINK OF IT...
WHY DID I, JUST NOW...
GLANCE GLANCE
...SAY I WANT TO HELP SAWAKO TOO?
Too?
AAUGH!
JOLT
Hmph Hmph

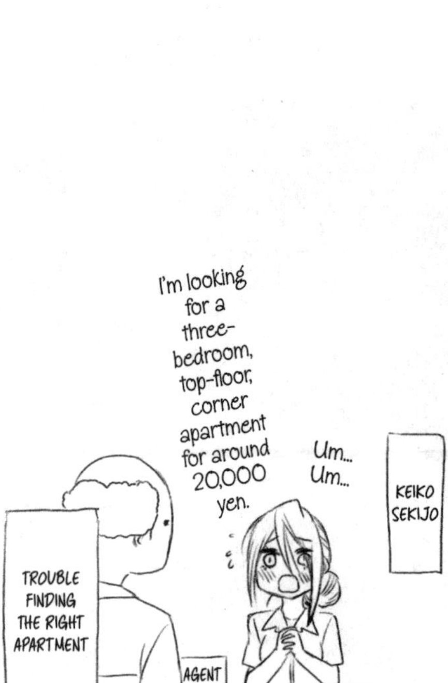
KEIKO SEKIJO
Um... Um...
I'm looking for a three-bedroom, top-floor, corner apartment for around 20,000 yen.
TROUBLE FINDING THE RIGHT APARTMENT
AGENT

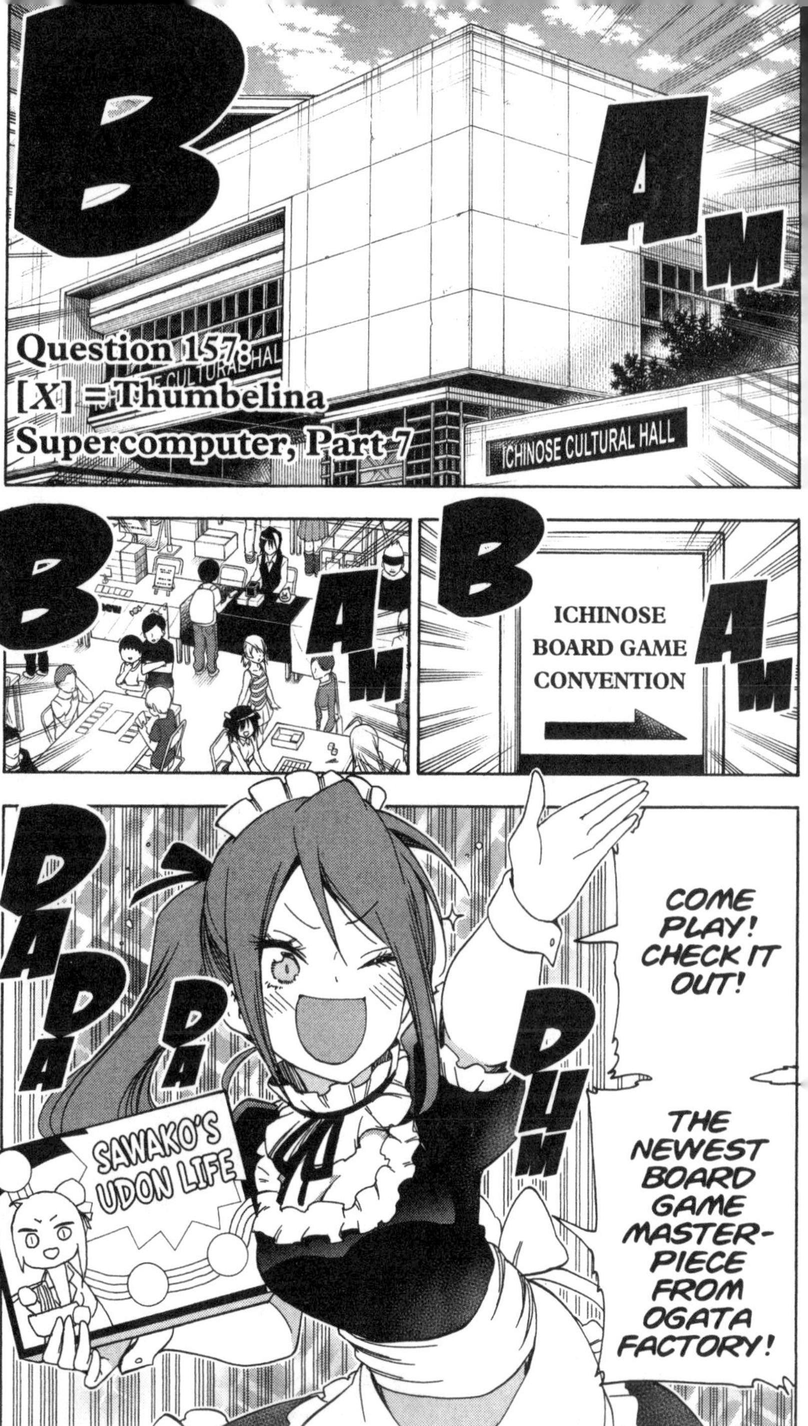
BAM
Question 157:
[X] = Thumbelina
Supercomputer, Part 7
ICHINOSE CULTURAL HALL
BAM
ICHINOSE
BOARD GAME
CONVENTION
BAM
DADADA DUM
COME PLAY! CHECK IT OUT!
THE NEWEST BOARD GAME MASTER-PIECE FROM OGATA FACTORY!
SAWAKO'S UDON LIFE

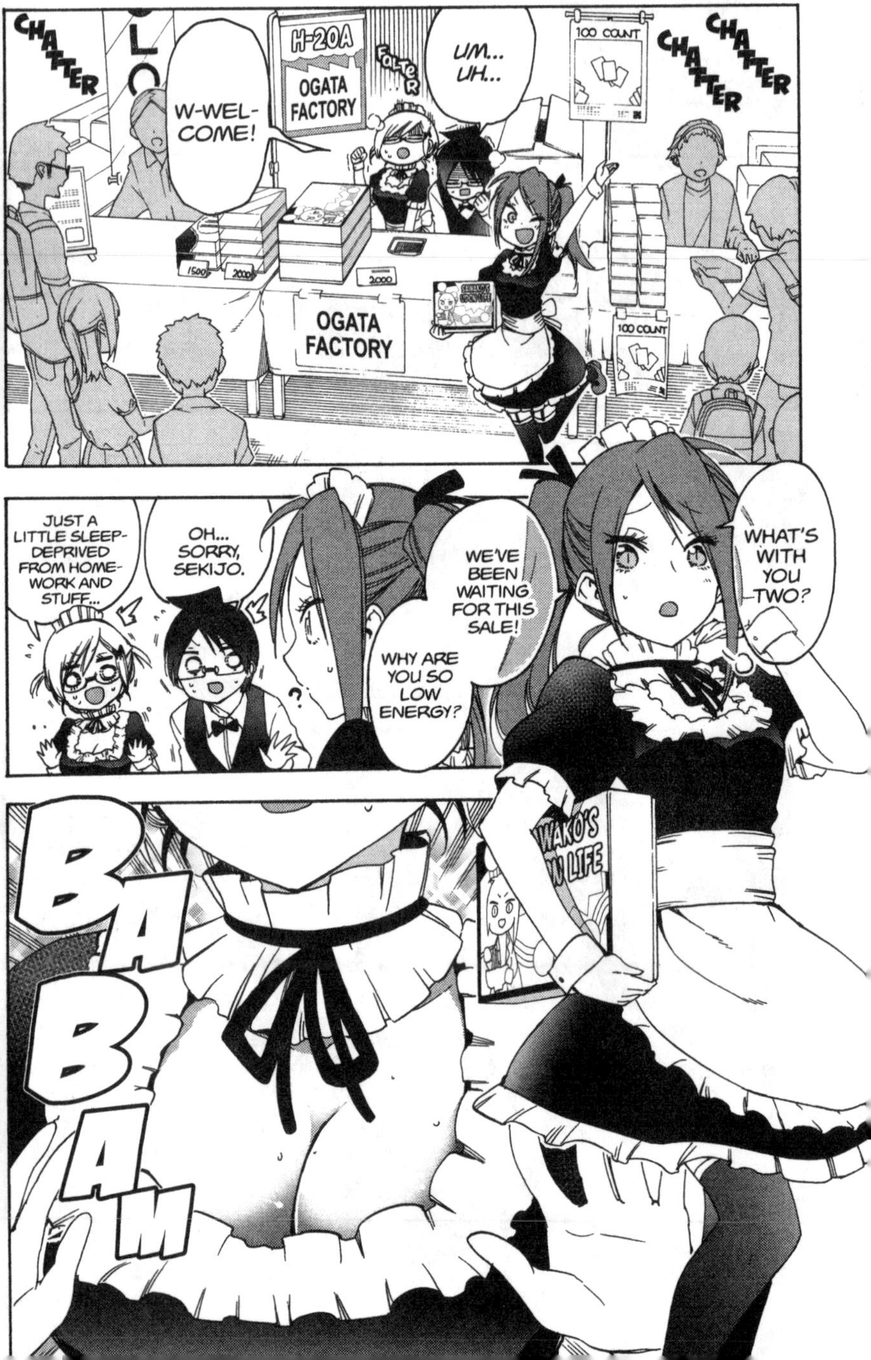
CHATTER CHATTER
100 COUNT
UM... UH...
Falter
H-20A
OGATA FACTORY
W-WEL-COME!
CHATTER
1500
2000
2000
OGATA FACTORY
SAWAKO'S UDON LIFE
100 COUNT
WHAT'S WITH YOU TWO?
WE'VE BEEN WAITING FOR THIS SALE!
WHY ARE YOU SO LOW ENERGY?
OH... SORRY, SEKIJO.
JUST A LITTLE SLEEP-DEPRIVED FROM HOME-WORK AND STUFF...
BA BAM

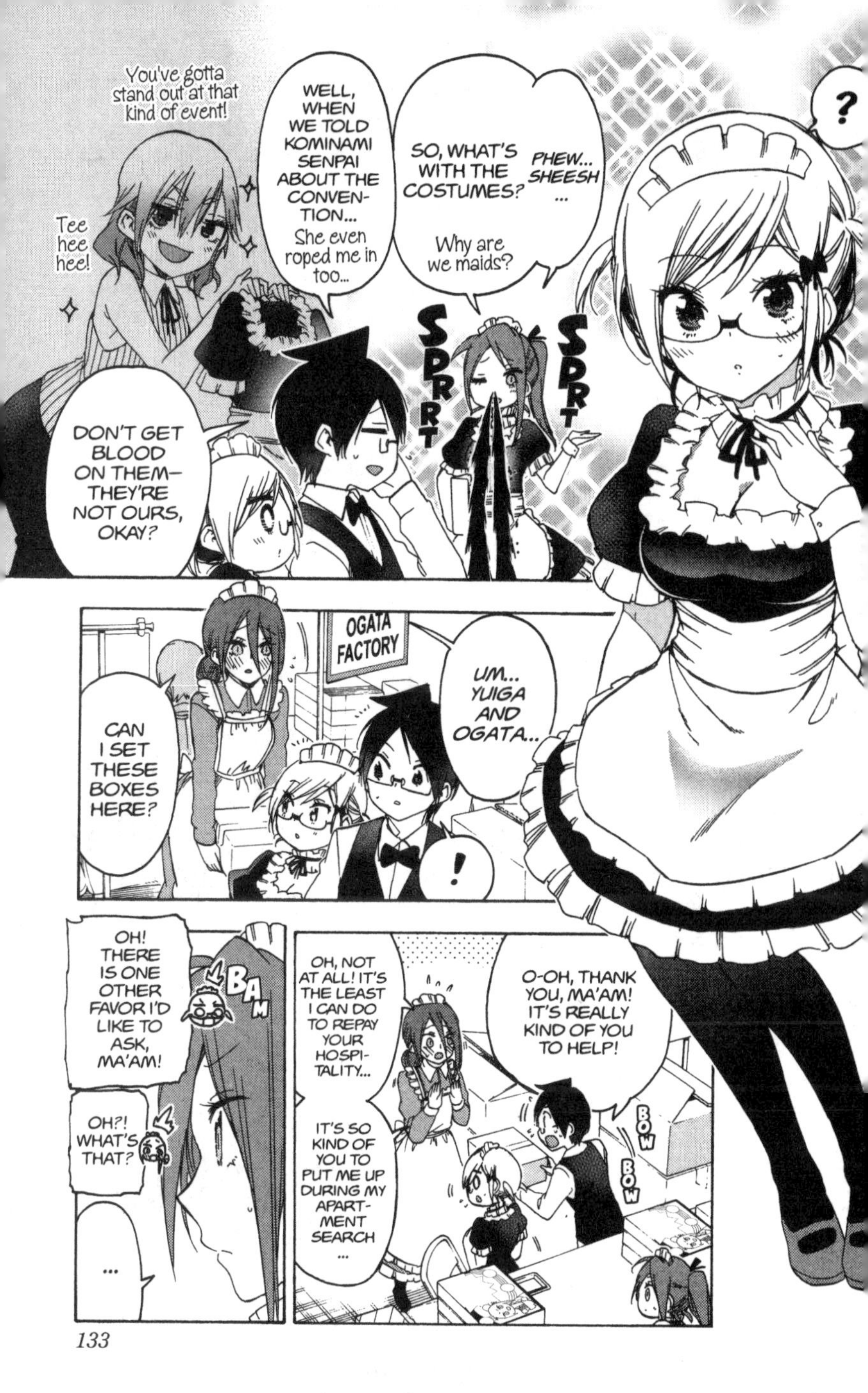
?
PHEW... SHEESH ...
SO, WHAT'S WITH THE COSTUMES?
Why are we maids?
WELL, WHEN WE TOLD KOMINAMI SENPAI ABOUT THE CONVENTION...
She even roped me in too...
You've gotta stand out at that kind of event!
Tee hee hee!
SPRT
SPRT
DON'T GET BLOOD ON THEM—THEY'RE NOT OURS, OKAY?
UM... YUIGA AND OGATA...
!
OGATA FACTORY
CAN I SET THESE BOXES HERE?
O-OH, THANK YOU, MA'AM! IT'S REALLY KIND OF YOU TO HELP!
BOW
BOW
OH, NOT AT ALL! IT'S THE LEAST I CAN DO TO REPAY YOUR HOSPITALITY...
IT'S SO KIND OF YOU TO PUT ME UP DURING MY APARTMENT SEARCH ...
OH! THERE IS ONE OTHER FAVOR I'D LIKE TO ASK, MA'AM!
BAM
OH?! WHAT'S THAT?
...

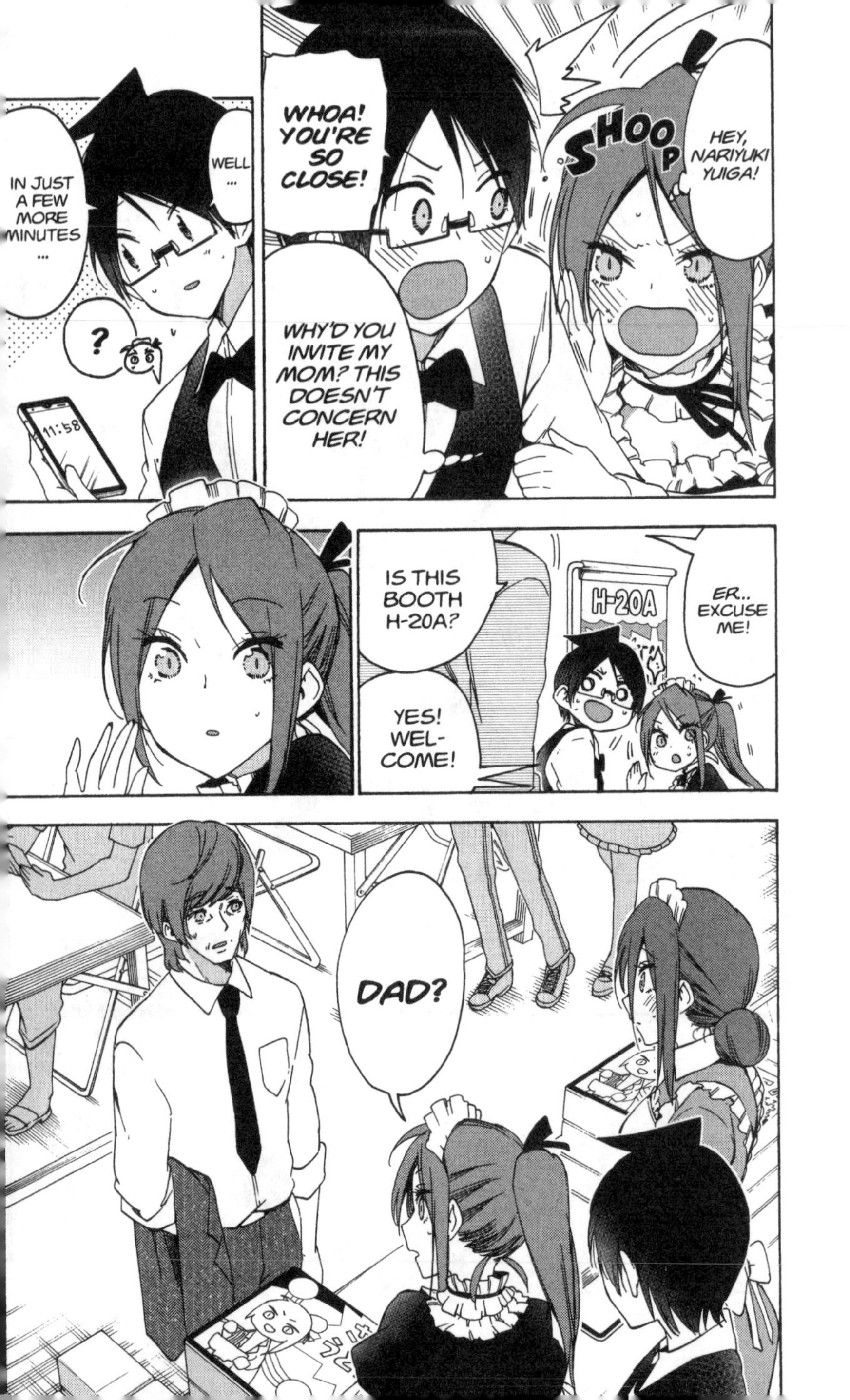
SHOOP
HEY, NARIYUKI YUIGA!
WHOA! YOU'RE SO CLOSE!
WHY'D YOU INVITE MY MOM? THIS DOESN'T CONCERN HER!
WELL...
IN JUST A FEW MORE MINUTES...
?
11:58
ER.. EXCUSE ME!
IS THIS BOOTH H-20A?
H-20A
YES! WEL-COME!
DAD?

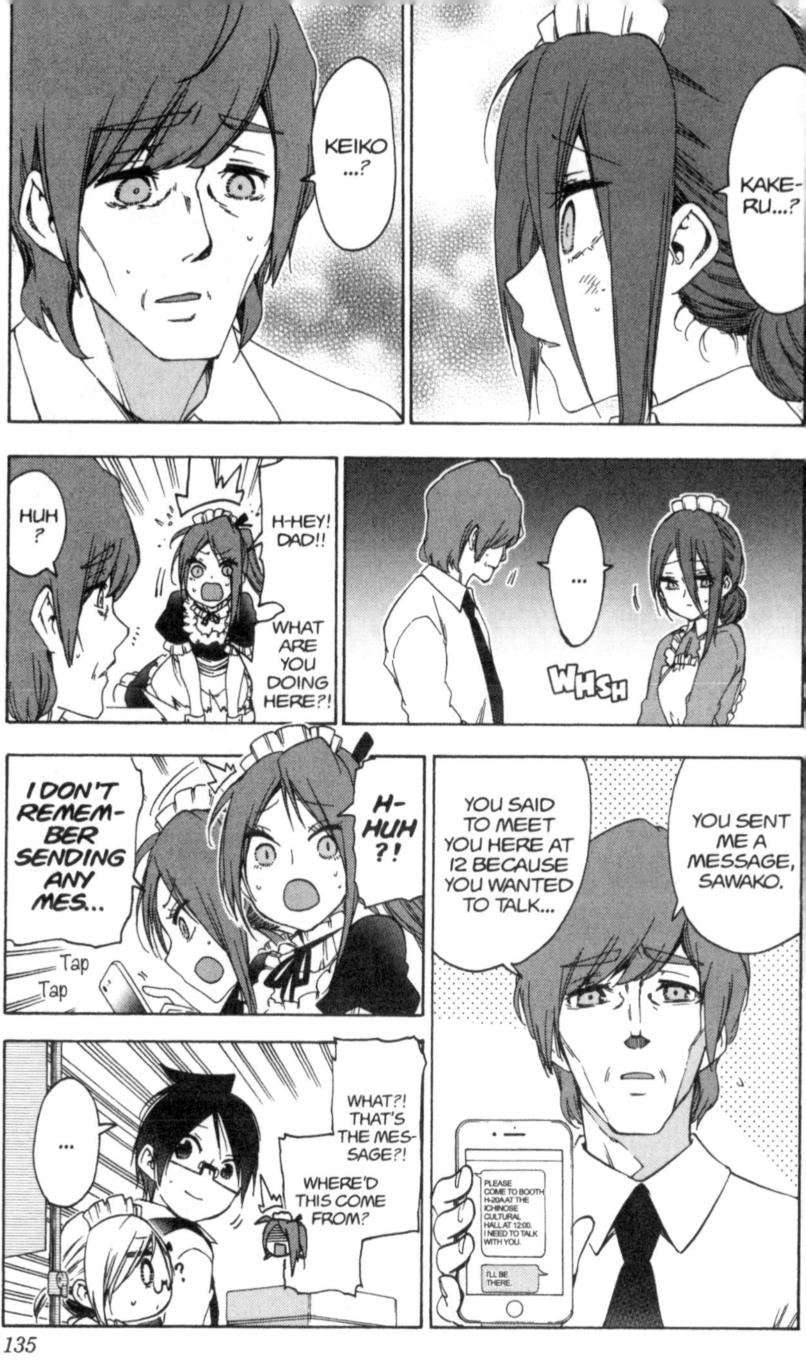

KAKE-RU...?
KEIKO ...?
...
WHSH
H-HEY! DAD!!
WHAT ARE YOU DOING HERE?!
HUH ?
YOU SENT ME A MESSAGE, SAWAKO.
YOU SAID TO MEET YOU HERE AT 12 BECAUSE YOU WANTED TO TALK...
PLEASE COME TO BOOTH H-20A AT THE ICHINOSE CULTURAL HALL AT 12:00. I NEED TO TALK WITH YOU.
I'LL BE THERE.
H-HUH ?!
I DON'T REMEMBER SENDING ANY MES...
Tap
Tap
WHAT?! THAT'S THE MESSAGE?!
WHERE'D THIS COME FROM?
...

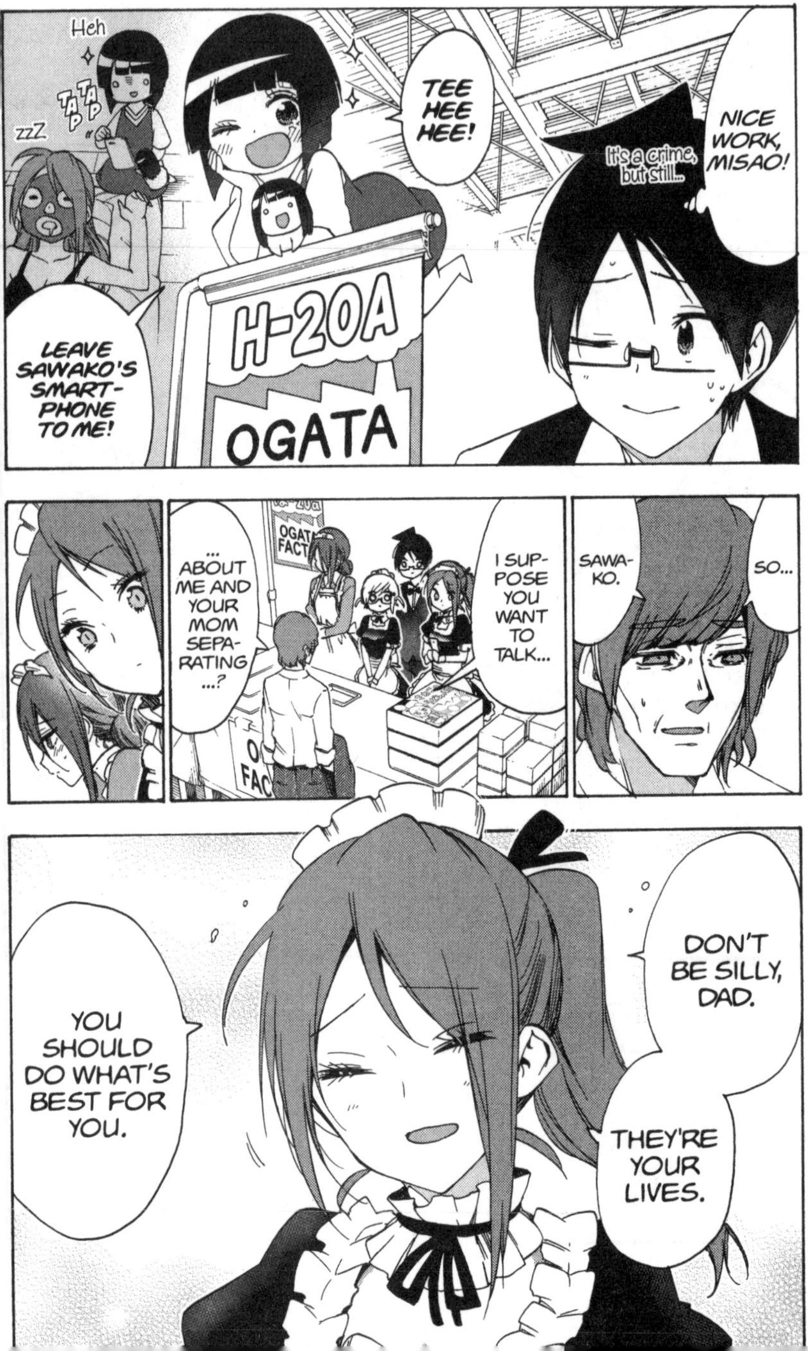
NICE WORK, MISAO!
It's a crime, but still...
TEE HEE HEE!
Heh
TAP TAP
zzZ
H-20A
OGATA
LEAVE SAWAKO'S SMART-PHONE TO ME!
SO...
SAWA-KO.
I SUP-POSE YOU WANT TO TALK...
...ABOUT ME AND YOUR MOM SEPA-RATING...?
DON'T BE SILLY, DAD.
THEY'RE YOUR LIVES.
YOU SHOULD DO WHAT'S BEST FOR YOU.

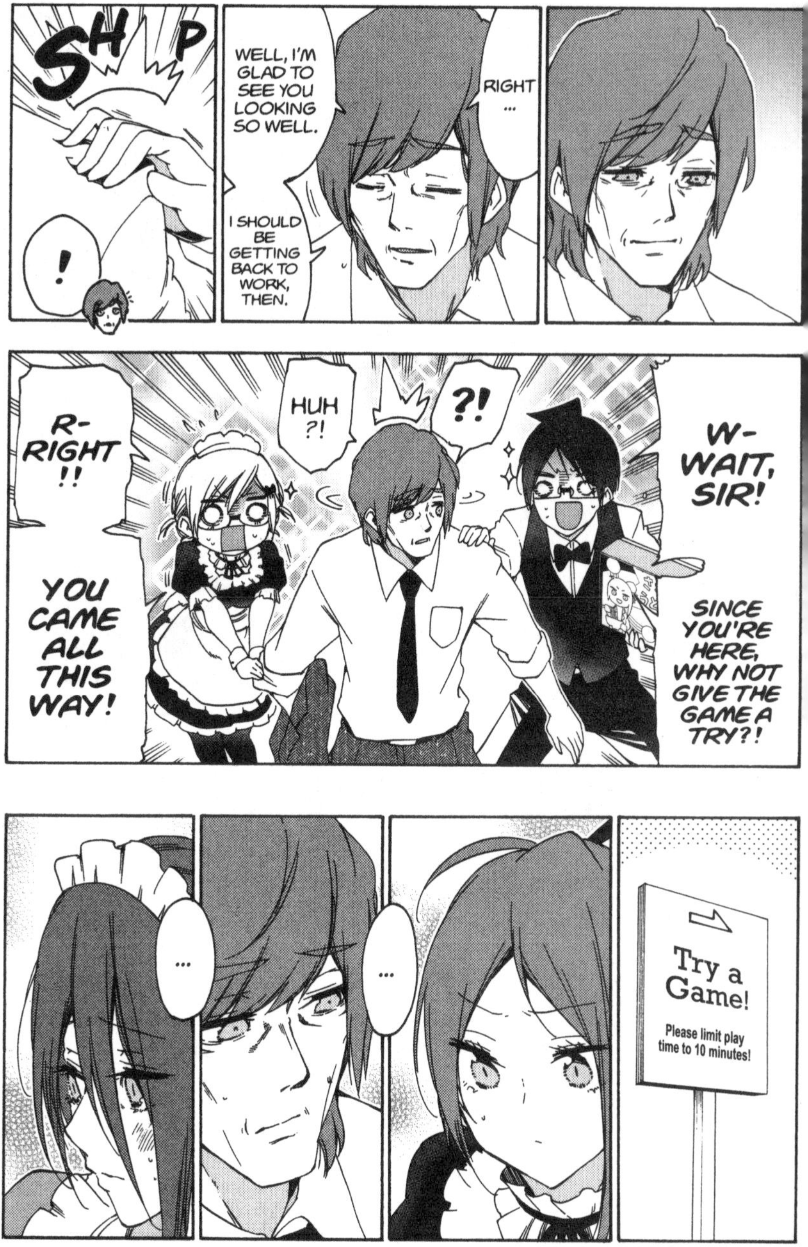
RIGHT ...
WELL, I'M GLAD TO SEE YOU LOOKING SO WELL.
I SHOULD BE GETTING BACK TO WORK, THEN.
SHP
!
W-WAIT, SIR!
SINCE YOU'RE HERE, WHY NOT GIVE THE GAME A TRY?!
?!
HUH ?!
R-RIGHT!!
YOU CAME ALL THIS WAY!
Try a Game!
Please limit play time to 10 minutes!
...
...

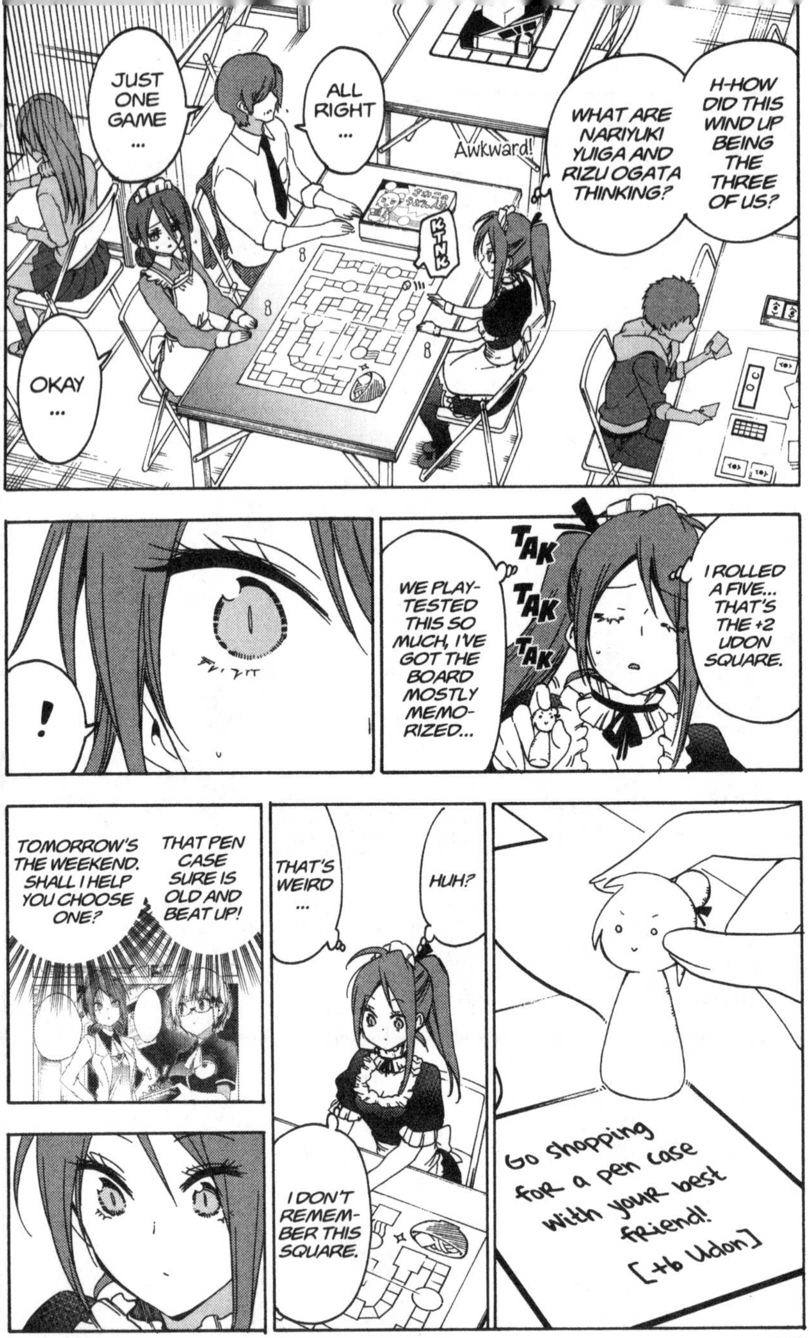
H-HOW DID THIS WIND UP BEING THE THREE OF US?
WHAT ARE NARIYUKI YUIGA AND RIZU OGATA THINKING?
Awkward!
ALL RIGHT ...
JUST ONE GAME ...
KTNK
OKAY ...
I ROLLED A FIVE... THAT'S THE +2 UDON SQUARE.
TAK TAK TAK
WE PLAY-TESTED THIS SO MUCH, I'VE GOT THE BOARD MOSTLY MEMORIZED...
!
Go shopping for a pen case with your best friend! [+6 Udon]
HUH?
THAT'S WEIRD ...
I DON'T REMEMBER THIS SQUARE.
THAT PEN CASE SURE IS OLD AND BEAT UP!
TOMORROW'S THE WEEKEND. SHALL I HELP YOU CHOOSE ONE?

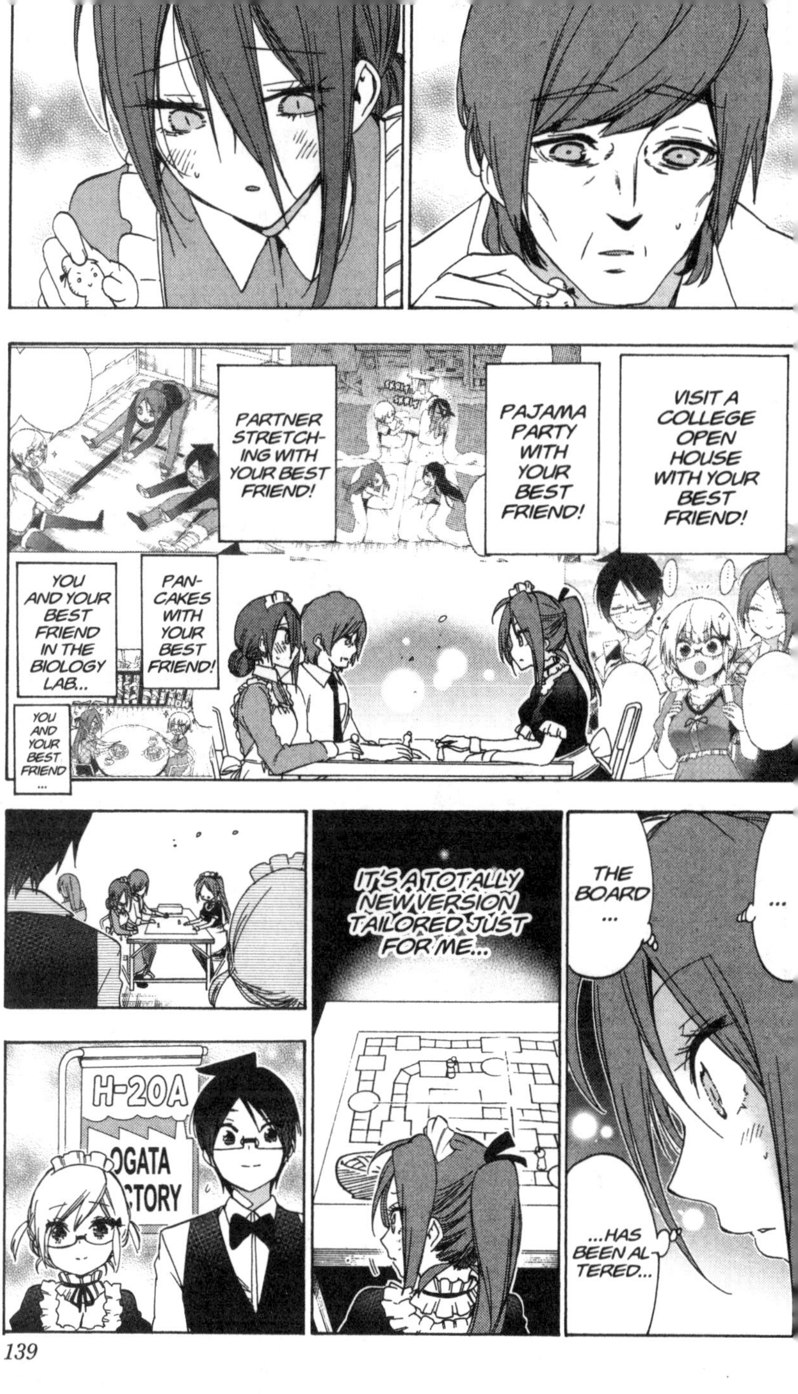
VISIT A COLLEGE OPEN HOUSE WITH YOUR BEST FRIEND!
PAJAMA PARTY WITH YOUR BEST FRIEND!
PARTNER STRETCHING WITH YOUR BEST FRIEND!
PANCAKES WITH YOUR BEST FRIEND!
YOU AND YOUR BEST FRIEND IN THE BIOLOGY LAB...
YOU AND YOUR BEST FRIEND ...
THE BOARD ...
...
...HAS BEEN ALTERED...
IT'S A TOTALLY NEW VERSION TAILORED JUST FOR ME...
H-20A
OGATA

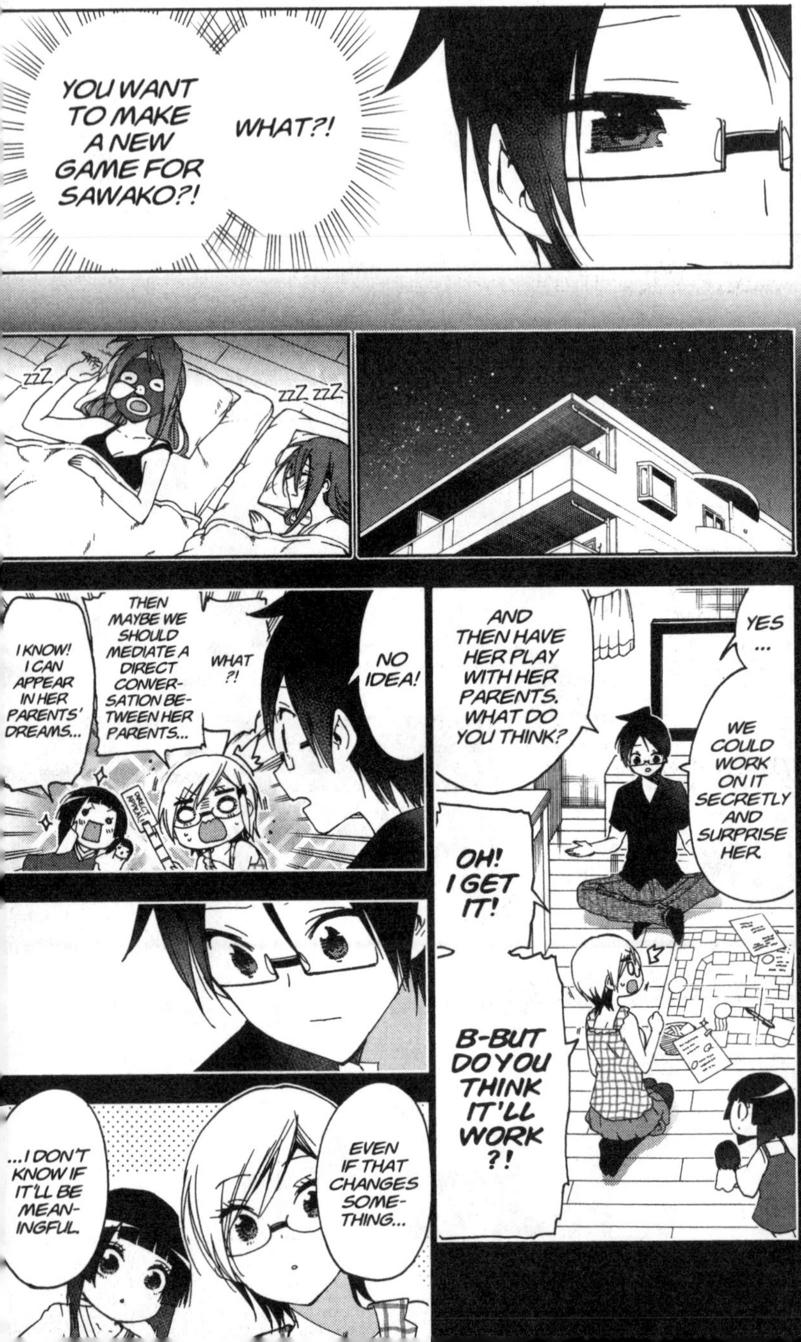
WHAT?!
YOU WANT TO MAKE A NEW GAME FOR SAWAKO?!
zzZ
zzZ zzZ
YES ...
WE COULD WORK ON IT SECRETLY AND SURPRISE HER.
AND THEN HAVE HER PLAY WITH HER PARENTS. WHAT DO YOU THINK?
OH! I GET IT!
B-BUT DO YOU THINK IT'LL WORK ?!
NO IDEA!
WHAT ?!
THEN MAYBE WE SHOULD MEDIATE A DIRECT CONVER-SATION BE-TWEEN HER PARENTS...
I KNOW! I CAN APPEAR IN HER PARENTS' DREAMS...
DIRECT APPEAL
EVEN IF THAT CHANGES SOME-THING...
...I DON'T KNOW IF IT'LL BE MEAN-INGFUL.

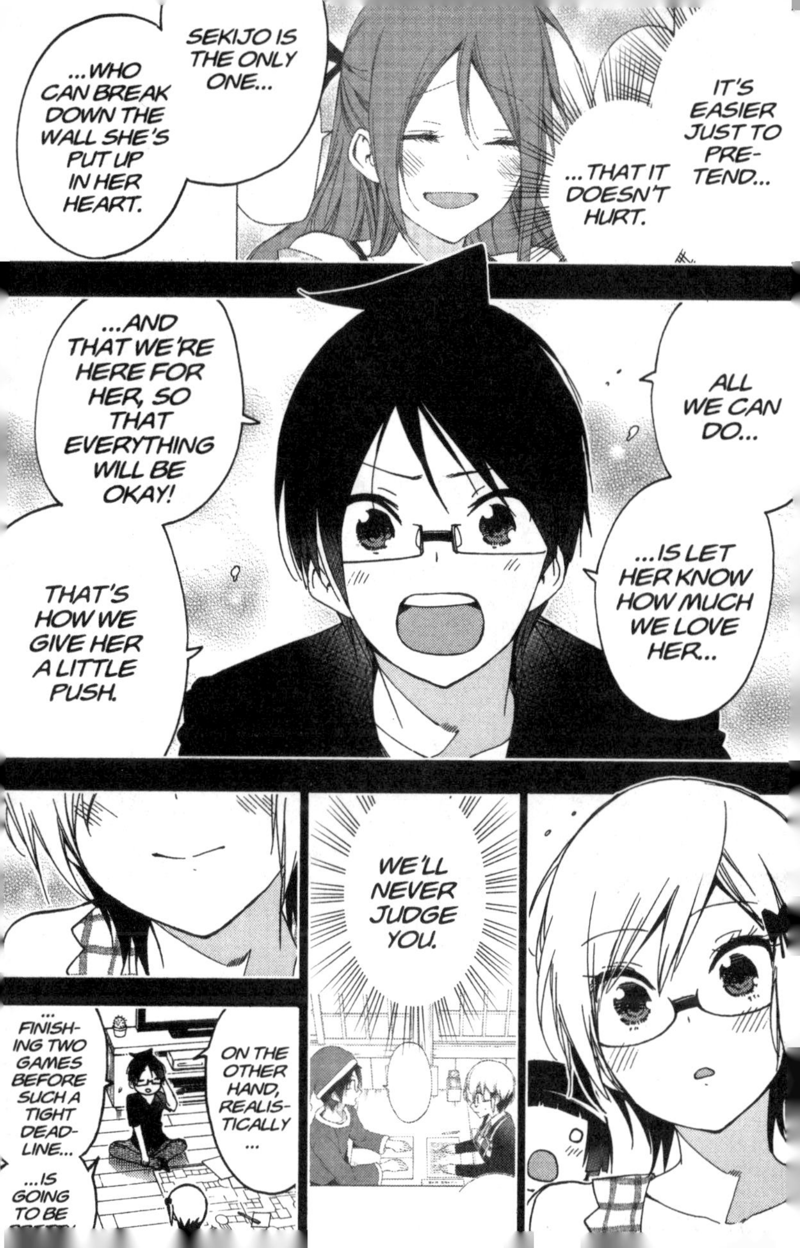
IT'S EASIER JUST TO PRE-TEND...
...THAT IT DOESN'T HURT.
SEKIJO IS THE ONLY ONE...
...WHO CAN BREAK DOWN THE WALL SHE'S PUT UP IN HER HEART.
ALL WE CAN DO...
...IS LET HER KNOW HOW MUCH WE LOVE HER...
...AND THAT WE'RE HERE FOR HER, SO THAT EVERYTHING WILL BE OKAY!
THAT'S HOW WE GIVE HER A LITTLE PUSH.
WE'LL NEVER JUDGE YOU.
ON THE OTHER HAND, REALIS-TICALLY...
...FINISH-ING TWO GAMES BEFORE SUCH A TIGHT DEAD-LINE...
...IS GOING TO BE

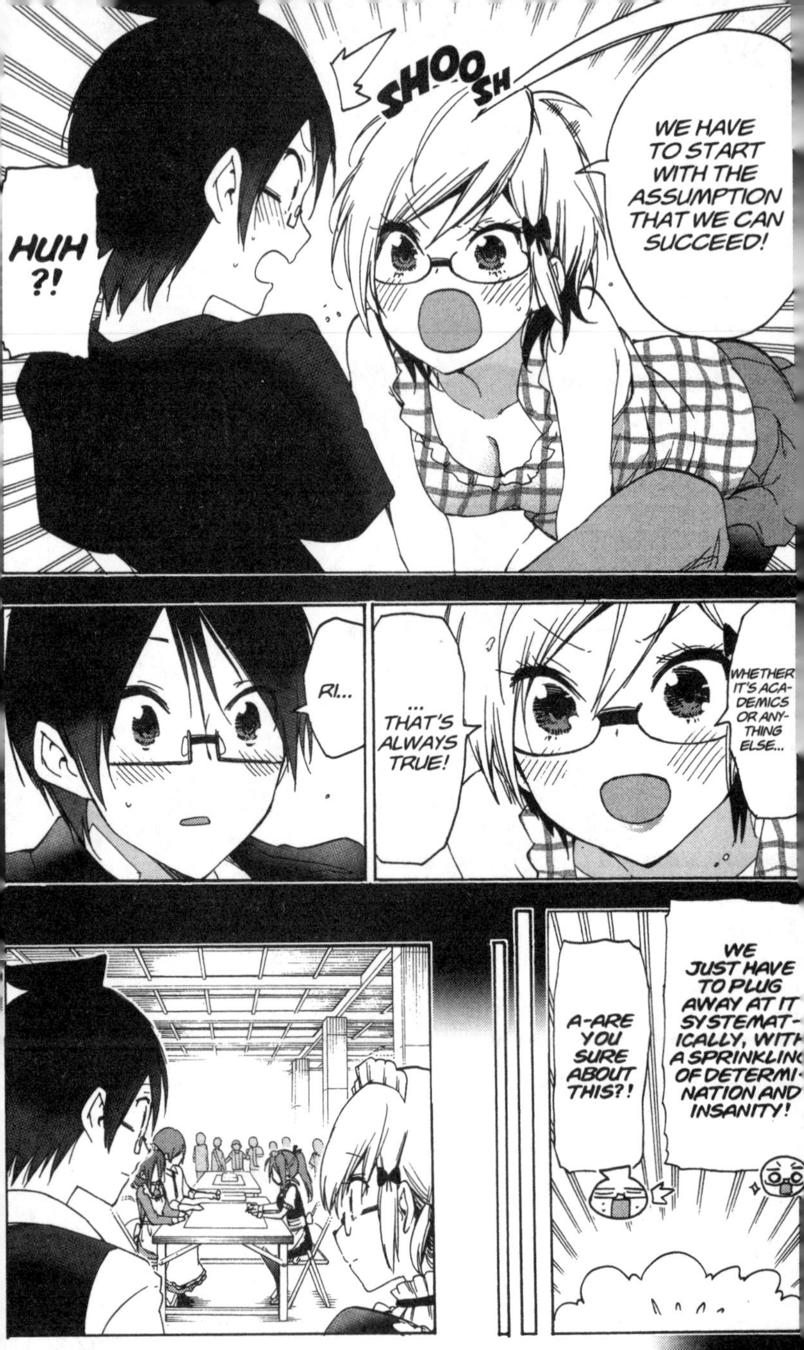
SHOOSH
WE HAVE TO START WITH THE ASSUMPTION THAT WE CAN SUCCEED!
HUH?!
WHETHER IT'S ACADEMICS OR ANYTHING ELSE...
... THAT'S ALWAYS TRUE!
RI...
WE JUST HAVE TO PLUG AWAY AT IT SYSTEMATICALLY, WITH A SPRINKLING OF DETERMINATION AND INSANITY!
A-ARE YOU SURE ABOUT THIS?!

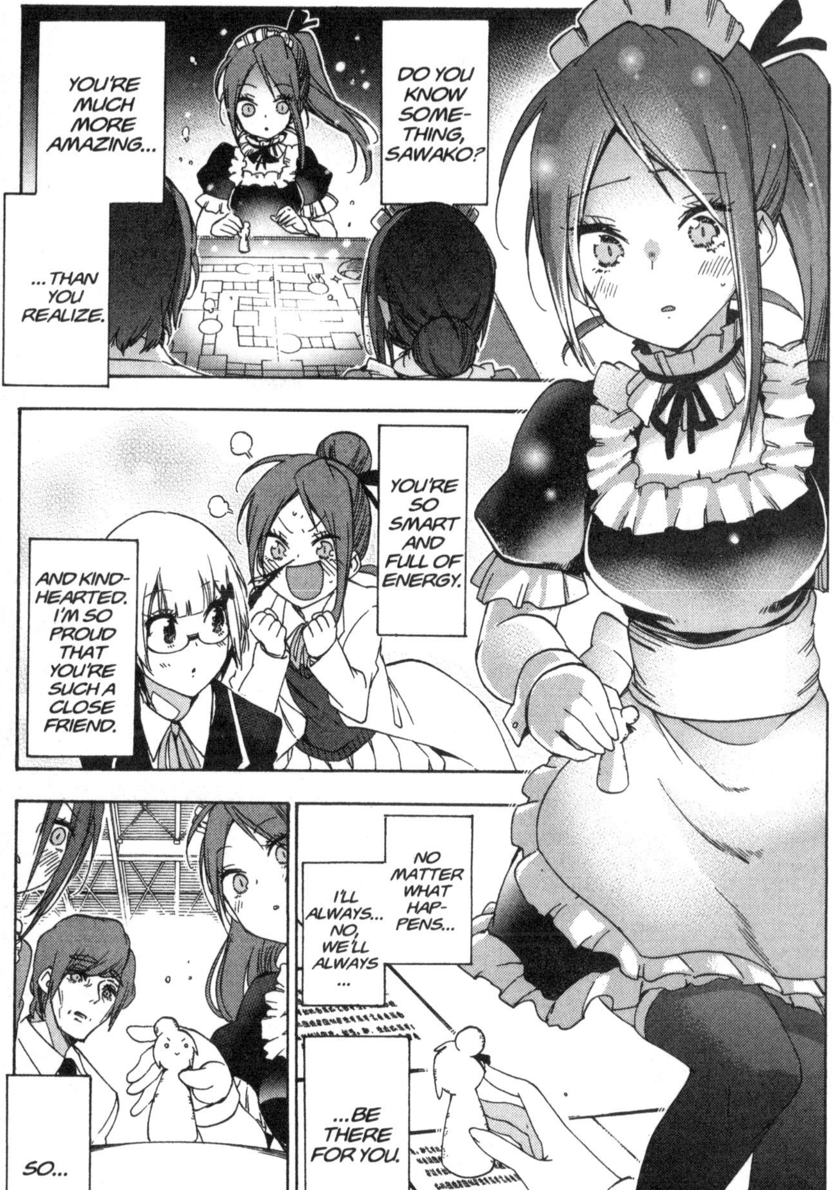
DO YOU KNOW SOME-THING, SAWAKO?
YOU'RE MUCH MORE AMAZING...
...THAN YOU REALIZE.
YOU'RE SO SMART AND FULL OF ENERGY.
AND KIND-HEARTED. I'M SO PROUD THAT YOU'RE SUCH A CLOSE FRIEND.
NO MATTER WHAT HAP-PENS...
I'LL ALWAYS... NO, WE'LL ALWAYS...
...BE THERE FOR YOU.
SO...

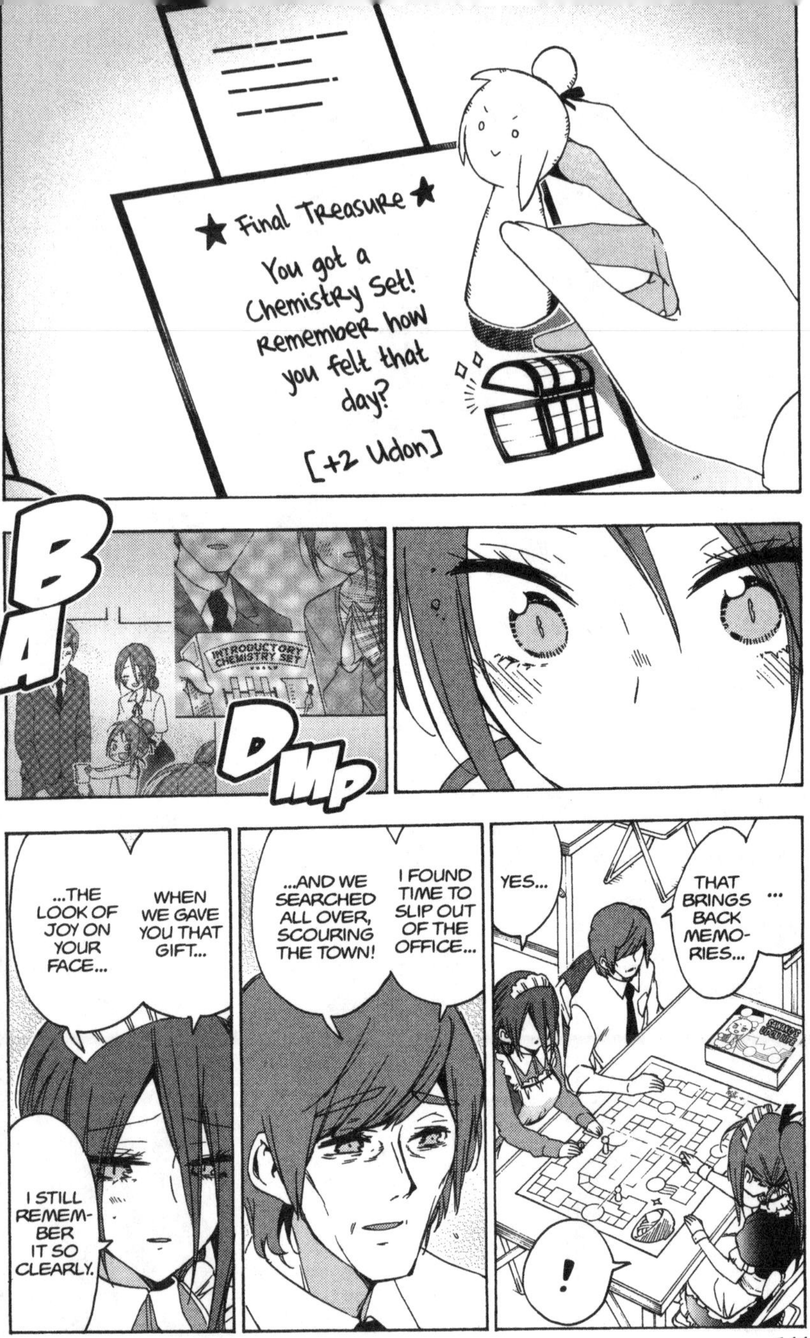
★ Final Treasure ★
You got a Chemistry Set! remember how you felt that day?
[+2 Udon]
BA
DMP
INTRODUCTORY CHEMISTRY SET
THAT BRINGS BACK MEMO-RIES... ...
YES...
!
I FOUND TIME TO SLIP OUT OF THE OFFICE...
...AND WE SEARCHED ALL OVER, SCOURING THE TOWN!
WHEN WE GAVE YOU THAT GIFT...
...THE LOOK OF JOY ON YOUR FACE...
I STILL REMEM-BER IT SO CLEARLY.

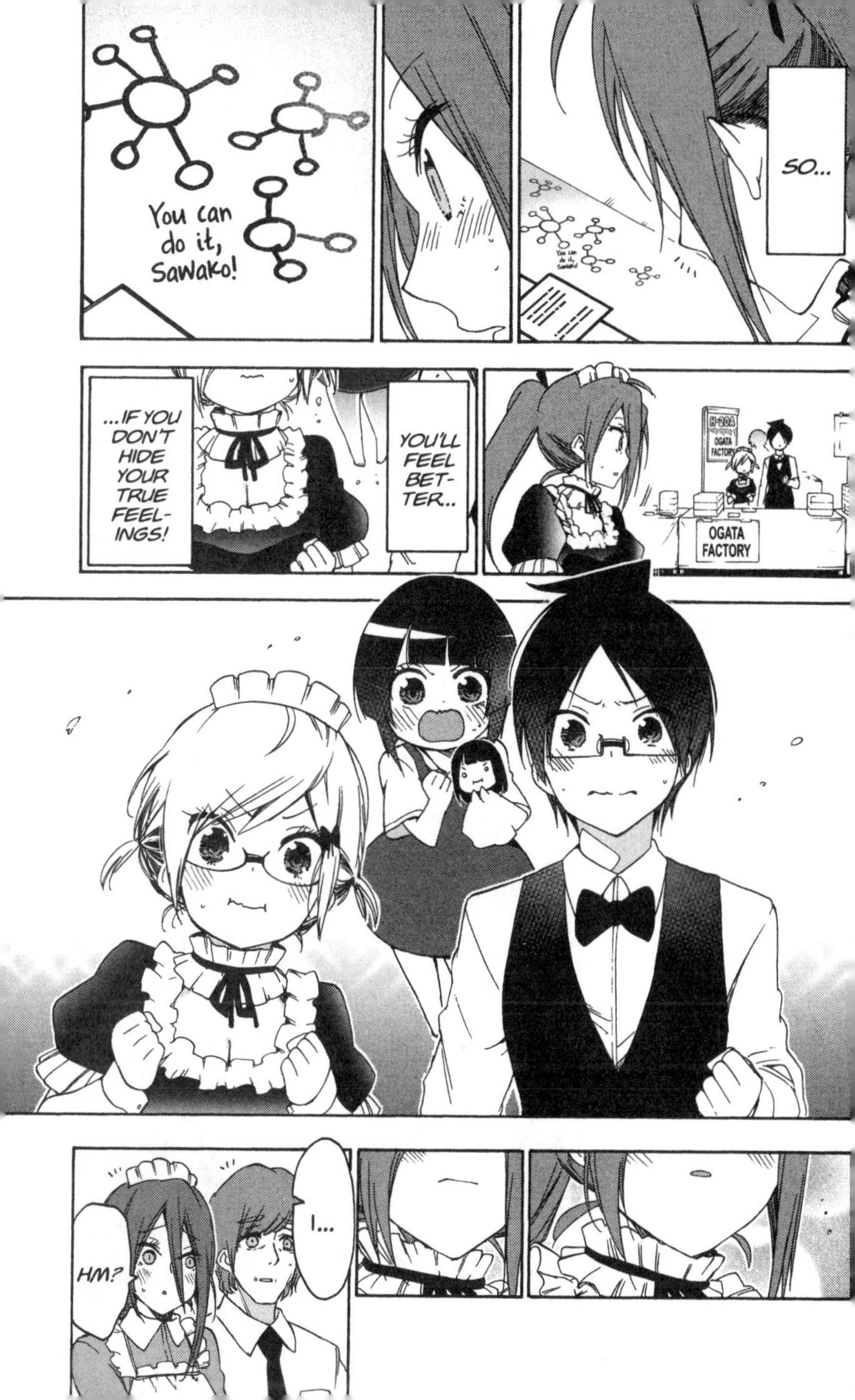
SO...
You can do it, Sawako!
H-20A
OGATA FACTORY
OGATA FACTORY
YOU'LL FEEL BETTER...
...IF YOU DON'T HIDE YOUR TRUE FEELINGS!
I...
HM?

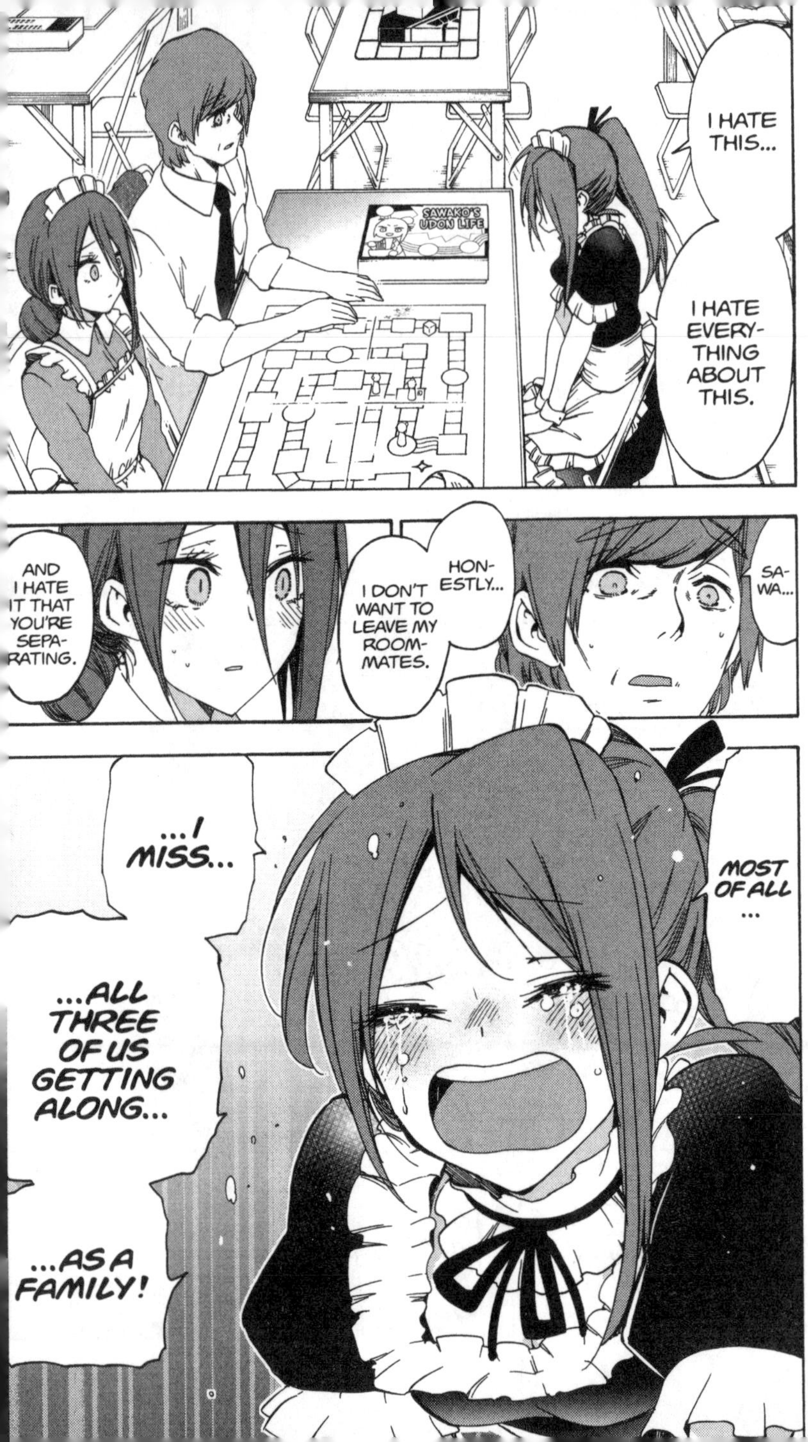
SAWAKO'S UDON LIFE
I HATE THIS...
I HATE EVERY-THING ABOUT THIS.
SA-WA...
HON-ESTLY...
I DON'T WANT TO LEAVE MY ROOM-MATES.
AND I HATE IT THAT YOU'RE SEPA-RATING.
MOST OF ALL ...
...I MISS...
...ALL THREE OF US GETTING ALONG...
...AS A FAMILY!

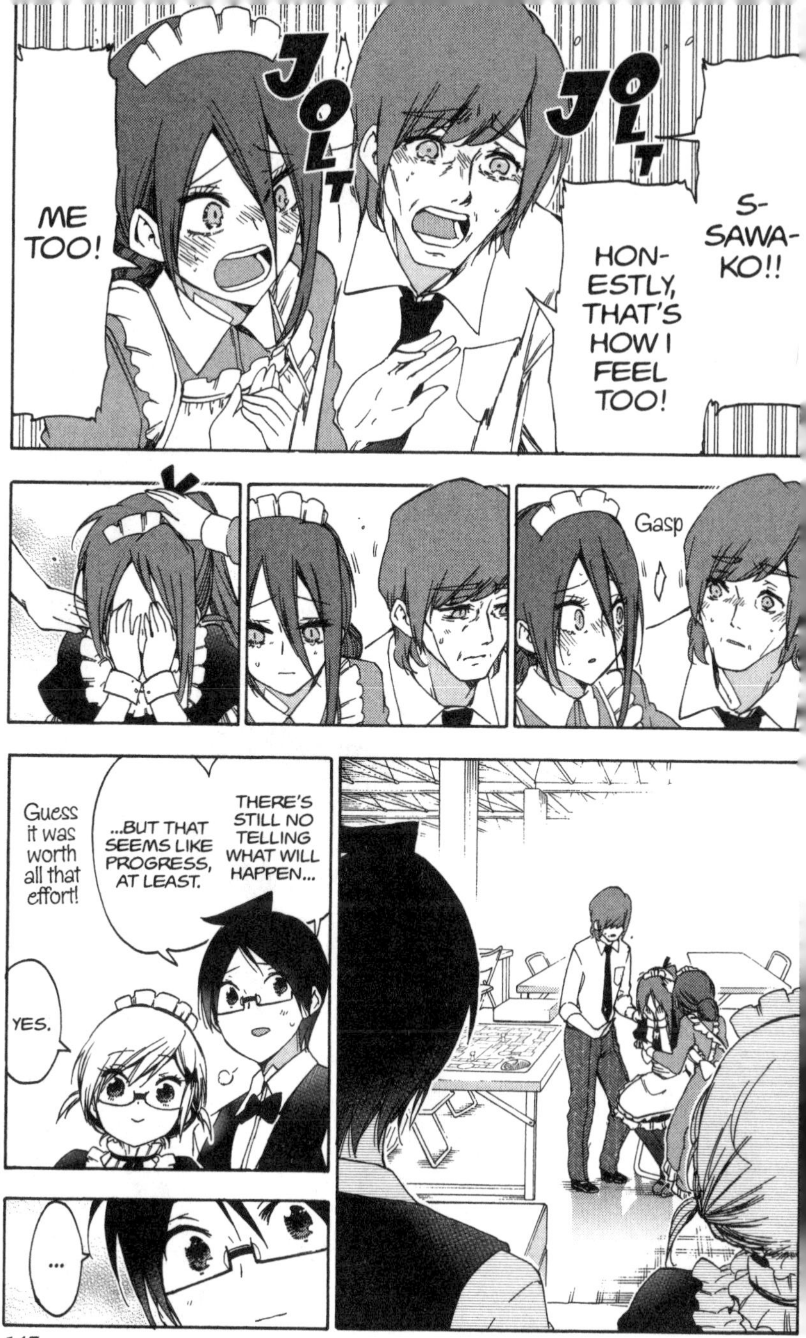
S-SAWAKO!!
HONESTLY, THAT'S HOW I FEEL TOO!
JOLT
JOLT
ME TOO!
Gasp
THERE'S STILL NO TELLING WHAT WILL HAPPEN...
...BUT THAT SEEMS LIKE PROGRESS, AT LEAST.
Guess it was worth all that effort!
YES.
...

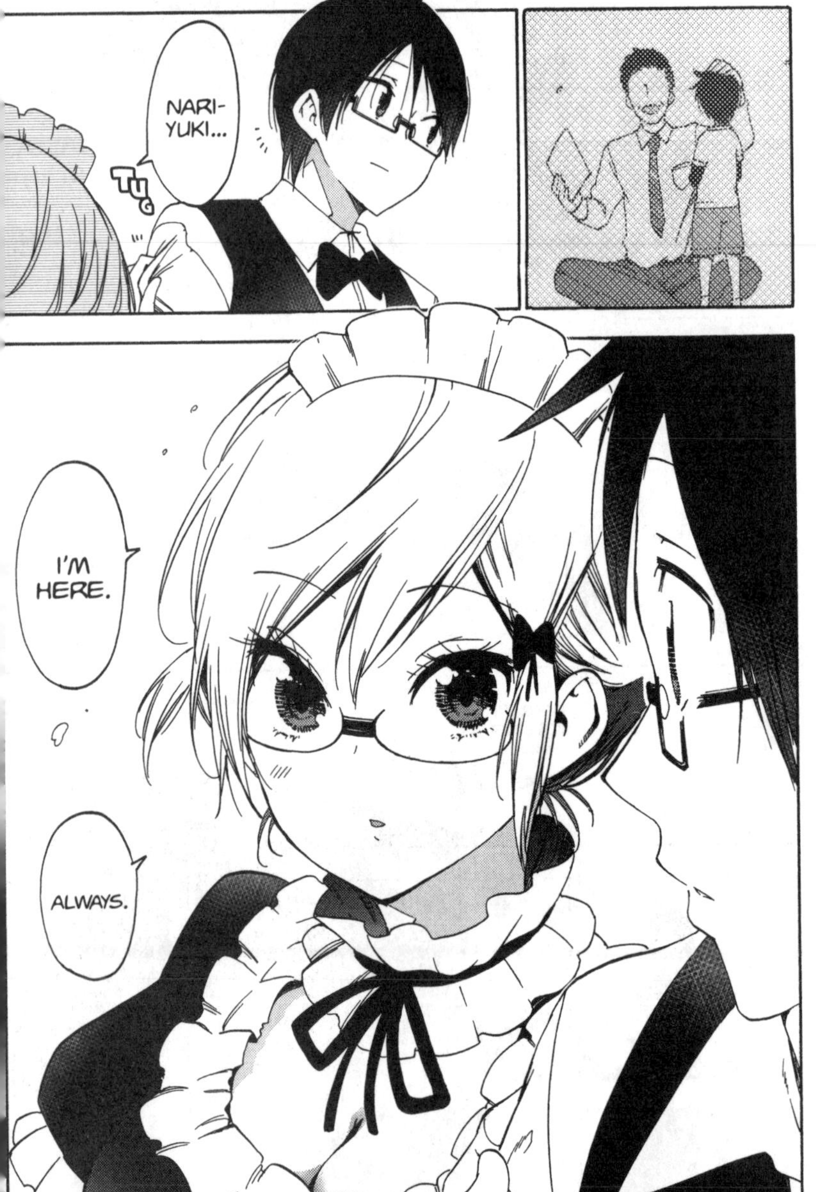
NARI-
YUKI...
TUG
I'M HERE.
ALWAYS.

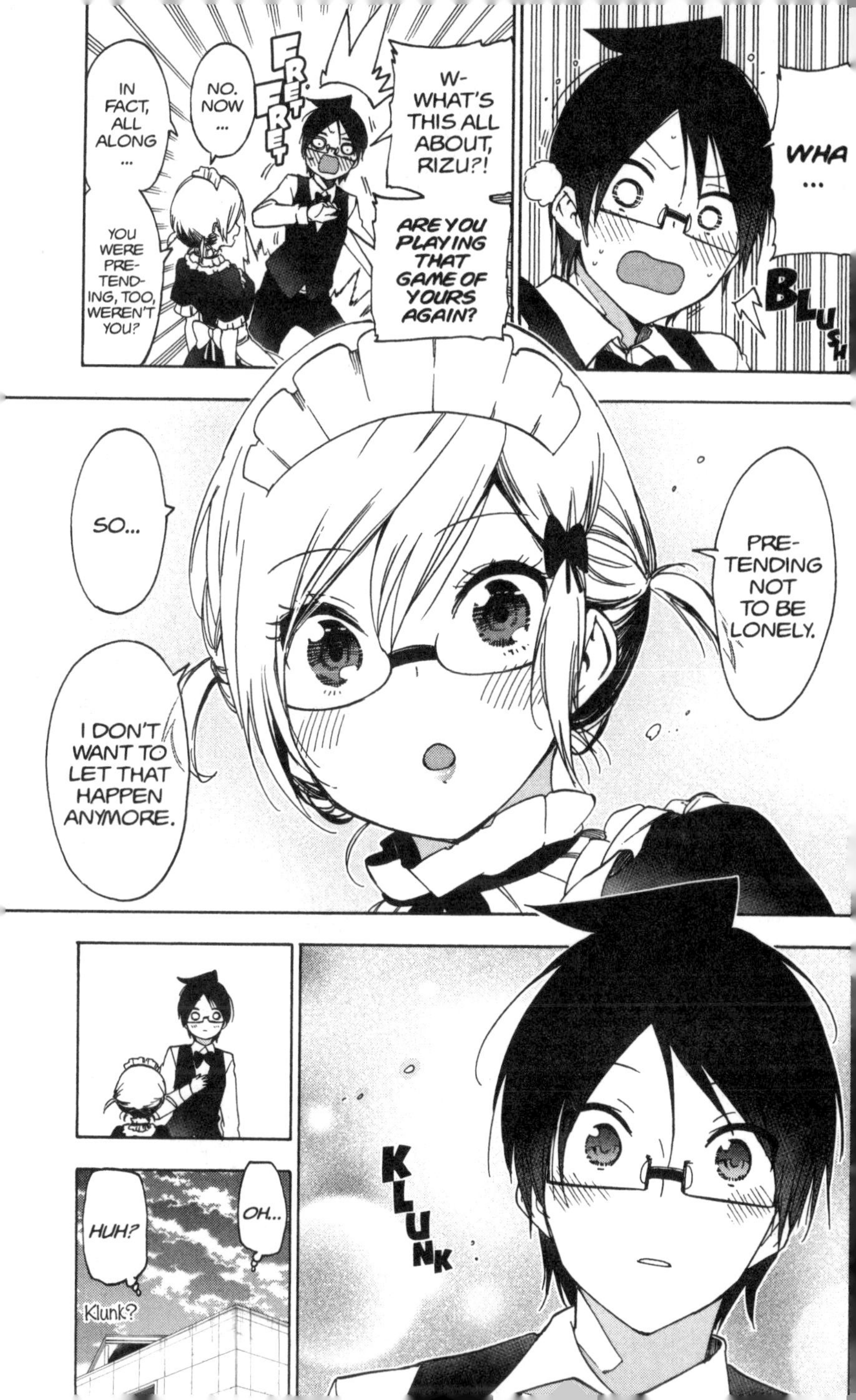
WHA ...
BLUSH
W-WHAT'S THIS ALL ABOUT, RIZU?!
ARE YOU PLAYING THAT GAME OF YOURS AGAIN?
FRET FRET
NO. NOW ...
IN FACT, ALL ALONG ...
YOU WERE PRE-TENDING, TOO, WEREN'T YOU?
PRE-TENDING NOT TO BE LONELY.
SO...
I DON'T WANT TO LET THAT HAPPEN ANYMORE.
KLUNK
OH...
HUH?
Klunk?

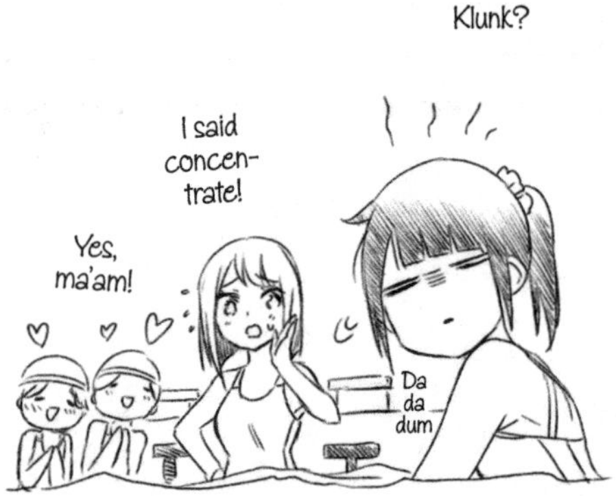
Klunk?
Da da dum
I said concen-trate!
Yes, ma'am!

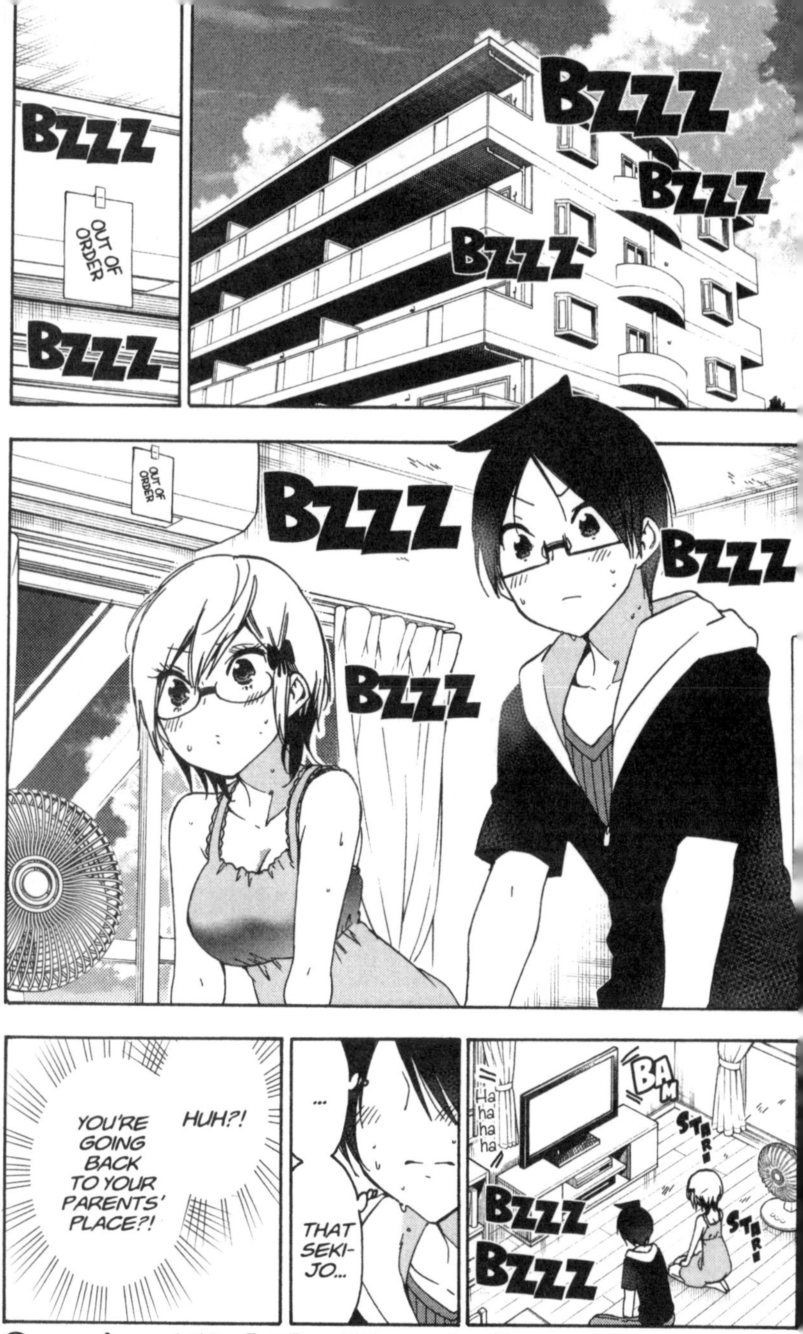
BZZZ
BZZZ
BZZZ
BZZZ
OUT OF ORDER
BZZZ
OUT OF ORDER
BZZZ
BZZZ
BZZZ
BAM
Ha ha ha ha
STARE
STARE
BZZZ
BZZZ
...
THAT SEKI-JO...
HUH?!
YOU'RE GOING BACK TO YOUR PARENTS' PLACE?!

Question 158: [X] = Thumbelina Supercomputer, Part 8

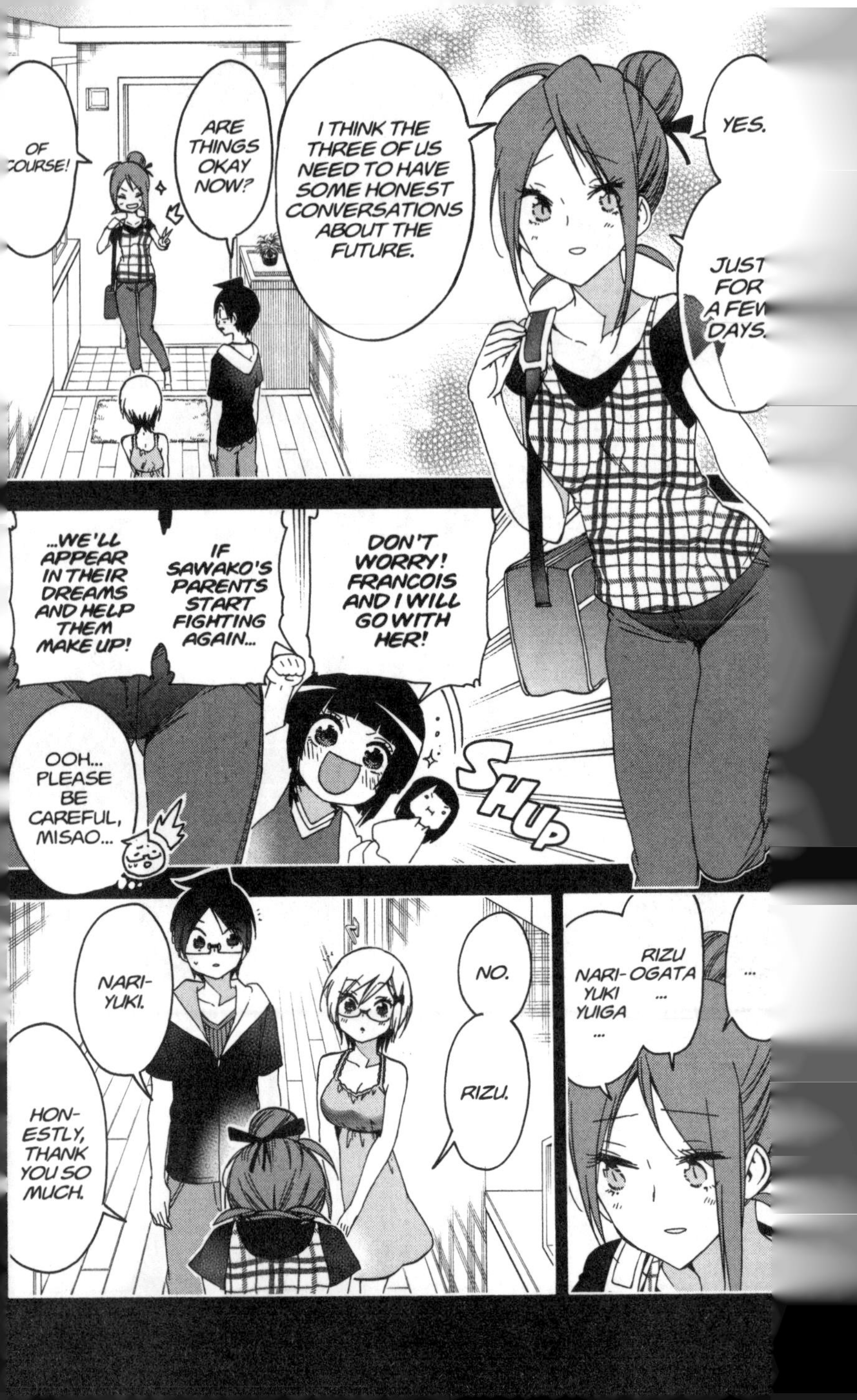
YES.
JUST FOR A FEW DAYS.
I THINK THE THREE OF US NEED TO HAVE SOME HONEST CONVERSATIONS ABOUT THE FUTURE.
ARE THINGS OKAY NOW?
OF COURSE!
DON'T WORRY! FRANCOIS AND I WILL GO WITH HER!
IF SAWAKO'S PARENTS START FIGHTING AGAIN...
...WE'LL APPEAR IN THEIR DREAMS AND HELP THEM MAKE UP!
SHUP
OOH... PLEASE BE CAREFUL, MISAO...
...
RIZU OGATA...
NARI-YUKI YUIGA...
NO.
RIZU.
NARI-YUKI.
HON-ESTLY, THANK YOU SO MUCH.

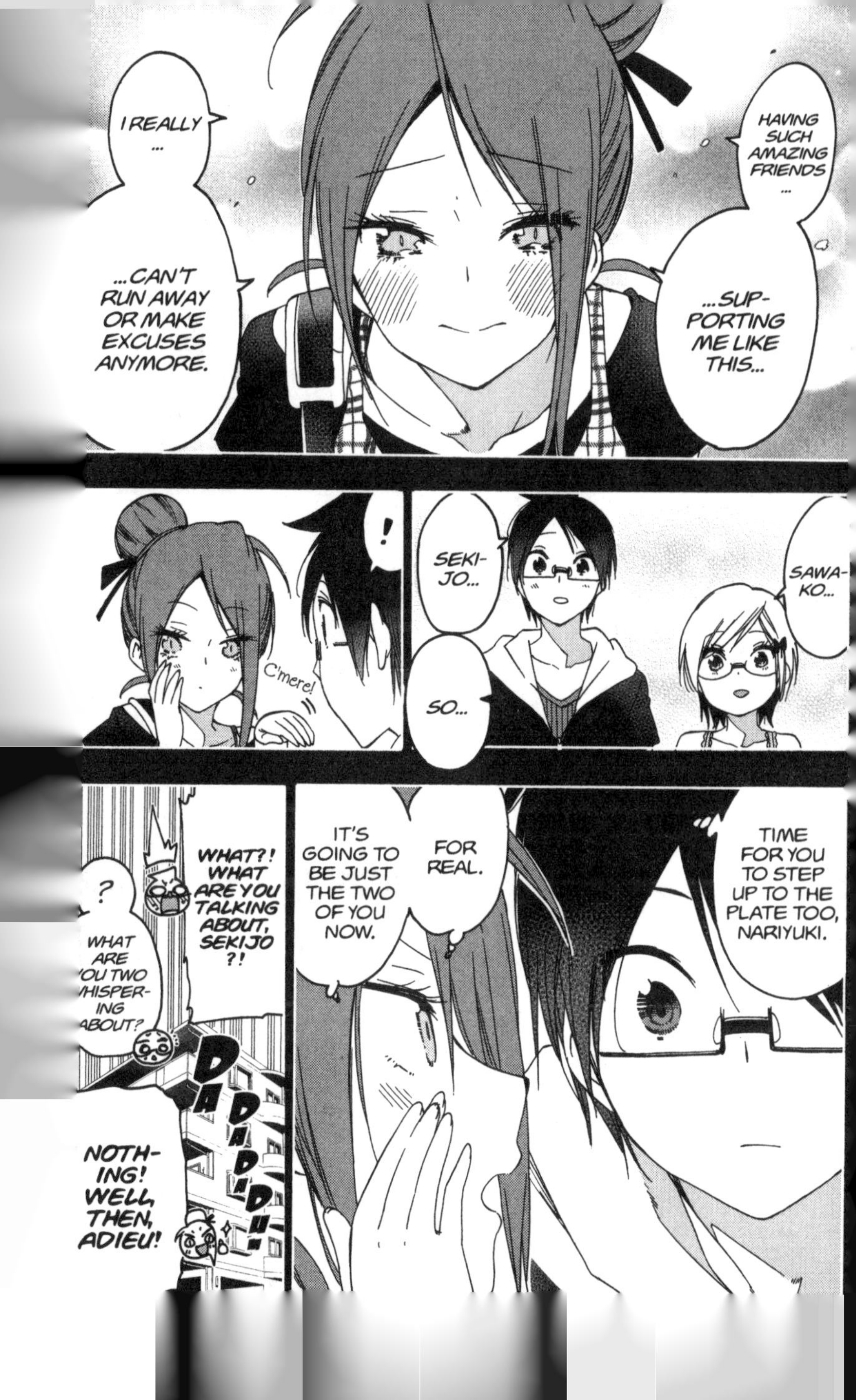

HAVING SUCH AMAZING FRIENDS...
...SUPPORTING ME LIKE THIS...
I REALLY...
...CAN'T RUN AWAY OR MAKE EXCUSES ANYMORE.
SAWAKO...
SEKIJO...
SO...
!
C'mere!
TIME FOR YOU TO STEP UP TO THE PLATE TOO, NARIYUKI.
FOR REAL.
IT'S GOING TO BE JUST THE TWO OF YOU NOW.
WHAT?! WHAT ARE YOU TALKING ABOUT, SEKIJO?!
?
WHAT ARE YOU TWO WHISPERING ABOUT?
DA DA DA DU
NOTHING! WELL, THEN, ADIEU!

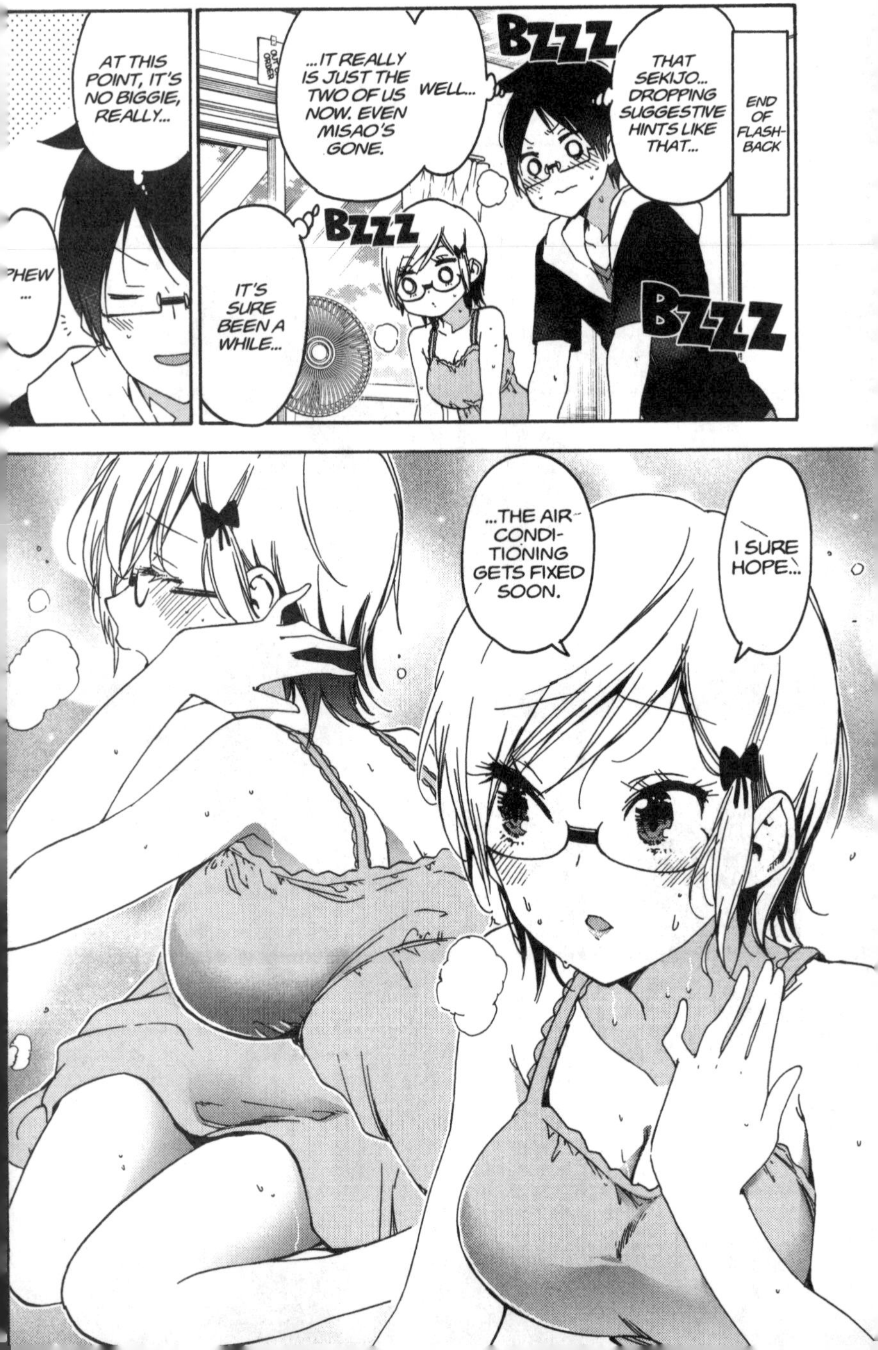
END OF FLASH-BACK
THAT SEKIJO... DROPPING SUGGESTIVE HINTS LIKE THAT...
BZZZ
WELL...
...IT REALLY IS JUST THE TWO OF US NOW. EVEN MISAO'S GONE.
OUT OF ORDER
BZZZ
IT'S SURE BEEN A WHILE...
BZZZ
AT THIS POINT, IT'S NO BIGGIE, REALLY...
PHEW ...
I SURE HOPE...
...THE AIR CONDITIONING GETS FIXED SOON.

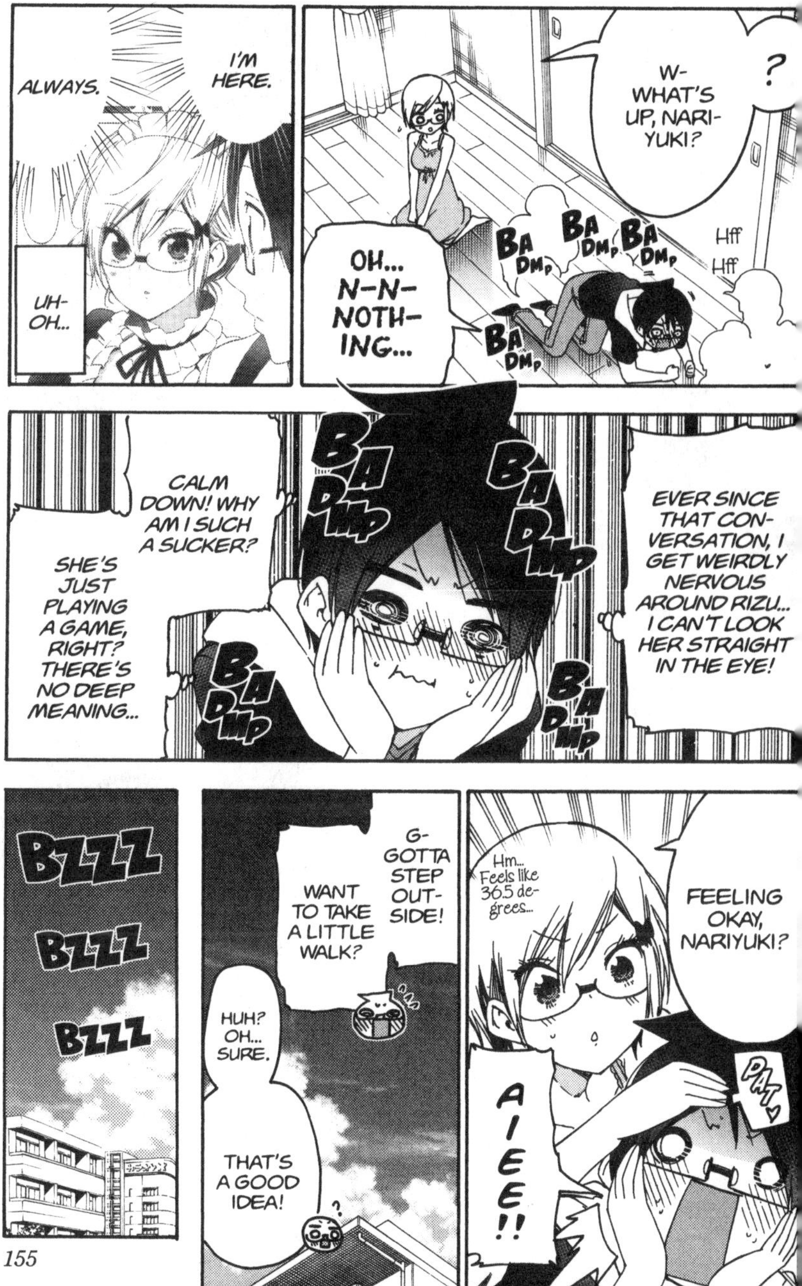
?
W-WHAT'S UP, NARI-YUKI?
BADMP BADMP BADMP
Hff Hff
OH... N-N-NOTHING...
BADMP
I'M HERE.
ALWAYS.
UH-OH...
BADMP BADMP
EVER SINCE THAT CONVERSATION, I GET WEIRDLY NERVOUS AROUND RIZU... I CAN'T LOOK HER STRAIGHT IN THE EYE!
CALM DOWN! WHY AM I SUCH A SUCKER?
SHE'S JUST PLAYING A GAME, RIGHT? THERE'S NO DEEP MEANING...
BADMP BADMP
FEELING OKAY, NARIYUKI?
Hm... Feels like 36.5 degrees...
PAT
AIEE!!
G-GOTTA STEP OUTSIDE!
WANT TO TAKE A LITTLE WALK?
HUH? OH... SURE.
THAT'S A GOOD IDEA!
BZZZ
BZZZ
BZZZ

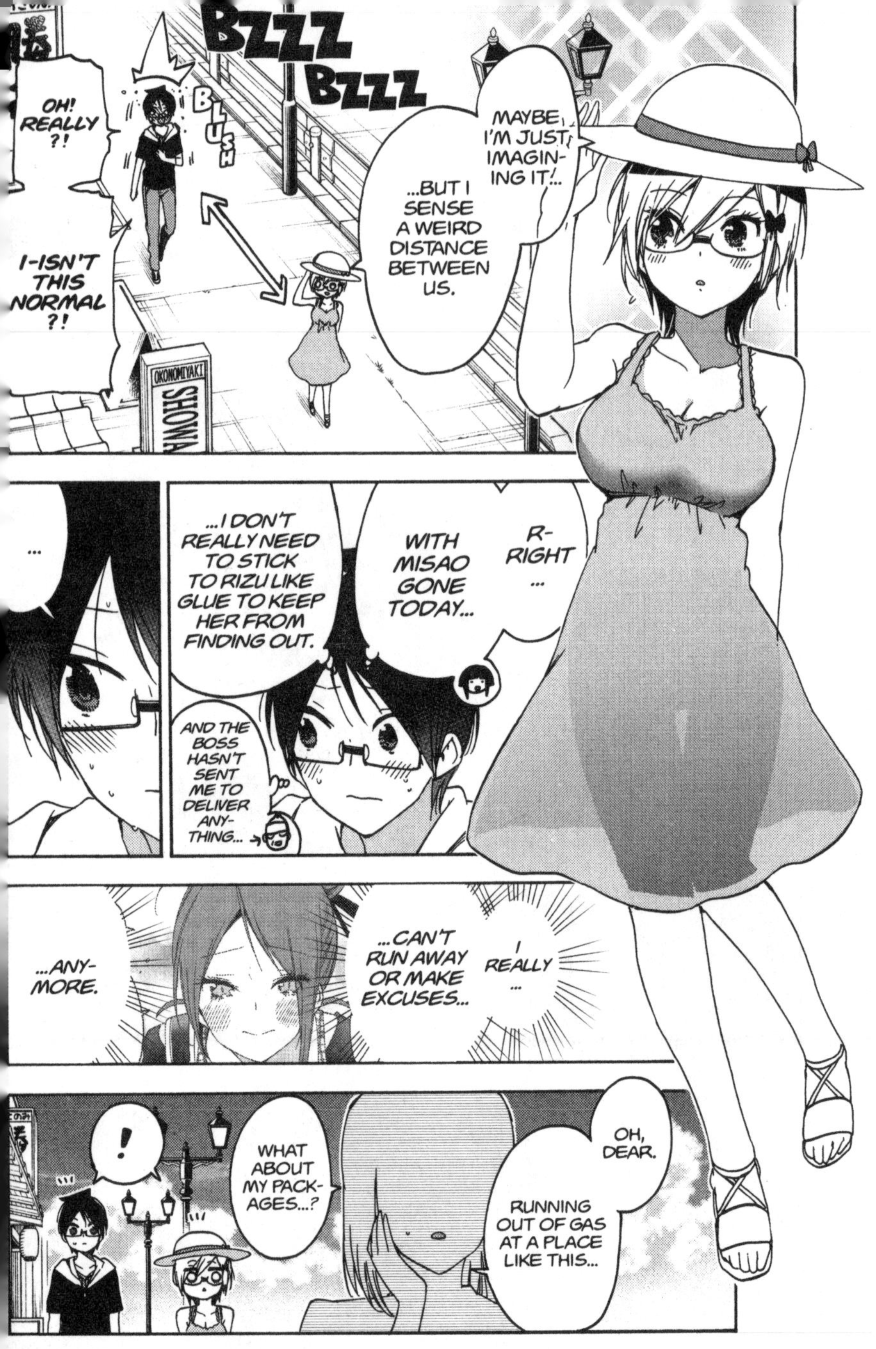
MAYBE I'M JUST IMAGINING IT!...
...BUT I SENSE A WEIRD DISTANCE BETWEEN US.
BZZZ BZZZ
BLUSH
OH! REALLY?!
I-ISN'T THIS NORMAL?!
OKONOMIYAKI
R-RIGHT...
WITH MISAO GONE TODAY...
...I DON'T REALLY NEED TO STICK TO RIZU LIKE GLUE TO KEEP HER FROM FINDING OUT.
AND THE BOSS HASN'T SENT ME TO DELIVER ANYTHING...
...
I REALLY...
...CAN'T RUN AWAY OR MAKE EXCUSES...
...ANYMORE.
OH, DEAR.
RUNNING OUT OF GAS AT A PLACE LIKE THIS...
WHAT ABOUT MY PACKAGES...?
!

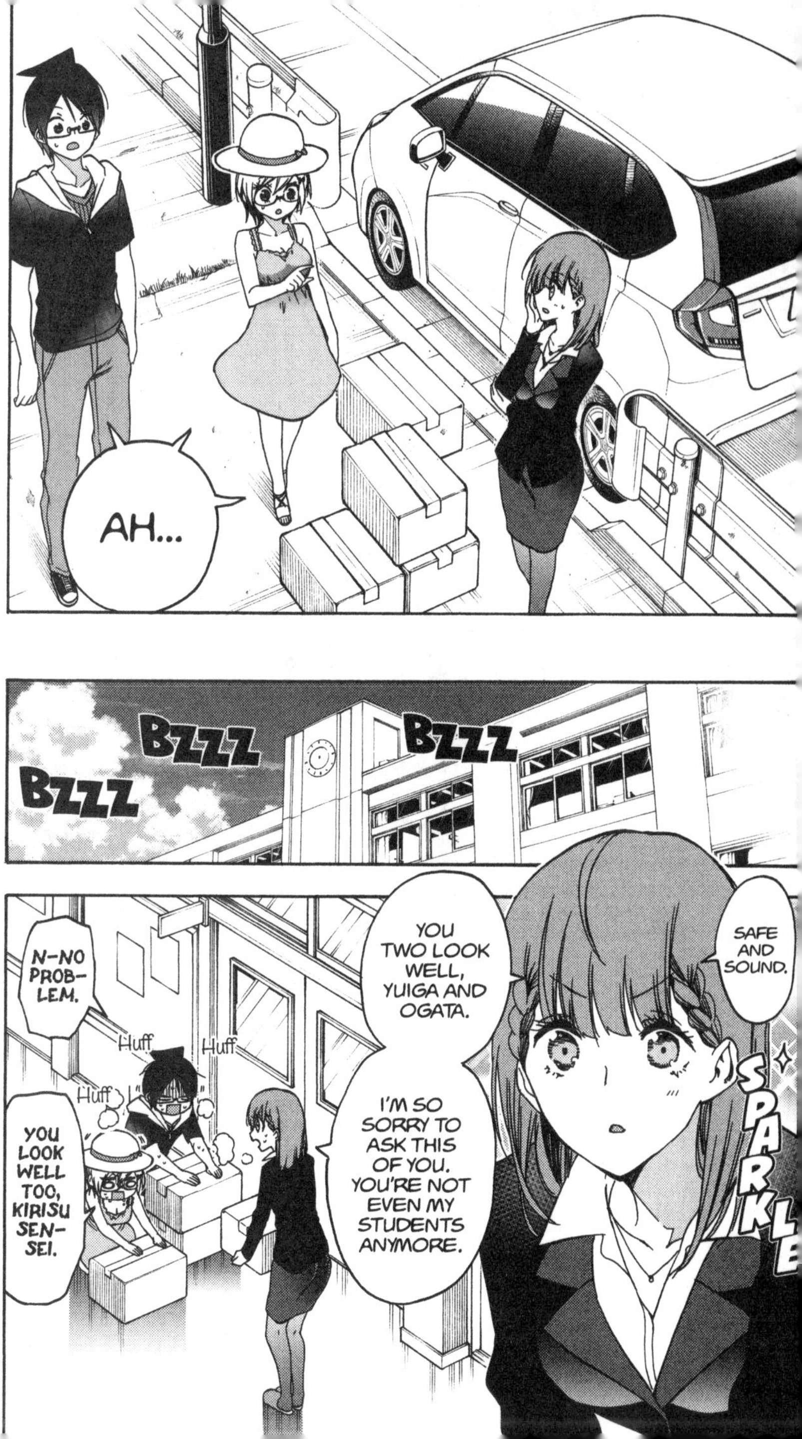
AH...
BZZZ
BZZZ
BZZZ
SAFE AND SOUND.
SPARKLE
YOU TWO LOOK WELL, YUIGA AND OGATA.
I'M SO SORRY TO ASK THIS OF YOU. YOU'RE NOT EVEN MY STUDENTS ANYMORE.
N-NO PROB-LEM.
Huff
Huff
Huff
YOU LOOK WELL TOO, KIRISU SEN-SEI.

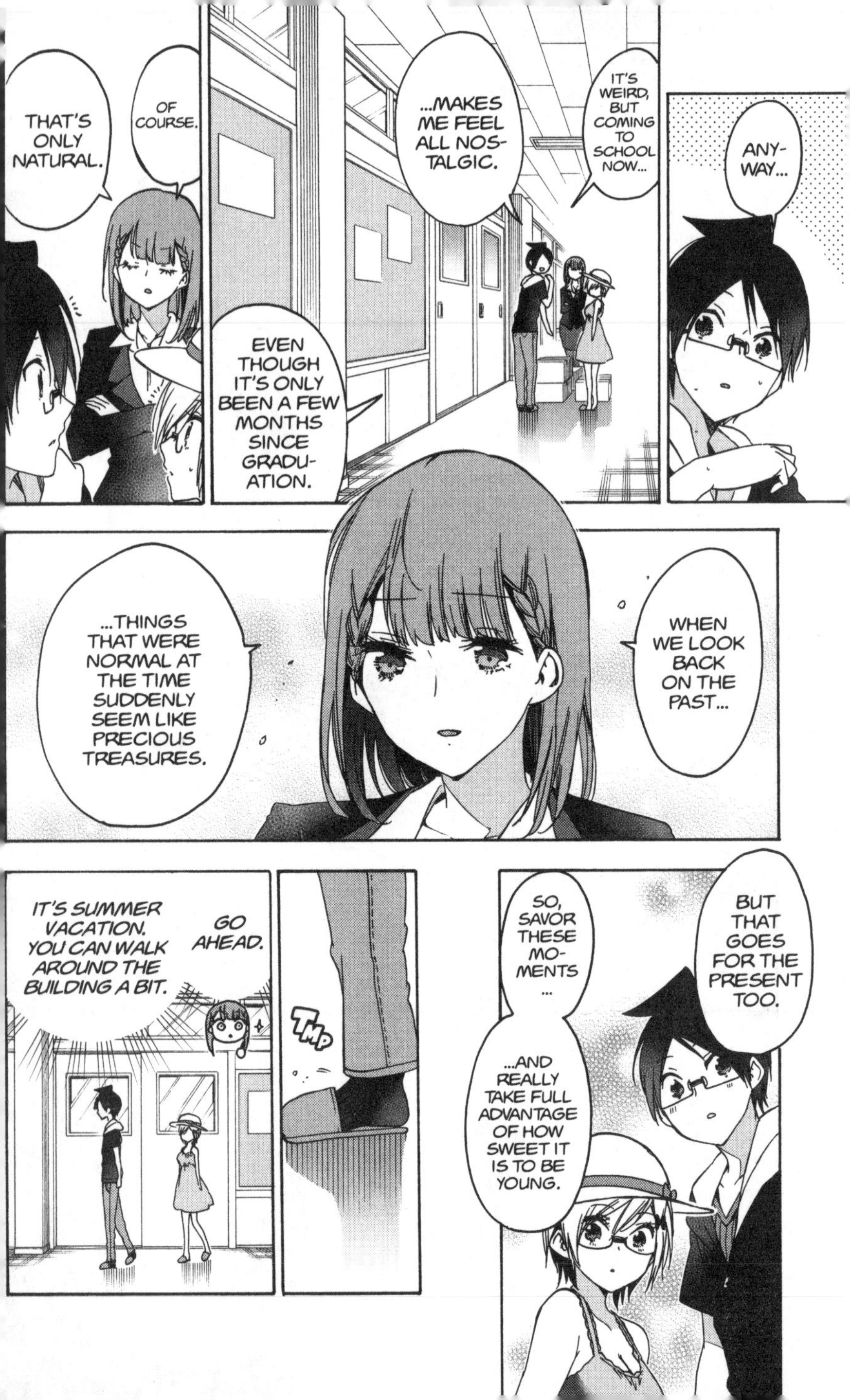
ANYWAY...
IT'S WEIRD, BUT COMING TO SCHOOL NOW...
...MAKES ME FEEL ALL NOSTALGIC.
EVEN THOUGH IT'S ONLY BEEN A FEW MONTHS SINCE GRADUATION.
OF COURSE.
THAT'S ONLY NATURAL.
WHEN WE LOOK BACK ON THE PAST...
...THINGS THAT WERE NORMAL AT THE TIME SUDDENLY SEEM LIKE PRECIOUS TREASURES.
BUT THAT GOES FOR THE PRESENT TOO.
SO, SAVOR THESE MOMENTS...
...AND REALLY TAKE FULL ADVANTAGE OF HOW SWEET IT IS TO BE YOUNG.
TMP
GO AHEAD.
IT'S SUMMER VACATION. YOU CAN WALK AROUND THE BUILDING A BIT.

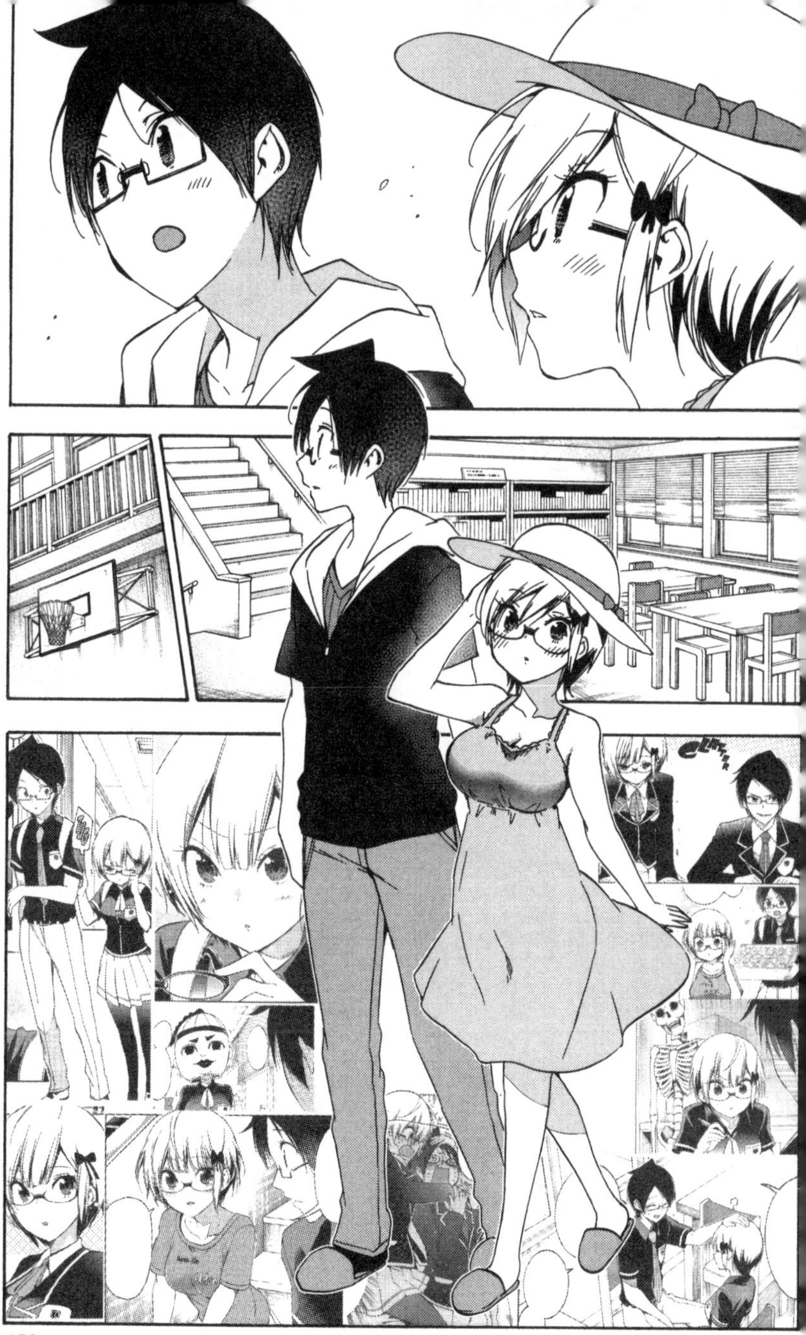
GLITTER

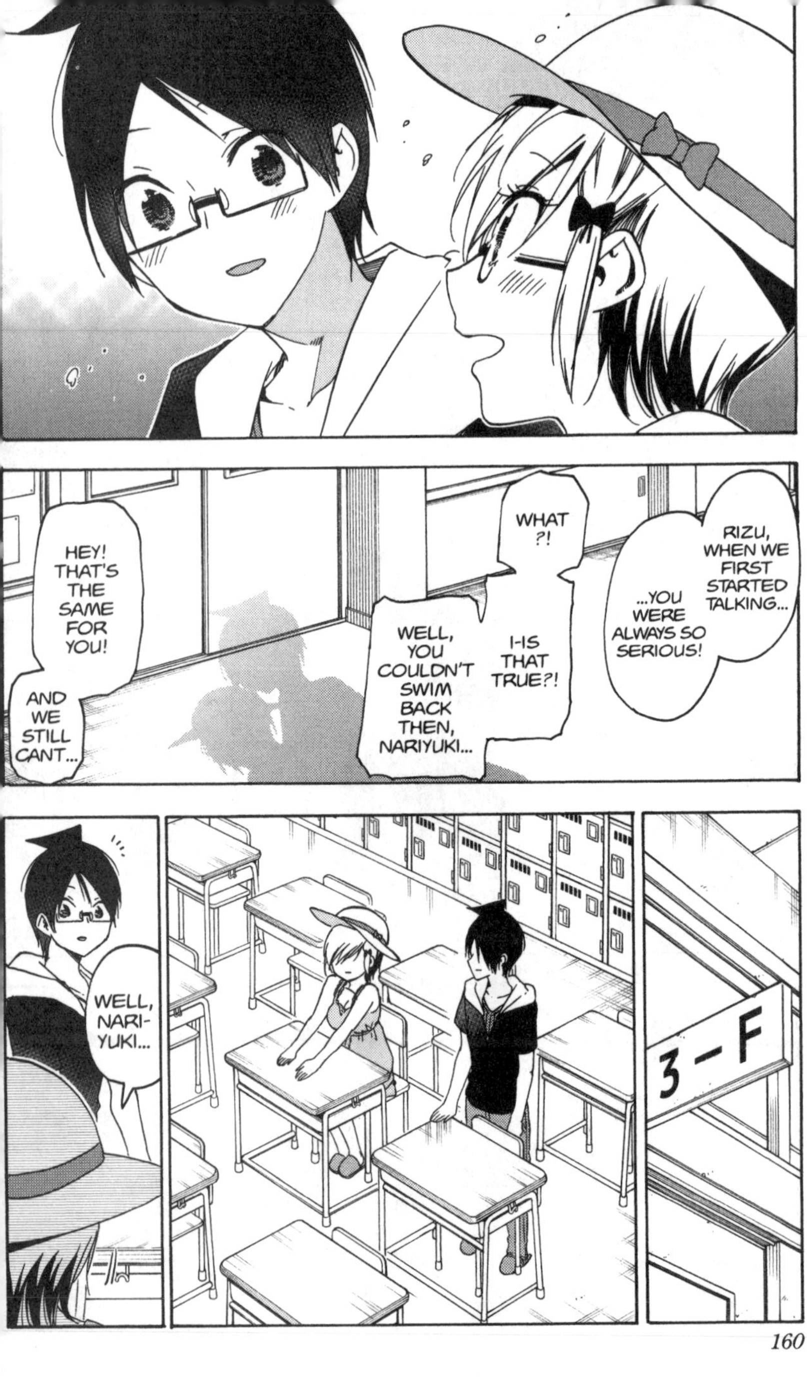
RIZU, WHEN WE FIRST STARTED TALKING...
...YOU WERE ALWAYS SO SERIOUS!
WHAT?!
I-IS THAT TRUE?!
WELL, YOU COULDN'T SWIM BACK THEN, NARIYUKI...
HEY! THAT'S THE SAME FOR YOU!
AND WE STILL CANT...
3-F
WELL, NARI-YUKI...

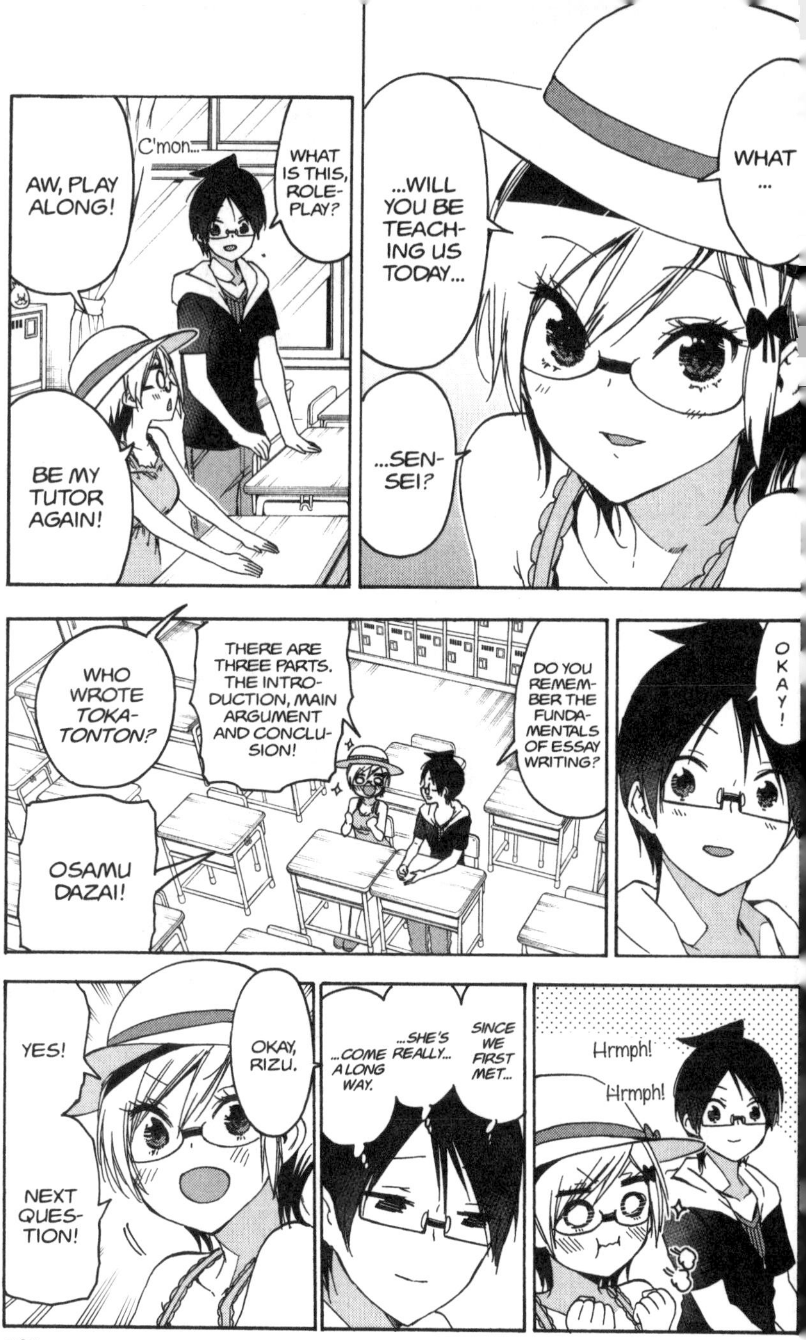
WHAT ...
...WILL YOU BE TEACHING US TODAY...
...SENSEI?
WHAT IS THIS, ROLE-PLAY?
C'mon...
AW, PLAY ALONG!
BE MY TUTOR AGAIN!
OKAY!
DO YOU REMEMBER THE FUNDAMENTALS OF ESSAY WRITING?
THERE ARE THREE PARTS. THE INTRODUCTION, MAIN ARGUMENT AND CONCLUSION!
WHO WROTE *TOKA-TONTON?*
OSAMU DAZAI!
Hrmph!
Hrmph!
SINCE WE FIRST MET...
...SHE'S REALLY...
...COME A LONG WAY.
OKAY, RIZU.
YES!
NEXT QUESTION!

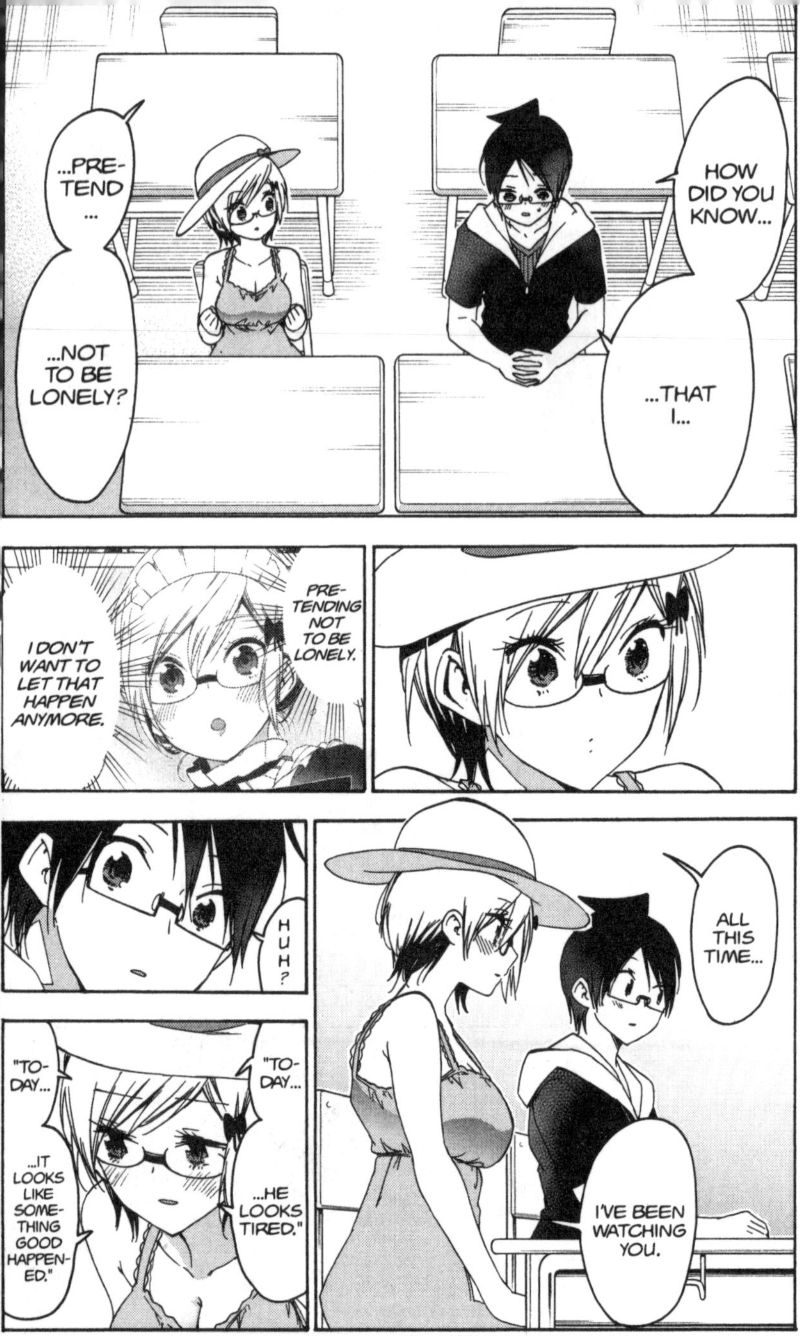
HOW DID YOU KNOW...
...THAT I...
...PRE-TEND...
...NOT TO BE LONELY?
PRE-TENDING NOT TO BE LONELY.
I DON'T WANT TO LET THAT HAPPEN ANYMORE.
ALL THIS TIME...
I'VE BEEN WATCHING YOU.
HUH?
"TO-DAY...
...HE LOOKS TIRED."
"TO-DAY...
...IT LOOKS LIKE SOME-THING GOOD HAPPEN-ED."

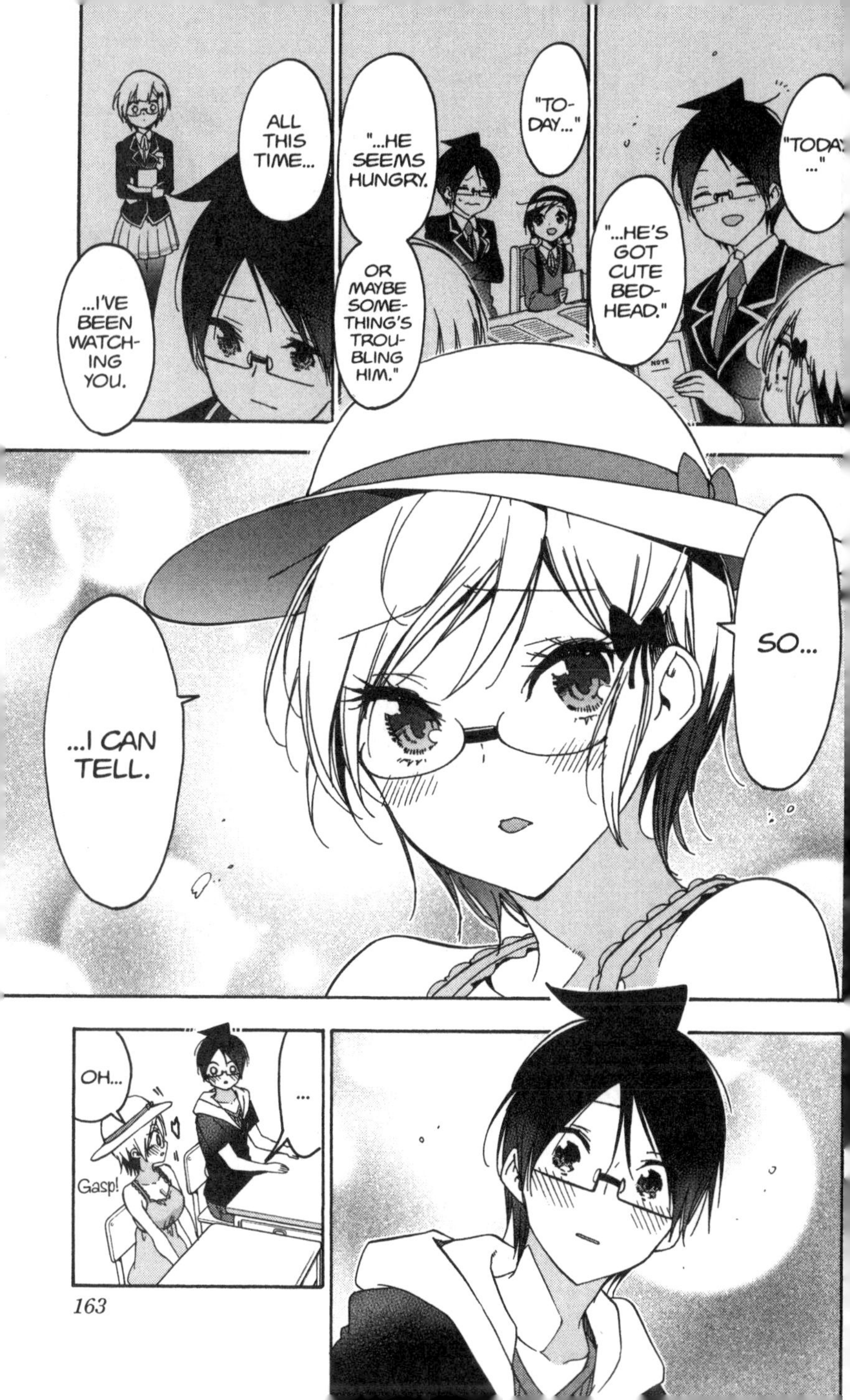
"TODAY..."
"...HE'S GOT CUTE BED-HEAD."
"TO-DAY..."
"...HE SEEMS HUNGRY.
OR MAYBE SOME-THING'S TROU-BLING HIM."
ALL THIS TIME...
...I'VE BEEN WATCH-ING YOU.
SO...
...I CAN TELL.
...
OH...
Gasp!

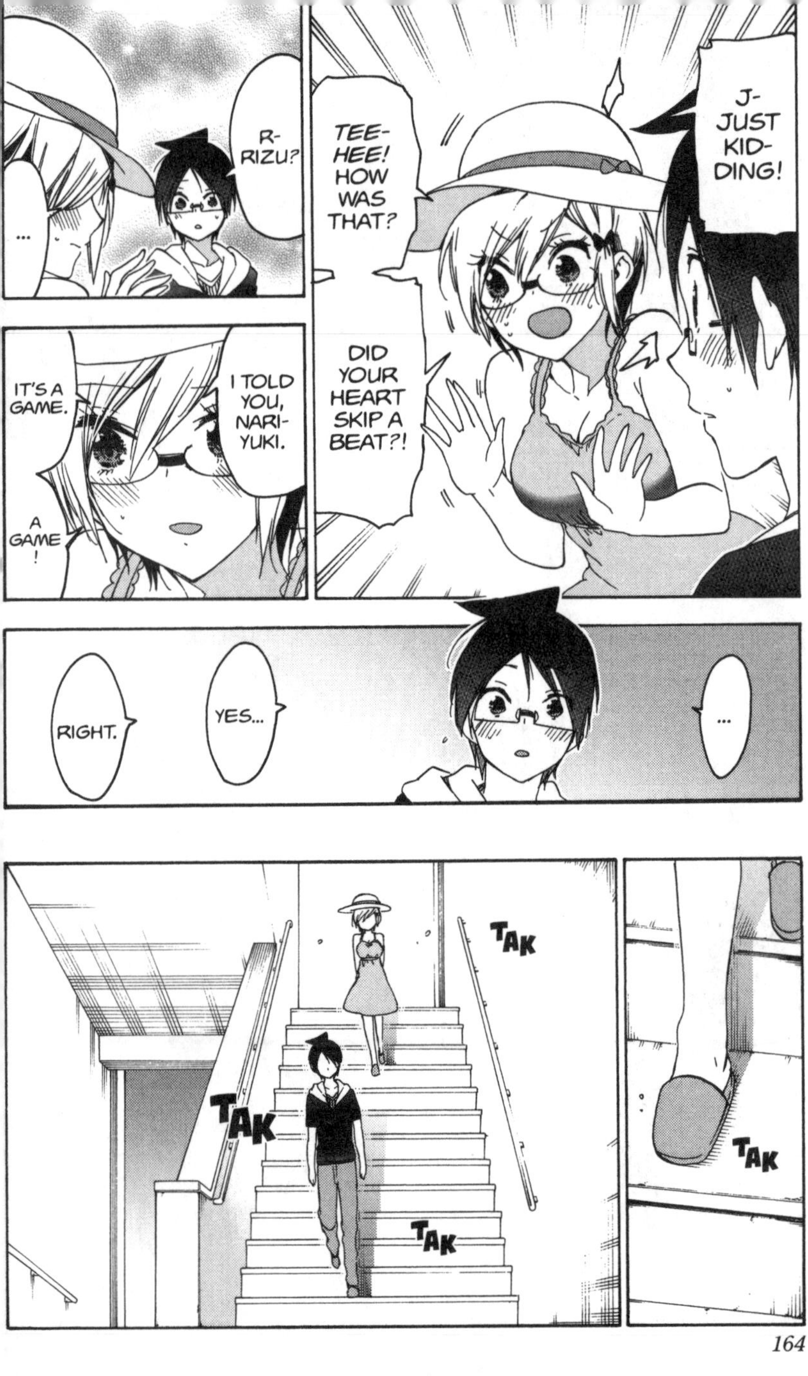
J-JUST KID-DING!
TEE-HEE! HOW WAS THAT?
DID YOUR HEART SKIP A BEAT?!
R-RIZU?
...
I TOLD YOU, NARI-YUKI.
IT'S A GAME.
A GAME!
...
YES...
RIGHT.
TAK
TAK
TAK
TAK

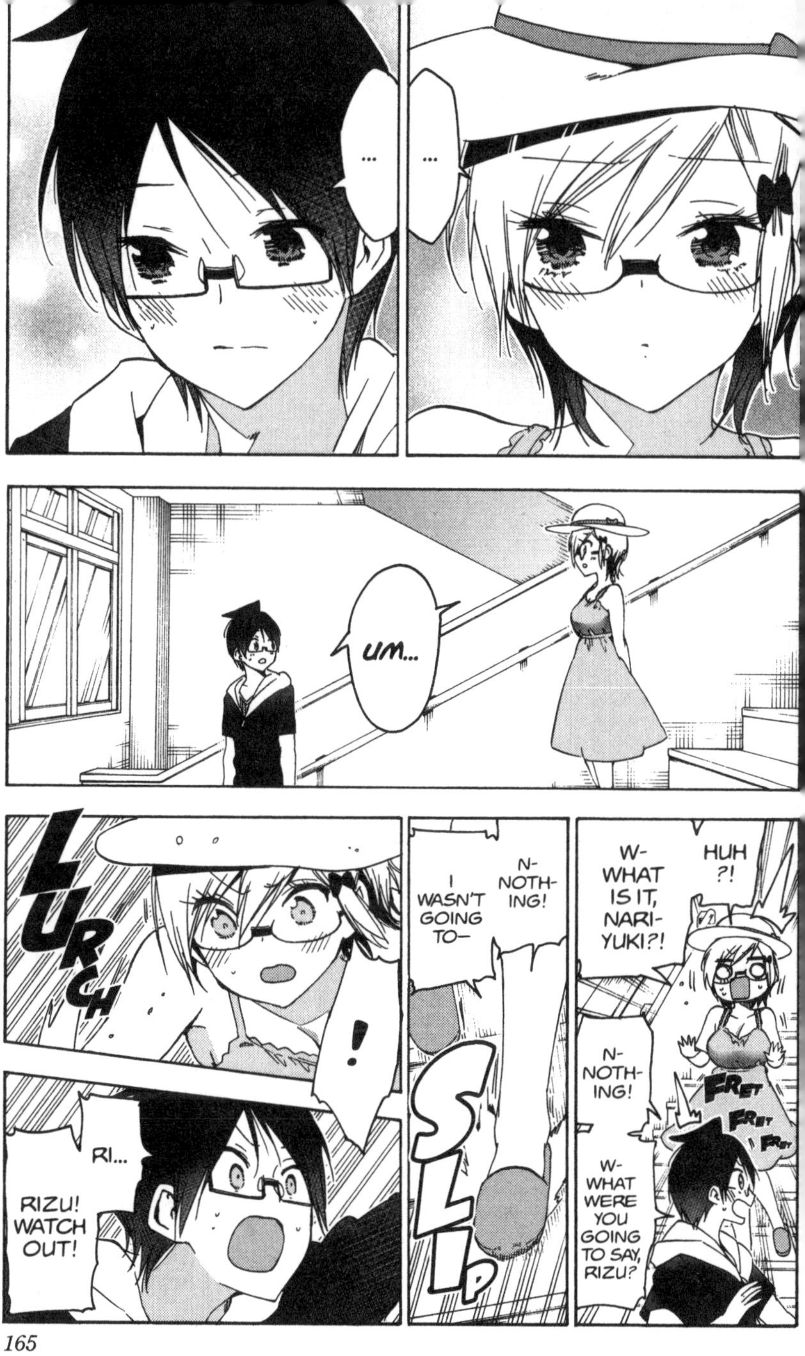
...
...
UM...
HUH?!
W-WHAT IS IT, NARIYUKI?!
N-NOTHING!
W-WHAT WERE YOU GOING TO SAY, RIZU?
FRET FRET FRET
N-NOTHING!
I WASN'T GOING TO—
SLIP
LURCH
!
RI...
RIZU! WATCH OUT!

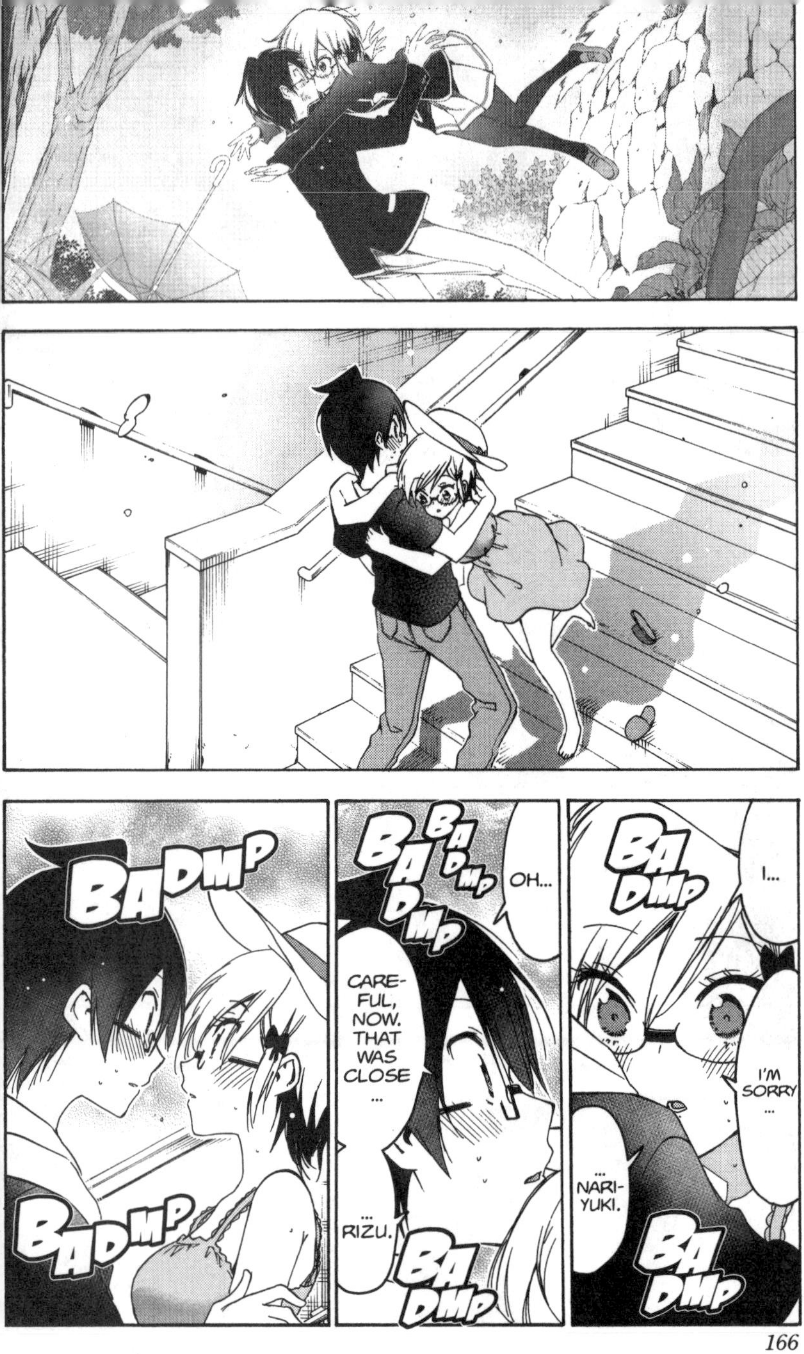
BADMP
I...
I'M SORRY...
...NARIYUKI.
BADMP
BADMP
BADMP
OH...
CAREFUL, NOW. THAT WAS CLOSE...
...RIZU.
BADMP
BADMP
BADMP

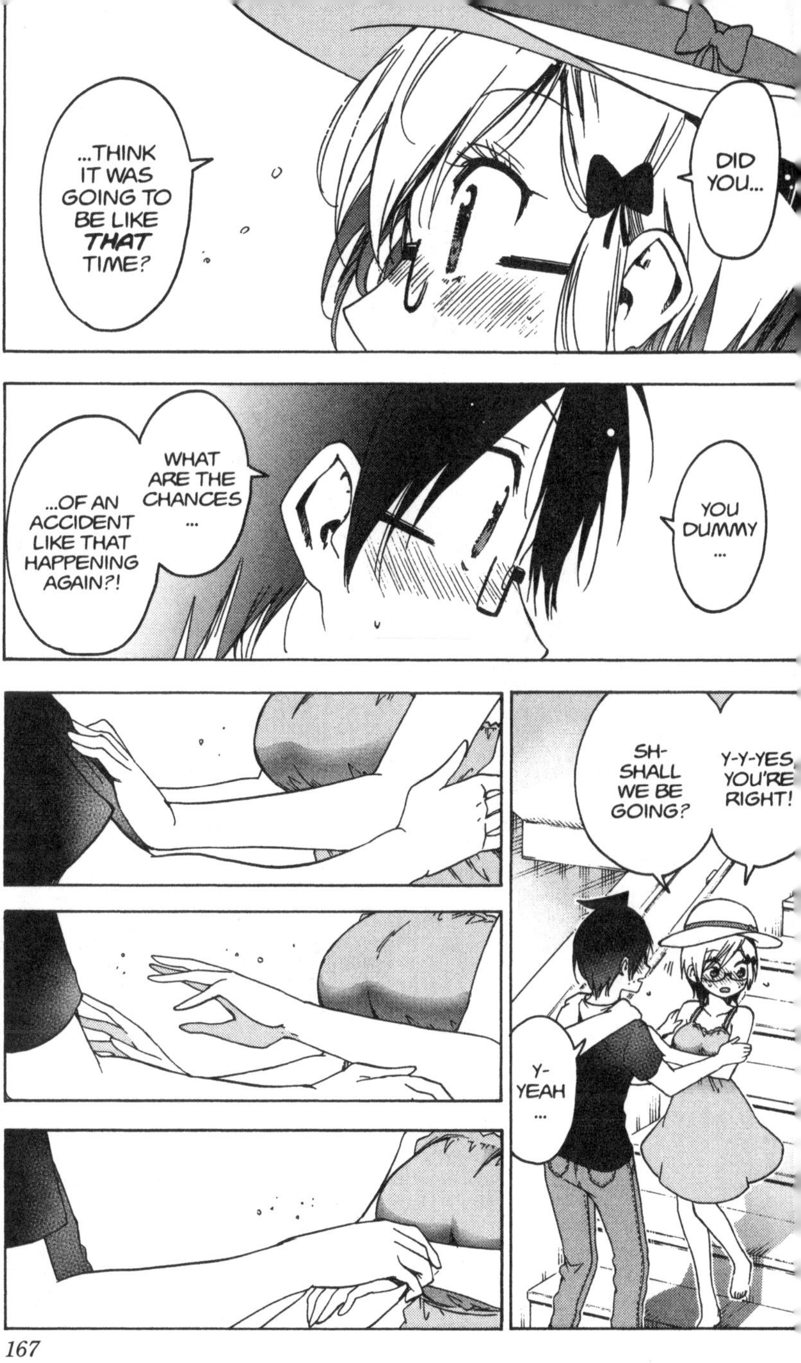
DID YOU...
...THINK IT WAS GOING TO BE LIKE *THAT* TIME?
YOU DUMMY ...
WHAT ARE THE CHANCES ...
...OF AN ACCIDENT LIKE THAT HAPPENING AGAIN?!
Y-Y-YES YOU'RE RIGHT!
SH-SHALL WE BE GOING?
Y-YEAH ...

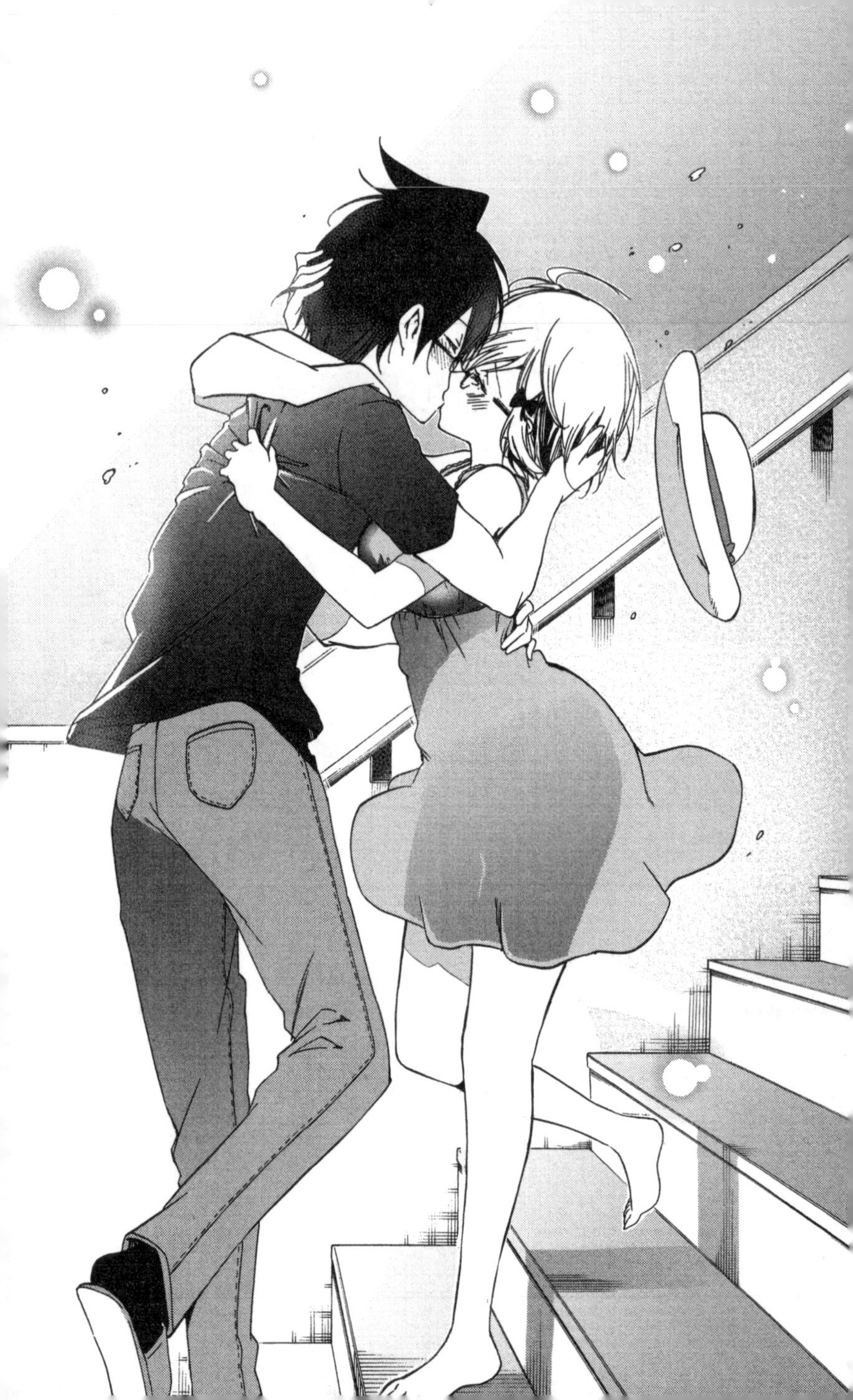

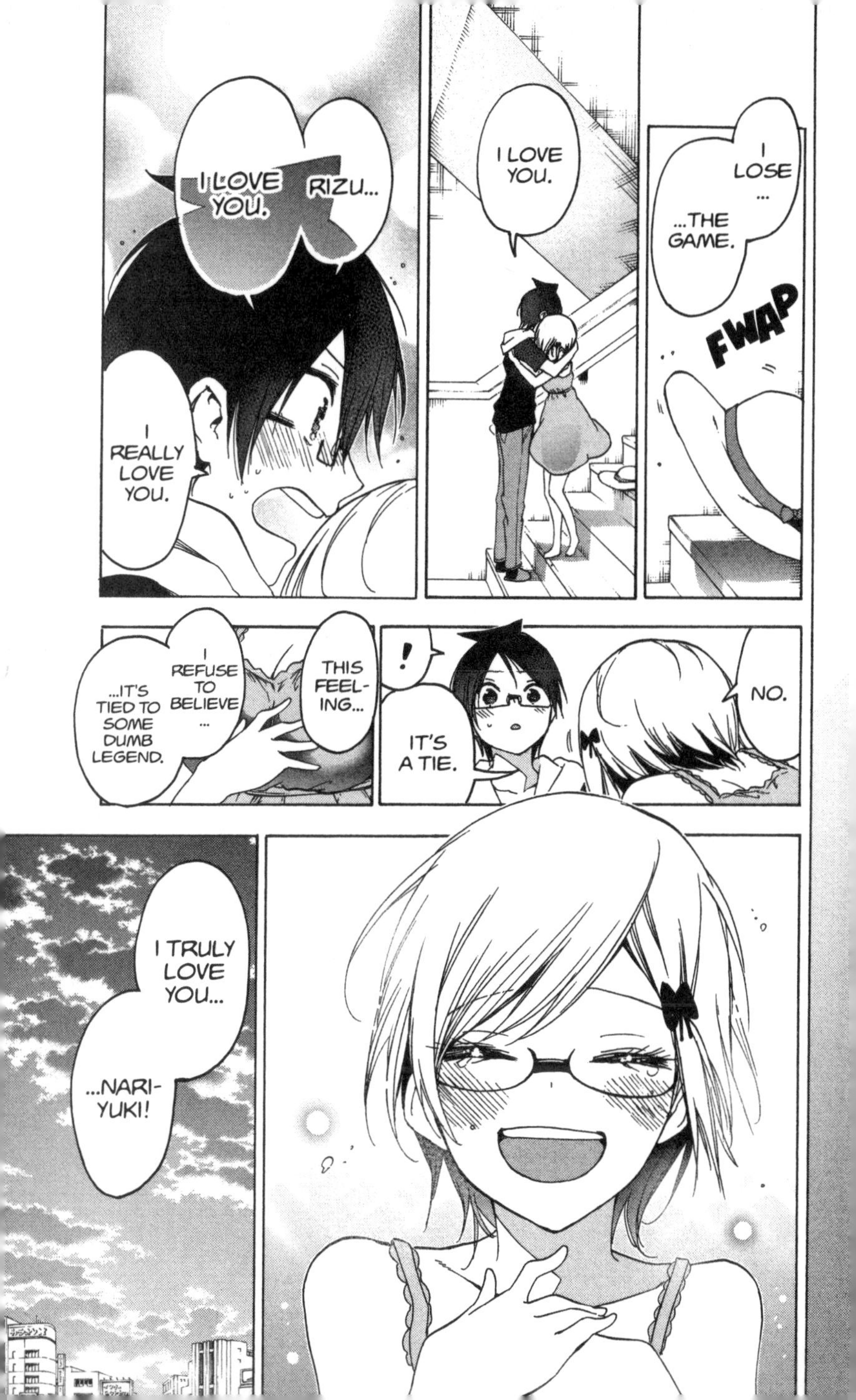
I LOSE ...
...THE GAME.
FWAP
I LOVE YOU.
RIZU...
I LOVE YOU.
I REALLY LOVE YOU.
NO.
!
IT'S A TIE.
THIS FEEL-ING...
I REFUSE TO BELIEVE ...
...IT'S TIED TO SOME DUMB LEGEND.
I TRULY LOVE YOU...
...NARI-YUKI!

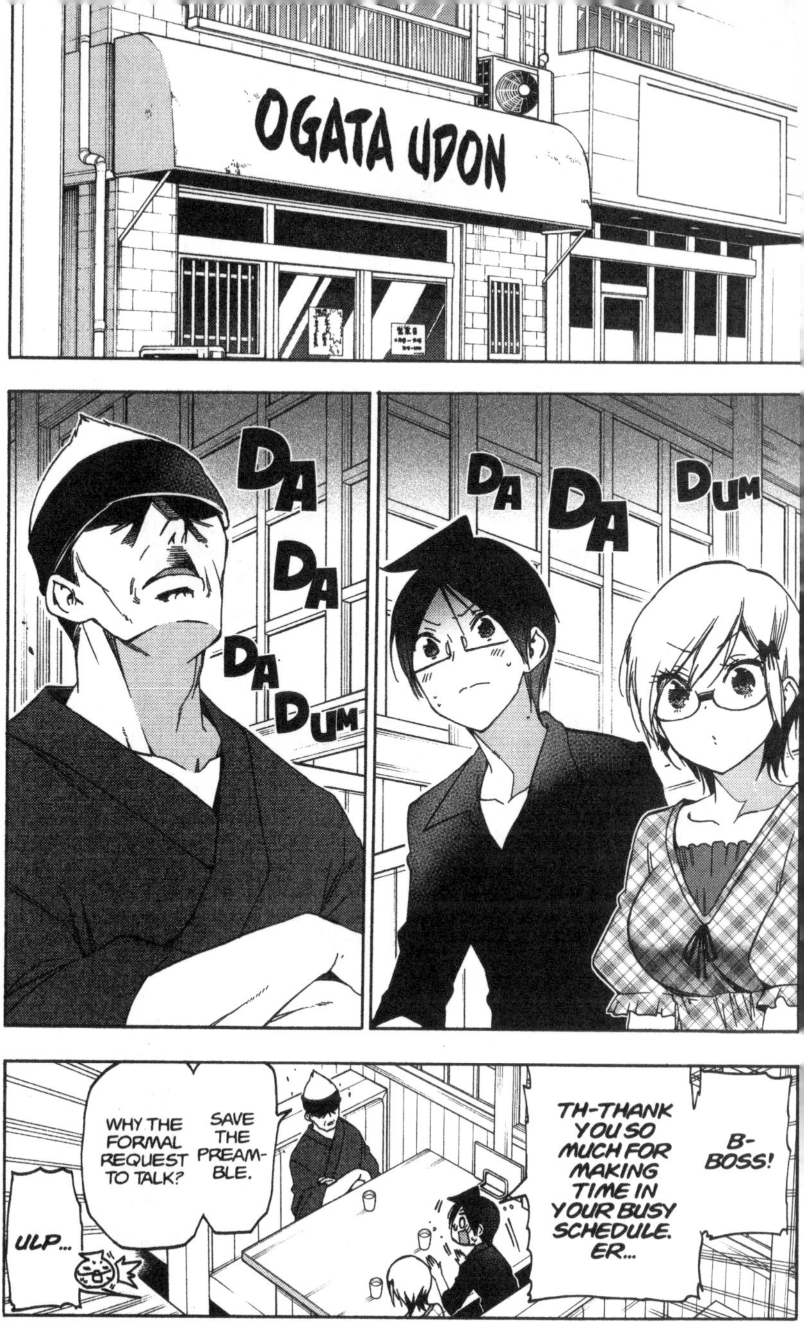
OGATA UDON
DA DA DUM
DA DA DA DUM
B-BOSS!
TH-THANK YOU SO MUCH FOR MAKING TIME IN YOUR BUSY SCHEDULE. ER...
SAVE THE PREAMBLE.
WHY THE FORMAL REQUEST TO TALK?
ULP...

Question 159: [*X*] = Thumbelina Supercomputer, Part 9

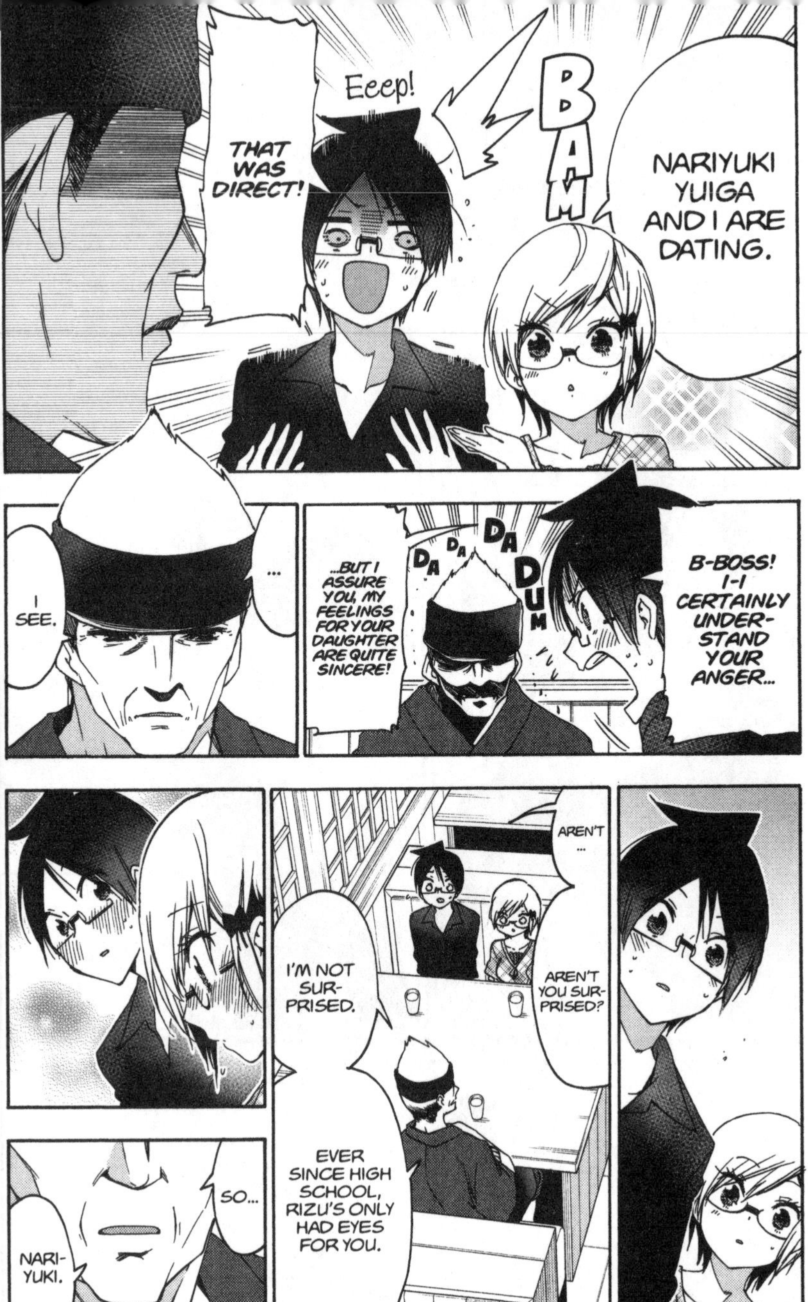
NARIYUKI YUIGA AND I ARE DATING.
BAM
Eeep!
THAT WAS DIRECT!
B-BOSS! I-I CERTAINLY UNDER-STAND YOUR ANGER...
DA DA DA DADUM
...BUT I ASSURE YOU, MY FEELINGS FOR YOUR DAUGHTER ARE QUITE SINCERE!
...
I SEE.
AREN'T ...
AREN'T YOU SUR-PRISED?
I'M NOT SUR-PRISED.
EVER SINCE HIGH SCHOOL, RIZU'S ONLY HAD EYES FOR YOU.
SO...
NARI-YUKI.

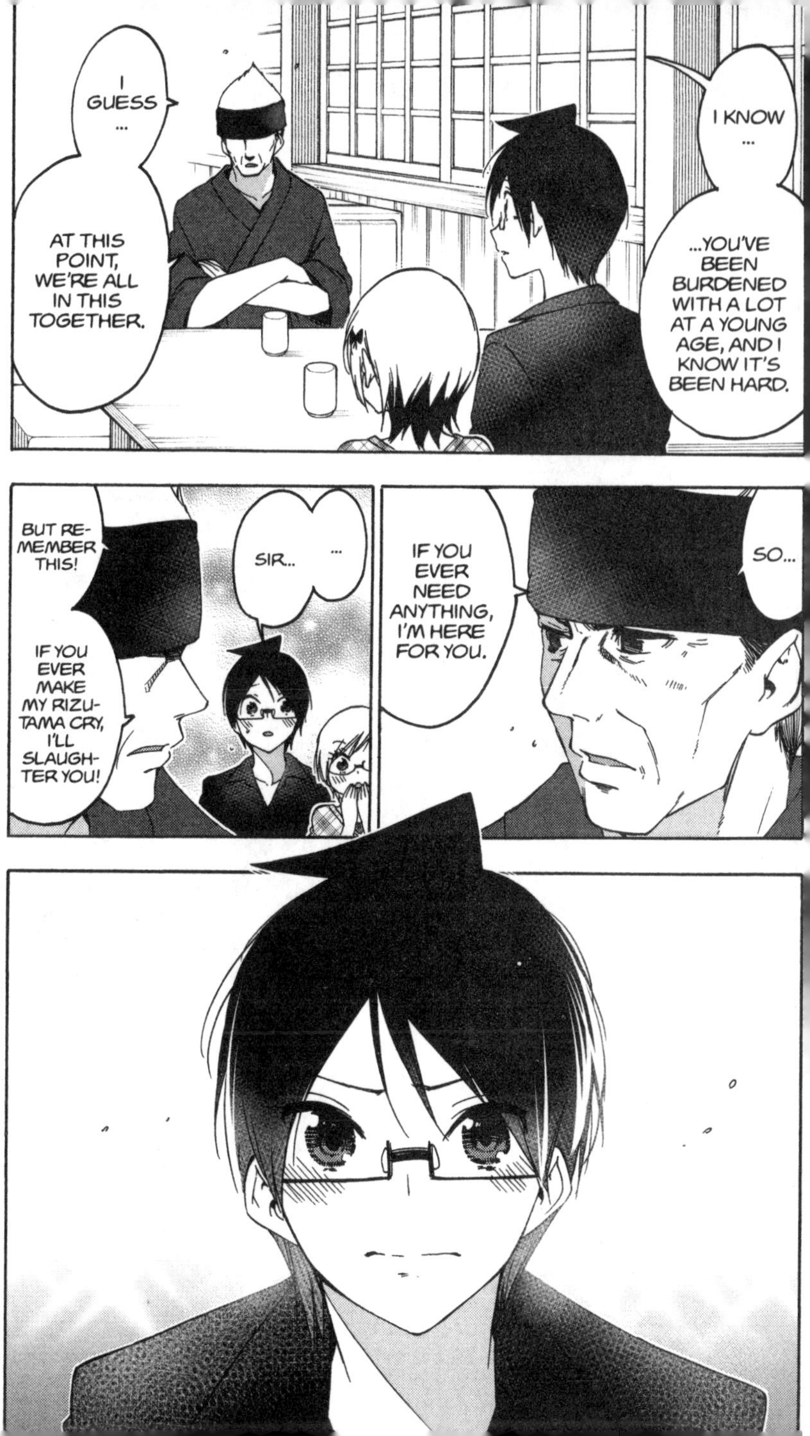
I KNOW ...
...YOU'VE BEEN BURDENED WITH A LOT AT A YOUNG AGE, AND I KNOW IT'S BEEN HARD.
I GUESS ...
AT THIS POINT, WE'RE ALL IN THIS TOGETHER.
SO...
IF YOU EVER NEED ANYTHING, I'M HERE FOR YOU.
SIR... ...
BUT RE-MEMBER THIS!
IF YOU EVER MAKE MY RIZU-TAMA CRY, I'LL SLAUGH-TER YOU!

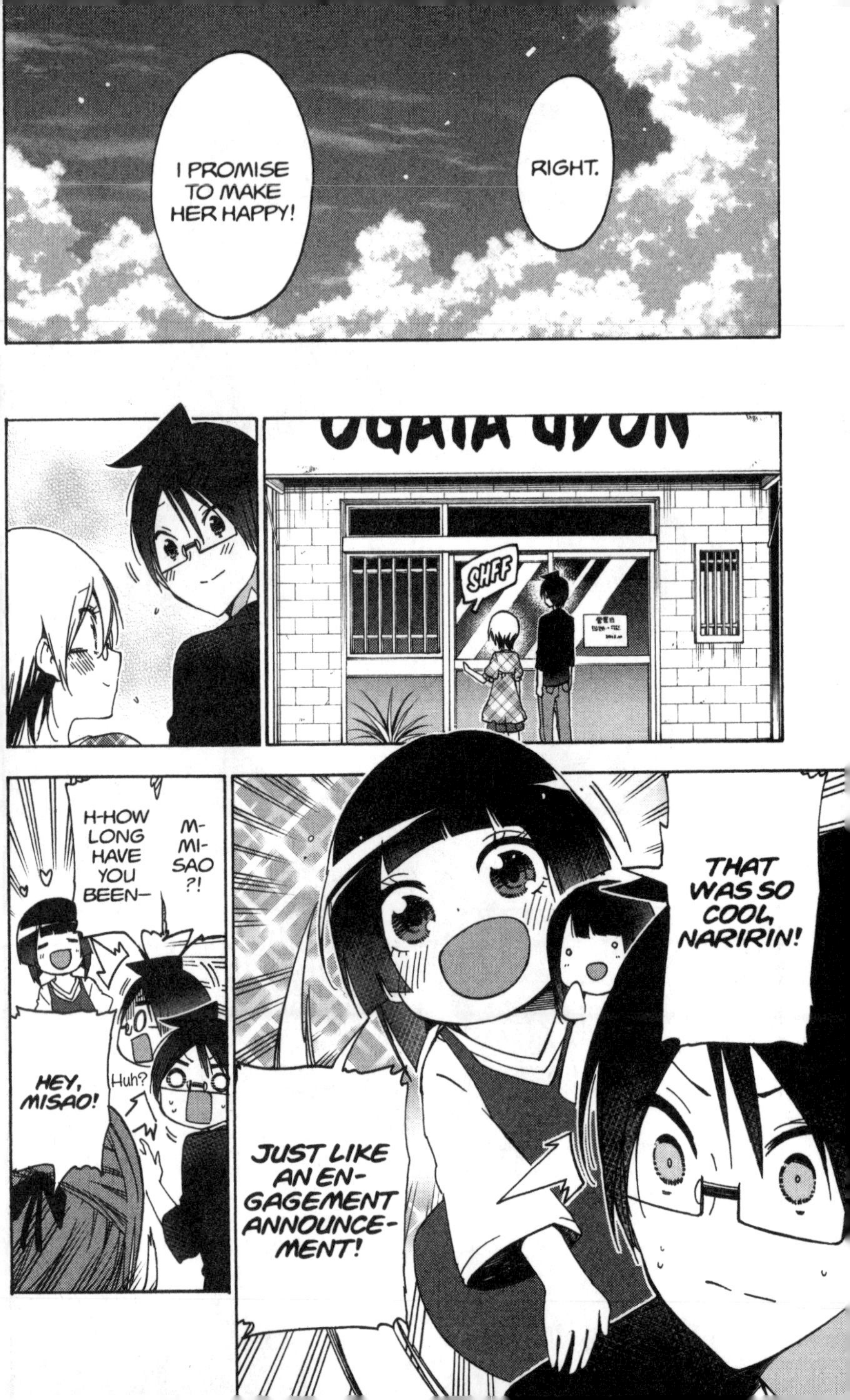
RIGHT.
I PROMISE TO MAKE HER HAPPY!
SHFF
THAT WAS SO COOL, NARIRIN!
JUST LIKE AN ENGAGEMENT ANNOUNCEMENT!
M-MI-SAO?!
H-HOW LONG HAVE YOU BEEN—
Huh?
HEY, MISAO!

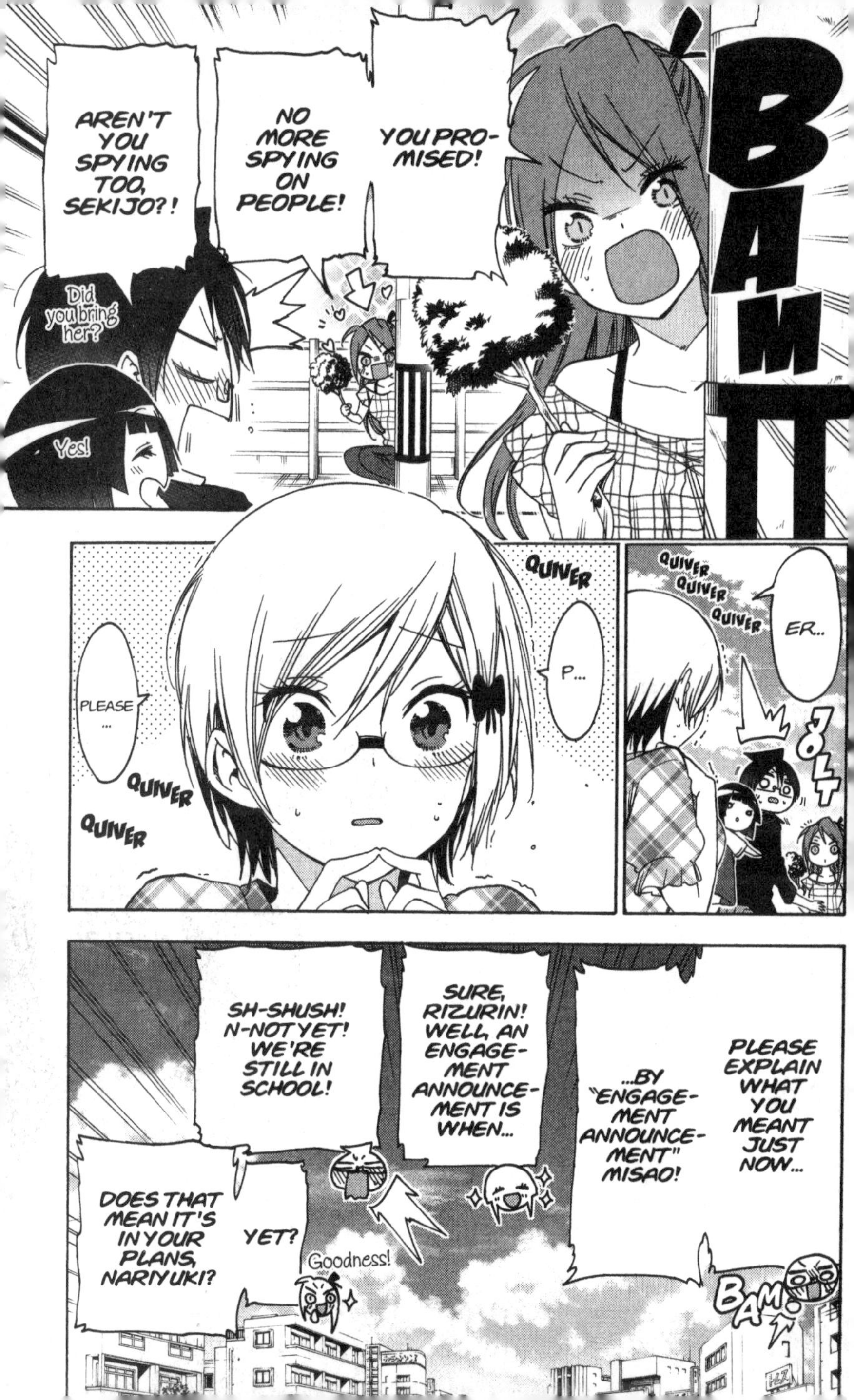
BAMTT
YOU PRO-MISED!
NO MORE SPYING ON PEOPLE!
AREN'T YOU SPYING TOO, SEKIJO?!
Did you bring her?
Yes!
ER...
QUIVER QUIVER QUIVER
JOLT
QUIVER
P...
PLEASE ...
QUIVER QUIVER
PLEASE EXPLAIN WHAT YOU MEANT JUST NOW...
BAM
...BY "ENGAGEMENT ANNOUNCEMENT" MISAO!
SURE, RIZURIN! WELL, AN ENGAGEMENT ANNOUNCEMENT IS WHEN...
SH-SHUSH! N-NOT YET! WE'RE STILL IN SCHOOL!
YET?
DOES THAT MEAN IT'S IN YOUR PLANS, NARIYUKI?
Goodness!

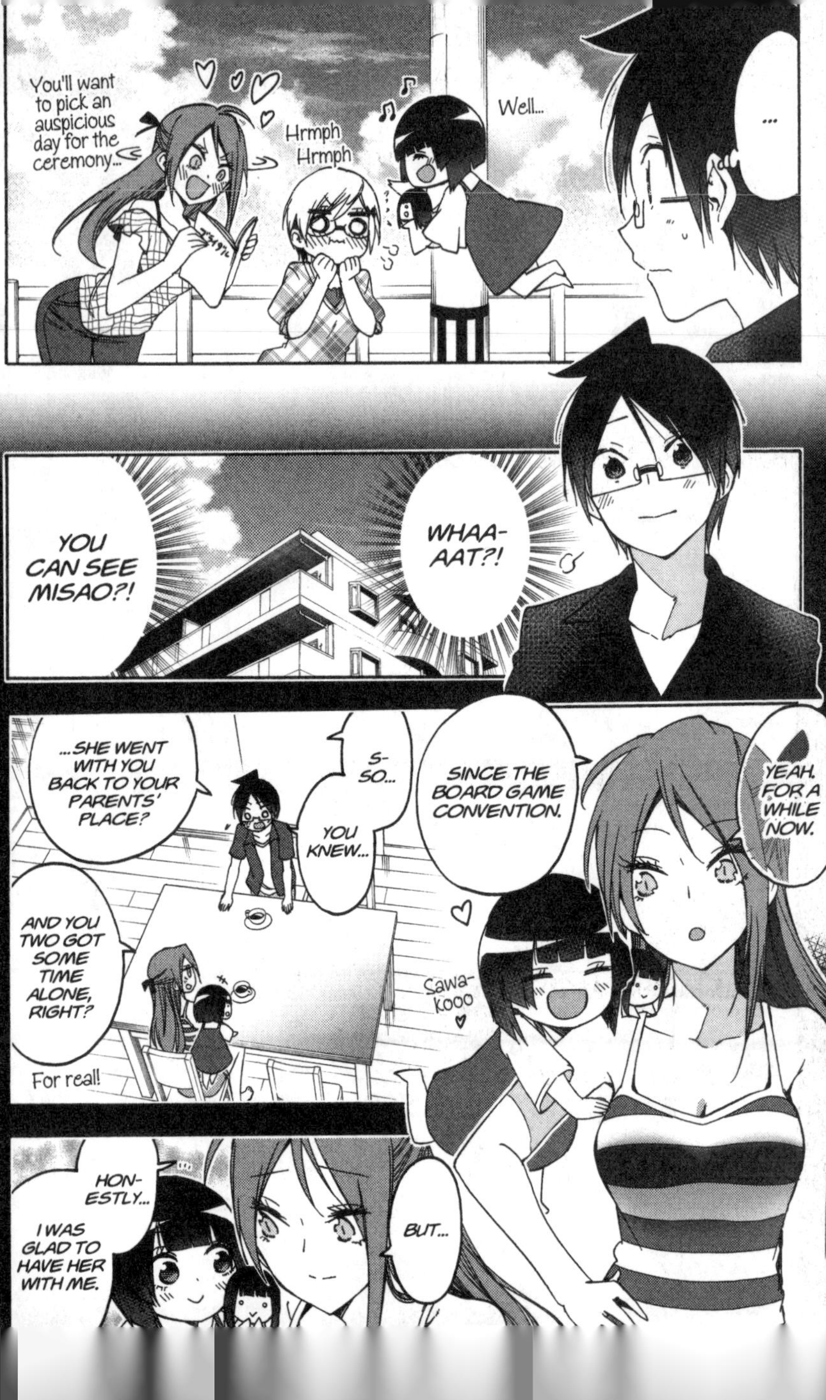
...
Well...
Hrmph Hrmph
You'll want to pick an auspicious day for the ceremony...
WHAAA-AAT?!
YOU CAN SEE MISAO?!
YEAH. FOR A WHILE NOW.
SINCE THE BOARD GAME CONVENTION.
S-SO... YOU KNEW...
...SHE WENT WITH YOU BACK TO YOUR PARENTS' PLACE?
Sawa-kooo
AND YOU TWO GOT SOME TIME ALONE, RIGHT?
For real!
BUT...
HON-ESTLY... I WAS GLAD TO HAVE HER WITH ME.

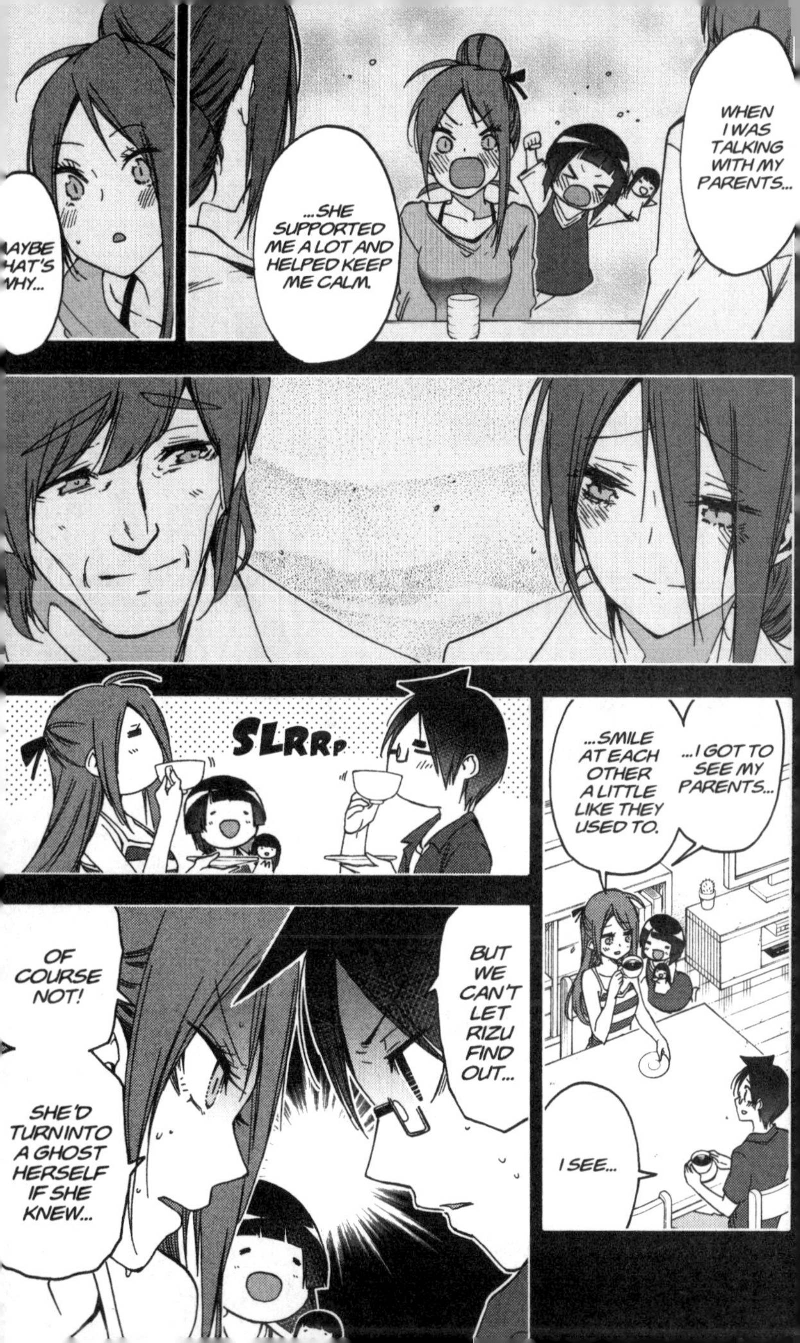
WHEN I WAS TALKING WITH MY PARENTS...
...SHE SUPPORTED ME A LOT AND HELPED KEEP ME CALM.
AYBE HAT'S WHY...
...I GOT TO SEE MY PARENTS...
...SMILE AT EACH OTHER A LITTLE LIKE THEY USED TO.
I SEE...
SLRRP
BUT WE CAN'T LET RIZU FIND OUT...
OF COURSE NOT!
SHE'D TURN INTO A GHOST HERSELF IF SHE KNEW...

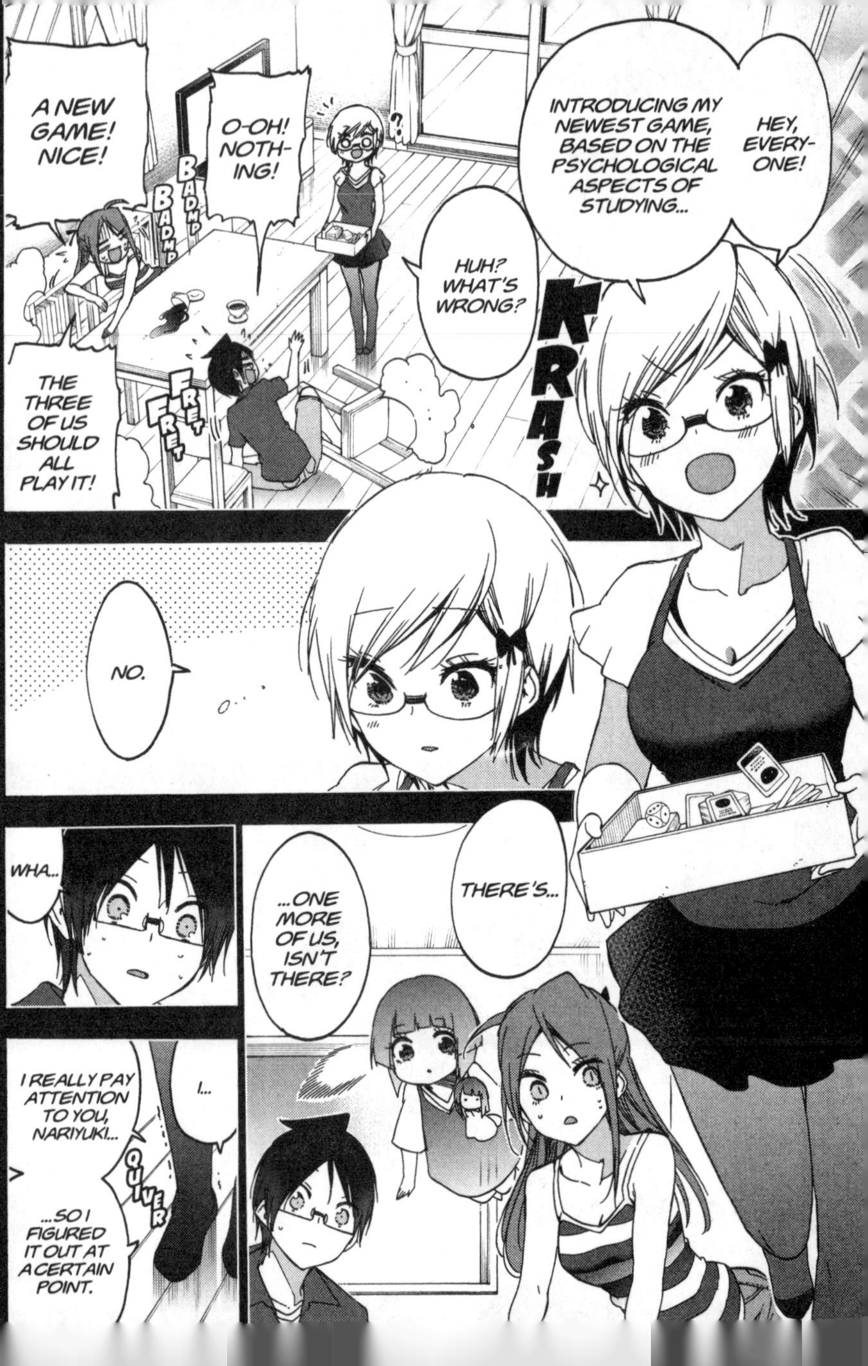
HEY, EVERY-ONE!
INTRODUCING MY NEWEST GAME, BASED ON THE PSYCHOLOGICAL ASPECTS OF STUDYING...
KRASH
HUH? WHAT'S WRONG?
O-OH! NOTHING!
BADMP BADMP
A NEW GAME! NICE!
THE THREE OF US SHOULD ALL PLAY IT!
FRET FRET
NO.
THERE'S...
...ONE MORE OF US, ISN'T THERE?
WHA...
I...
I REALLY PAY ATTENTION TO YOU, NARIYUKI...
QUIVER
...SO I FIGURED IT OUT AT A CERTAIN POINT.

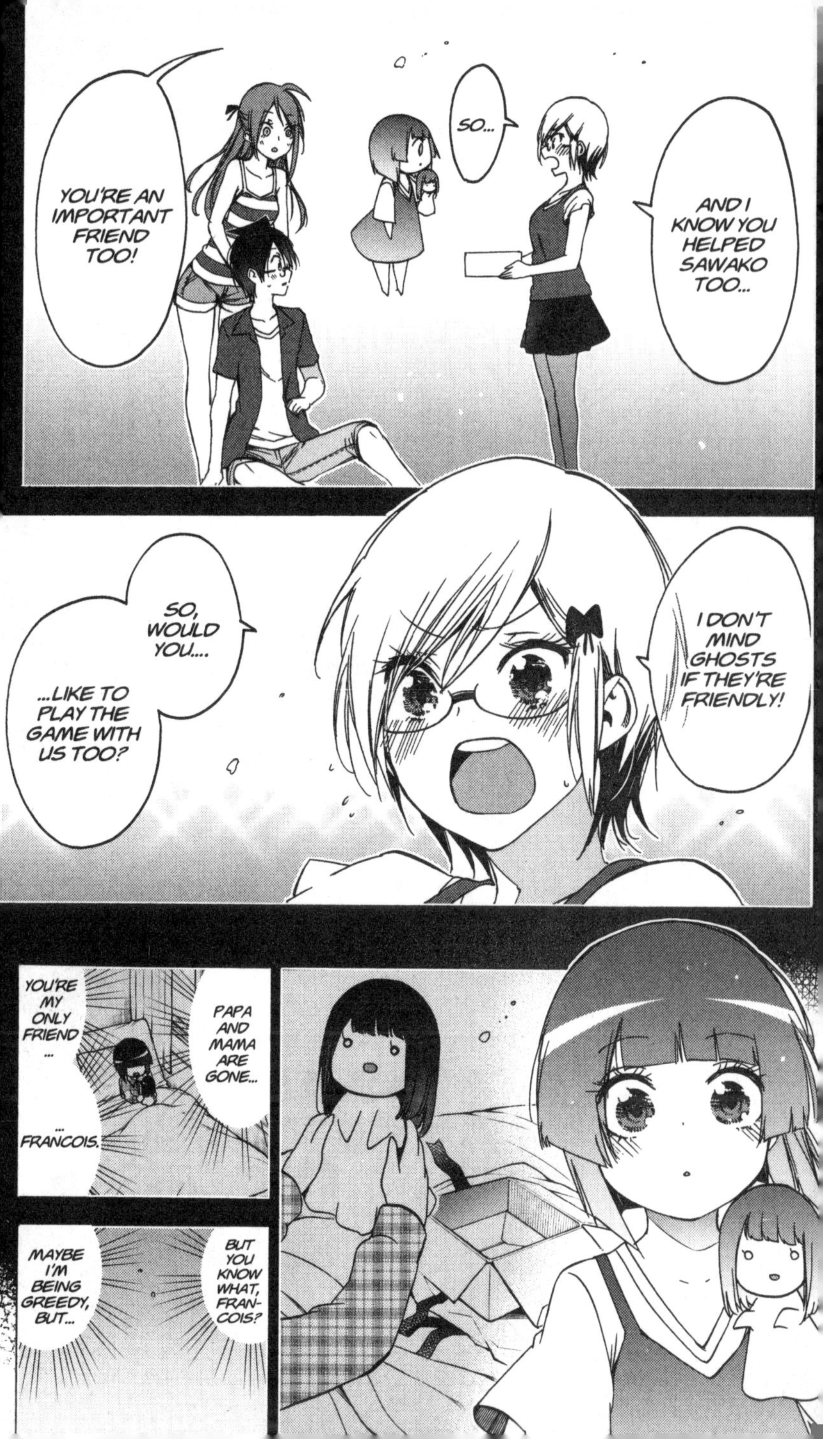
AND I KNOW YOU HELPED SAWAKO TOO...
SO...
YOU'RE AN IMPORTANT FRIEND TOO!
I DON'T MIND GHOSTS IF THEY'RE FRIENDLY!
SO, WOULD YOU....
...LIKE TO PLAY THE GAME WITH US TOO?
PAPA AND MAMA ARE GONE...
YOU'RE MY ONLY FRIEND ...
... FRANCOIS.
BUT YOU KNOW WHAT, FRAN-COIS?
MAYBE I'M BEING GREEDY, BUT...

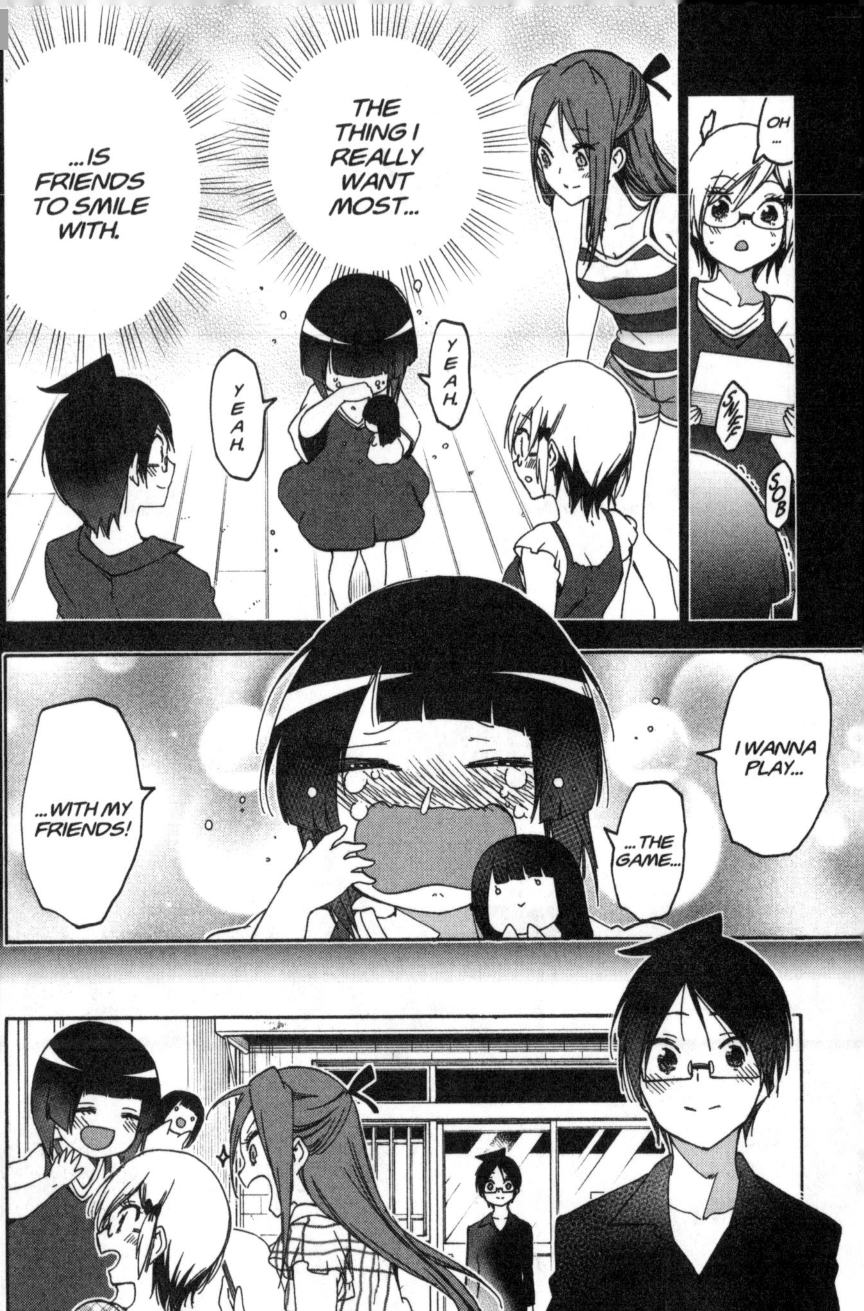
OH ...
SNIFF
SOB
THE THING I REALLY WANT MOST...
...IS FRIENDS TO SMILE WITH.
YEAH.
YEAH.
I WANNA PLAY...
...THE GAME...
...WITH MY FRIENDS!

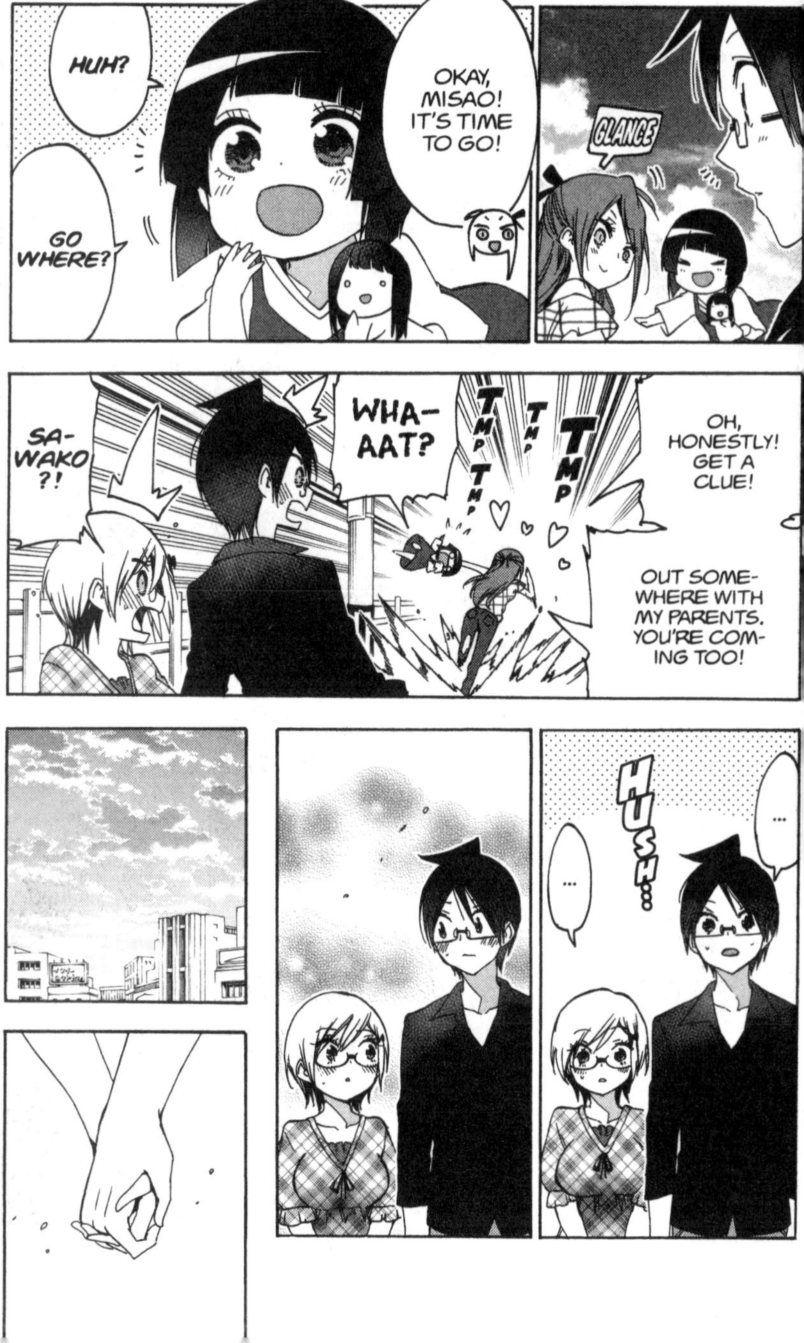
GLANCE
OKAY, MISAO! IT'S TIME TO GO!
HUH?
GO WHERE?
OH, HONESTLY! GET A CLUE!
OUT SOME-WHERE WITH MY PARENTS. YOU'RE COM-ING TOO!
TMP
TMP
TMP TMP
WHA-AAT?
SA-WAKO?!
...
HUSH...
...

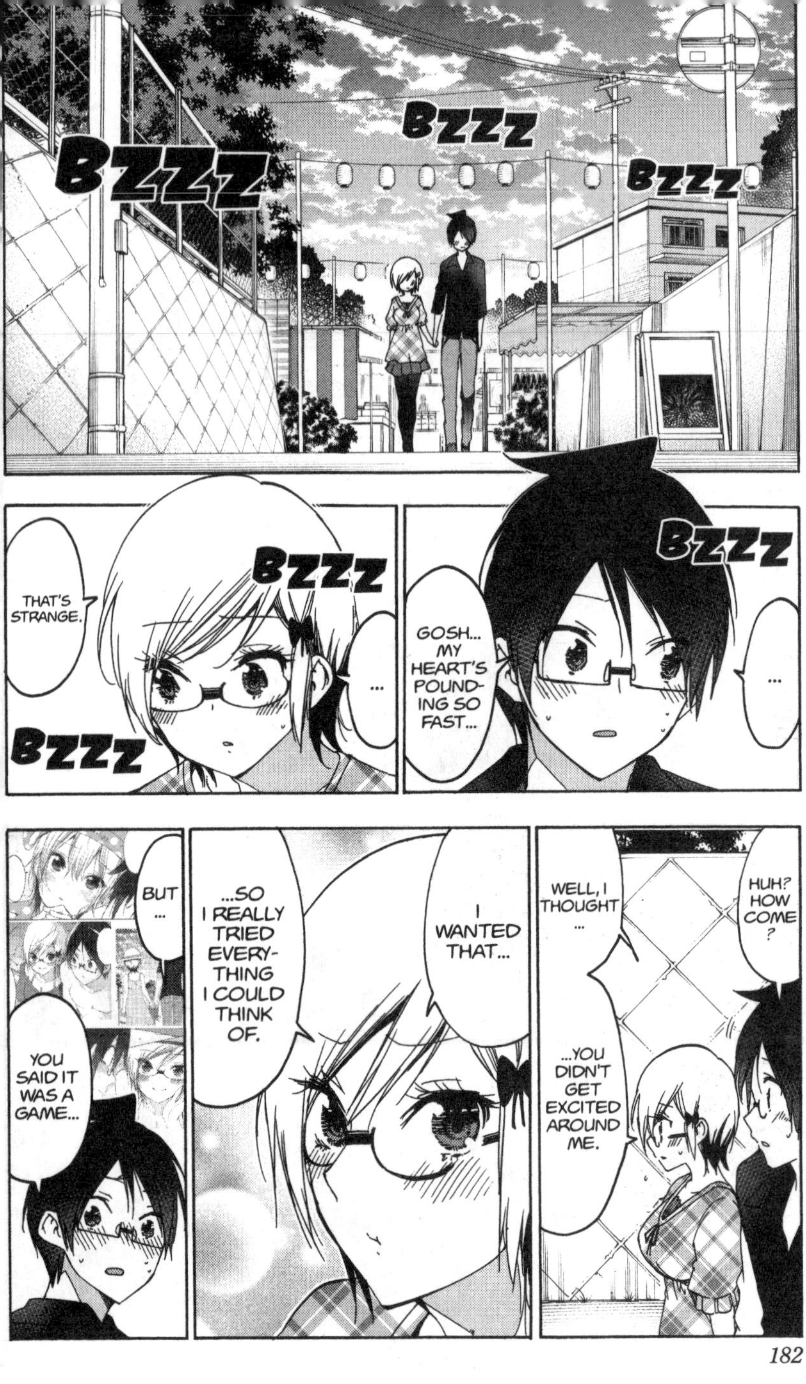
BZZZ
BZZZ
BZZZ
BZZZ
...
GOSH... MY HEART'S POUNDING SO FAST...
BZZZ
...
THAT'S STRANGE.
BZZZ
HUH? HOW COME?
WELL, I THOUGHT...
...YOU DIDN'T GET EXCITED AROUND ME.
I WANTED THAT...
...SO I REALLY TRIED EVERYTHING I COULD THINK OF.
BUT...
YOU SAID IT WAS A GAME...

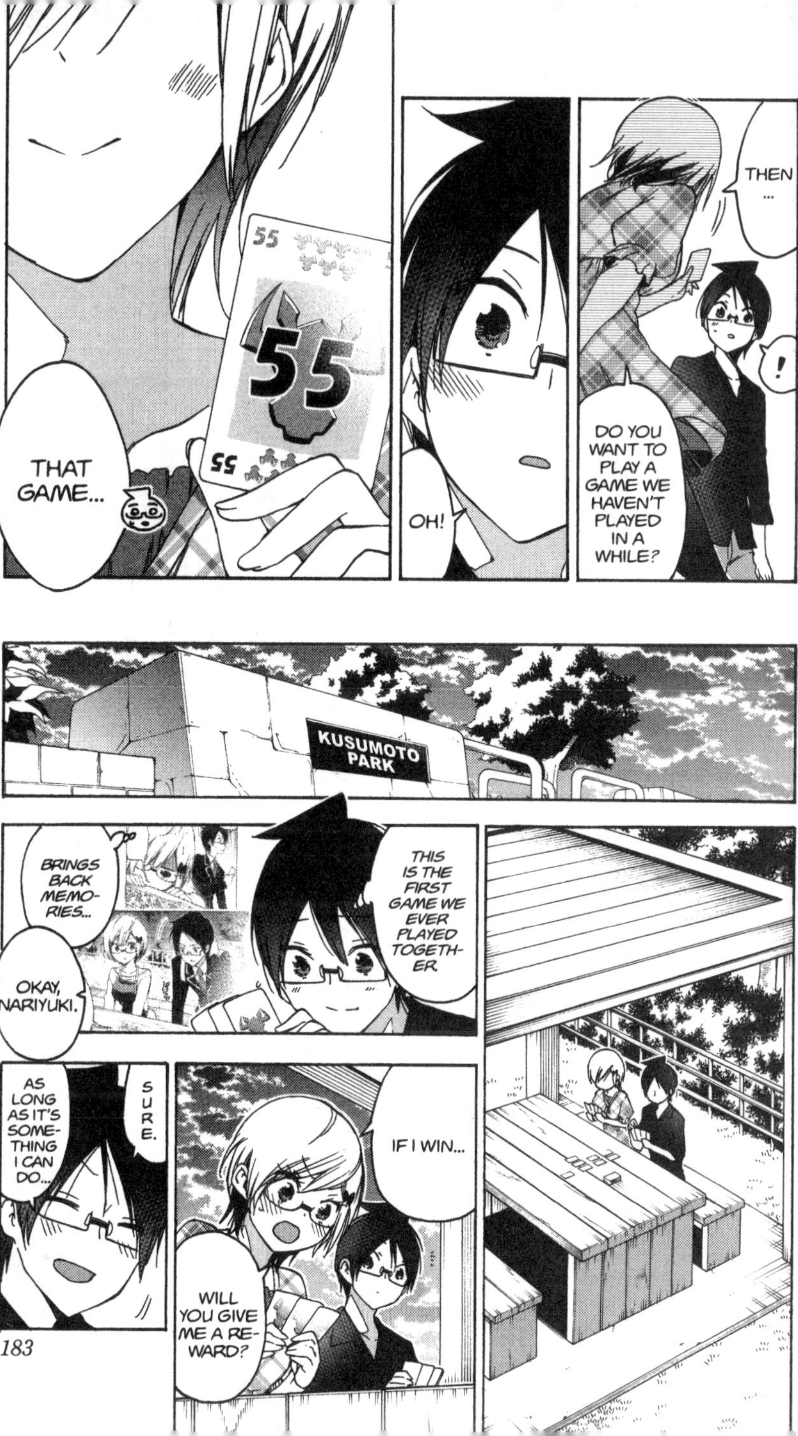
THEN...
!
DO YOU WANT TO PLAY A GAME WE HAVEN'T PLAYED IN A WHILE?
OH!
55
THAT GAME...
KUSUMOTO PARK
THIS IS THE FIRST GAME WE EVER PLAYED TOGETHER.
BRINGS BACK MEMORIES...
OKAY, NARIYUKI.
IF I WIN...
WILL YOU GIVE ME A REWARD?
SURE.
AS LONG AS IT'S SOMETHING I CAN DO...

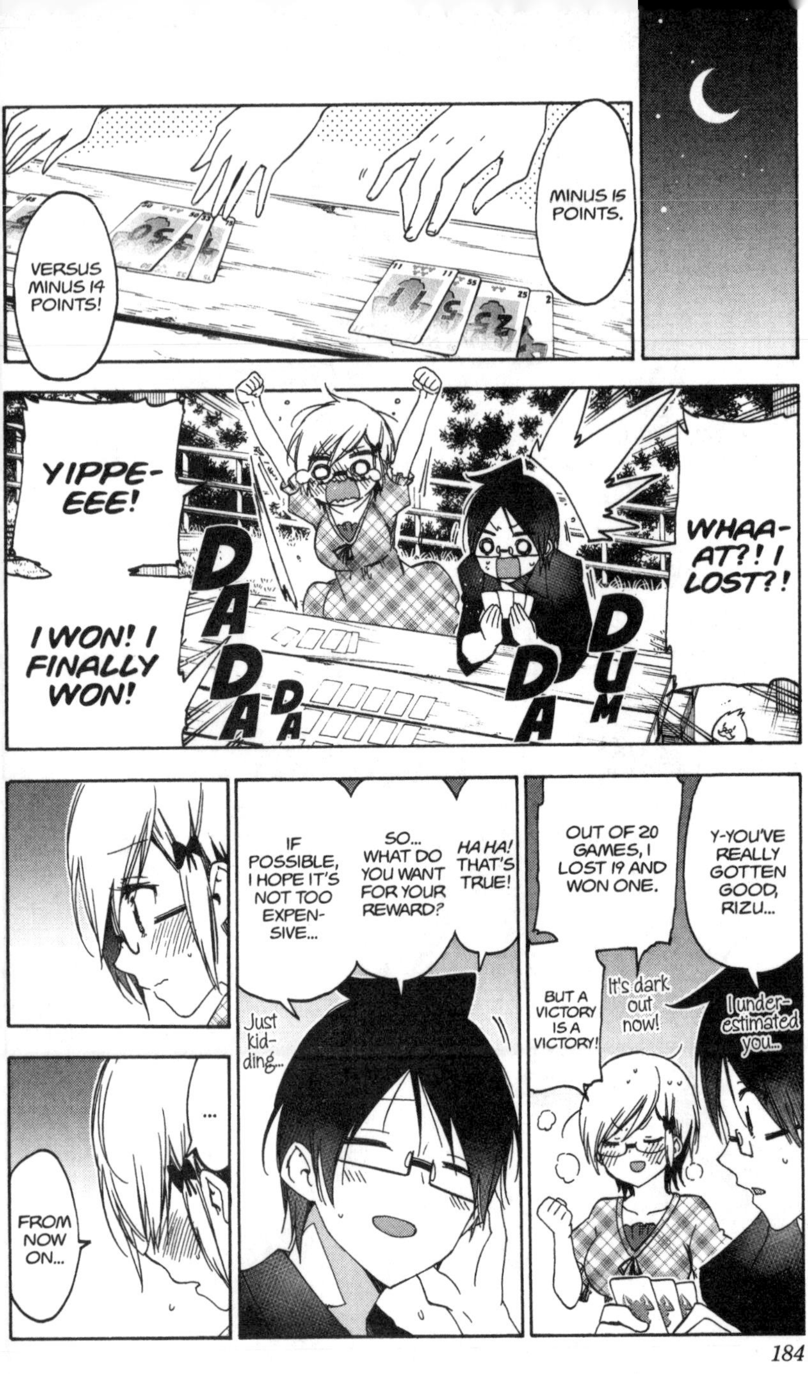
MINUS 15 POINTS.
VERSUS MINUS 14 POINTS!
WHAAA-AT?! I LOST?!
DA DA DA DA DUM
YIPPE-EEE!
I WON! I FINALLY WON!
Y-YOU'VE REALLY GOTTEN GOOD, RIZU...
I under-estimated you...
OUT OF 20 GAMES, I LOST 19 AND WON ONE.
It's dark out now!
BUT A VICTORY IS A VICTORY!
HA HA! THAT'S TRUE!
SO... WHAT DO YOU WANT FOR YOUR REWARD?
IF POSSIBLE, I HOPE IT'S NOT TOO EXPEN-SIVE...
Just kid-ding...
...
FROM NOW ON...

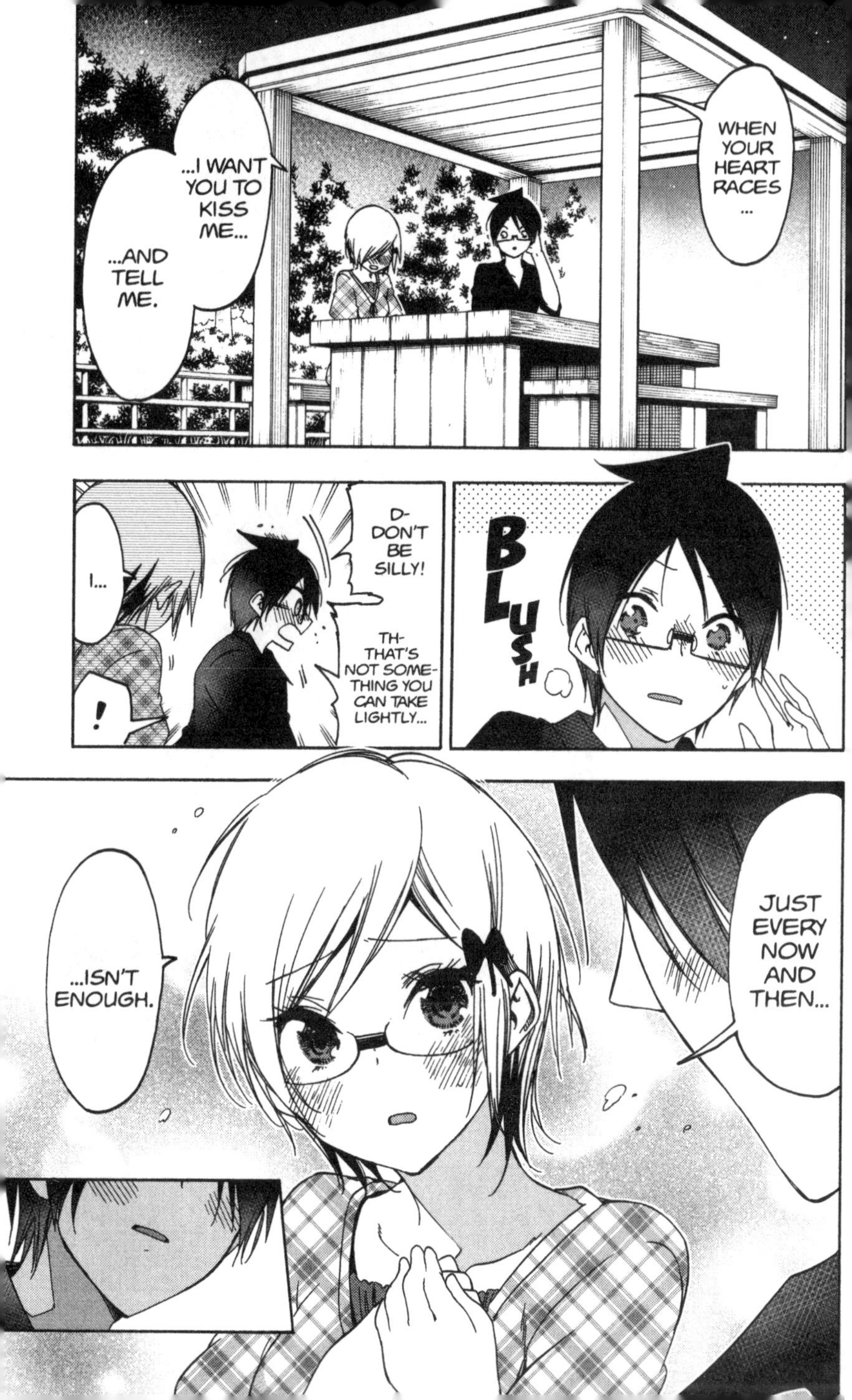
WHEN YOUR HEART RACES ...
...I WANT YOU TO KISS ME...
...AND TELL ME.
BLUSH
D-DON'T BE SILLY!
TH-THAT'S NOT SOMETHING YOU CAN TAKE LIGHTLY...
I...
!
JUST EVERY NOW AND THEN...
...ISN'T ENOUGH.

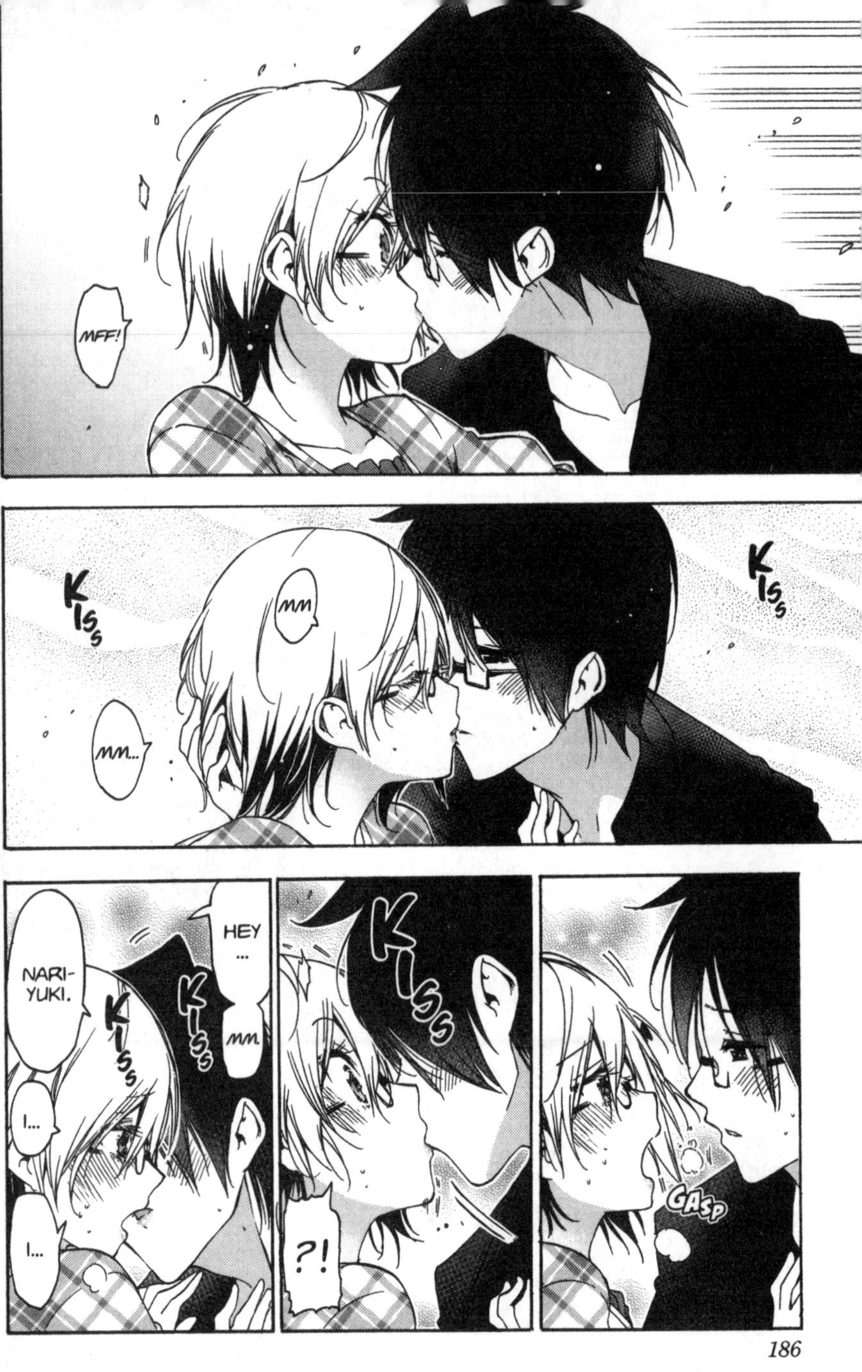
MFF!
KISS
MM
KISS
MM...
GASP
KISS
?!
HEY... MM.
NARI-YUKI.
KISS
I...
I...

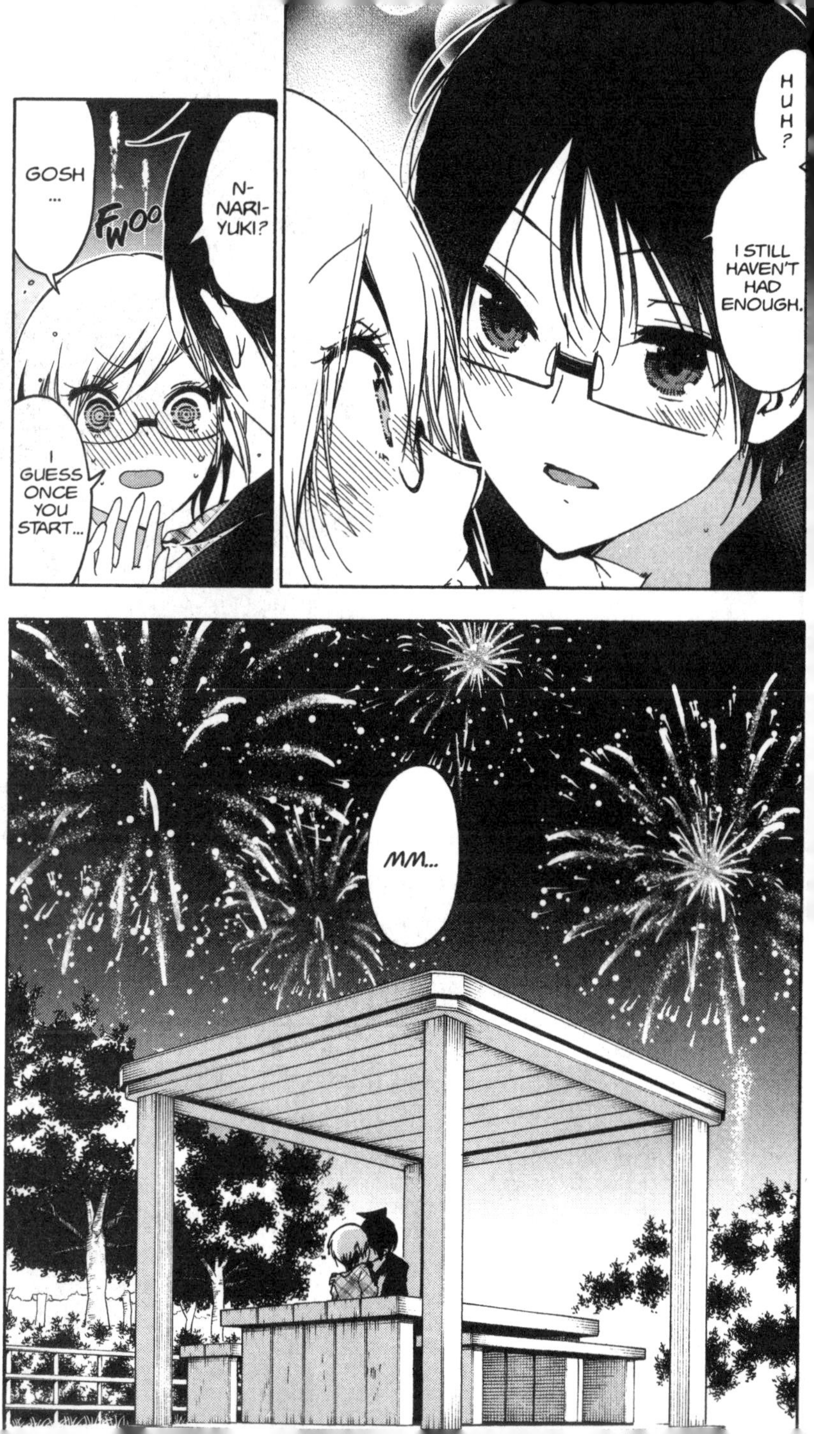
HUH?
I STILL HAVEN'T HAD ENOUGH.
N-NARI-YUKI?
GOSH...
FWOO
I GUESS ONCE YOU START...
MM...

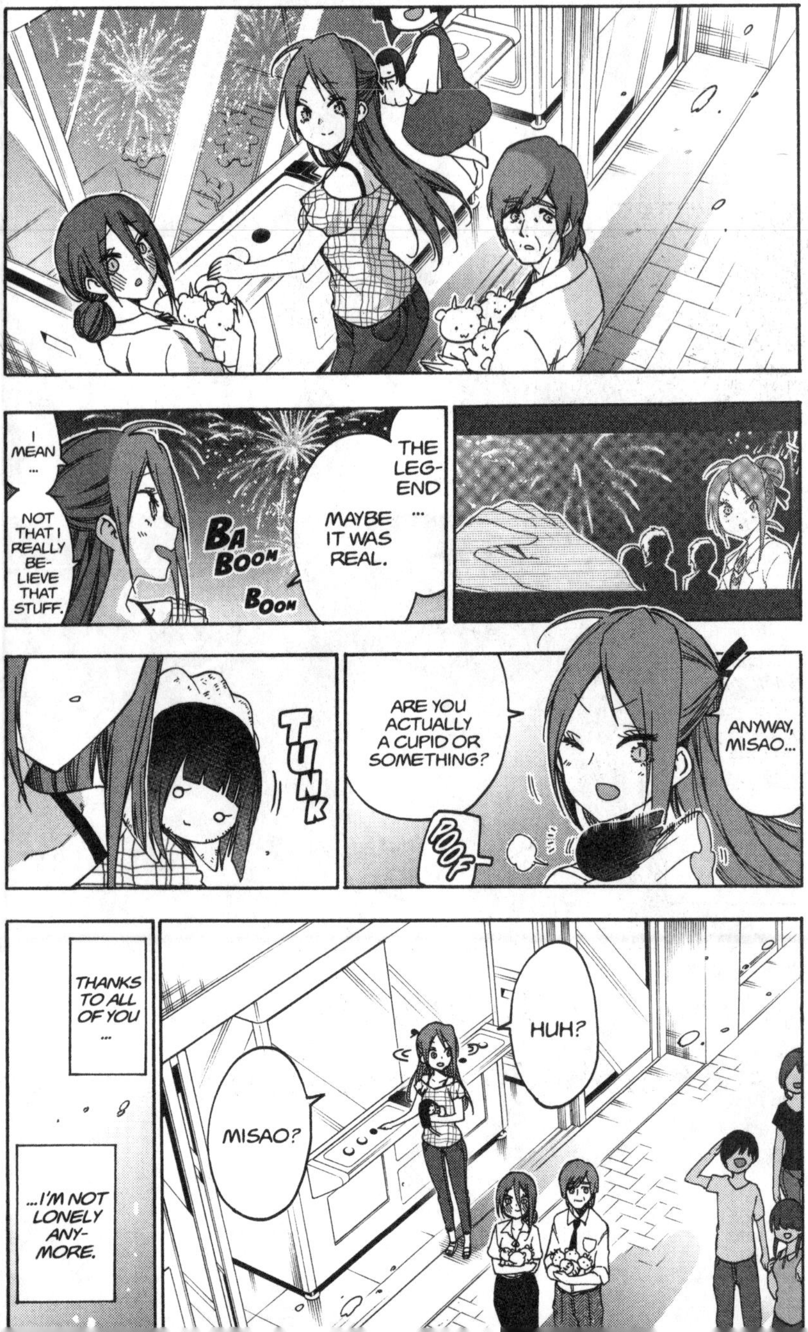
THE LEGEND...
MAYBE IT WAS REAL.
BA BOOM
BOOM
I MEAN...
NOT THAT I REALLY BELIEVE THAT STUFF.
ANYWAY, MISAO...
ARE YOU ACTUALLY A CUPID OR SOMETHING?
POOF
TUNK
HUH?
MISAO?
THANKS TO ALL OF YOU...
...I'M NOT LONELY ANYMORE.

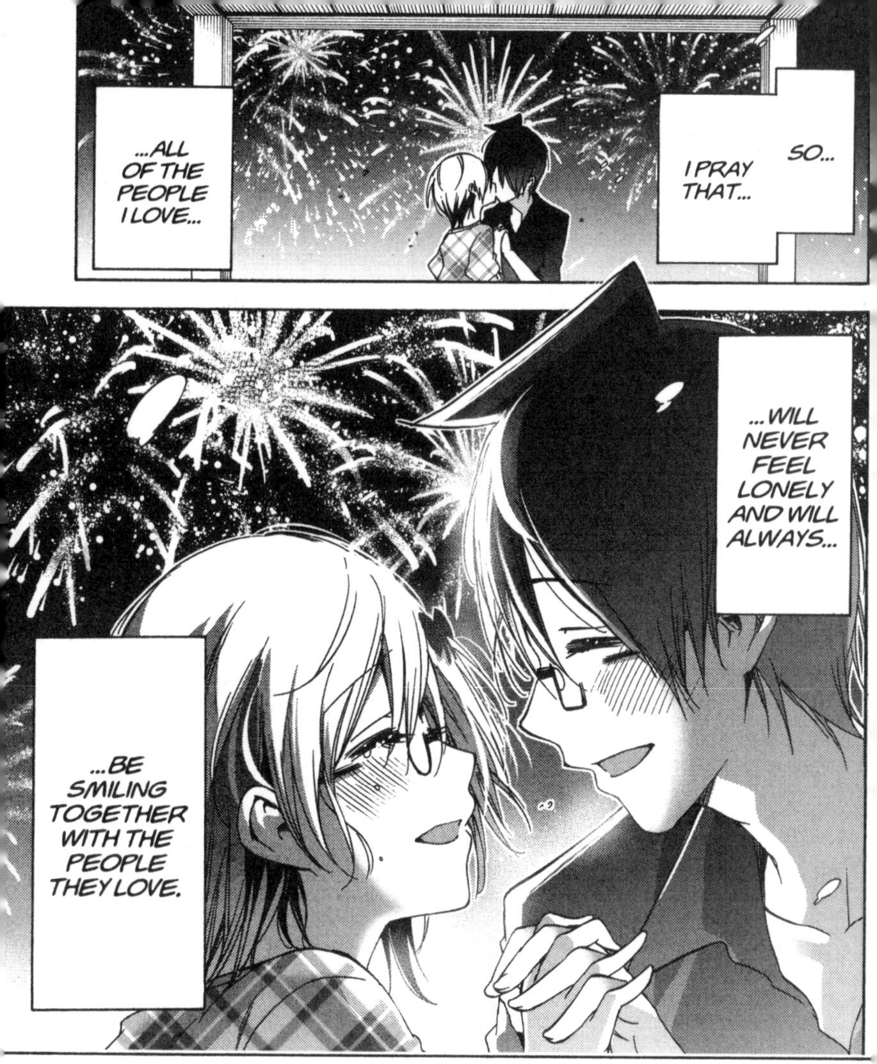
SO...
I PRAY THAT...
...ALL OF THE PEOPLE I LOVE...
...WILL NEVER FEEL LONELY AND WILL ALWAYS...
...BE SMILING TOGETHER WITH THE PEOPLE THEY LOVE.

Route: 2/5

[X] = Thumbelina Supercomputer Arc

- END -